Distributional
Cost-Effectiveness Analysis

Handbooks in Health Economic Evaluation Series

Series editors: Alastair Gray and Andrew Briggs

Existing volumes in the series:

Decision Modelling for Health Economic Evaluation

Andrew Briggs, Mark Sculpher, and Karl Claxton

Applied Methods of Cost-Effectiveness Analysis in Healthcare

Alastair M. Gray, Philip M. Clarke, Jane L. Wolstenholme, and Sarah Wordsworth

Applied Methods of Cost-Benefit Analysis in Healthcare

Emma McIntosh, Philip Clarke, Emma Frew, and Jordan Louviere

Economic Evaluation in Clinical Trials

Henry A. Glick, Jalpa A. Doshi, Seema S. Sonnad, and Daniel Polsky

Applied Health Economics for Public Health Practice and Research

Rhiannon Tudor Edwards and Emma McIntosh

Distributional Cost-Effectiveness Analysis
Quantifying Health Equity Impacts and Trade-Offs

Edited by

Richard Cookson
Professor, Centre for Health Economics,
University of York, UK

Susan Griffin
Senior Research Fellow, Centre for Health Economics,
University of York, UK

Ole F. Norheim
Professor, Department of Global Public Health,
University of Bergen, Norway, and Adjunct Professor,
Harvard University, USA

Anthony J. Culyer
Professor Emeritus, University of York, UK,
and Visiting Professor, Imperial College, London
Adjunct Professor, University of Toronto, Canada

OXFORD
UNIVERSITY PRESS

Great Clarendon Street, Oxford, OX2 6DP,
United Kingdom

Oxford University Press is a department of the University of Oxford.
It furthers the University's objective of excellence in research, scholarship,
and education by publishing worldwide. Oxford is a registered trade mark of
Oxford University Press in the UK and in certain other countries

© Oxford University Press 2021

The moral rights of the authors have been asserted

First Edition published in 2021

Impression: 2

All rights reserved. No part of this publication may be reproduced, stored in
a retrieval system, or transmitted, in any form or by any means, without the
prior permission in writing of Oxford University Press, or as expressly permitted
by law, by licence or under terms agreed with the appropriate reprographics
rights organization. Enquiries concerning reproduction outside the scope of the
above should be sent to the Rights Department, Oxford University Press, at the
address above

You must not circulate this work in any other form
and you must impose this same condition on any acquirer

Published in the United States of America by Oxford University Press
198 Madison Avenue, New York, NY 10016, United States of America

British Library Cataloguing in Publication Data

Data available

Library of Congress Control Number: 2020938124

ISBN 978-0-19-883819-7

Printed and bound by
CPI Group (UK) Ltd, Croydon, CR0 4YY

The authors and the publishers do not accept responsibility or legal liability for any
errors in the text or for the misuse or misapplication of material in this work.

Links to third party websites are provided by Oxford in good faith and
for information only. Oxford disclaims any responsibility for the materials
contained in any third party website referenced in this work.

Series Preface

Health economic evaluation is a thriving international activity that is increasingly used to allocate scarce health resources, and within which applied and methodological research, teaching, and publication are flourishing. Several widely respected texts are already well established in the market, so what is the rationale for not just one more book, but for a series? We believe that the books in the series Handbooks in Health Economic Evaluation share a strong distinguishing feature, which is to cover as much as possible of this broad field with a much stronger practical flavour than existing texts, using plenty of illustrative material and worked examples. We hope that readers will use this series not only for authoritative views on the current practice of economic evaluation and likely future developments, but for practical and detailed guidance on how to undertake an analysis. The books in the series are textbooks, but first and foremost they are handbooks.

Our conviction that there is a place for the series has been nurtured by the continuing success of two short courses we helped develop—Advanced Methods of Cost-Effectiveness Analysis, and Advanced Modelling Methods for Economic Evaluation. Advanced Methods was developed in Oxford in 1999 and has run several times a year ever since, in Oxford, Canberra, and Hong Kong. Advanced Modelling was developed in York and Oxford in 2002 and has also run several times a year ever since, in Oxford, York, Glasgow, and Toronto. Both courses were explicitly designed to provide computer-based teaching that would take participants through the theory but also the methods and practical steps required to undertake a robust economic evaluation or construct a decision-analytic model to current standards. The proof of concept was the strong international demand for the courses—from academic researchers, government agencies, and the pharmaceutical industry—and the very positive feedback on their practical orientation.

So the original concept of the handbooks series, as well as many of the specific ideas and illustrative material, can be traced to these courses. The Advanced Modelling course is in the phenotype of the first book in the series, *Decision Modelling for Health Economic Evaluation,* which focuses on the role and methods of decision analysis in economic evaluation. The Advanced Methods course has been an equally important influence on *Applied Methods of Cost-Effectiveness,* the third book in the series which sets out the key elements of analysing costs and outcomes, calculating cost-effectiveness, and reporting results. The concept was then extended to cover several other important topic areas. First, the design, conduct, and analysis of economic evaluations alongside clinical trials have become a specialized area of activity with distinctive methodological and practical issues, and its own debates and controversies. It seemed worthy of a dedicated volume, hence the second book in the series, *Economic Evaluation in Clinical Trials*. Next, while the use of cost-benefit analysis in healthcare has spawned a substantial literature, this is mostly theoretical, polemical, or focused on specific issues such as willingness to pay. We believe the fourth book in the series, *Applied Methods of Cost-Benefit Analysis in Health Care*, fills an important gap in the literature by providing a comprehensive guide to the theory but also the practical conduct of cost-benefit analysis, again with copious illustrative material and worked out examples.

The fifth book in the series, *Applied Health Economics for Public Health Practice and Research*, addresses the specific challenges of applying economic evaluation to public health. Finally, the current book—the sixth in the series—addresses the long-standing challenge of equity and health inequality. Equity concerns are central to healthcare and public health policy, and it is widely acknowledged that large health inequalities exist everywhere. However, standard economic evaluation focuses on efficiency in terms of aggregate costs and effects rather than equity in the distribution of costs and effects. This book is an all-in-one guide for researchers, policy advisers, policy makers and research funders who wish to learn about, commission and use equity-informative or "distributional" cost-effectiveness analysis to promote both equity and efficiency in health and healthcare.

Each book in the series is an integrated text prepared by several contributing authors, widely drawn from academic centres in the UK, the USA, Australia, and elsewhere. Part of our role as editors has been to foster a consistent style, but not to try to impose any particular line: that would have been unwelcome and also unwise amidst the diversity of an evolving field. News and information about the series, as well as supplementary material for each book, can be found at the series website: <http://www.herc.ox.ac.uk/books>.

Alastair Gray
Oxford

Andrew Briggs
London

Preface

'How to' books of this kind are usually based on course materials produced by colleagues from the same institution who have all been teaching together for several years. We did things differently by asking leading lights in the field from different institutions across the world to work together to develop the materials from scratch. This was partly to avoid parochialism: we wanted the book to be useful for analysts and decision makers working in a wide variety of different organizations in high-, middle-, and low-income countries. It was also because we wanted to use the collaborative writing process as a way of moving the field on, refining our thinking, and developing a degree of international consensus on concepts and terminology.

We did not simply let our authors do their own thing, as we were determined to produce a coherent teaching resource with chapters that hang together and build on each other in a cumulative sequence. We therefore adopted a decidedly heavy-handed editorial approach involving intensive consultation, thorough peer review, and incessant editorial commenting on successive drafts.

As any experienced professional knows, complete consensus on terminology is impossible—but at least we now have a reasonably consistent terminology across the handbook and a better idea of what we disagree about. How far we have succeeded in our other aims we leave the reader to judge.

We hope you find this book useful and enjoy learning about distributional cost-effectiveness analysis.

Richard Cookson
Susan Griffin
Ole F. Norheim
Anthony J. Culyer
University of York, UK and University of Bergen, Norway

Acknowledgements

First and foremost we are most grateful to the lead authors of the handbook methods chapters and training exercises—Colin Angus, Kjell Arne Johannsen, James Love-Koh, Andrew Mirelman, Owen O'Donnell, Mike Paulden, and Tom van Ourti—for putting up with our hands-on editorial approach, for responding so co-operatively to requests, and for contributing so generously and enthusiastically towards this collective endeavour. It has been great fun and we have learned a lot from you.

We are also especially grateful to Miqdad Asaria for producing the accompanying web-based DCEA tool, to James Lomas and James Love-Koh for helping to co-ordinate the production of the spreadsheet training exercises, to Alec Morton and Martin Forster for helpful comments on the whole manuscript, and to Christopher McCabe, Michael Drummond, Jeremy Lauer, Emma McIntosh, Alec Morton, Frida Nagalsoni, and Milton Weinstein for detailed comments on all the introductory chapters.

For helpful comments on individual chapters we would also like to thank John Broome, Maria Merritt, Dan Hausman, Alex Voorhoeve, Erik Schokkaeart, Andrew Mirelman, and Alessandro Grosso (Chapter 2); John Britton and Kamran Siddiqi (Chapter 5); Amani Mori, Erik Nord, and Mike Paulden (Chapter 6); Amanda Sacker, Dominic Nkhoma, Martin Forster, and Alec Morton (Chapter 7); Solomon Memirie and James Love-Koh (Chapter 8); Jessica Ochalek, Susan Cleary, Martin Forster, and Alec Morton (Chapter 9); Ijeoma Edoka, Owen O'Donnell, Bryony Dawkins, and Stephane Verguet (Chapter 10); Matthias Arnold and Yukiko Asada (Chapters 11 and 12); Mieraf Taddesse Tolla, Owen O'Donnell, Matthew Adler, and Finn McGuire (Chapter 13); Bjarne Robberstad, Christopher McCabe, Wandrudee Isaranuwatcha, and Aki Tsuchiya (Chapter 14); Colin Angus and Marta Soares (Chapter 15); and Graham Medley, Anna Vassall, and Richard White (Chapter 16). We would also like to thank Helen Cohen and Elizabeth Grant for excellent administrative support in organizing the peer review process, our editors from Oxford University Press, Nic Wilson, Hillevi Sellén, Sean McLeod and Susan Crowhurst, our copyeditor, Rosalind Wall, our typesetter, Kalpana Sagayanathan from Newgen, and our indexer, Kim Stringer, for their kindness, patience and flexibility at various stages of the process.

We would like to thank Owen O'Donnell, James Lomas, James Love-Koh, Andrew Mirelman, Ieva Skarda, and Fan Yang for help in running short courses on distributional cost-effectiveness analysis during the development of this book, and to the many students who have given us feedback.

We would also like to thank the Brocher Foundation for sponsoring our three-day planning workshop in Geneva in November 2017; Kalipso Chalkidou for advice on organizing the planning workshop; Kay Fountain, Alex Rollinger, and Marie Grosclaude for excellent administrative support; and to all the participants at this workshop for their help in shaping our thinking about the handbook design, including Matthew Adler, Colin Angus, Robert Baltussen, Maxim Berdnikov, Melanie Bertram, Michael Borowitz, Andrew Briggs, Christine Clavien, Mark Dusheiko, Samia Hurst, Raymond Hutubessy, Kjell Arne Johansson, Matthew Jowett, Carleigh Krubiner, Ross Leach, Ryan Li, James Love-Koh, Emma McIntosh, Andrew Mirelman, Ole Norheim, Owen O'Donnell, Breshna Orya, Trygve Ottersen, Mike Paulden, Maria Petro Brunal, Yoonie Sim, Erik Schokkaert, Ieva Skarda, Karin Stenberg, Mieraf Taddesse Tolla, Tessa Tan Torres-Edejer, Nertila Tavanxhi, Aki Tsuchiya, Anna Vassall, Stephane Verguet, Adam Wagstaff, Ning Wang, and Shufang Zhang.

Richard Cookson is grateful to the Brocher Foundation for hosting him as a visiting fellow for the month of July 2018 to undertake key handbook editorial tasks, and to the UK National Institute for Health Research (2016–2017) and the Wellcome Trust (2018–2020) for fellowship support during the course of this handbook project.

Neither we nor the authors have always followed the advice given and so we must absolve all the individuals as well as all the organizations listed above from responsibility for errors and misjudgments.

Contents

Contributors *xiii*

Part I: **Preliminaries**

1. Introduction *3*
   Richard Cookson, Susan Griffin, Ole F. Norheim, and Anthony J. Culyer

2. Principles of health equity *18*
   Richard Cookson, Anthony J. Culyer, and Ole F. Norheim

3. Designing a distributional cost-effectiveness analysis *44*
   Richard Cookson, Susan Griffin, Ole F. Norheim, and Anthony J. Culyer

4. Describing equity impacts and trade-offs *69*
   Richard Cookson, Susan Griffin, Ole F. Norheim, and Anthony J. Culyer

5. Introduction to the training exercises *92*
   Richard Cookson, James Love-Koh, Colin Angus, and James Lomas

Part II: **Simulating distributions**

6. Health by disease categories *105*
   Kjell Arne Johansson, Matthew M. Coates, Jan-Magnus Økland, Aki Tsuchiya, Gene Bukhman, Ole F. Norheim, and Øystein Haaland

7. Health by social variables *130*
   James Love-Koh and Andrew Mirelman

8. Costs and health effects *152*
   Colin Angus

9. Health opportunity costs *174*
   James Love-Koh

10. Financial protection *195*
    Andrew Mirelman and Richard Cookson

Part III: **Evaluating distributions**

11. Dominance analysis *213*
    Owen O'Donnell and Tom Van Ourti

12. Rank-dependent equity weights *237*
    Owen O'Donnell and Tom Van Ourti

13. Level-dependent equity weights 253
   Ole F. Norheim, Miqdad Asaria, Kjell Arne Johansson, Trygve Ottersen, and Aki Tsuchiya
14. Direct equity weights 275
   Mike Paulden, James O'Mahony, and Jeff Round

Part IV: **Next steps**

15. Uncertainty about facts and heterogeneity in values 303
   Susan Griffin
16. Future challenges 321
   Richard Cookson, Alec Morton, Erik Schokkaert, Gabriela B. Gomez, Maria W. Merritt, Ole F. Norheim, Susan Griffin, and Anthony J. Culyer

Glossary 345
Index 353

Contributors

Colin Angus
Senior Research Fellow
School of Health and Related Research
University of Sheffield, UK

Miqdad Asaria
Assistant Professorial Research Fellow
London School of Economics and Political Science
London, UK

Gene Bukhman
Assistant Professor
Harvard Medical School
Boston, USA

Matthew M. Coates
Research Associate
Harvard Medical School
Boston, USA

Richard Cookson
Professor
Centre for Health Economics
University of York
York, UK

Anthony J. Culyer
Professor Emeritus
University of York
York, UK
Visiting Professor
Imperial College
London

Gabriela B. Gomez
Honorary Associate Professor
Department of Global Health and Development
London School of Hygiene and Tropical Medicine
London, UK

Susan Griffin
Senior Research Fellow
Centre for Health Economics
University of York
York, UK

Øystein Haaland
Associate Professor
Department of Global Public Health and Primary Care
University of Bergen
Bergen, Norway

Kjell Arne Johansson
Professor
Department of Global Public Health and Primary Care
University of Bergen
Bergen, Norway

James Lomas
Research Fellow
Centre for Health Economics
University of York
York, UK

James Love-Koh
Research Fellow

Centre for Health Economics
University of York
York, UK

Maria W. Merritt
Associate Professor
Johns Hopkins Bloomberg School of Public Health
Baltimore, USA

Andrew Mirelman
Research Fellow
Centre for Health Economics
University of York
York, UK

Alec Morton
Professor and Head of Department
Management Science
University of Strathclyde
Glasgow, UK

Ole F. Norheim
Professor
Department of Global Public Health
University of Bergen
Bergen, Norway
Adjunct Professor
Harvard University
Boston, USA

Owen O'Donnell
Professor
Erasmus School of Economics
Erasmus University
Rotterdam, Netherlands

James O'Mahony
Research Assistant Professor
Public Health and Primary Care
Trinty College Dublin
Dublin, Ireland

Jan-Magnus Økland
Chief Engineer
Department of Global Health and Social Medicine
University of Bergen
Bergen, Norway

Trygve Ottersen
Executive Director
Norwegian Institute of Public Health
Oslo, Norway

Tom van Ourti
Professor
Erasmus School of Economics
Erasmus University
Rotterdam, Netherlands

Mike Paulden
Assistant Professor
School of Public Health
University of Alberta
Edmonton, Canada

Jeff Round
Director of Economics
Institute of Health Economics
Edmonton, Canada

Erik Schokkaert
Professor
Faculty of Economics and Business
University of Leuven
Leuven, Belgium

Aki Tsuchiya
Professor
School of Health and Related Research and Department of Economics
University of Sheffield
Sheffield, UK

Part I
Preliminaries

Chapter 1
Introduction

Richard Cookson, Susan Griffin,
Ole F. Norheim, and Anthony J. Culyer

Equity concerns are central to healthcare and public health policy. They have been highlighted in recent years by international reports on Universal Health Coverage (UHC) (Jamison et al., 2013; Ottersen & Norheim, 2014; World Health Organization, 2015) and the social determinants of health (Marmot et al., 2008). Systematic differences have been documented between advantaged and disadvantaged people in health, use of health services, and financial protection from hardship due to the out-of-pocket (OOP) costs of using health services. Concern to reduce unfair differences in health, healthcare, and financial protection has been expressed in relation to numerous equity-relevant variables—including severity of illness, disability, proximity to death, rarity of condition, socioeconomic status, geographical location, ethnicity, indigenous status, migrant status, gender, and age—of varying salience to decision makers in different countries and organizations.

Historically, the mainstream teaching and practice of economic evaluation in the health sector has focused on efficiency[1] in terms of aggregate costs and effects rather than equity in the distribution of costs and effects. Cost-effectiveness analysis (CEA) is now routinely used across the globe to inform health sector priority-setting decisions, and published cost-effectiveness evidence is available about thousands of healthcare and public health programmes (World Health Organization, 2018; Tufts Medical Center, 2019). Until recently CEA studies focused on providing information about the aggregate costs and effects of alternative decisions. They have not provided information about equity in the distribution of costs and effects between more and less disadvantaged people. Nor have they provided information about the trade-offs that may

---

[1] As explained in the handbook glossary, we typically use the term 'efficiency' informally to mean net health benefit—i.e. total health benefits minus total health opportunity costs. However, efficiency can mean different things in different contexts, and one can even talk about efficiency in the pursuit of an equity objective.

arise between efficiency and equity objectives. An unfortunate disconnect has thus emerged between what health decision makers often want to know about equity and what economic evaluation evidence usually tells them. This disconnect matters. Research that fails to address decision makers' concerns will not have impact, even though the CEA evidence may have been soundly based as far as it went. And decision makers who are poorly informed about the equity impacts of their decisions may not achieve their equity objectives.

A substantial and growing literature has, however, now emerged on practical methods of conducting CEA that provide information about distributional equity impacts and trade-offs (Van de Wetering et al., 2013; Asaria et al., 2015; Ottersen et al., 2016; Verguet et al., 2016; Cookson et al., 2017). This literature has yet to be brought together into the general texts on CEA and its application. Our handbook pulls the material together into an all-in-one guide for educational and reference purposes. It describes the principles and methods, with illustrative examples from high-, middle-, and low-income countries, and provides practical training exercises with step-by-step instructions. We hope this will help raise awareness of the principles and methods among research commissioners and users as well as increasing the capacity for applying them among analysts. As well as increasing the quantity of applied studies, we hope this will also help to improve their quality and relevance to decision-making. Although in places we are critical of simplistic and misleading approaches to equity analysis, we wish to encourage a pragmatic approach—inability to conduct a perfect equity analysis should not be a barrier to conducting an imperfect but useful analysis.

We use the phrase 'distributional cost-effectiveness analysis' (DCEA) as a broad umbrella term to cover all types of CEA that provide information about both equity in the distribution of costs and effects, and efficiency in terms of aggregate costs and effects. DCEA can involve simply exploring the implications of giving special priority or 'equity weight' to improving the health of programme recipients compared with the health of non-recipients. It can also involve more detailed simulation of the distribution of benefits and burdens within the general population by equity-relevant variables, simulation of distributional consequences other than health, and formal evaluation of distributional consequences including potential trade-offs between equity and efficiency objectives. A similar phrase is 'extended cost-effectiveness analysis' (ECEA), which is effectively a synonym for distributional cost-effectiveness analysis.[2] The essential feature of DCEA that distinguishes it from other ways of addressing equity concerns is that it

---

[2] For those interested in terminological nuance, an explanation of the precise relationship between the terms DCEA and ECEA is given in Chapter 3.

provides information about distributional consequences, that is, differences in the benefits and burdens of alternative decisions for different people. CEA provides the total costs and effects. DCEA indicates who gains and who loses and by how much.

DCEA is potentially useful in any priority setting decision in healthcare or public health, since almost any decision will have different consequences for different people. Such decisions include:

- Purchasing costly new health technologies—for example whether to fund new drugs for cancer, at what price, and for which patient subgroups.
- Designing healthcare benefit packages—for example whether to cover diabetes in a public health insurance plan and, if so, which treatments and with what co-payments.
- Investing in health service delivery infrastructure—for example whether to invest in a community health worker programme, and if so how to prioritize investments targeting different geographical areas.
- Public health—for example whether to implement a sugar-sweetened beverage tax, which will have different impacts on consumption and expenditure across households.

The methods are applicable to conventional health technology assessment (HTA) decision-making about the pricing and reimbursement of new pharmaceuticals, devices and treatments for specific conditions. They are also applicable to a broader swathe of health sector priority setting decisions involving specific interventions for specific populations, including decisions about the funding and delivery of existing treatments; about screening, vaccination, and other preventive healthcare programmes; and about broader public health programmes such as safety regulations, 'sin' taxes, and investments in healthy living environments. However, challenges remain in applying both CEA and DCEA convincingly to 'macro level' questions of health system reform involving complex behavioural responses and system dynamics—for example whether to increase national health expenditure, change the public-private expenditure mix, or change the way that doctors are paid—and to health service infrastructure investments with complex economies of scale and scope across many different treatments and disease areas. We thus refer to analysing 'decisions' or 'programmes' throughout the handbook and generally avoid the terms 'technology' (too narrow) and 'policy' (too broad).

The handbook has two complementary aims. The first is to equip health decision makers in government and other agencies to be more effective commissioners of DCEA studies; to be constructive partners as the research proceeds, for example by discussing the variety of possible social value judgments to be used during the process; to be able to evaluate the quality, relevance, and limitations of the studies when complete; and to use the findings to inform healthcare and public health priority-setting decisions. The second is to help postgraduate students and practitioners of CEA to produce good quality DCEA studies suitable for informing healthcare and public health priority-setting decisions in the different contexts provided by low-, middle-, and high-income countries.

The text of the book is designed to be useful for CEA specialists, but also accessible to anyone who is comfortable reading graphs, tables, and simple mathematical formulae and who is familiar with basic CEA principles (Drummond et al., 2015). Our intended readership includes health sector postgraduate students, researchers, advocates, practitioners and policy advisers in health-related disciplines, from any country. Completing the practical training exercises requires a high degree of proficiency in spreadsheet manipulation, including the ability to use complex spreadsheet functions and graph formatting options. It does not, however, require advanced modelling or programming skills such as the ability to construct a Markov or microsimulation model, or conduct probabilistic sensitivity analysis.

We show how different methods are useful for different purposes and highlight their strengths and limitations, including weaknesses in the evidence base and remaining unresolved methodological challenges. The methods are imperfect, and likely to continue developing rapidly in the decades to come, and we anticipate some of those developments in a concluding chapter on 'future challenges' for the field.

Analysing equity raises controversial issues because reasonable people disagree on appropriate value judgments that define equity. We have therefore sought to identify key areas of ethical controversy and, without taking sides, to help readers make up their own minds. Our approach is to design distributional analyses that reflect the specific equity concerns of decision makers and research users in their own specific decision-making context, and to be as clear and explicit as possible about the underpinning value judgments. The tools of DCEA are available to anyone, whatever their ethical or political views.

1.1 Economic evaluation

Economic evaluation aims to support decision-making by appraising the costs and benefits of alternative decisions before resources are committed. Health economic evaluation is the branch of economic evaluation that supports decision-making in healthcare and public health. There are numerous well-established guides to health economic evaluation, including a basic principles textbook known informally among health economists as the 'blue book'

(Drummond et al., 2015) and a modelling handbook known informally as the 'green book' (Briggs et al., 2006).

Economic evaluation of healthcare decisions often draws upon effectiveness evidence from randomized controlled trials, quasi-experimental studies, and other well-designed evaluations of health technologies and policies. However, economic evaluation almost always needs to go beyond evidence provided by effectiveness studies. Trials and quasi-experiments are incomplete methods of informing expenditure decisions. Trials contribute usefully to the testing of causal hypotheses about 'what works' under controlled study conditions (efficacy), and hence to internal validity. Quasi-experiments can assess the consequences of a specific health programme in a specific setting. However, they have limited external validity in terms of predicting the consequences of a similar programme involving the delivery of services in different ways to different people under different conditions. Usually they provide information only about short-run consequences, rather than long-run consequences for mortality, morbidity, and public cost that can accumulate for many years or decades into the future. Often, they provide evidence about health benefits only in terms of biochemical or clinical outcomes that do not help comparisons across diseases. Rarely do they provide information about the opportunity costs of spending public money that could have been used in other beneficial ways. More rarely still do they provide information about the distribution of benefits and burdens within either the recipient population or the wider population served by the decision-making organization. Economic evaluation is needed to provide a more complete picture.

The standard approach to health economic evaluation is CEA based on a general summary measure of health outcome that can be used to make comparisons between disease areas, such as the quality-adjusted life year (QALY) gained or the disability-adjusted life year (DALY) averted. From now on we will use the term health-adjusted life year (HALY) to mean either a QALY or an averted DALY or other similar general measure of health outcome in terms of healthy years.

When making priority-setting decisions, health sector decision makers implicitly or explicitly compare condition-specific clinical effects for people with different conditions—for example a five-point gain in a mental health symptom score versus a ten per cent reduction in the risk of dying from cardiovascular disease. General summary measures of health outcome provide a systematic method for comparing condition-specific effects in terms of gains in healthy years of life, based on evidence and explicit value judgments that are open to scrutiny. They also allow value for money to be assessed in a standardized way, by establishing a common cost-effectiveness benchmark (e.g. in terms of cost per HALY gained) that can be used for deciding which services are best included in healthcare coverage (Culyer, 2016a).

In this handbook we show how standard CEA methods can be used to analyse the consequences of health decisions for distributional equity. The fundamental ethical imperative underpinning standard CEA is an efficiency objective: to improve the sum total of population health (Cookson, 2015). We show how CEA can also be used to analyse distributional equity objectives, such as reducing inequality in health, promoting equal access to health services, and providing equal protection from financial hardship arising from OOP healthcare expenditure. We also show how tensions can arise between different equity and efficiency objectives, how trade-offs can be explored, and how equity impacts can be measured and summarized in general ways that allow comparisons across disease areas and decisions.

The handbook focuses on distributional analysis in the context of CEA, which remains the dominant form of economic evaluation in the health sector. However, the methods of simulation and evaluation that we describe can also be applied in the context of other forms of economic evaluation that are sometimes used in the health sector, including cost-benefit analysis, multi-criteria decision analysis, and mathematical programming (Morton, 2014). For example, a simple form of multi-criteria decision analysis might include equity as one of the criteria, by seeking stakeholder views about equity impact in terms of a subjective rating scale. DCEA could be used to provide a more analytical, evidence-based measure of equity impact by simulating the distribution of costs and benefits and formally evaluating equity impact using a summary index of inequality.

When analysing equity impacts and trade-offs it is often useful to adopt the net health benefit framework, which combines effects and costs into a single summary measure of net health benefit (Drummond et al., 2015). This provides an aggregate measure of 'efficiency impact' which can then be compared with aggregate measures of 'equity impact'. Unlike a cost-effectiveness ratio, it also provides a sense of the scale of the benefits. However, it is often important also to provide disaggregated information about specific effects and costs—for example decision makers will often want to know the total health benefit and the total cost, as well as the net health benefit.

1.2 Distributional cost-effectiveness analysis

The usual convention in economics is that evaluation of specific public expenditure decisions should focus exclusively on 'efficiency' and the analysis of total or marginal costs and benefits (Blackorby & Donaldson, 1990; Brouwer et al., 2008; Atkinson, 2011). Matters of equity are usually dealt with in the context of general fiscal policies on taxes, transfers, and market regulations and their consequences for the distribution of income and wealth (Atkinson, 2015). There is, however, considerable demand from health sector decision makers for information about the health-related distributional consequences of healthcare and public health programmes, and that is our concern in this book. The economist James Tobin has argued that it is not unreasonable to have 'specific egalitarian' concerns about equity in the distribution of specific goods—for example food, shelter, healthcare, education, and legal services—as well as 'general egalitarian' concerns about equity in the distribution of income and wealth (Tobin, 1970). The philosopher Michael Walzer has argued that different principles of distributional equity should be applied to the distribution of different kinds of goods (Walzer, 2008). And the philosopher-economist Amartya Sen has argued that the informational basis for assessing inequality should not be narrowed exclusively to income and wealth but should also include information on the distribution of specific components of human flourishing, including health (Sen, 1999).

DCEA provides information about distributional consequences that can be broken down by one or more equity-relevant variables—including disease variables (e.g. disease classification, severity of illness, proximity to death, rarity of condition), social variables (e.g. socioeconomic status, geographical location, indigenous status, ethnicity, gender, age), and other variables of special interest in a particular country or decision-making context. It offers ways of thinking and techniques of measurement that can be used by different decision-making organizations to reflect different ideas of fairness. Some organizations may wish to apply a consistent approach to equity analysis across all decisions within their remit. However, organizations in different countries may wish to use different approaches, and this book does not prescribe a one-size-fits-all solution.

DCEA is only one useful source of quantitative information for policymakers concerned about equity. Other methods are available to help provide other kinds of quantitative information about equity, including information that is needed as an input to DCEA. This includes methods of measuring inequalities in health, health services, and financial protection (O'Donnell et al., 2008); incorporating distributional health equity concerns into health system monitoring (World Health Organization, 2013; Cookson et al., 2018); using trials and quasi-experiments to evaluate the differential impacts of health technologies and policies on more and less disadvantaged subgroups of programme recipients (Khandker et al., 2010; Welch et al., 2017); and using systematic review methods to synthesize information from such trials and quasi-experiments (O'Neill et al., 2014).

DCEA, however, provides additional information about the distribution of costs and effects that is not provided by these other methods of applied health research. Decision makers may need information not only on who benefits from a policy but also on who bears the opportunity costs of diverting scarce resources from other uses; they are likely to be concerned about distributional impacts within the entire general population they serve, not merely within a specific population of programme recipients; they usually need information about long-term as well as short-term equity impacts; they need ways of comparing equity impacts between disease areas and programmes; and they need information about trade-offs between equity and efficiency objectives.

Although DCEA can provide useful information and insight about all these matters, the methods are imperfect and will require ongoing development and improvement in decades to come. At present, for example, the methods proposed in this book examine equity in the distribution of health separately from equity in the distribution of non-health benefits and burdens (such as financial protection, income, education, employment, the quality of personal relationships), rather than attempting to integrate the full range of distributional consequences into an overall equity analysis. Important methodological challenges also remain in explicitly modelling real-world complexities such as economies of scale and system dynamics in ways that help to produce more accurate and credible simulations of distributional consequences, in simulating and evaluating *ex post* distributions of realized health as well as *ex ante* distributions of expected health, and in analysing ethical principles based on respecting rights and proportionally satisfying needs rather than maximizing social value. There are also substantial limitations in the evidence base for simulating the distribution of health-related benefits and burdens, with little information currently available about who bears the opportunity costs of expenditure decisions in terms of health forgone. These and other limitations are noted in the relevant methods chapters and discussed in Chapter 16 on future challenges. Many of these problems are likely to arise in practice. Anyone embarking on DCEA must therefore be prepared from time to time to adopt a pragmatic and locally sensitive approach, and to avoid letting a desire to conduct a perfect study become the enemy of a merely useful one.

A common misconception is that the distinctive aim of DCEA is to incorporate a pre-specified set of equity weights and other social value judgments about equity into the analysis. All economic evaluation studies do this, including standard CEA studies. Most obviously, standard CEA specifies that all healthy years count the same, no matter who gains or loses them— 'a HALY is a HALY is a HALY'. In other words, standard CEA specifies a uniform set of equity weights. Standard CEA also implicitly makes other social value judgments about equity, in scoping decisions about the relevant policy options and comparators, which costs and effects to measure, how to compare costs and effects of different kinds, how to aggregate costs and effects for different people and organizations, and how to value future costs and effects (Shah et al., 2013). These value judgments are rarely mentioned in applied studies and reports to decision makers, though they are extensively discussed in textbooks, methods guidance documents and other underpinning literature that may be unfamiliar to the decision maker. To improve transparency and accountability, therefore, it is important to ensure that decision makers are closely involved in making these value judgments and that, when reporting or publishing, documentation is cited that describes and justifies the value judgments that have been made.

This handbook shows how to go beyond incorporating pre-specified value judgments about equity into the analysis. DCEA is not simply about specifying a new set of equity weights to replace the standard uniform ones. DCEA does not have to use equity weights at all—it can just provide a breakdown of distributional consequences. If equity weights are used, extensive sensitivity analysis can be conducted around the implications of different weights without necessarily recommending base case benchmark weights. If a 'preferrred' set of weights is endorsed by the decision maker, this choice does not have to be pre-specified but can be a context-specific decision made either during the scoping phase of a study or at a later stage in the light of the initial DCEA findings and stakeholder consultation.

DCEA focuses on generating new information about distributional consequences that will facilitate deliberation among decision makers and stakeholders. What is distinctive about DCEA is not that equity weights and other value judgments are incorporated 'in' to the analysis, but that new information about equity in the distribution of costs and effects is extracted 'out' of the analysis. DCEA is thus an 'equity-informative' kind of health economic evaluation, in which the role of the analyst is to provide information rather than to judge what is fair. Decision makers and the populations they serve are the ultimate arbiters of these value judgments—including judgments about the 'who' and the 'what' of the relevant distributions (e.g. which equity-relevant characteristics, what costs and effects) as well as judgments about the weights to be attached to gains and losses. Analysts inform, decision makers decide (Culyer, 2016b).

Designing an approach to equity analysis that is useful in a specific decision-making context is likely to take the analyst into broader managerial issues around the decision-making structure and process and the research base that supports it. When considering social value judgments and the scope of a DCEA it will often be useful to engage stakeholders through some form of consultation. A critically important characteristic of good evaluations is their credibility and acceptability both to decision makers and the populations they serve. Identifying relevant stakeholders and allowing them to participate at various points in the decision-making process is of value not only for credibility and wider 'ownership' of the process, but can also be a means by which decision-makers learn—by having their preconceptions challenged and their knowledge base widened (Culyer & Lomas, 2006). These are matters taken up further in Chapter 3.

We focus on presenting a set of basic tools that can be combined and used in different ways for different purposes, rather than a set of pre-packaged solutions. To use a culinary analogy, this is a cooking skills manual rather than a recipe book. Once you have learned the basic skills, you can cook any dish according to any recipe you like. You can even give your recipe a brand-name—though the proliferation of different brand names (and associated acronyms) for similar methods can cause confusion for students and decision makers.

1.3 Summary of the book contents

Part I of the book is an introduction and overview for healthcare and public health officials wanting to commission and use DCEA findings, as well as for students and analysts wanting to learn how to conduct DCEA. Parts II and III provide step-by-step guides to the methods for students and analysts, with accompanying hands-on spreadsheet training exercises. Part II focuses on methods for simulating distributions—finding out who gains and loses—and Part III focuses on valuing distributions—valuing the gains and losses. Part IV concludes with discussions about how to handle uncertainty about facts and disagreement about values, and some of the future challenges facing this young and rapidly evolving field of study.

Part I, 'Preliminaries', continues with Chapter 2 on equity principles. This sets out ways of thinking about equity and what kinds of equity issues can and cannot be addressed by DCEA. It also shows how to translate the equity concerns expressed informally by decision makers into formal equity objectives that are clear, coherent, and amenable to quantitative analysis. Chapter 3, on designing a DCEA, then shows how different equity objectives can be analysed by combining different components of analysis in various ways. Chapter 4, on describing equity impacts and trade-offs, reviews the value judgments underpinning the selection and presentation of information about distributional consequences and shows how to interpret the key equity metrics and diagrams used in DCEA to analyse trade-offs between equity and efficiency impacts. Chapter 5 introduces the training exercises, explaining how the exercises fit together and introducing the example of nicotine replacement therapy that we use in a cumulative sequence of training exercises throughout the rest of this book.

Part II, 'Simulating distributions', starts with two chapters on how to simulate baseline distributions of health prior to implementation of a new health programme. Chapter 6 introduces different concepts of health with different equity implications—for example lifetime health from birth to death versus future health remaining from disease onset to death—and shows how to compare disease groups using those different concepts. Chapter 7 then shows how to simulate the baseline distribution of lifetime health broken down by one or more equity-relevant social variables, using socioeconomic status and geography to illustrate. Chapter 8 shows how to analyse the distribution of health effects—including effects on health service utilization as well as health outcome. Chapter 9 examines the distribution of health opportunity costs—the health benefits forgone as a result of displacing resources from alternative uses in order to fund a new health programme. Finally, Chapter 10 shows how to analyse the distribution of financial protection effects, focusing on protection from catastrophic and impoverishing OOP healthcare bills.

Part III, 'Valuing distributions', introduces several ways of summarizing, evaluating, and ranking distributions in a manner that is founded on explicit, challengeable, and consistent ethical principles. Chapter 11, on dominance analysis, explains how to establish whether one distribution is dominant over another according to general ethical principles. Chapters 12 and 13 explain how to compare distributions using indirect equity weights based on an equity parameter reflecting the degree of priority given to less healthy individuals or groups. Chapter 12 explains how to compare distributions using rank-dependent equity weights, which give priority to the worse-off depending on their rank in the health distribution. Chapter 13 explains how to compare distributions using level-dependent equity weights, which give priority to the worse-off depending on their absolute level of health. Chapter 14 introduces direct equity weights that can be set in whatever *ad hoc* pattern the decision maker prefers. A key theme throughout is the need to pay explicit attention to who bears the opportunity costs of health programmes as well as who gains the benefits, so that equity weights can be applied in an even-handed way to all those who share the same equity-relevant characteristics rather than in a one-sided way favouring programme recipients only.

Finally, Part IV, 'Next steps', concludes with Chapter 15 on handling uncertainty about facts and heterogeneity of values and Chapter 16 on future challenges.

1.4 How to use this book

All readers will benefit from reading Chapter 2 on principles of equity, especially the first section on four different ways of thinking about equity. In our experience students are sometimes impatient with introductory material on basic principles, and keen to skip ahead. However, we recommend resisting this temptation. Equity is a complicated concept which often generates more heat than light. Diving in to a discussion or analysis of equity without a clear and shared understanding of what you are talking or thinking about is a recipe for confusion.

Research commissioners will then want to read Chapter 3 on designing a DCEA, which shows the different elements of DCEA and how they can be combined in applied DCEA studies. They may also be interested in Chapter 16 on future challenges for ideas on commissioning research.

Research users will want to read Chapter 4 on equity impacts and trade-offs, which describes the main equity metrics and graphs needed to understand and critically appraise DCEA findings.

Research producers will first need to read the introductory Chapters 2, 3, 4, and 5 and then decide what kind of DCEA they want to produce. They will then be able to choose which of the remaining chapters and training exercises will be most useful to them, depending on which components of DCEA they need. In deciding which of the methods chapters to read, the key questions are as follows:

1. *Do you need to simulate distributions by disease categories or social variables?* Distributional concern may focus on unfair differences related to disease categories such as severity of illness or rarity (Chapter 6) or social variables such as socioeconomic status or region (Chapter 7).

2. *Do you need to simulate baseline distributions or incremental distributions or both?* Decision makers may just want to compare how badly-off different people are in terms of their health in the baseline pre-decision situation (Chapters 6 and 7). However, they may also want information about the incremental distribution of health effects (Chapter 8) and health opportunity costs (Chapter 9).

3. *Do you need to simulate distributions of financial protection outcomes?* It may be enough to focus on health outcomes. However, decision makers may also want information about distributions of financial protection outcomes (Chapter 10), especially in countries where many people face financial hardship due to OOP healthcare costs.

4. *Do you need to conduct a formal evaluation of distributional consequences?* It may be enough to provide decision makers with detailed distributional breakdowns of each outcome for each decision option. However, since distributional consequences can be complicated and hard to interpret, it may help to conduct a formal evaluation using dominance analysis (Chapter 11), rank-dependent equity weights (Chapter 12), level-dependent equity weights (Chapter 13), direct equity weights (Chapter 14), or a combination thereof.

Each methods chapter has an accompanying spreadsheet training exercise to give you hands-on practice in using the methods. These exercises are introduced in Chapter 5 and are freely available at this website along with a web-based DCEA research tool which automates the calculations: https://www.york.ac.uk/che/research/equity/handbook

References

Asaria M., Griffin S., Cookson R., Whyte S., & Tappenden P. (2015). Distributional cost-effectiveness analysis of healthcare programmes—a methodological case study of the UK Bowel Cancer Screening Programme. *Health Economics,* **24,** 742–754.

Atkinson A. (2011). The restoration of welfare economics. *American Economic Review,* 157–161.

Atkinson A. (2015). *Inequality: What Can Be Done?* Harvard University Press, Cambridge, MA.

Blackorby C. & Donaldson D. (1990). A review article: the case against the use of the sum of compensating variations in cost-benefit analysis. *Canadian Journal of Economics,* **23**(3), 471–494.

Briggs A., Sculpher M., & Claxton K. (2006). *Decision Modelling for Health Economic Evaluation.* Oxford University Press, Oxford.

Brouwer W., Culyer A., van Exel N., & Rutten F. (2008). Welfarism vs extra-welfarism. *Journal of Health Economics,* **27,** 325–338.

Cookson R. (2015). Justice and the NICE approach. *Journal of Medical Ethics,* **41,** 99–102.

Cookson R, Mirelman A., Griffin S., Asaria M., Dawkins B., Norheim O., et al. (2017). Using cost-effectiveness analysis to address health equity concerns. *Value in Health,* **20,** 206–212.

Cookson R, Asaria M., Ali S., Shaw R., Doran T., & Goldblatt P. (2018). Health equity monitoring for healthcare quality assurance. *Social Science & Medicine,* **198,** 148–156.

Culyer A. & Lomas J. (2006). Deliberative processes and evidence-informed decision making in healthcare: do they work and how might we know? *Evidence & Policy: A Journal of Research, Debate and Practice,* **2,** 357–371 (reprinted in **R. Cookson** and **K. Claxton** (eds) (2012). *Humble Economist,* 283–300, https://www.york.ac.uk/che/publications/books/the-humble-economist/.)

Culyer A. (2016a). Cost-effectiveness thresholds in healthcare: a bookshelf guide to their meaning and use. *Health Economics, Policy and Law,* **11,** 415–432.

Culyer A. (2016b). HTA—Algorithm or process? Comment on 'Expanded HTA: Enhancing fairness and legitimacy'. *International Journal of Health Policy and Management*, 5, 501–505.

Drummond M., Sculpher M., Claxton K., Stoddart G., & Torrance G. (2015). *Methods for the Economic Evaluation of Healthcare Programmes*. Oxford University Press, Oxford.

Jamison D., Summers L., Alleyne G., Arrow K., Berkley S., Binagwaho A., et al. (2013). Global health 2035: a world converging within a generation. *Lancet*, 382, 1898–1955.

Khandker S., Koolwal G., & Samad H. (2010). *Handbook on Impact Evaluation: Quantitative Methods and Practices*: World Bank Publications, Washington, DC.

Marmot M., Friel S., Bell R., Houweling T., & Taylor S. (2008). Closing the gap in a generation: health equity through action on the social determinants of health. *Lancet*, 372, 1661–1669.

Morton A. (2014). Aversion to health inequalities in healthcare prioritisation: a multicriteria optimisation perspective. *Journal of Health Economics*, 36, 164–173.

O'Donnell O, van Doorslaer E., Wagstaff A., & Lindelow M. (2008). *Analyzing Health Equity Using Household Survey Data: a Guide to Techniques and their Implementation*. World Bank Publications, Washington, DC.

O'Neill J., Tabish H., Welch V., Petticrew M., Pottie K., Clarke M., et al. (2014). Applying an equity lens to interventions: using PROGRESS ensures consideration of socially stratifying factors to illuminate inequities in health. *Journal of Clinical Epidemiology*, 67, 56–64.

Ottersen T. & Norheim O. (2014). Making fair choices on the path to universal health coverage. *Bulletin of the World Health Organization*, 92, 389.

Ottersen T., Ford R., Kakad M., Kjellevold A., Melberg H., Moen A., et al. (2016). A new proposal for priority setting in Norway: open and fair. *Health Policy*, 120(3), 246–251.

Sen A. (1999). *Commodities and Capabilities*: Oxford University Press, New Delhi.

Shah K., Cookson R., Culyer A., & Littlejohns P. (2013). NICE's social value judgments about equity in health and healthcare. *Health Economic Policy Law*, 8, 145–165.

Tobin J. (1970). On limiting the domain of inequality. *Journal of Law and Economics*, 13(2), 263–277.

Tufts Medical Center (2019). CEA Registry. Center for the Evaluation of Value and Risk in Health. https://cevr.tuftsmedicalcenter.org/databases/cea-registry

Van de Wetering E., Stolk E., Van Exel N., & Brouwer W. (2013). Balancing equity and efficiency in the Dutch basic benefits package using the principle of proportional shortfall. *European Journal of Health Economics*, 14, 107–115.

Verguet S., Kim J., & Jamison D. (2016). Extended cost-effectiveness analysis for health policy assessment: a tutorial. *Pharmacoeconomics*, 34, 913–923.

Walzer M. (2008). *Spheres of Justice: A Defense of Pluralism and Equality*. Basic Books, New York.

Welch V., Norheim O., Jull J., Cookson R., Sommerfelt H., & Tugwell P. (2017). CONSORT-Equity 2017 extension and elaboration for better reporting of health equity in randomised trials. *British Medical Journal*, 2017;359:j5085.

World Health Organization. (2018). WHO-CHOICE. World Health Organization, Geneva. https://www.who.int/choice/cost-effectiveness/en/

World Health Organization (2013). *Handbook on Health Inequality Monitoring with a Special Focus on Low-and Middle-income Countries.* World Health Organization, Geneva.

World Health Organization (2015). *Tracking Universal Health Coverage: First Global Monitoring Report.* World Health Organization, Geneva.

Chapter 2

Principles of health equity

Richard Cookson, Anthony J. Culyer, and Ole F. Norheim

This chapter shows how informal normative concerns about health equity raised by decision makers can be translated into formal health equity objectives amenable to quantitative analysis using distributional cost-effectiveness analysis (DCEA). It also clarifies the kinds of ethical concerns that can and cannot be addressed using the methods in this handbook. Technical details and variants are described later in the methods chapters in Parts II and III.

2.1 Introduction

Amongst the commonly met criteria for making decisions about investments in healthcare and public health are equity concerns to reduce unfair differences in people's health, access to health services, and financial protection from the risk of large and unexpected out-of-pocket (OOP) healthcare costs (Whitehead, 1992). DCEA can provide information about each of these.

There are substantial differences in what decision makers have in mind when they speak of 'fairness', 'justice', and 'equity'. DCEA must therefore have a sufficiently broad scope to be of service in a variety of decision contexts. The contexts vary according to the role and function of the decision makers, their values (personal, social, and political), the historical and cultural context of their particular society or jurisdiction, local governance and accountability, and the sophistication of the available data and of the analysts at hand for analysing it.

DCEA provides information about the distributional consequences of decisions that can be useful to any decision maker or stakeholder, whatever their political persuasion and philosophical views. Distributional consequences usually matter to some extent, whatever philosophical view is adopted. There are many ways of thinking about the ethics of priority-setting, as we shall see, and fair decision-making is often a matter of making pragmatic compromises between different considerations and different ways of thinking.

DCEA provides a useful framework for thinking about complex and often emotionally challenging decisions, as well as useful quantitative information for decision makers and other stakeholders. The information that is useful in a particular context requires judgment. Some of these judgments relate to what it is that the decision maker is asking of the analyst, some relate to what is possible, financially and politically, and some are social value judgments about what is good for society. DCEA is best used in the context of a deliberative decision-making process involving all relevant stakeholders. It is not a computer-based algorithm that tells decision makers what the right decision is, 'all things considered'. It provides some useful information about equity but not all the information that decision makers could possibly ever need. Because reasonable people can disagree about equity, the methods of equity-informative health economic evaluation are designed to be useful in the presence of such disagreement, for example by identifying the relevant ethical issues about which there is disagreement and by making empirical assessments of relevant factual matters, thereby facilitating a discussion. This may not result in a consensus. Nevertheless, a clearer understanding about who disagrees, and why, may be important in implementing decisions and explaining them to health professionals and the general public.

Schematically, DCEA proceeds as follows: First, one establishes a framework for thinking about the decision problem and the options to be evaluated, in consultation with the decision maker. Then one finds out the relevant facts about the distributional consequences of each option—estimates, for example, of who is likely to gain and who to lose, and by how much. Then one evaluates the options, wherever possible based on objectives that are chosen by the decision maker. Finally, one presents the quantitative findings—along with the conventional cost-effective analysis (CEA) efficiency results and perhaps alongside other relevant but more qualitative kinds of information (such as likely barriers to implementation). Chronologically, of course, the process can be as iterative and flexible as needed—for example discussion of interim findings may reveal ethical or factual issues that merit further analysis, and may even throw up new options that decision makers wish to consider.

2.2 Four ways of thinking about ethics

We distinguish four ways of thinking about the ethics of priority-setting, as listed in Fig 2.1. When considering whether and how to handle an equity concern in DCEA, it is important to consider which of these four ways of thinking is most relevant. Trying to analyse an equity concern without recognizing the relevant way of thinking is rather like trying to talk with someone without

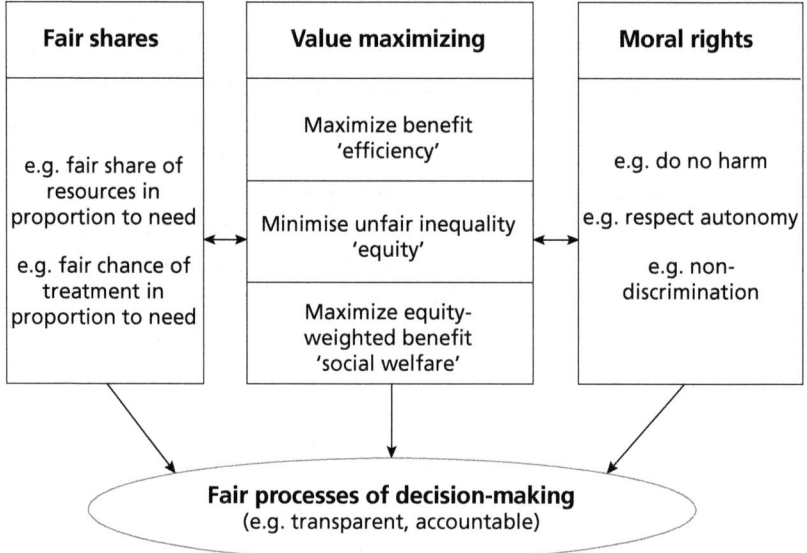

Figure 2.1 Ways of thinking about ethics.

recognizing their language—more likely to result in confusion than useful information.

DCEA methods are primarily based on the 'value maximizing' way of thinking, which seeks to evaluate which decision option has the best consequences (or the greatest 'social value') after considering both efficiency in terms of sum total benefits and burdens and equity in their distribution. However, the information provided about distributional consequences can also be a useful input into deliberations based on other ways of thinking.

When having to justify a priority-setting decision that may be unpopular, like saying 'No' to providing a treatment under a public health insurance scheme, it would normally be an advantage to be able to defend it by arguing that its consequences were inferior to all other options considered, as well as by claiming that the decision respected people's rights, that everyone received a fair share of resources, and that all appropriate steps had been taken in the process of making the decision. Furthermore, information about consequences is required to make appropriate compromises between different people's conflicting rights, to assess what constitutes a fair share of scarce resources, and to design and follow a fair process of decision-making.

The value maximizing way of thinking underpins most of the economics literature on equity, and most of the evaluation methods described in Part III of this handbook. The idea is to compare options by ranking them according to how well their consequences succeed in fulfilling one or more policy objectives. If there are several objectives that cannot all be simultaneously fulfilled—as is often the case in practice—then options are ranked by making trade-offs between the different objectives to maximize overall value or 'social welfare'. For example, suppose we have two objectives: to maximize total health benefit and to reduce unfair health inequality. Mathematically, the optimal pursuit of these twin objectives is then a matter of maximizing social welfare as measured by a numerical index that ranks health distributions according to specific value judgments about the appropriate trade-off between reducing unfair health inequality and improving total health. These judgments can be summarized mathematically using an inequality aversion parameter. In the context of a specific decision, this can also be thought of as maximizing what we shall call the equity-weighted sum of health benefits, where equity weights have been set to reflect the baseline distribution of health as well as a specific value of the inequality aversion parameter. The same degree of concern for unfair health inequality—that is, the same inequality aversion parameter value—may imply different equity weights in the context of different decisions with different baseline distributions of health.

The 'moral rights' way of thinking focuses on normative rules about what duties individuals owe to each other and hence what actions are just (required by the duties) and unjust (prohibited by the duties). For example, a doctor may owe patients a duty of care, and a manager may owe staff, clients, and the wider public a duty of non-discrimination. Respecting such rights may conflict with the principle of cost-effectiveness. For example, it may not be cost-effective to save workers trapped in a mine but respecting a moral duty of care may require decision makers to do so. Respecting moral rights is a way of thinking that appeals to many decision makers and that may be more salient in some cultures than others. In some cultures, for example, a duty of care for older people is deeply embedded. In the presence of resource constraints, however, this may not imply that older patients have an absolute right to all needed medical care irrespective of cost-effectiveness. Rather, it may require that decision makers should consider the consequences of their funding decisions for different age groups and ask themselves whether assigning a high equity weight on consequences for older people relative to younger people is acceptable in view of the health consequences for the young. Respecting rights may also rule out some options as unacceptable. For example, an option might be considered wrong if it seriously violates some people's rights to autonomy or invidiously discriminates against disabled people. Again, however, there are trade-off possibilities. Rights need not be 'hard' constraints that dominate all other considerations: they may be overruled when they clash with other rights, or when they impose unreasonable costs or harms (Rumbold et al., 2017). A DCEA may not be able to determine what is an 'unreasonable' or 'reasonable' harm but it can seek to quantify the health opportunity costs borne by different people and thereby help decision makers to form a judgment.

Equity concerns about respecting rights can sometimes be addressed by adjusting the health outcome metric used to measure aggregate costs and effects rather than by analysing distributions of costs and effects. For example, the US Affordable Care Act prohibits the use of research evidence to inform decision-making 'in a manner that treats extending the life of an elderly, disabled, or terminally ill individual as of lower value than extending the life of an individual who is younger, nondisabled, or not terminally ill' (Patient Protection and Affordable Care Act, 2010). The healthy year metric used in standard CEA falls foul of this prohibition, and so various reformulated health outcome metrics have been proposed to satisfy this prohibition and thereby reduce the theoretical risk that incautious use of CEA information might lead to discrimination against elderly, disabled, and terminally ill patients (Basu et al., 2020). Use of these reformulated health outcome metrics to provide information about aggregate costs and effects may help to address concerns about potential discrimination without providing any information about the distribution of costs and effects by disability, age, or proximity to death. However, respecting rights to non-discrimination is not necessarily the same thing as reducing health inequality—use of a reformulated health outcome metric may or may not yield recommendations that reduce inequality in health between disabled and non-disabled people: to find out, one would need to conduct DCEA.

The 'fair shares' way of thinking insists that all individuals and groups should receive a fair share of resources in proportion to the strength of their claim. This is similar to the value maximizing approach insofar as the focus of concern is squarely on distributional consequences: has everyone received their fair share? The crucial difference is that the fair shares approach will not allow the claim of any individual or group to be completely overridden by the greater good of society. Rather, all claims must be partially met in proportion to their strength—even claims to effective health services that are not cost-effective and do not reduce health inequality. In this respect, the fair shares approach is closer to the rights approach than the maximizing approach: decision makers can be thought of as having a duty to provide all individuals with their fair share of resources. They may, however, choose not to if the opportunity cost is deemed too high. Once more this is a matter for judgment and compromise. Box 2.1 illustrates this important difference between maximizing and fair shares principles, using a fictional example. This fictional example is loosely based on findings from a pioneering paper on healthy life years by Alan Williams, published in 1985 (Economics of coronary artery bypass grafting. *British Medical Journal* (Clin Res Ed) 291, 6491, 326–9).

Box 2.1 Value maximizing versus fair shares—fictional example of renal dialysis versus heart bypass

You are a hospital chief executive with a small amount of discretionary funding available over the next 5–10 years. Your renal department requests this funding for dialysis for one more kidney failure patient, while your cardiovascular department request it for 30 more coronary artery bypass graft (CABG) operations for patients with severe heart disease. The cost is the same, but the cardiovascular option benefits more patients and delivers a much larger total health gain. A kidney failure patient on dialysis is expected to live 7.5 years at an average health quality of 0.66, yielding an expected gain of 5 HALYs (7.5 times 0.66). Each heart patient is expected to gain 2.75 HALYs, yielding a total of 82.5 HALYs (30 patients times 2.75 HALYs each). The costs and benefits are summarized below.

	Total cost	Cost per patient	Number of patients	HALY gain per patient	Total HALY gain	Cost per HALY
Heart bypass	90,000	3,000	30	2.75	82.5	1,100
Dialysis	90,000	90,000	1	5	5	18,000

A simple value maximizing principle would recommend funding heart bypass, as it is much more cost-effective. A more complex equity-sensitive value maximizing principle could in principle recommend funding dialysis. However, this would require weighting each healthy year nearly 18 times more highly for the dialysis patient compared with the heart bypass patients. By contrast, a fair shares principle might recommend dividing the funding between dialysis and heart bypass. It is not clear, however, whether the division should be 50:50 or otherwise set to reflect strength of need claim. Does a dialysis patient have a stronger claim than a heart patient, since they are more certain to die soon without treatment and gain more HALYs per patient? Does a heart patient have a stronger claim, since they gain more HALYs per unit of cost? Or do both types of patient have roughly equal strengths of claim—both being severely ill with substantial capacity to benefit?

The logic of maximization will always recommend funding one of the two departmental claims and completely over-riding the other claim. By contrast, the logic of fair shares will always recommend dividing up the funding in some fashion or holding a lottery.

The value maximizing, moral rights, and fair shares ways of thinking are all *substantive* ethical principles concerning the benefits, harms, rights, and wrongs associated with alternative health programmes. By contrast, the fair processes way of thinking is about following a fair procedure for choosing. If correct procedure is all that matters, then the right decision is whatever emerges from following the correct procedure, irrespective of substantive consequences. Fair procedures can include statutory processes (laid down by law), institutional process (set by the relevant policymaking body), and social processes (social norms of policymaking behaviour).

US philosopher Normal Daniels and the psychiatrist Jim Sabin have developed a theory of procedural fairness in health policy that they call 'accountability for reasonableness' (A4R) (Daniels & Sabin, 1998; Daniels, 2000). They argue that it is often easier to agree on a fair procedure for making priority-setting decisions in the health sector than to agree on the substantive principles and the appropriate weight to be given to different considerations (Daniels & Sabin, 2008).

A4R proposes that publicly financed healthcare and public health priority setting should be governed by four requirements. These are:

- Transparency—public accessibility of decisions and the rationales for them.
- Relevance—reasonableness of rationales in the sense both of giving reasons and applying relevant principles.
- Challengeability—through appeal and provision of the possibility of revision of decisions.
- Enforceability—the presence of mechanisms to ensure that the foregoing requirements are met.

This proposal has been endorsed by various health priority-setting institutions, including the UK National Institute for Health and Care Excellence (NICE) (Culyer, 2006a; Culyer & Lomas, 2006), the Mexican *Seguro Popular* health insurance programme, the Oregon Health Fund Board in the US (Daniels & Sabin, 2008), and the guidance on priority setting in Norway (Ottersen et al., 2016). This is not the only possible theory of procedural fairness in health policy, of course, and other requirements may be relevant—for example requirements of democratic accountability according to context and locally relevant traditions and values. Moreover, procedural equity may require policymakers to pay attention to substantive ethical principles when framing their supporting arguments and evidence—perhaps going beyond the requirement of relevance towards a requirement of clarity, coherence, and factual accuracy. A process that pays no attention to substantive ethical issues about consequences, moral rights, and fair shares runs the risk of being vacuous and non-transparent.

Different ways of thinking about ethics can sometimes be combined in a clear, coherent and analytically tractable manner—for example, rights principles may be used to define the set of ethically acceptable decision options, and maximizing principles then used to evaluate which of those options has the best consequences. More often, however, different ways of thinking conflict with one another and yield contradictory recommendations. It is tempting for analysts to imagine that such conflicts can in principle always be resolved by using the value maximizing way of thinking to seek an optimal trade-off between all the other different kinds of consideration. However, this runs the risk of riding rough-shod over the non-maximizing logical structures of the other three ways of thinking, and privileging one way of thinking as the ultimate arbiter may not be acceptable to people who endorse other ways of thinking. In practice, therefore, conflicts between different ways of thinking are likely to require pragmatic compromises through a process of consultation and deliberation—including compromises that may seem illogical or inconsistent from a value maximizing perspective.

2.3 Informal equity concerns

As with any kind of economic evaluation, one needs to sift and translate the concerns that may be informally expressed by decision makers into more clearly stated formal principles that are amenable to quantitative analysis. In the case of DCEA, one needs to translate informal equity concerns into formal principles about equity in the distribution of benefits and burdens in terms of one or more health-related outcome variables (e.g. health, health service delivery, financial protection) between population groups that differ in terms of one or more equity-relevant variables (e.g. severity of illness, disability, rarity of disease, proximity to death, socioeconomic status, geographical location, ethnicity, gender, age). This translation process requires investigation and discussion with official representatives of the decision-making organization, consultation with stakeholders, and review of relevant information about public values within the general population being served.

Box 2.2 lists a variety of issues that often crop up in health sector priority-setting decisions and that are sometimes labelled 'equity' concerns. Informal equity concerns of this kind are rather like a bucket of sediment that needs refining to extract the precious minerals inside. The 'equity bucketful' needs refining and translating into clearly defined equity objectives. The trick is to extract the right minerals—the ones that decision makers, stakeholders, and the public are most concerned about and that can be most appropriately handled in the analysis. Where important equity concerns cannot be appropriately handled through DCEA it may be possible to address them in other ways, for example by providing qualitative evidence and intelligence. One must resist succumbing to 'quantophrenia'—excessive reliance on quantitative information (Sorokin, 1956). As the old adage goes, 'Not everything that counts, can be counted, and not everything that can be counted, counts' (Cameron, 1963).

The first step in sifting the contents of the equity bucket is to consider whether a concern would be more appropriately handled by including additional total costs and effects within a standard CEA analysis, rather than providing an explicit DCEA breakdown of the distribution of costs and effects. For example, concern to give priority to urgent cases may relate to the health benefits of early intervention, as in the adage that 'a stitch in time saves nine'. If so, this may primarily be an efficiency concern to do with maximizing health benefit that can be handled in standard CEA by explicitly modelling the greater health benefits of earlier intervention. Or concern for non-health and non-patient costs and effects may be primarily motivated by a desire to seek a more complete and accurate assessment of total benefits and burdens. One way of doing this would be to produce an 'impact inventory' of these additional costs and effects (Sanders et al., 2016). There may also be a distributional equity concern that omitting non-health and non-patient outcomes gives too much or too little attention to burdens borne disproportionately by specific population groups, such as low-income groups and women doing unpaid care for relatives (McCabe, 2019). If so, a question arises as to whether this equity concern can be satisfactorily addressed through an 'impact inventory' approach, or whether the decision maker also wants to see an explicit DCEA breakdown of the distributional consequences to verify the nature and direction of the distributional impact.

Innovation is sometimes suggested as an important non-health consequence. Innovative technology seems primarily a matter of concern not for distributional equity but for benefits that are missing from the conventional cost-effectiveness calculus—for example the additional employment, business opportunities, and tax revenues from a thriving biotechnology industry, and the additional future net health benefits when the technology comes off patent with a substantially reduced price and increased cost-effectiveness. The distribution of these missing effects, including transfer payments, might be relevant

Box 2.2 Some examples of informal equity concerns

Disadvantaged patients or service users

Biological factors

- Severity of illness (e.g. end-of-life, current and prospective pain and suffering)
- Co-morbidity and biological risk factors

Social factors

- Income, poverty, education, neighbourhood deprivation
- Geographical location (e.g. rural, disadvantaged area)

Mixed factors

- Ethnicity
- Gender
- Disability
- Age (e.g. children, older adults)

Special health benefits

- Life-saving (i.e. permanently restored to normal life expectancy)
- Large individual health benefit (e.g. many healthy years gained)
- Urgency (e.g. timely intervention is more beneficial)

Special treatments

- Innovative technology
- Unavailability of alternative treatment

Special illnesses or causes of illness

- Rare illness (e.g. 'orphan' drug, hard to recoup development cost)
- Dreaded illness (e.g. cancer)
- Under-funded illness (e.g. mental health)
- Government responsibility (e.g. hospital infection)
- Individual responsibility (e.g. self-inflicted illness)

> **Some examples of informal equity concerns** *(Continued)*
>
> ### Non-health and non-patient benefits
>
> - Impact on household finances
> - Impact on productivity
> - Impact on informal carers' health and well-being
> - Impact on dependents' health and well-being
> - Impact on patient experience
>
> ### Other considerations
>
> - Non-discrimination, e.g. by age; disability; gender reassignment; marriage and civil partnership; pregnancy and maternity; race; religion or belief; sex; sexual orientation
> - Fair chance of treatment despite high cost
>
> ### Decision making process
>
> - Equal opportunity for all stakeholders to participate
> - Unbiased process of reviewing evidence and professional opinion

if there were important additional equity concerns about who gains and who loses from a thriving biotechnology industry and the future fall in price of the technology. However, there is then a question as to whether including wider costs and effects (e.g. employment, tax revenues, long-term price reductions) in a standard CEA would suffice to address those concerns, or whether an explicit DCEA breakdown of costs and effects by population group is required. Further discussion is needed with the decision maker to clarify the precise nature of the concern and how far it may or may not relate to specific kinds of distributional consequences.

The second step is to consider which of the four ways of thinking about equity is most relevant to the equity concern under consideration—that is, does the concern relate to maximizing value, respecting moral rights, providing fair shares, or following fair procedures of decision-making? Some equity concerns—for example concern to prevent discrimination by disability, age, or other 'protected characteristics'—may be primarily to do with individual rights that can be understood and respected without needing additional DCEA information about distributional consequences. Whether a specific form of discrimination is acceptable in a specific decision-making context can usually be assessed competently by the decision maker without requiring an economic analysis of costs and effects. When decision makers are unsure whether an option is unacceptably discriminatory, they will usually turn to a lawyer or ethicist for advice—or, perhaps, a public relations expert—rather than an economist. Nevertheless, there may be cases where a DCEA analysis of the benefits and burdens of decisions for particular 'protected' groups might prove useful in defending the decision-making organization against a charge of discrimination.

The final step is to consider whether the concern relates to reducing unfair differences in a health-related consequence (e.g. health service delivery, financial risk protection, or health itself), or to giving priority to a special group such as patients with cancer or a severe illness. If the former, it may be possible to apply the full apparatus of DCEA as described in Chapter 3 and applied in Chapters 5–13. If the latter, then it may be possible to apply direct equity weighting, as described in Chapter 14, to give additional priority to special categories of patient (e.g. 'cancer or not', 'severe illness or not'). Rather than applying a pre-determined equity weight, however, it is often more useful to conduct sensitivity analysis to find out how much additional weight one would have to give to this special group to change the policy recommendation. If the severity of a condition is defined by lifetime health, concerns for the worst-off (those with least lifetime health) can also be handled by social welfare functions as discussed in Chapters 12 and 13.

We now turn to the main policy objectives that can be analysed using DCEA. We start with total health benefit maximization, the objective analysed by standard cost-effectiveness analysis, before turning to the additional objectives that can be analysed by DCEA, that is, equity in health service delivery, equity in financial risk protection, and equity in health.

2.4 Total health benefit maximization

Health maximization can be thought of as the ethical imperative underpinning CEA (Culyer, 2006b; Cookson, 2015). CEA compares the costs and effects of two or more mutually exclusive policy options (Drummond et al., 2015). To facilitate comparison between programmes for people with different diseases with diverse mortality and morbidity impacts, health effects are often measured using a composite summary index of health, such as the quality-adjusted life year (QALY) or the disability-adjusted life year (DALY) averted. Health effects are simply added up across different people and different time periods—though future health effects are sometimes systematically discounted (i.e. given a lower value) compared with earlier health effects (Claxton et al., 2011).

Historically, QALYs have been used for health technology assessment in high-income countries and averted DALYs in low- and middle-income countries. QALYs and DALYs can differ in various respects. QALYs, for example, tend to be based on health state valuation surveys that are more closely tailored to the individual country (Airoldi & Morton, 2009). However, methods are converging and the only essential conceptual difference is that DALYs are health losses whereas QALYs are health gains. The choice is thus primarily a matter of convenience and taste. We will use the term health-adjusted life year (HALY) to mean either a QALY gain or a DALY averted or other similar generic measure of health benefit.

A HALY index allows the effectiveness of health programmes to be compared in terms of healthy years gained. It also allows cost-effectiveness to be compared in terms of the incremental cost per HALY of one programme compared with an alternative. When assessing effectiveness and cost-effectiveness in this way, the process of adding up HALY gains and opportunity costs across individuals and groups embodies the value judgment that all healthy years count the same, no matter who gains or loses them—that is, 'a HALY is a HALY is a HALY'. The one caveat to this statement relates to the discounting of future costs and effects—a HALY in ten years' time may be considered less valuable than a HALY this year. There are various reasons for discounting future costs and effects on efficiency grounds related to producing a more accurate estimate of sum total health and well-being—for example 'pure' time preference, allowing for the risk of a future 'apocalyptic event' causing mass extinction, and allowing for economic growth and technological innovation (Claxton et al., 2011). There are also further equity considerations related to intergenerational equity in the distribution of costs and effects between age groups and birth cohort groups, which can be addressed using DCEA methods.

A HALY index allows one to compare any two individuals, or any two groups, in terms of whether their health is better, worse, or about the same. The foundation on which a HALY index is built is a general descriptive system that classifies all possible health states in terms of multiple dimensions of health-related quality of life. This descriptive system needs to be carefully assessed for construct validity by the relevant decision makers and stakeholders and, in particular, by the patients, carers, and disease specialists who have direct and vicarious experience of the disease and sequelae after various treatments.

The HALY index combines length of life with these multiple dimensions of health-related quality of life to produce a single number on a ratio scale anchored at 0 (as bad as death and bounded above at 1 (full health). Normalizing the scale of health in this way for economic evaluation purposes is rather like choosing a standard unit for measuring distance – for example, using light-years to measure distance in astronomy. Other units are available – such as kilometers – but light-years are convenient for certain purposes. In principle you can even go below 0 for states of health considered to be worse than being alive and conscious; although thankfully such states are rarely encountered in practice.

The resemblance that a HALY has to some usages of 'utility' in welfare economics has led some to describe HALYs as utilities, which can be misleading on a number of grounds. The term 'utility' in welfare economics generally refers to an index of individual preference ('decision utility') or well-being ('experienced utility'). The typical use of a HALY, however, is not necessarily as in indication of what any individual wants, thinks, feels, or chooses, or how well their life is going overall, but rather as a measure of health (of which, doubtless, more will indeed usually be preferred). The HALY is not a value-free measure of health, however, as the process of selecting, scoring, and weighting the different dimensions of health requires a series of social value judgments. The most relevant normative test of the validity of this value-laden health construct is whether the relevant decision makers and stakeholders see the HALY as an adequate representation of what they understand by 'health' and are willing to accept the value judgments embodied in its construction.

The HALY might be seen as a component of well-being, or as a partial indicator of health-related well-being, but it is by no means a complete measure of well-being. For most practical applications of DCEA in the health sector, the objective is cast entirely in terms of health, with other outcomes at most considered only for their impact on health or the effectiveness of health interventions. To avoid confusion with the standard usage of the word 'utility' in economics to mean preference or well-being, we avoid the use of terms like 'cost-utility analysis' and do not refer to HALYs, QALYs, or DALYs as 'utilities'.[1]

---

[1] This also helps us to avoid a linguistic confusion that could otherwise arise in relation to level-dependent equity weights, as described in Chapter 13. To compute level-dependent equity weights, individual HALYs are converted into individual contributions to social welfare using a transformation function that could be called a 'utility function'. If we were to call HALYs 'utilities', and the transformation function a 'utility function', then we would have to talk about a 'utility of a utility'.

A cost-increasing policy option can be considered 'cost-effective' if its health gain per unit of cost compares favourably with (i.e. is higher than) the most attractive alternative way of using resources. The recognition of opportunity costs—that is, that resources used in the provision of a programme would have generated value if used in their most highly valued use elsewhere—is fundamental to cost-effectiveness analysis. Every benefit attributed to a programme must be assessed relative to the benefits displaced when resources are diverted from alternative activities. In well-ordered markets, it is usually assumed that any use displaced will represent the best alternative use as assessed by potential buyers and sellers. When this simplification is too unrealistic, the true opportunity cost may be lower, since the resources in question were not delivering as much health benefit as they could have delivered. Indeed, if they were being used to no good effect at all, the true opportunity cost would be zero.

In a public health system with an exogenously fixed budget, the displaced activities will usually be alternative health programmes that would otherwise have been producing health benefits. This is as true when the budget is due to expand or contract over time as it is when it is due to remain constant. If the budget is set to grow, then the question is: 'where to spend the next dollar?' The displaced activity is then the alternative health programme the next dollar could otherwise have been spent on. In this context, 'exogenously fixed' does not necessarily mean 'constant over time'. Rather, it means 'beyond the control of the health sector decision maker who is making the priority setting decision'.

Things are different if the health budget is endogenous, however, in the sense that the decision maker can choose to increase the health budget rather than displace other health programmes. In such settings, the displaced activities may include alternative health services, but they may also include other activities having both health and non-health benefits—such as other forms of public expenditure (e.g. education, transport, poverty reduction) or reduced taxes or insurance premiums allowing people to enjoy improved material living conditions. Whatever activity is displaced, there may be both health and non-health opportunity costs. Cost-effectiveness in healthcare and public health can then be interpreted as a test of whether the overall net effect of a programme will be to improve total health—allowing for the health opportunity costs as well as the health benefits.

A cost-effective policy will have a positive net health impact because its health gains will always (by definition) outweigh the health losses from shifting expenditure away from other uses. By contrast, a cost-ineffective policy will have a negative net health impact, because the health losses from shifting expenditure away from other uses will outweigh the health gains. Conventional CEA can help decision makers to choose cost-effective investments that increase total health and to avoid cost-ineffective investments that reduce total health. The estimation of health opportunity costs is more problematic if opportunity costs do in fact primarily fall on household consumption (via increased taxes or insurance premiums) or on reductions in public expenditure on programmes not primarily designed to improve health. In that case, it may be more helpful to conduct cost-benefit analysis rather than cost-effectiveness analysis. This will entail enumerating the kinds of benefits displaced and assigning a monetary value to each, which may (or may not) be adequately revealed in markets, so that the total opportunity cost is revealed.

Differences in cost-effectiveness can be large, both between and within countries, especially in low-income ones where public resources are sometimes devoted to high-cost specialized care in urban hospitals, while rural populations lack access to highly effective low-cost basic care. The WHO Consultative Group on Equity and Universal Health Coverage give a striking example (Ottersen et al., 2014). They cite evidence that fortification of foods with vitamin A and zinc to reduce malnutrition produces about 60 healthy years per $1000 spent, while dialysis for kidney failure only produces about 0.02 healthy years per $1000 spent. This implies that spending $1m on kidney dialysis rather than food fortification loses 99.97% of the total health benefit that could have been produced—a sacrifice of nearly 59,980 healthy years (60,000 minus 20). Like all empirical estimates, these figures are vulnerable to bias and need to be interpreted in the appropriate institutional context. For example, the health benefits of additional spending on food fortification will be much lower in countries with low rates of malnutrition, or in settings where expenditure is likely to be wasted through corruption. Nevertheless, this example points to a large difference in total health benefit and reveals an important truth—namely that neglecting cost-effectiveness can have catastrophic consequences.

2.5 Equity in health

Equity in health can be defined and measured in substantially different ways, with substantially different implications for decision-making, raising thorny issues of value judgment. Various health equity metrics are available, which are introduced in Chapter 4 and detailed in Chapters 11–13. The most fundamental issue is the concept of health that is being used and in particular whether the focus is on *lifetime health* from birth to death or *future health* remaining from the time of disease onset (Culyer et al., 1971; Williams, 1997; Ottersen et al., 2014; Olsen, 2017). Fig 2.2 illustrates different concepts of health.

Lifetime health is the number of healthy years from birth to death. By contrast, future health is the number of healthy years remaining at the time of observation

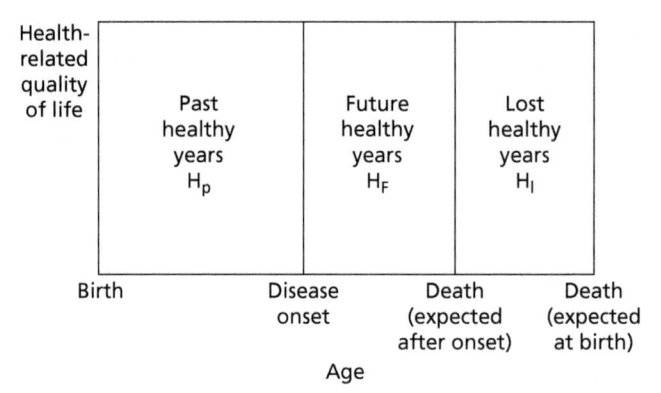

```
Health-
related
quality
of life    Past          Future         Lost
           healthy       healthy        healthy
           years         years          years
           H_P           H_F            H_L


           Birth         Disease        Death          Death
                         onset          (expected      (expected
                                        after onset)   at birth)
                              Age
```

Figure 2.2 Different concepts of health.

(e.g. at birth, disease onset, or decision to treat) excluding past health. Future health is uncertain until death—we cannot know for sure how many healthy years an individual or group will experience until they have died—and so decision makers have to rely on expectations. However, expectations depend on the information available at the time of observation when the expectation is formed. At birth, expected future health is the same as expected lifetime health and is represented by the sum of all three boxes. But now suppose a disease develops after birth. At disease onset, expected future health is represented by the middle box, H_F, which can also be referred to as health-adjusted life expectancy at disease onset. This excludes both past health prior to disease onset, H_P, and the expected health loss from the disease, H_L. At disease onset, expected lifetime health is also shortened by the expected health loss, H_L, but still includes past health, H_P. Expected lifetime health at disease onset is thus equal to the sum of the first two boxes: past health, H_P, plus health-adjusted life expectancy at disease onset, H_F. In each case, realized health can be thought of as expected health plus an error component representing uncertainty about future health.

Different concepts of health can have substantially different equity implications and require different kinds of analysis. People who are badly off from a future health perspective (e.g. old and sick people) may be well off from a lifetime health perspective, while people who are badly off from a lifetime health perspective (e.g. young and poor people) may be well off from a future health perspective. Furthermore, people who are badly off from a future health perspective (e.g. those suffering from incapacitating terminal illnesses) are usually considered to merit special priority and attention whatever their social background or cause of illness, whereas social factors and causal pathways are usually considered to be of central importance when assessing the fairness of inequalities in lifetime health (Deaton, 2013).

The choice of health concept can have important implications for age discrimination. Is an older person 'worse-off' because she has fewer HALYs to look forward to, or 'better off' because she has already enjoyed a long and healthy life? According to the 'fair innings' argument, equity concern should focus on reducing inequality in realized lifetime health (Williams, 1997). This implies that older people who have already lived a long, healthy lifespan should receive low priority. An alternative viewpoint is that only future health matters, and so older people with limited remaining future health should receive high priority. A third viewpoint is that the focus should be on reducing inequality in expected lifetime health at birth, in which case current age is treated as a neutral variable and taken out of the equation. In that case, all that matters are the equity-relevant variables used to calculate expected lifetime health at birth.

Most of the handbook chapters use an illustrative example based on expected lifetime health at birth, in which the equity-relevant variables are socioeconomic status and geographical location. However, we also include material on future health in Chapter 6 (on how to simulate baseline distributions of different health concepts between disease groups) and Chapter 14 (on how to set direct equity weights based on these concepts), and in principle the methods can be applied to any concept of health.

The appropriate health concept may depend upon the nature of the health programme and its principal recipients. For example, when making decisions about healthcare technologies the focus is often on comparing future health or health loss between disease groups, while when making decisions about public health interventions the focus is often on comparing lifetime health between social groups. The appropriate perspective may also vary between different cultures. For example, UK guidelines for appraising healthcare technologies give preferential treatment based on short remaining life expectancy—commonly referred to as the 'end-of-life' criterion (Cookson, 2013). By contrast, Norwegian guidelines focus on health loss and define this more broadly to include absolute loss of health-related quality of life as well as loss of life expectancy (Ottersen et al., 2016). And Dutch guidelines look at relative loss of health-related quality of life and loss of life expectancy (Van de Wetering et al., 2013).

Throughout the handbook, we maintain the fundamental axiom that resources, and therefore our ability to achieve all that we would like, are constrained. Some authors have proposed the idea of a 'right to healthcare' or a 'right to health'. A key challenge for this idea is the 'bottomless pit' problem raised by US economist Kenneth Arrow (Arrow, 1973). Due to modern medical advances, keeping all citizens alive for as long as technologically possible could potentially consume all of society's resources. This means that a universal right to all effective healthcare cannot be secured even in high-income countries. It rings hollow to say that all people have a right that not all people can secure, even if all of society's resources were devoted to it. The 'bottomless pit' problem applies even more strongly to the concept of a right to the highest possible standard of health. There is mounting evidence, for example, that the super-rich live longer than the merely rich—for instance, the richest 1% of US citizens live longer than the richest 10% (Chetty et al., 2016). Yet making everyone super-rich is hardly a practical proposition.

Internationally, the 'right to health' is stated in Article 12 of the International Covenant on Economic, Social and Cultural Rights (United Nations, 1966), under which ratifying states are committed to delivering, for all, the highest attainable standard of physical and mental health. The adjective 'attainable' is crucial because what is attainable depends on choices about the use of resources that are limited and have valued uses other than promoting or sustaining health (Rumbold et al., 2017).

In some countries, however, national 'right to health' legislation has led the courts to require publicly funded healthcare to be made available regardless of its cost-effectiveness and sometimes even regardless of its effectiveness. When legislation of this kind is incautiously worded and over-zealously interpreted, it denies the existence of limited resources and assigns a higher duty to meet health needs than other needs. This can increase the arbitrary availability of treatments and skew priorities towards those who are willing and able to pursue their healthcare claims through legal action. It is thus likely to reduce both the population's health and fairness in its distribution. In such jurisdictions, there may be little point seeking rational prioritization through CEA and DCEA (Gruskin & Daniels, 2008).

The Scottish epidemiologist, and founder of evidence-based medicine, Archie Cochrane, made a radical proposal in 1972 that all (and only) effective procedures should be free (specifically in the UK National Health Service) (Cochrane, 1972). While this proposal comes up against the 'bottomless pit' problem, two modest adjustments avoid it: replacing 'effective' with 'cost-effective' and adding a realistic cost-effectiveness threshold. English philosopher James Wilson has proposed a similar solution. He proposes a right to 'public health risk reduction measures that would be practicable and cost-effective to implement' (Wilson, 2016). According to Wilson, what counts as 'practicable and cost-effective' is to be decided through a 'transparent and reasonable system for setting priorities for public risk reduction'. The right thus imposes a duty on public officials to implement a fair priority-setting process. Wilson's proposal thus retains the key characteristics of a right—it imposes specific duties on specific individuals to uphold the right-holder's claim. So, for example, this right would give government officials a duty to implement practicable and cost-effective air pollution controls. If you live in an area of high pollution that lacks controls of this kind, you would then be wronged as an individual by the government officials' failure to implement such controls and have legitimate cause for complaint. Furthermore, your right would involve a tangible claim on policy action in the here and now, rather than being a matter for 'progressive realization' at some unspecified time in the future.

Insofar as a 'reasonable system for setting priorities' requires consideration of distributional consequences, as well as aggregate costs and effects, DCEA could then play a useful role in supporting a right to health by providing additional information for consideration in the priority setting process.

2.6 Equity in health service delivery

Equity in health service delivery is an important goal of all health systems, which is often phrased in terms of providing equal access to services (Culyer et al., 1992; Fiscella et al., 2000; Sen, 2002; O'Donnell et al., 2008; Fleurbaey & Schokkaert, 2011; Cookson et al., 2016). In principle, equity in health service delivery has two aspects—horizontal and vertical. Horizontal equity requires appropriately equal health service delivery for people with equal needs, and vertical equity requires appropriately greater health service delivery for people with greater needs. In practice, however, analysis typically focuses on the horizontal aspect—as do most of the methods described in this handbook. Analysis of horizontal equity aims to measure inequalities in health service delivery for people with equal needs, broken down by equity-relevant variables such as socioeconomic status, geographical location, gender, and ethnicity. Health service delivery is commonly measured using data on service utilization—sometimes referred to as 'coverage' or 'uptake'—with suitable adjustment for the different needs in different groups. However, equity in health service delivery can also be measured using data on health service resource inputs (e.g. doctors per population), process quality (e.g. proportion of patients receiving appropriate standards of care), or risk-adjusted outcomes (e.g. risk-adjusted mortality rates following surgery).

In Chapter 7 we show how to simulate impacts of the choice of health programmes on differences in health service utilization by socioeconomic and geographical groups. We use the example of a preventive service—nicotine replacement therapy—to help people quit smoking and, for the sake of the illustration, assume that all smokers are in equal need of this preventive service. In relation to other health services, however, some social groups may have substantial additional needs—for example disadvantaged people may have greater need for cardiovascular medication due to higher rates of cardiovascular morbidity. If so, careful adjustment for need would be required using detailed information about morbidity. Useful training resources for doing this are freely available elsewhere (O'Donnell et al., 2008).

Vertical equity in health service delivery is hard to measure because the definition of 'need' is hotly contested. We must first distinguish the amount of resource needed from the strength of the need claim. The latter is more contestable than the former. English economists Culyer and Wagstaff have proposed a definition of the amount of resource needed as the expenditure required to exhaust expected health benefit from a specific intervention: further expenditures by definition generate no benefit and therefore cannot be needed for health (Culyer & Wagstaff, 1993; Culyer, 1998). However, no one believes that all claims for potentially health-improving expenditure should be fully met, and so this still leaves open the more contested question of how far different need claims for different amounts of expenditure should be met. According to the fair shares way of thinking, claims on resources should be met in proportion to the strength of the need claim (thus, an equal proportion for equal strength of need and a greater proportion if the strength is greater). However, there is no consensus on how to define the strength of the need claim and hence the proportion of the claim that should be satisfied. Views about strength of need can be influenced by various factors, including urgency of care to prevent imminent suffering, death, or deterioration; severity of illness in terms of loss of healthy years; and capacity to benefit in terms of potential healthy years gained from health expenditure. These factors can have diametrically opposed implications. For example, someone about to die of cancer may have high severity of illness but low capacity to benefit from treatment. By contrast, someone with early stage diabetes may have low severity of illness but high capacity to benefit from long-term medication and lifestyle change. Who has the stronger need claim—and thus who should receive an appropriately greater proportion of the expenditure required to exhaust capacity to benefit—is a controversial value judgment. Developing DCEA methods to handle vertical equity in healthcare delivery and the fair shares way of thinking are challenges discussed further in Chapter 16.

2.7 Equity in financial risk protection

Out-of-pocket (OOP) payments continue to be the main source of healthcare financing in most low- and middle-income countries and a non-negligible source in many high-income countries—not only the USA (Baird, 2016; Palladino et al., 2016). In such countries, falling ill can put people at risk of serious financial hardship due to large and unexpected OOP medical bills (Van Doorslaer et al., 2006; Saksena et al., 2014). This risk is not evenly distributed across the population—poorer people are typically at higher risk both of falling ill and of suffering financial hardship as a result. Health policymakers are thus not only concerned about *average* levels of financial risk as measured, for example by the proportion of the general population facing 'catastrophic' or 'impoverishing' OOP healthcare bills. They are also concerned about the *distribution* of those financial risks by equity-relevant variables such as socioeconomic status, rural location, gender, and ethnicity.

We describe methods for analysing the distribution of financial risk protection consequences in Chapter 10. The underpinning equity objective is to reduce unfair differences in the risk of financial hardship due to OOP medical bills. One limitation of these methods is that they do not address broader health policy concerns about equity in the distribution of tax and insurance premium payments for healthcare, as well as the distribution of OOP payments. Such concerns often have a vertical equity dimension (e.g. that people with greater ability to pay and fewer family responsibilities should pay more for healthcare) as well as horizontal dimension (e.g. that people with equal ability to pay and equal family commitments should pay the same). In principle it would be possible to conduct distributional impact analysis of these broader concerns by applying standard methods for measuring equity in healthcare financing (O'Donnell et al., 2008). Fortunately, for purposes of DCEA the problems are more contained since we will be concerned only with measuring the impact on financial exposure (positive or negative) that arises from the use, and scale of use, of a specific health service.

Another limitation of existing methods used in the health sector is that they focus on OOP medical expenditure rather than the other ways that illness can lead to financial hardship through lost earnings and lost household production—for example childcare, household chores, and other time-consuming activities of daily living. Methods have developed this way because responsibility for insuring people against these broader costs of illness is typically shared with decision makers working outside the health sector—for example those responsible for unemployment and disability benefits, sick pay regulations, and disability discrimination laws—rather than being seen as primarily a matter for health policy. So although healthcare costs are only one of the important costs of falling ill, they are the costs that health sector decision makers are most able to modify using the policy instruments at their disposal. In principle, however, it would be possible to address these issues, if decision makers so desired, by incorporating these broader effects into the analysis: the data sources will be different but the basic analytical steps are the same.

2.8 Conclusion

DCEA extends the scope of CEA by including 'equity' as a criterion of choice in making decisions about the funding, organization, and delivery of healthcare services and public health programmes. DCEA does not commit the analyst to any particular set of social value judgments but it does provide a range of empirical techniques for quantifying common equity concerns. This chapter started by reviewing four main ways of thinking about equity—value maximizing, moral rights, fair shares, and fair processes. It then discussed the four main categories of health equity principles that can be analysed in DCEA: health maximization, equity in health, equity in health service delivery, and equity in financial risk protection. The first of these is the conventional focus of standard cost-effectiveness analysis and embodies the assumption that a 'HALY is a HALY is a HALY'. The other three remove this assumption. All four are covered in this handbook.

The bulk of the handbook is devoted to the many technical challenges involved in simulating and valuing the impacts of alternative decisions on equity in health, health service delivery, and financial protection—including methodological, statistical, and data availability challenges. However, underpinning these technical challenges are conceptual challenges about the meaning and measurement of equity in a specific decision-making context.

DCEA is a rich territory for the exercise of judgment—social value judgments about equity and efficiency and the further high-level value judgments about how far these criteria conflict and how they might be traded off. There are also many other types of judgment required, as will be seen. For example, a recurring question is whether the available data are an adequate representation of what is of interest to decision makers (construct validity). Another is the extent to which summary measures (say, of inequality and the impact of a decision on it) adequately capture a nuanced understanding of the politics of distribution. Yet another is the assessment of the value of an analysis that is strong on concepts but weak on evidence. Like CEA, DCEA is designed to be an aid to thought, not a substitute for it. Being a territory in which political values are prominent it is also one in which analysts will normally need to restrain their own political leanings and policy preferences. The exception to this is when the analyst turns advocate. We assume in the handbook that the usual role for the analyst is not as advocate but as a servant of 'the decision maker', whose identity, whether real or imagined, should always be made clear in the specification of the perspective of a study and whose social values are the principal value content of the analysis.

2.9 Further reading

A gentle introduction to principles of equity in health is Cookson and Dolan (2000). A more comprehensive and technically difficult treatment is Fleurbaey and Schokkaert (2011). Examples of all four ways of thinking about health equity are as follows: Williams describes a 'value maximizing' approach (1997), Rumbold and colleagues describe a 'moral rights' approach (2017), Broome describes a 'fair shares' approach (1990), and Culyer and Lomas describe a 'fair process' approach (2006).

References

Airoldi M. & **Morton A.** (2009). Adjusting life for quality or disability: stylistic difference or substantial dispute? *Health Economics*, **18**, 1237–1247.

Arrow K. (1973). Some ordinalist-utilitarian notes on Rawls's theory of justice. *Journal of Philosophy*, **70**, 245–263.

Baird K. (2016). High out-of-pocket medical spending among the poor and elderly in nine developed countries. *Health Services Research*, **51**, 1467–1488.

Basu A., **Carlson J.**, & **Veenstra D.** (2020). Health years in total: a new health objective function for cost-effectiveness analysis. *Value in Health*, **23**(1), 96–103. doi:https://doi.org/10.1016/j.jval.2019.10.014

Broome J. (1990). *Fairness*. Proceedings of the Aristotelian Society, JSTOR. pp. 87–101.

Cameron B. (1963). *Informal Sociology: a Casual Introduction to Sociological Thinking*. Random House, New York.

Chetty R., **Stepner M.**, **Abraham S.**, **Lin S.**, **Scuderi B.**, **Turner N.**, et al. (2016). The association between income and life expectancy in the United States, 2001–2014. *Journal of the American Medical Association*, **315**, 1750–1766.

Claxton K., **Paulden M.**, **Gravelle H.**, **Brouwer W.**, & **Culyer A.** (2011). Discounting and decision-making in the economic evaluation of health-care technologies. *Health Economics*, **20**, 2–15.

Cochrane A. (1972). *Effectiveness and Efficiency: Random Reflections on Health Services*. Nuffield Provincial Hospitals Trust, London.

Cookson R. & **Dolan P.** (2000). Principles of justice in healthcare rationing. *Journal of Medical Ethics*, **26**, 323–329.

Cookson R. (2013). Can the NICE 'end-of-life premium' be given a coherent ethical justification? *Journal Health Politics Policy Law*, **38**, 1129–1148.

Cookson R. (2015). Justice and the NICE approach. *Journal of Medical Ethics*, **41**, 99–102.

Cookson R., **Propper C.**, **Asaria M.**, & **Raine R.** (2016). Socioeconomic inequalities in healthcare in England. *Fiscal Studies*, **37**, 371–403.

Culyer A., **Lavers R.**, & **Williams A.** (1971). Social indicators: health. *Social Trends*, **2**, 31–42.

Culyer A., **Van Doorslaer E.**, & **Wagstaff A.** (1992). Comment: utilisation as a measure of equity by Mooney, Hall, Donaldson and Gerard. *Journal of Health Economics*, **11**, 93–98.

Culyer A. & **Wagstaff A.** (1993). Equity and equality in health and healthcare. *Journal of Health Economics*, **12**, 431–457.

Culyer A. (1998). Need—is a consensus possible? *Journal of Medical Ethics*, **24**, 77.

Culyer A. (2006a). NICE's use of cost effectiveness as an exemplar of a deliberative process. *Health Economics, Policy and Law*, **1**, 299–318 (reprinted in **R. Cookson** and **K. Claxton** (eds) (2012). *Humble Economist*, 283–300, https://www.york.ac.uk/che/publications/books/the-humble-economist/)

Culyer A. (2006b). The bogus conflict between efficiency and vertical equity. *Health Economics*, **15**, 1155–1158.

Culyer A. & Lomas J. (2006). Deliberative processes and evidence-informed decision-making in healthcare: do they work and how might we know? *Evidence & Policy: a Journal of Research, Debate and Practice*, **2**, 357–371. (reprinted in **R. Cookson** and **K. Claxton** (eds) (2012). *Humble Economist*, 283–300, https://www.york.ac.uk/che/publications/books/the-humble-economist/)

Daniels N. & Sabin J. (1998). The ethics of accountability in managed care reform. *Health Affairs (Millwood)*, **17**, 50–64.

Daniels N. (2000). Accountability for reasonableness. *British Medical Journal*, **321**, 1300–1301.

Daniels N. & Sabin J. (2008). Accountability for reasonableness: an update. *British Medical Journal*, **337**, a1850.

Deaton A. (2013). What does the empirical evidence tell us about the injustice of health inequalities? In **N. Eyal, S. Hurst, O.F. Norheim, & D. Wikler** (eds), *Inequalities in Health: Concepts, Measures, and Ethics*. Oxford University Press, New York.

Drummond M., Sculpher M., Claxton K., Stoddart G., & Torrance G. (2015). *Methods for the Economic Evaluation of Healthcare Programmes*. Oxford University Press, Oxford.

Fiscella K., Franks P., Gold M., & Clancy C. (2000). Inequality in quality: addressing socioeconomic, racial, and ethnic disparities in healthcare. *Journal of American Medical Association*, **283**, 2579–2584.

Fleurbaey M. & Schokkaert E. (2011). Chapter 16—Equity in health and healthcare. In T. Mark, V. Pauly, & P. Pedro (eds), *Handbook of Health Economics*. Elsevier, Amsterdam. pp. 1003–1092.

Gruskin S. & Daniels N. (2008). Process is the point: justice and human rights: priority setting and fair deliberative process. *American Journal of Public Health*, **98**, 1573–1577.

McCabe C. (2019). Expanding the scope of costs and benefits for economic evaluations in health: some words of caution. *Pharmacoeconomics*, **37**, 457–60.

O'Donnell O., van Doorslaer E., Wagstaff A., & Lindelow M. (2008). *Analyzing Health Equity Using Household Survey Data: a Guide to Techniques and Their Implementation*. World Bank, Washington, DC. https://openknowledge.worldbank.org/handle/10986/6896

Olsen J. (2017). Chapter 20: Beyond cost-effectiveness: priority setting. *Principles in Health Economics and Policy*. Oxford University Press, Oxford.

Ottersen T., Norheim O., Chitah B., Cookson R., Daniels N., Defaye, F., et al. (2014). *Making Fair Choices on the Path to Universal Health Coverage: Final Report of the WHO Consultative Group on Equity and Universal Health Coverage*. World Health Organization, Geneva.

Ottersen T., Ford R., Kakad M., Kjellevold A., Melberg H., Moen A., et al. (2016). A new proposal for priority setting in Norway: open and fair. *Health Policy*, **120**(3), 246–251.

Palladino R., Lee J., Hone T., Filippidis F., & Millett C. (2016). The great recession and increased cost sharing in European health systems. *Health Affairs*, 35, 1204–1213.

Patient Protection and Affordable Care Act (2010). Public Law 111–148. *Public Law*, 111, 759–762.

Rumbold B., Baker R., Ferraz O., Hawkes S., Krubiner C., Littlejohns P., et al. (2017). Universal health coverage, priority setting, and the human right to health. *Lancet*, 390, 712–714.

Saksena P., Hsu J., & Evans D. (2014). Financial risk protection and universal health coverage: evidence and measurement challenges. *PLoS Medicine*, 11, e1001701.

Sanders G., Neumann P., Basu A., Brock D., Feeny D., Krahn M., et al. (2016). Recommendations for conduct, methodological practices, and reporting of cost-effectiveness analyses: second panel on cost-effectiveness in health and medicine. *Journal of the American Medical Association*, 316, 1093–1103.

Sen A. (2002). Why health equity? *Health Economics*, 11, 659–666.

Sorokin P. (1956). Quantophrenia. *Fads and Foibles in Modern Sociology and Related Sciences*. Greenwood Press, Westport, Connecticut. pp. 102–30.

United Nations. (1966). *International Covenant on Economic, Social and Cultural Rights*. United Nations Human Rights Office of the High Commissioner. https://www.ohchr.org/en/professionalinterest/pages/cescr.aspx

Van de Wetering E., Stolk E., Van Exel N., & Brouwer W. (2013). Balancing equity and efficiency in the Dutch basic benefits package using the principle of proportional shortfall. *European Journal of Health Economics*, 14, 107–115.

Van Doorslaer E., O'Donell. O, Rannan-Eliya R., Somanathan A., Adhikari S., Garg C., et al. (2006). Effect of payments for healthcare on poverty estimates in 11 countries in Asia: an analysis of household survey data. *Lancet*, 368, 1357–1364.

Whitehead M. (1992). The concepts and principles of equity and health. *International Journal of Health Services*, 22, 429–445.

Williams A. (1997). Intergenerational equity: an exploration of the 'fair innings' argument. *Health Economics*, 6, 117–132.

Wilson J. (2016). The right to public health. *Journal of Medical Ethics*, 42, 367–375.

Chapter 3

Designing a distributional cost-effectiveness analysis

Richard Cookson, Susan Griffin,
Ole F. Norheim, and Anthony J. Culyer

The aim of this chapter is to guide the design of a distributional cost-effective analysis (DCEA) study intended to inform decision-making in a specific context. The appropriate design will depend on the remit and objectives of the relevant decision-making authorities; the political, economic, and institutional environment; and the prevailing social norms in the population being served, as well as the resources available for the analysis.

The previous chapter introduced different ways of thinking about equity and the issues that need to be considered when assessing whether to address a specific equity concern using DCEA or in some other way. In this chapter we assume that decision makers have equity concerns that can usefully be addressed using DCEA and are now considering how to select and assemble various components of the DCEA toolkit to provide useful information.

We start by discussing the decision-making context, which is always the first thing to consider when designing any economic evaluation study intended to inform decision-making. We then present the equity-efficiency impact plane. This is a visual tool for illustrating the relationship between the impact of a decision on efficiency (in the sense of improving total health) and equity (in the sense of reducing unfair differences in health) compared with a baseline decision. Informally sketching out how the decision options might be located relative to one another on an equity-efficiency impact plane can be a useful exercise to clarify the potential equity trade-offs to be informed by the DCEA.

We then describe the main components of DCEA and explain how they can be combined in different ways for different purposes, including simple, low-cost forms of equity analysis that may be useful when detailed bespoke modelling of distributional consequences is not a practical option—for example due to constraints on time, analytical capacity, or data availability.

3.1 The decision-making context

The appropriate selection of DCEA components depends on the decision-making context and the scope of the analysis. The first questions to ask are about the main decision-making body that will be making the resource allocation decision(s) to be informed by DCEA. What is the main organization that will be using the analysis to inform its decision-making? What objectives is it trying to achieve? What is its remit, what resources can it reallocate, and what other policy levers are under its control? Answering these questions requires at least some direct or indirect liaison with officials working for the decision-making body.

The decision-making unit is not necessarily the same as the organization that funds the analysis or initiates the research question. The analysis might be commissioned by a stakeholder group such as research funding body, a pharmaceutical company seeking to influence a reimbursement decision by a healthcare funding agency, or a local health agency seeking to understand the local implication of a national decision. Insofar as the decision-making body is responsible for consulting with stakeholders and considering their interests, it may be important to ensure the analysis addresses the concerns of stakeholder organizations. The process of designing and conducting DCEA may thus require a degree of 'co-production' between the analysts conducting the study, the decision makers using the findings to inform their decision, and the stakeholders with an interest in the decision.

Once background questions have been answered about the decision-making and stakeholder groups, it is then possible to start scoping out the analysis: the topic to be addressed, the menu of options to be evaluated, the equity objectives to be analysed, and the consequences to be simulated. Sometimes proceeding with some preliminary literature review and analysis may help decision makers to answer background questions which they may not previously have thought much about—for example by revealing inequalities that are surprisingly large, or counter-intuitively shaped, or associated with groups that normally pass under the policy radar.

Throughout this book we assume that the main decision-making organization is a healthcare or public health body with official objectives that include both improving health equity and increasing total health. We also assume that the decision-making body has at least some genuine interest in pursuing its official objectives. As far as possible, however, we leave the nature of the equity objectives to the decision-making authority. Whether and how analysts should serve a decision-making organization with equity objectives they disagree with, or that they consider to be thoroughly corrupt, is a matter we leave to the conscience of analysts: this handbook is a technical guide to doing equity analysis, not an ethical code of conduct for analysts.

By 'improving health equity' we mean reducing unfair differences in health-related consequences in a population—potentially including consequences for health service delivery and protection against the financial risks of out-of-pocket (OOP) healthcare costs as well as consequences for health itself. Most national healthcare and public health organizations have health equity objectives of this kind, among other objectives such as improving total health (Crombie et al., 2005; Marmot et al., 2008; 2012). For national authorities, the relevant population will often be the whole general civilian population of the relevant nation-state comprising many millions of people. However, DCEA methods can also be applied to smaller subnational populations (e.g. a subnational administrative area, public employees, military personnel, the rural poor) or larger supra-national populations.

The main decision-making body might be a government authority, such as a ministry of health, a public health agency, a healthcare advisory body, a development aid agency, a hospital, or a community health centre responsible for a local population. It might also be an inter-governmental authority such as the World Health Organization, a non-government organization (NGO) such as Médecins Sans Frontières, a philanthropic unit such as the Bill and Melinda Gates Foundation, or a commercial body such as a health insurance firm or health plan, pharmaceutical company or private equity firm. These groups may also commission DCEA analyses in their capacity as stakeholder organizations. Although commercial organizations cannot survive for long without making a profit, they often have wider social missions of their own and are often interested in demonstrating their corporate responsibility and the value of their products and services to large and important customer groups with health equity objectives.

To illustrate how the remit and objectives of the decision-making unit can shape the appropriate design of a DCEA, let us consider an example. In this example, the decision-making authority is the National Health Service (NHS) in England, and the policy topic is public funding of nicotine replacement therapy (NRT) to help adults quit smoking. This example is used as the basis for several of the training exercises in the handbook, which are summarized in Chapter 5. The remit of the NHS is assumed to be the allocation of a budget for universal health services, and the objectives of the NHS include improving total health and reducing unfair inequality in lifetime health within the general population of England. The minister of health has a legal duty to 'have regard to the need to reduce inequalities between the people of England with respect to the benefits that they can obtain from the health service' (Health and Social Care Act 2012) and the NHS in England has 'a wider social duty to promote equality through the services it provides and to pay particular attention to groups or sections of society where improvements in health and life expectancy are not keeping pace with the rest of the population' (Department of Health, 2012). Rates of smoking and smoking related illness are higher in socioeconomically disadvantaged individuals and are also geographically concentrated in the historically disadvantaged northern region of England, which tends to be less prosperous and less healthy than the southern region. Equity concerns relating to socioeconomic and geographical differences in lifetime health are thus especially relevant. To address these health equity objectives, our DCEA training exercise simulates lifetime health consequences for the English population broken down by ten social subgroups based on five socioeconomic groups and location either in the north or south.

This example illustrates how DCEA can be used to help redesign a preventive healthcare programme to reduce health inequality without sacrificing too much total health. We use this example because it illustrates a common situation faced by health sector decision makers and funding bodies who commission economic evaluations. Health equity might be served better by looking at other decision options, including options outside the health sector. For example, rather than investing in helping adults to quit smoking, the money could instead be invested in a cash transfer programme to reduce child poverty and thereby discourage children from taking up smoking in the first place. Or investments in preschool and primary education might have more impact on health than further investment in health services. These policy options could be relevant if the decision-making organization were the finance ministry, responsible for the allocation of government funding between health, education, social protection, and other policy sectors, rather than just the health ministry. However, policy options of this kind are unlikely to be within the remit of a health ministry.

3.2 Equity-efficiency impact plane

The equity-efficiency impact plane can help analysts and policy advisers think about potential trade-offs or compromises between efficiency and equity and consider whether it is worth doing a detailed equity analysis. The plane can also be used as a tool for visualizing the quantitative findings of a DCEA study (Allen et al., 2015; Kypridemos et al., 2016) and can also be used as a visual device to help advisory committees keep both objectives in sight when seeking a consensus or, in its absence, a reasonable way forward.

The equity-efficiency impact plane draws on the basic cost-effective analysis (CEA) concept of net health benefit. Before describing the equity-efficiency impact plane, therefore, it is worth reminding ourselves about the nuts and bolts of

CEA (Briggs et al., 2006; Drummond et al., 2015) and net health benefit (Hoch et al., 2002).

CEA of a single decision option entails estimating the incremental or additional costs and health effects of that option compared to the current or reference situation. If these consequences are estimated to be reduced costs and increased health, it is the 'dominant' option (a 'win-win'). If the consequences are estimated to be increased costs and reduced health, it is 'dominated' (a 'lose-lose'). If the consequences are estimated to be either increased costs accompanied by increased health, or reduced costs accompanied by reduced health, then an additional piece of information is required to determine whether the decision is cost-effective, that is, the 'threshold value' at which investments are considered cost-effective.

This can be shown diagrammatically using a cost-effectiveness plane (see Fig 3.1). The origin represents a baseline comparator of no change from the reference situation. Other points in the plane represent the total expected incremental costs and effects of alternative decisions compared with this baseline decision. The cost-effectiveness plane thus has four quadrants representing four logically possible cases: (1) north-east for cost-increasing and health-improving; (2) north-west for cost-increasing and health-harming (i.e. 'dominated' in the cost-effectiveness sense); (3) south-east for cost-saving and health-improving (i.e. 'dominant' in the cost-effectiveness sense), and (4) south-west for cost-saving and health-harming ('win-lose').

Fig 3.2 restricts attention to the first of these cases, that is, the NE quadrant of the cost-effectiveness plane. It plots a new decision Y that is cost-increasing and health-improving. Health effects are typically measured using a 'health adjusted life year' (HALY) metric such as a QALY or a DALY. This allows cost-effectiveness comparisons to be made between different health conditions, and

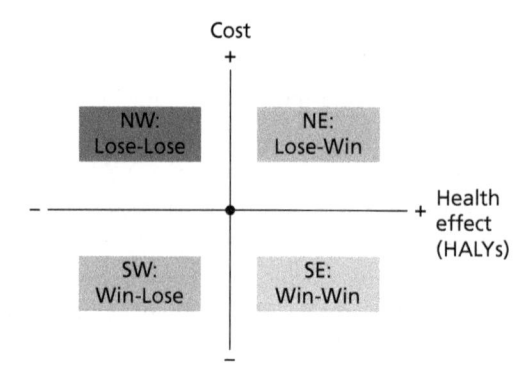

Figure 3.1 Cost-effectiveness plane.

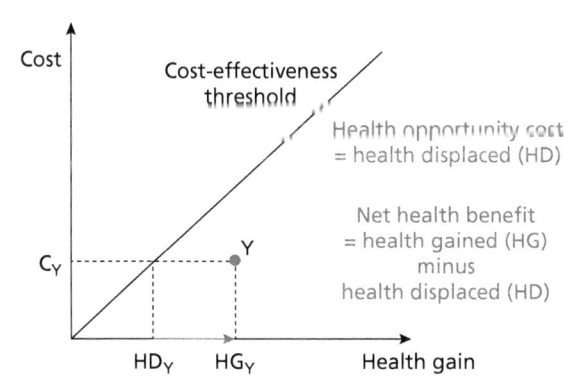

Figure 3.2 Policy Y is cost-effective with positive net health benefit.

for a common 'cost-per-HALY' threshold value to be developed for assessing value for money. We can then draw a threshold line passing through the origin with a slope equal to the threshold value. This value can be given a 'demand-side' interpretation as society's willingness to pay for a HALY. In this handbook, however, we adopt a 'supply-side' interpretation in which the threshold cost-per-HALY value is set equal to the marginal production cost of a HALY from forgone activity that can no longer be undertaken if resources are allocated to option Y. Put the other way around, we interpret the inverse of this value—that is, the threshold HALY-per-cost value—as the marginal productivity of forgone activity in terms of health produced per unit of cost. The health opportunity cost of Y is its total cost divided by the threshold cost-per-HALY value. Net health benefit is health benefit minus health opportunity cost. If net health benefit is positive then Y is cost-effective. The concept of net health benefit thus collapses the two dimensions of cost and health effect into a single dimension. It does this by translating financial costs into health opportunity costs, so that costs and benefits can be compared on a common scale. Typically, this is done with a single threshold value applied to all costs, but in principle it can be extended to allow for differing marginal productivity by type of resource. One can also go the other way around by using the cost-per-HALY threshold value to translate health effects into costs and compute net monetary benefit—the two approaches are mathematically equivalent.

The interpretation of the cost-effectiveness threshold value as the marginal production cost of a HALY fits most comfortably in decision-making contexts where opportunity costs fall on a fixed health budget from which alternative health programmes would otherwise be funded. However, it can still be useful in broader contexts where opportunity costs fall on private consumption or other publicly funded programmes—as when a health insurance plan can choose to raise premiums, or a health ministry can successfully lobby the finance ministry for additional funding. Insurance premiums cannot be raised indefinitely, and the health ministry cannot lobby indefinitely for additional funding. At some point budget constraints will become binding, and some (or all) of the opportunity costs will fall on other health services. Furthermore, increases in insurance premiums may cause some individuals to reduce their coverage and access to care, which may harm their health and shift costs on to public healthcare budgets for statutory provision of necessary care. In addition, private consumption and non-health public programmes often produce health benefits as well as non-health benefits. Opportunity costs falling outside health budgets often imply forgone health benefits as well as forgone non-health benefits. The challenge is to understand where the opportunity costs are likely to fall and to calibrate the marginal production cost of a HALY accordingly. Since there will always be uncertainty about this parameter, it is conventional to conduct sensitivity analysis using a range of values (Drummond et al., 2015).

The idea of thinking about costs as forgone health may be uncomfortable for decision makers unfamiliar with health economic concepts, because health opportunity costs to unspecified anonymous people are less visible and tangible than the health benefits to programme recipients. If the consequences of decisions are to be taken seriously, however, then costs need to be weighed against benefits.

Fig 3.3 shows a decision that is not cost-effective. The health displaced by shifting resources towards X and away from alternative uses is greater than the health gains. So option X is not cost-effective and its net health benefit is negative—it harms total health.

However, this standard cost-effectiveness analysis says nothing about equity. If the net health benefit of a decision is negative, that is, if the health opportunity

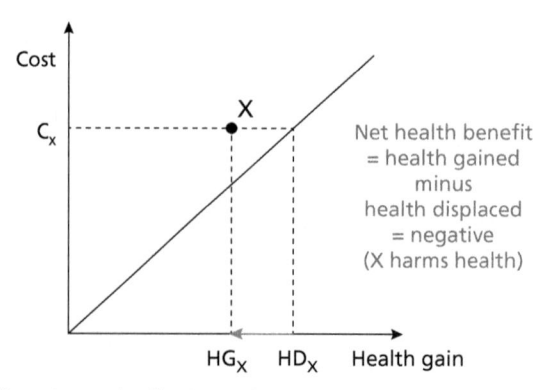

Figure 3.3 Policy X is cost-ineffective with negative net health benefit.

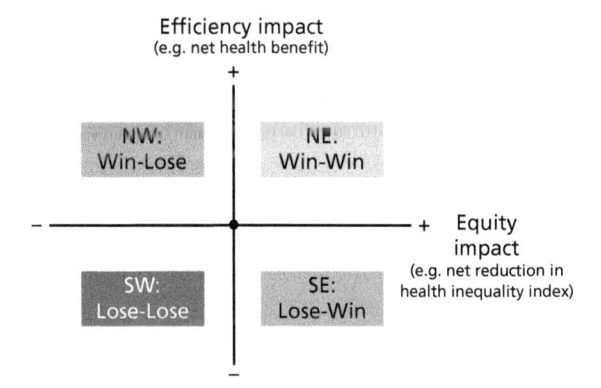

Figure 3.4 Equity-efficiency impact plane.

costs are greater than the benefits to programme recipients, then it would not be deemed cost-effective. However, if that decision improves equity, then it might be worth doing despite not being cost-effective. And if a decision with positive net health benefit harms equity, then it might not be worth doing despite being cost-effective. The equity-efficiency impact plane in Fig 3.4 sets out the four logical possibilities in a systematic manner.

The origin of the equity-efficiency impact plane is the comparator decision. The vertical axis tells us whether a decision option is better than the comparator in terms of efficiency, and the horizontal axis tells us whether it is better in terms of equity. The vertical axis collapses information about cost and effect into a single dimension of 'efficiency impact'—for example net health benefit. The horizontal axis collapses information about health-related distributional consequences into a single dimension of 'equity impact'—for example reduction in an index of health inequality. Both axes represent value-laden summary indices that can be defined in different ways to suit different policy contexts. This flexibility is an advantage but also a challenge—'equity impact' is a particularly complex concept requiring careful specification and sensitivity analysis. An important point when calculating equity impact is to account for not only the distribution of health effects but also the distribution of health opportunity costs. That is, the net equity impact is the relevant quantity, and this requires information not only about inequality in the distribution of benefits to programme recipients but also about inequality in the distribution of opportunity cost burdens within the wider population.

The common meaning of 'efficiency' in economics is to do with the impact of inputs on outputs. Thus, if it is possible to generate a bigger increase in population health with strategy Y than with equally costly strategy X, one would say that strategy Y was the more efficient. One would conclude similarly if strategy

Y generated the same outcome as strategy X but at a lower cost. 'Efficiency impact' can therefore be defined variously as the impact of a decision on an outcome (like population health) given a budget (e.g. a total effect or effect-cost ratio), or on cost given a target outcome (e.g. a total cost or cost-effect ratio), or on the difference between benefit and cost when measured in common units (e.g. net health benefit or net monetary benefit). In a typical health sector context it is often useful to define 'efficiency impact' in the latter manner as the increase in sum total population health after allowing for health opportunity costs—also known as 'net health benefit' (Hoch et al., 2002).

A policy that falls in the NE 'win-win' quadrant improves both total health and health equity, and one that falls in the SW 'lose-lose' quadrant harms both. In low- and middle-income countries, for example, vaccination programmes (e.g. rotavirus immunization (Verguet et al., 2013)) and infectious disease control programmes (e.g. tuberculosis (Verguet et al., 2015)) often fall into the 'win-win' quadrant. Programmes of this kind typically deliver large health gains per unit cost and reduce health inequity, insofar as they disproportionately benefit socially disadvantaged groups. By contrast, investments in high-cost treatments for late-stage chronic disease may fall into the 'lose-lose' quadrant of being neither cost-effective nor likely to improve health equity: they may deliver small health gains per unit of cost and disproportionately benefit groups who are well off in terms of both lifetime health and social status (Asante et al., 2016). In these two cases, the efficiency and equity impacts are in the same direction, so compromises or trade-offs are irrelevant[1].

By contrast, impacts on total health and health equity in the other two quadrants are opposed and some form of reconciliation is required. In NW 'win-lose' quadrant, the option is good for total health but bad for equity, and in the SE 'lose-win' quadrant, the option is bad for total health but good for equity. If we had a guarantee that all decision options would always fall either in the NE or SW quadrants ('win-win' and 'lose-lose') then there would be no need to analyse health equity impacts. An option identified as cost-effective using standard CEA would then always improve health equity, and a cost-ineffective option would always harm health equity. Unfortunately, however, we have no such guarantee and many decision options do indeed fall into the NW and SE 'trade-off' quadrants. Sometimes socially disadvantaged groups may gain

---

[1] The direction of equity effect is often disputable, however, by choosing a different concept of equity. For example, patients with late-stage chronic disease are badly off in terms of future health remaining, and so it can be argued that improving their health improves health equity—in which case there is a trade-off.

less than advantaged groups from a decision to fund a medical technology, due to unequal access or quality of healthcare. Access costs may be relatively high and healthcare coverage relatively low in remote rural areas that lack well-resourced health facilities. In such cases, decision makers may wish to consider re-designing delivery strategies to increase utilization and quality in disadvantaged communities. They may even wish to consider equity-oriented strategies that produce less health overall than standard delivery strategies and lie in the 'lose-win' quadrant. Our NRT training example illustrates one such case, as we shall see later. In our example, proportional universal delivery of NRT, with more delivery effort for deprived communities, is a 'lose-win' option compared with standard universal delivery.

Conflicts between equity and efficiency often arise in relation to preventive health programmes that seek behaviour change—including changes in smoking, diet, physical exercise, and other lifestyle behaviours, as well as participation in vaccination and screening programmes. Preventive interventions may have more success in improving health in advantaged communities which face fewer barriers to behaviour change (Frohlich & Potvin, 2008; Lorenc et al., 2012; McLaren et al., 2010). Such preventive public health programmes lie in the 'win-lose' quadrant—cost-effective but harmful to health equity—a phenomenon sometimes referred to as 'intervention-generated inequality' (Lorenc et al., 2012). A key role of DCEA is then in helping to re-design health programmes to avoid harmful equity impacts through appropriate targeting of additional delivery resources to disadvantaged populations—for example people in rural or deprived inner-city areas with limited access to clinical services. This can help to shift programmes away from the equity-harming side of the plane without sacrificing too much net health benefit.

The equity-efficiency impact plane thus provides a simple visual tool for understanding when compromises and trade-offs may be necessary between efficiency and equity objectives.

3.3 Components of distributional cost-effectiveness analysis

As described in Chapter 2, DCEA can provide information about equity in the distribution of costs and effects on health, health service delivery, and financial risk protection, broken down by one or more equity-relevant variables such as disease variables (e.g. disease classification, severity of illness, rarity of condition) and social variables (e.g. socioeconomic status, geography, ethnicity). The design of the study will depend upon which distributional consequences are to be simulated, which equity-relevant variables are to be examined, and how the

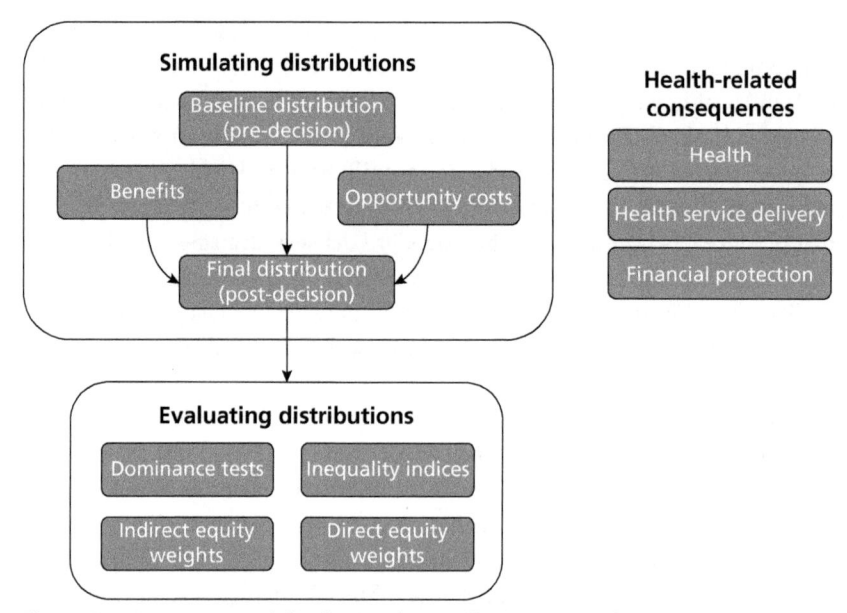

Figure 3.5 Components of distributional cost-effectiveness analysis.

distributional consequences are to be evaluated. This then guides the design of the economic evaluation model and the search for evidence.

The main components of DCEA are shown in Fig 3.5.

Simulating distributions is about breaking down the consequences of alternative decision options by equity-relevant variables. To conduct a full DCEA, we need to simulate the pre-decision baseline distribution, the distribution of benefits, and the distribution of opportunity costs. We then put these together to simulate the post-decision distribution. The resulting pre- and post-decision distributions can then be evaluated and ranked in terms of efficiency, equity, and an overall assessment of social welfare, taking into account both efficiency and equity. This evaluation can be done informally or by using one of the four formal approaches listed in Fig 3.5 as described further below.

Simulating distributions is arguably the most important stage of DCEA, since everything else depends upon it. There is not much point conducting a formal evaluation of distributions that are badly estimated or irrelevant to decision makers. As well as requiring access to data and technical modelling skills, simulating distributions also requires prior consultation with decision makers about various contestable value judgments—for example choices about which outcomes to simulate, broken down by which equity-relevant variables.

Distributions of costs and effects can be simulated through careful decision analytical modelling based on detailed disaggregated information. The basic approach is to characterize and model the 'inequality staircase' leading to variations in costs and effects by equity relevant group—for example differences by equity-relevant variable in need (e.g. smoking prevalence), receipt (e.g. uptake of smoking cessation therapy), short-term effect (e.g. 12-month quit rate), and long-term effect (e.g. lifetime HALYs gained). How many steps to model in a particular application is a tricky judgment call, requiring consideration of which steps are likely to be important in driving overall distributional consequences as well as analytical resource constraints and data availability.

Distributions of health opportunity cost are harder to simulate with the same degree of detail and accuracy. However, they are an important element of net health benefit and must be considered. When empirical estimates of the distribution of health opportunity costs are not available, scenario analysis based on expert assumptions will often be necessary. However, some relevant pieces of evidence may be available to inform the design of the scenario analysis, rule out certain distributional patterns as implausible, and narrow down the range of key parameters. For example, overall health opportunity cost for different health expenditure categories has been carefully estimated using micro data for England (Claxton et al., 2015) and, by combining this with aggregate country-level data, estimates of health opportunity cost are available in terms of a cost-effectiveness threshold for a range of high-, middle-, and low-income countries (Woods et al., 2016). This can be combined with information on current average levels of disease prevalence and service utilization by social group to give a crude indication of how far opportunity costs fall on different social groups. This is only a crude indication, however, since current average levels may differ from future marginal changes. Where more detailed data are available, however, it is possible to go further than this in estimating marginal distributions, as explained in Chapter 9 (Love-Koh et al., 2020). Consultation with experts and decision makers will likely be required to design suitable scenario analyses.

Due to constraints of time and analytical capacity, it is not always possible to conduct a thorough analysis of the distribution of effects. In such cases, it is possible to produce approximate distributional breakdowns of programme benefits by using readily available aggregate data (the 'aggregate approach'). This approach has been applied to both public health investments (Griffin et al., 2019) and clinical technologies (Love-Koh et al., 2019). It simplifies the analysis by using aggregate data rather than conducing *de novo* decision analytical modelling, and by focusing primarily on the first two steps in the inequality staircase. It uses available aggregate level information about average costs and health effects, the characteristics of the targeted population or disease, and variation in healthcare use and health opportunity cost by equity-relevant variables (e.g. socioeconomic status, geography).

Cost-effectiveness analysis evidence on average costs and health outcomes is available for a range of healthcare interventions through national health technology assessment bodies and international cost-effectiveness databases such as Tufts Global Health Cost-Effectiveness Analysis Registry, the Disease Control Priorities project, and WHO CHOICE. To support inference on differences in need, national census and survey data can be used to estimate the overall size of the relevant target population (e.g. by disease group, demography group, and/or risk factor group) and to describe variation in the incidence or prevalence of the relevant health condition by equity-relevant variables. To find out how many people in need of care actually receive care, one can use aggregate data from surveys (e.g. Demographic and Health Surveys) and routine administrative data which link healthcare utilization to equity-relevant characteristics. If the intervention is expected to have similar health effects across population groups, then total health benefits can simply be broken down by population group according to indicators of need and utilization. A full analysis of distributional consequences can then be produced by combining this with available information or assumptions about the baseline distribution and the distribution of health opportunity costs.

Care must be taken with the aggregate approach, however, as it is subject to various potential biases. For example, the distribution of uptake of a new treatment may differ from the historical distribution of uptake of previous treatments for the same condition. And health effects may not be uniform for different social groups. For example, people from disadvantaged communities may have lower capacity to benefit from using a specific health service, since they may be less able to co-invest their own resources in the care process (e.g. time, money, a supportive home and work environment conducive to recovery, and adherence to treatment) and may suffer a greater burden of co-morbidity (Cookson et al., 2016).

Nevertheless, the aggregate approach can provide simple, low-cost information about the likely health equity impacts and as such may be a useful starting point for deliberation. Careful consideration then needs to be given as to whether the aggregate approach is likely to be biased—for example whether expert opinion and evidence suggests that uptake, adherence, or effectiveness may differ across social groups. If so, this may indicate the need for more in-depth equity analysis.

Once the distributions have been simulated, evaluation can be done informally by visualizing and tabulating the results in a 'dashboard' of distributional breakdowns. This can also be done formally using the methods listed in Fig 3.5 and described in Part III. Dominance analysis checks whether one distribution is better than another for all groups, or under almost any definition of equity and efficiency. Inequality indices can be used to measure and compare equity impact of different decision options, alongside efficiency impact, and determine whether there are trade-offs between equity and efficiency. If trade-offs exist, equity weighting may be useful. Direct equity weights give priority directly to specific groups (e.g. patients with severe or rare illness, children, or disadvantaged socioeconomic groups) defined in terms of their characteristics. Indirect equity weights give priority to specific groups as a function of their health outcomes, with greater weight to people who are worse-off in terms of health. The way that decision makers' value judgments about health equity translate into different values for health gains to different groups can be characterized mathematically or algebraically using a social welfare function. Direct equity weighting is more flexible in the sense that equity weights can be set in whatever ad hoc pattern is preferred, while indirect equity weighting is more systematic: it facilitates impartiality between different disadvantaged groups and consistency between different decisions in the pursuit of health equity. There are two main kinds of indirect equity weights. Rank-dependent weights (e.g. 'extended Gini' weights) depend on how badly off the group is in terms of health rank. By contrast, level-dependent weights (e.g. 'Atkinson' weights) depend on how badly off the group is in terms of health level. In both cases sensitivity analysis can test the effects of alternative value judgments by varying the degree of priority given to the worse-off.

The flowchart in Fig 3.6 is a guide to the key design questions in selecting appropriate components of DCEA.

The first design question is whether to provide a distributional breakdown by simulating distributions of effects and opportunity costs broken down by one or more equity-relevant variables. In some cases it may not be practical to do this, and a simpler approach may be preferred. For example, some HTA agencies use a simple two-group form of DCEA that compares programme recipients and non-recipients using direct equity weights. In this kind of analysis, programme recipients are considered to merit special priority over non-recipients due to an equity-relevant characteristic such having a severe illness—with the degree of priority potentially depending on the average level or intensity of the characteristic within the recipient group (e.g. the average degree of severity). Priority can then be given either by weighting benefits more highly than usual or by using a more generous cost-effectiveness threshold value than usual. In effect, this simple approach creates an approximate distributional breakdown between two groups: recipients, who receive higher priority, and non-recipients,

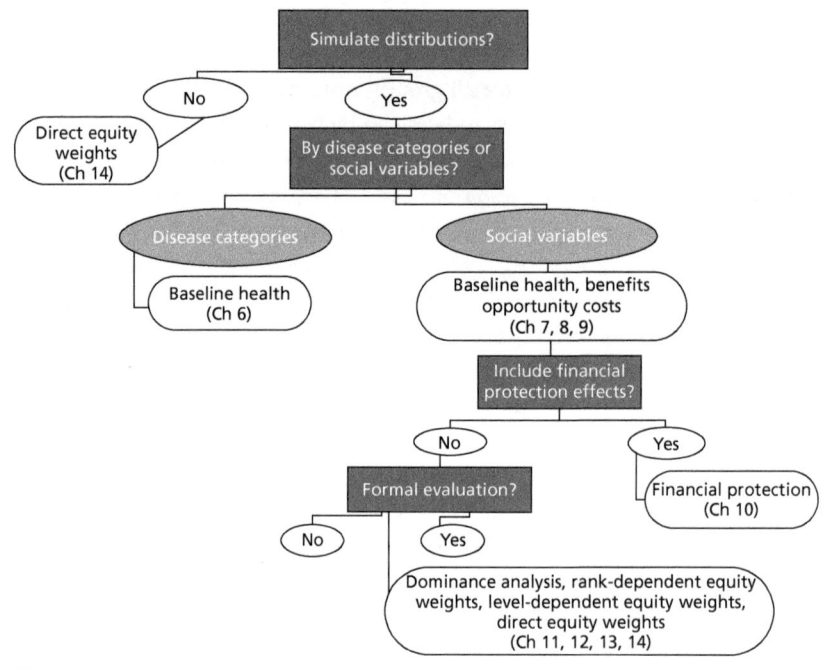

Figure 3.6 Flowchart guide to designing a DCEA.

who receive lower priority. As explained further in Chapter 14, this simple approach has various biases and limitations. For example, some non-recipients may also qualify for higher priority based on the same equity-relevant characteristic (e.g. a severe illness) and some recipients may qualify only to a limited extent (e.g. their illness may be less severe than some non-recipients). Moreover, the decision maker may wish to give priority to people with more than one equity-relevant characteristic—for example they may be interested in health disadvantage related to social group (e.g. income, geographical location, or ethnicity) as well as disease group. More generally, equity concern is not simply about reducing health differences between recipients and non-recipients of a specific health service. Rather, decision makers usually have underlying distributional concerns about reducing unfair health differences between groups defined by equity-relevant variables (e.g. severity of illness or socioeconomic status). Fully addressing these underlying concerns may therefore merit the more intricate modelling required to simulate these distributional impacts directly.

If distributional breakdowns are to be simulated, the second design question is: which ones? One key design question is whether to focus on disease variables or social variables—that is, does policy concern focuses on reducing inequality in health between people with different diseases or people from different social groups? This will then shape the next key design question: which concept of health to use. When comparing health across social groups, the focus is often on lifetime health expected at birth. However, when comparing health across diseases the focus is usually on lifetime or future health expected at the time of disease onset. These different concepts of health disadvantage may in turn have different implications for priority setting and may require the use of different equity weights and inequality aversion parameters.

Health decision makers are often interested in reducing unfair differences in health service delivery and health outcomes and may also be interested in reducing unfair differences in financial protection—especially, but not exclusively, in low-, and middle-income countries where OOP payments are the main means of financing healthcare. When the analysis looks at distributions of health and financial protection together in the same study, this is also known as 'extended' cost-effectiveness analysis (ECEA) (Verguet et al., 2016).

The relationship between DCEA and ECEA is illustrated in Fig 3.7.

DCEA includes areas (1) and (2), that is, any CEA studies with distributions of health outcomes, distributions of non-health outcomes such as financial protection, or both. In principle, ECEA includes all three areas, all of which can be seen as 'extensions' to standard CEA. Area (3) refers to studies that look at aggregate costs and effects of various kinds—including both health and non-health effects—but do not look at equity in the distribution of consequences, a form of analysis sometimes known as 'cost-consequence analysis'. In practice, studies labelled as ECEA studies have hitherto tended to lie in area (2). So one

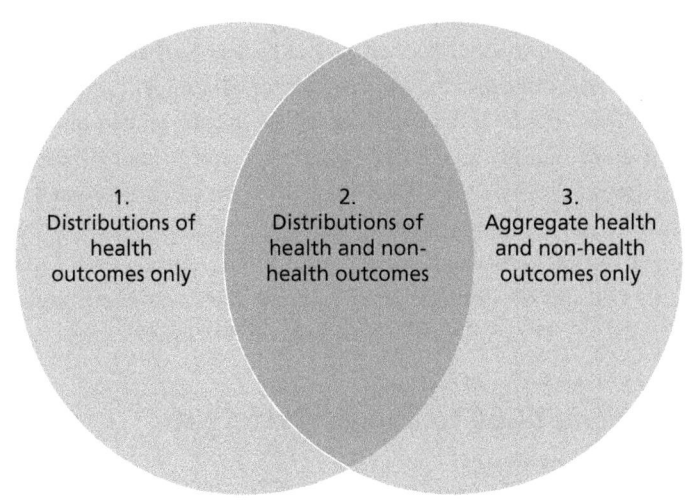

Figure 3.7 Relationship between DCEA and ECEA.
Note: DCEA is (1) + (2); ECEA is (1) + (2) + (3).

could interpret DCEA and ECEA more narrowly by restricting DCEA to area (1) and ECEA to area (2). However, this narrow interpretation is somewhat unintuitive, since areas (1) and (2) both involve 'distributions' and areas (1), (2), and (3) all involve 'extensions'.

Another design question is whether to simulate baseline distributions or incremental distributions or both, and whether to simulate distributions of opportunity cost as well as distributions of effect. A full simulation produces information about all the relevant distributions—including the incremental distribution of health effects and health opportunity costs as well as the baseline distribution of health. A partial simulation may just focus on the baseline distribution or the distribution of health effects. However, this information on its own may be misleading, since it does not provide a complete picture of the distribution of benefits and burdens.

The final design question is whether to conduct a formal evaluation of health distributions and, if so, what kind. A formal evaluation is only possible once one has undertaken a full simulation of distributional consequences. Evaluating distributions formally means using the simulated information about distributional consequences to rank the decision alternatives formally in order of efficiency, equity, and social welfare. Evaluating distributions can be done informally, based on eyeballing graphs and tables of the different distributions. However, expert intuitions can be misleading, and different ways of presenting the same information can lead people to draw different conclusions (Kahneman, 2011). So it can be helpful to conduct formal analyses of how well the distributions succeed in meeting different criteria. Distributions can be compared in terms of efficiency impact (e.g. impact on sum total health), equity impact (e.g. impact on an index of unfair inequality), and various concepts of distributional dominance (e.g. whether one distribution is better for all groups).

A full DCEA provides information on all the health-related distributional consequences of interest to the decision maker and formally evaluates the health distributions. A partial DCEA may be useful when this is not feasible or worthwhile. Some information on some of the health-related distributional consequences of interest may be better than no information. The main thing is to ensure that the key limitations are acknowledged, and their implications carefully considered to avoid drawing misleading conclusions.

3.4 Designing DCEA to address different equity concerns

We now discuss how to assemble the components of DCEA to address different kinds of equity concern. We discuss four kinds of concern in turn: equity in health between disease categories, equity in health between social groups, equity in health service delivery, and equity in financial protection.

3.4.1 Equity in health between disease categories

Various arguments can be made to prioritise patients with specific diseases, including rarity, unavailability of alternative treatments and severity of illness. Concern for severity may include not only concern for those facing immediate pain, suffering, or death—sometimes referred to as the 'rule of rescue' (Cookson et al., 2008)—but also those facing severely accelerated future decline in health (e.g. someone diagnosed with a rapidly progressive illness). This kind of concern can be addressed in two stages. First, by comparing the baseline level of health disadvantage suffered by different disease groups using one or more concepts of health—for example current health (morbidity and mortality risk in the current period), future health (health remaining from disease onset until death), and lifetime health (from birth to death, including past health prior to disease onset). Second, by applying direct equity weights to give priority to disease groups that are worse-off in terms of the chosen concept of health. The focus is usually on giving priority to people with the disease in question, irrespective of their social characteristics and how or why they came to be ill. Concern for equity in health between disease groups can also be analysed using indirect equity weights, as described in Chapters 12 and 13, with the worst-off group or the most severe disease defined as those with the least health.

3.4.2 Equity in health between social groups

Concern for equity in health between social groups usually focuses on people's whole lifetime experience of health from birth to death, including health-related quality of life as well as length of life. In DCEA, lifetime health is often defined as health-adjusted life expectancy (HALE) at birth, though expectations can also be taken from later points in the life. Realized lifetime health—known as health-adjusted age at death (HAAD)—can also be simulated with uncertainty prior to death by taking the expectation plus an appropriate random error. However, methods for doing this and integrating the findings into DCEA are not yet well developed—a research challenge taken up in Chapter 16.

To conduct a full appraisal of distributional impacts on lifetime health, we need to match the same individuals or groups across the elements under the 'simulating distributions' heading in Fig 3.5:

- Baseline distribution of lifetime health (i.e. the distribution of lifetime health in the baseline pre-decision situation).

- Lifetime health benefits (i.e. the distribution of incremental health benefits of the new decision option compared with the baseline decision).
- Lifetime health opportunity costs (i.e. the distribution of incremental health harms of the new decision option, generated by diverting resources from alternative uses that would otherwise have delivered health benefits under the baseline scenario).
- The final distribution of lifetime health (i.e. the distribution under the new decision option) is formed by adding the first three elements together.

If two conditions are fulfilled, it is possible to avoid having to measure baseline health. The first is that equity concern relates exclusively to reducing absolute differences in health. The second condition is that the relevant groups are social groups whose ranking in terms of social status or disadvantage is known in advance, rather than having to be discovered by analysing which groups are worse-off in terms of health. Impacts on absolute differences in health between social groups are simplified because they depend only on changes in health, whereas impacts on relative differences (e.g. the health ratio between advantaged and disadvantaged groups) also depend upon levels of health. The analysis can in this special case proceed simply by looking at the distribution of health benefits and health opportunity costs by social group, without worrying about the baseline distribution. However, the baseline distribution may still be worth undertaking as a separate analysis, to give policymakers an indication of the scale and importance of the baseline health inequality problem.

We can then evaluate the resulting distributions to address three questions: which policy is fairer, which policy is better for total health, and which policy is better overall? This can be done informally through visualization and tabulation of the relevant distributions, that is, by making intuitive judgments based on the pre- and post-policy distributions, and differences between the two, while bearing in mind the limitations of expert intuition. This can also be done formally using:

- Dominance tests (i.e. conducting formal tests to see if the new decision option is better for everyone concerned, or fairer according to any inequality index that satisfies reasonable ethical axioms).
- Inequality indices (i.e. quantifying equity impact using one or more specific inequality indices).
- Indirect equity weighting (i.e. formally comparing the two policies using an equity parameter within a social welfare function, reflecting degree of concern for the worse-off, which then indirectly implies weights for special groups).

- Direct equity weighting (i.e. formally comparing the two policies by setting direct equity weights on health benefits for special groups).

3.4.3 Equity in health service delivery

Methods for analysing equity in health service delivery in the baseline situation are covered extensively in other training resources (O'Donnell et al., 2008). In principle, distributions of effects on equity in health service delivery can be evaluated in DCEA using the same steps as for analysing equity in health. The only difference is that the focus is on the distribution of health service availability or utilization rather than health outcomes. Estimating the distribution of effects on utilization or coverage of the specific health service being evaluated is straightforward, using the 'staircase' approach to modelling costs and effects as described in Chapter 7. However, it is hard to estimate the distribution of opportunity costs in comparable units, since the opportunity costs are likely to fall on different services. Analysis of equity impacts on health service utilization is therefore likely to be incomplete, focusing primarily on the effects rather than the opportunity costs. A more complete analysis requires a focus on health outcomes, where it is possible to compare distributions of effects and opportunity costs using the same common unit of HALYs.

3.4.4 Equity in financial protection

Concern for equity in financial protection can be addressed by looking at the distribution of impacts on household finances. In many countries, large and unpredictable OOP payments for healthcare can cause severe financial difficulty and impoverishment, with harmful effects on the well-being of all family members. This has important equity implications, because disadvantaged families are often the most financially insecure. Financial protection impacts therefore become an important element of the overall equity impact, which may differ from impacts on equity in lifetime health. As with all DCEA analyses, however, it is important to consider not only the distribution of effects but also the distribution of opportunity costs—that is, the forgone financial protection benefits that would have been delivered through alternative use of scarce resources.

Hitherto, the focus of financial protection analysis in a health policy context has typically been on the OOP healthcare costs of illness, rather than the productivity costs of illness (i.e. lost earnings and lost ability to perform household tasks). This may partly be because health policymakers see healthcare costs as lying clearly within their remit, whereas responsibility for insuring people against loss of earnings due to illness is considered a matter for policymakers in the employment and social protection sectors. In principle there is no reason why such information could not be included in DCEA if health decision makers so wished. However, analysts would then need to access data about employment, wages, and household production costs, and would face the methodological challenge of disentangling the effects of illness on earnings from the effects of individual labour market choices. Financial protection from the consumption costs of unhealthy behaviours—such as smoking, use of alcohol and illegal drugs—may also be of interest to health decision makers, especially if there are catastrophic costs attributable to mental illness and addiction. However, decision makers may be less concerned about costs of unhealthy behaviour they consider to be a matter of personal responsibility.

Analyses of distributional consequences for financial protection have typically eschewed formal evaluation of distributions, focusing instead on a 'dashboard' approach that provides breakdowns of the costs, health, and financial protection effects by socioeconomic status. However, a future research challenge is to integrate outcomes for individual health and household finances into a unified framework that allows formal evaluation of equity in both outcomes simultaneously.

3.5 Partial or full DCEA?

Hitherto, DCEA has tended to be applied in practice in a simple, partial way by using direct equity weights for programme recipients considered to be disadvantaged in terms of their health—for example because they are diagnosed with a severe or terminal or rare illness. This approach focuses on ascertaining how badly-off programme recipients are in terms of baseline health compared with the wider population served by the decision-making organization. If programme recipients are worse-off than non-recipients, then this provides a simple indication that the programme may tend to improve health equity. It does not provide a guarantee, however, since the equity impact will depend on the distribution of effects and opportunity costs—that is, how much recipients gain and non-recipients lose, and how those gains and losses are distributed within those two groups by equity-relevant characteristics. For example, if many non-recipients also have a severe, terminal, or rare illness, and if they are likely to bear a substantial proportion of the opportunity cost of the programme, the programme could conceivably harm equity or have a broadly neutral equity impact—a case of robbing Peter (badly-off non-recipients bearing health opportunity costs) to pay Paul (badly-off recipients gaining health benefits). This is only a partial approach to DCEA because it only makes a two-group comparison between programme recipients and non-recipients and does not provide distributional breakdowns within these groups by equity-relevant variables. A full DCEA would require simulation of the baseline distribution of health within the programme recipient and non-recipient groups by equity-relevant variables, simulation of the distributions of benefits and opportunity costs by equity-relevant variables, and putting this all together to calculate the post-decision distribution of health by equity-relevant variables.

A partial DCEA approach has been used to inform health technology reimbursement decisions in Norway and the Netherlands (Van de Wetering et al., 2013; Ottersen et al., 2016). Future health metrics are used to assess the baseline health of programme recipients compared with non-recipients and make a judgment about severity of illness. A more generous cost-effectiveness threshold is then used when assessing treatments for patients with relatively severe illnesses, as a simple form of direct equity weighting.

One issue is that this approach focuses on future health and so does not provide information about equity in lifetime health. For example, bowel cancer patients are badly off in terms of future health but tend to be well-off in terms of lifetime health since onset usually occurs relatively late in life. By contrast, patients with bipolar illness will tend to be badly-off in terms of lifetime health, since onset is usually in young adulthood and can cause substantially impaired and shortened lives. Even if a lifetime health metric were used, however, this approach would still have numerous limitations, as summarized below and discussed in detail in Chapter 14.

Other things equal, prioritizing investment in treatment for bipolar illness rather than bowel cancer may tend to reduce inequality in lifetime health. However, other things may not be equal depending on the effects and costs of the relevant treatments and how they are distributed between different patient subgroups and by social risk factors. For example, there may be important social inequalities in lifetime health within the same health condition. Socially disadvantaged children with mental illness may be worse-off from a lifetime health perspective than advantaged children with the same illness, whose parents and families are better able to provide them with the additional financial and social support they need to live long and healthy lives.

Another issue is that focusing on baseline health cannot help to analyse the equity impacts of different programme delivery options for the same health condition or treatment—for example options for re-designing childhood mental health services to increase diagnosis and uptake among socially disadvantaged groups. Furthermore, partial DCEA provides information about only the likely direction of the equity impact if the programme is cost-effective, not its likely size. It only compares how badly-off different people are pre-decision, not the size of their likely health benefits and opportunity costs and the size of the impact on reducing health inequality. Decision makers may be interested in targeting resources more effectively to achieve larger reductions in health inequality, and not merely targeting resources in a well-intentioned way towards the worse-off.

These considerations militate in favour of considering some of the more sophisticated methods of DCEA described in this handbook, which explicitly simulate the relevant distributions of effect and opportunity cost by equity-relevant variables. There may of course be insufficient resource or skills or time available to design and undertake a full DCEA involving detailed modelling of distributional consequences. However, pragmatic compromises and shortcuts are available and there is a wide spectrum of alternatives between the simplest forms of 'partial' DCEA and the most complicated forms of 'full' DCEA. We therefore encourage readers to make a pragmatic assessment of which elements of DCEA are appropriate and useful in their specific decision-making context, given the analytical resources at their disposal.

3.6 Further reading

An overview is provided by Cookson and colleagues (2017). A simple DCEA approach to severity weighting by disease group as applied in practice in Norway is provided by Ottersen and colleagues (2016). A full DCEA approach based on social distributions of lifetime health is described by Asaria and colleagues (2016). A simplified 'aggregate' version of this approach is described by Griffin and colleagues (2019). An ECEA approach based on social distributions of health effect and financial protection effect is described by Verguet and colleagues (2016).

References

Allen K., Pearson-Stuttard J., Hooton P., Diggle W., Capewell S., & O'Flaherty M. (2015). Potential of trans fats policies to reduce socioeconomic inequalities in mortality from coronary heart disease in England: cost effectiveness modelling study. *British Medical Journal*, 351, h4583.

Asante A., Price J., Hayen A., Jan S., & Wiseman V. (2016). Equity in healthcare financing in low- and middle-income countries: a systematic review of evidence from studies using benefit and financing incidence analyses. *PLoS One*, 11, e0152866.

Asaria M., Griffin S., & Cookson R. (2016). Distributional cost-effectiveness analysis: a tutorial. *Medical Decision Making*, 36, 8–19.

Briggs A., Sculpher M., & Claxton K. (2006). *Decision Modelling for Health Economic Evaluation*. Oxford University Press, Oxford.

Claxton K., Martin S., Soares M., Rice N., Spackman E., Hinde S., et al. (2015). Methods for the estimation of the National Institute for Health and Care Excellence cost-effectiveness threshold. *Health Technology Assessment* (Winchester, England), 19, 1.

Cookson R., McCabe C., & Tsuchiya A. (2008). Public healthcare resource allocation and the Rule of Rescue. *Journal of Medical Ethics*, 34(7), 540–544.

Cookson R., Mirelman A., Griffin S., Asaria M., Dawkins B, Norheim O., et al. (2017). Using cost-effectiveness analysis to address health equity concerns. *Value in Health*, 20, 206–212.

Cookson R., Propper C., Asaria M., & Raine R. (2016). Socioeconomic inequalities in healthcare in England. *Fiscal Studies*, 37, 371–403.

Crombie I., Irvine L., Elliott L., & Wallace H. (2005). *Closing the Health Inequalities Gap: an International Perspective*. WHO Europe, Copenhagen.

Department of Health (2012). *The NHS Constitution*. London, DH.

Drummond M., Sculpher M., Claxton K., Stoddart G., & Torrance G. (2015). *Methods for the Economic Evaluation of Healthcare Programmes*. Oxford University Press, Oxford.

Frohlich K. & Potvin L. (2008). Transcending the known in public health practice: the inequality paradox: the population approach and vulnerable populations. *American Journal of Public Health*, 98, 216–221.

Griffin S., Love-Koh J., Pennington B., & Owen L. (2019). Evaluation of intervention impact on health inequality for resource allocation. *Medical Decision Making*, 39(3), 171–182.

Hoch J., Briggs A., & Willan A. (2002). Something old, something new, something borrowed, something blue: a framework for the marriage of health econometrics and cost-effectiveness analysis. *Health Economics*, 11, 415–430.

Kahneman D. (2011). *Thinking, Fast and Slow*. Macmillan, New York.

Kypridemos C., Allen K., Hickey G., Guzman-Castillo M., Bandosz P., Buchan I., et al. (2016). Cardiovascular screening to reduce the burden from cardiovascular disease: microsimulation study to quantify policy options. *British Medical Journal*, 353, i2793.

Lorenc T., Petticrew M., Welch V., & Tugwell P. (2012). What types of interventions generate inequalities? Evidence from systematic reviews. *Journal of Epidemiology and Community Health*, 67(2), 190–193.

Love-Koh J., Cookson R., Gutacker N., Patton T., & Griffin S. (2019). Aggregate distributional cost-effectiveness analysis of health technologies. *Value in Health*, 22(5), 518–526.

Love-Koh J., Cookson R., Claxton K., & Griffin S. (2020). Estimating social variation in the health effects of changes in health care. *Medical Decision Making*, https://doi.org/10.1177/0272989X20904360

Marmot M., Allen J., Bell R., Bloomer E., & Goldblatt P. (2012). WHO European review of social determinants of health and the health divide. *Lancet*, 380, 1011–1029.

Marmot M., Friel S., Bell R., Houweling T., & Taylor S. (2008). Closing the gap in a generation: health equity through action on the social determinants of health. *Lancet*, 372, 1661–1669.

McLaren L., McIntyre L., & Kirkpatrick S. (2010). Rose's population strategy of prevention need not increase social inequalities in health. *International Journal of Epidemiology*, 39, 372–377.

O'Donnell O., van Doorslaer E., Wagstaff A., & Lindelow M. (2008). *Analyzing Health Equity Using Household Survey Data: a Guide to Techniques and Their Implementation*.

World Bank, Washington, DC. https://openknowledge.worldbank.org/handle/10986/6896

Ottersen T., Forde R., Kakad M., Kjellevold A., Melberg H., Moen A., et al. (2016). A new proposal for priority setting in Norway: open and fair. *Health Policy*, **120**(3), 246–251.

Van de Wetering E., Stolk E., Van Exel N., & Brouwer W. (2013). Balancing equity and efficiency in the Dutch basic benefits package using the principle of proportional shortfall. *European Journal of Health Economics*, **14**, 107–115.

Verguet S., Kim J., & Jamison D. (2016). Extended cost-effectiveness analysis for health policy assessment: a tutorial. *Pharmacoeconomics*, **34**, 913–923.

Verguet S., Laxminarayan R., & Jamison D. (2015). Universal public finance of tuberculosis treatment in India: an extended cost-effectiveness analysis. *Health Economics*, **24**, 318–332.

Verguet S., Murphy S., Anderson B., Johansson K., Glass R., & Rheingans R. (2013). Public finance of rotavirus vaccination in India and Ethiopia: an extended cost-effectiveness analysis. *Vaccine*, **31**, 4902–4910.

Woods B., Revill P., Sculpher M., & Claxton K. (2016). Country-level cost-effectiveness thresholds: initial estimates and the need for further research. *Value in Health*, **19**, 929–935.

Chapter 4

Describing equity impacts and trade-offs

Richard Cookson, Susan Griffin,
Ole F. Norheim, and Anthony J. Culyer

This chapter introduces the basic concepts needed to understand and critically appraise distributional cost-effective analysis (DCEA) findings about equity impacts and trade-offs, with careful attention to the underpinning social value judgments. Technical details of specific summary metrics of equity impact are provided later in the relevant methods chapters. The chapter starts with ways of selecting the distributional breakdowns of interest before turning to ways of evaluating equity impacts and trade-offs using summary indices and graphs.

4.1 Selecting distributional breakdowns

One of the main functions of DCEA is to produce distributional breakdowns of the expected costs and effects of alternative decision options. Decision makers may also want information about how well or badly off different people are in the baseline situation before any decision is taken. Selecting the main distributional breakdowns of interest is a key task for the design stage of a project (also known as the scoping stage), requiring numerous value judgments to be made in consultation with decision makers and stakeholders.

Distributional breakdowns can rapidly become complicated and hard to interpret, as each new way of splitting the data multiplies the number of potentially relevant pieces of information. For any given primary outcome variable (e.g. lifetime health) there are at least five different types of distribution (baseline, effect, opportunity cost, net benefit, final). There may also be secondary outcome variables (e.g. health service delivery, financial protection) and input variables along the staircase of inequality (e.g. prevalence, short-term effect). These additional variables may be of interest to decision makers as intermediate outcomes that help them to understand and critically appraise the headline findings. Each outcome variable and each type of distribution can potentially be split by each of the equity-relevant variables (e.g. disease category, socioeconomic status, geographical location).

Analysts need to take a close look at the detail to understand what is going on, to spot potential measurement errors, and to reveal unexpected patterns in the data—including unexpected forms of unfairness. A close look can also reveal important gaps in the available data, some of which may be fixable but others not. In the latter case, one has advance warning of a possibly significant limitation to the distributional analysis.

Decision makers will not usually need to examine distributional breakdowns in as much detail as their analysts and technical advisers, especially not distributional breakdowns of input variables. However, equity can be complex and summary statistics can be misleading: the devil is in the detail and it is unwise to rely exclusively on a single 'one-size-fits-all' equity metric (Kjellsson et al., 2015). Decision makers are therefore likely to welcome a judiciously crafted 'dashboard' of tables and graphs showing what is going on underneath the headline findings, presenting the most relevant and informative types of distribution for selected primary, secondary, and intermediate outcome variables.

Selecting the most important distributional breakdowns to present to decision makers in their 'dashboard' is not a value-free process. Neither analysts nor decision makers can look at all possible distributional breakdowns of all possible variables that could have been included in the analysis—the permutations are endless. Value-laden editorial decisions are required to decide what distributions to present, what to include in the underpinning analysis for technical advisers, and what to leave out of the analysis altogether. As emphasized in previous chapters, our recommendation is that value-laden decisions should as far as possible reflect the value judgments of decision makers rather than analysts, which is why selecting the relevant distributional breakdowns requires consultation between analysts and decision makers.

In this section we set out the main value-laden choices in a step-by-step manner below, by asking the following six questions:

- Distributional breakdowns of which outcome variable(s)?
- Distributional breakdowns of incremental changes or levels or both?
- Distributional breakdowns within which population?
- Distributional breakdowns between which equity-relevant population groups?
- Distributional breakdowns adjusted how?
- Distributional breakdowns observed when?

When these issues have been resolved and suitable distributions simulated, a further question arises:

- Distributional breakdowns summarized and evaluated how?

4.1.1 Distributions of which outcome variable(s)?

The primary distributional outcome of interest will usually concern health, health service delivery, and/or financial protection, though distributions of other outcomes can also be examined in DCEA as deemed appropriate, following scoping discussions between decision makers and analysts. Within each broad category of outcome variable there are further choices, for example whether to report health in health-adjusted life years (HALYs), life-years or some other unit such as equity-weighted HALYs. These choices often need to be informed by the social value judgments of decision makers as well as the availability of data. For example, presenting distributions of lifetime health when the concern relates to future health could be misleading.

4.1.2 Distributions of incremental changes or levels or both?

Standard cost-effective analysis (CEA) usually focuses on incremental changes like the incremental costs and health effects of a decision compared with an alternative. In DCEA, however, the levels of health are usually also of interest. Decision makers can have equity concerns about inequality in health levels ('level egalitarianism') as well as the incremental health changes resulting from a decision ('change egalitarianism'). For example, decision makers might be concerned about the poor health of groups in deprived regions, groups with multiple disadvantages, vulnerable populations, people with orphan diseases, and HIV positive people. If so, the equity goal may not be to equalize net health benefits—reducing inequality in health levels may require larger net health benefits for disadvantaged groups. This issue also has implications for the computation of equity impact indices, as discussed below in the section on inequality metrics. The 'level egalitarian' approach is to compute the difference in the index of inequality in health levels pre-decision and post-decision. Whereas the 'change egalitarian' approach is to compute an index of inequality in incremental net health benefits. If concern focuses on equality in health levels, then the former is the appropriate approach.

4.1.3 Distributions within which population?

Equity is a population level concept. The relevant population for equity assessment is usually not just the intended recipient population targeted by a specific health programme (e.g. bowel cancer patients or smokers) but the broader population served by the decision-making organization. Viewing a group as disadvantaged or worse-off in terms of their health usually implies a comparison with some absolute general population standard (like a poverty line which may be set by statute), with other groups within the general population, or with the general population average. When evaluating the equity implications of a national human immunodeficiency virus (HIV) programme, for example, it would not normally be sufficient to analyse the distribution of effects within the intended recipient group of HIV patients. A ministry of health responsible for distribution of health resources within the general national population would also want to know how severely ill HIV patients are compared with patients with other diseases who could potentially gain health benefits from additional funding, and how they compare in terms of equity-relevant characteristics such as socioeconomic status and geographical location. More ambitiously, the ministry might also want to know how the distribution of health benefits within the HIV population combines with the distribution of health opportunity costs across the whole population to yield a general population distribution of net health benefits.

Defining the equity-relevant population is not as simple as it may first appear. The scope of equity is a normative question, and different choices can have implications for the whole process of undertaking a DCEA. For example, should refugees, illegal immigrants, homeless people, travellers, prisoners, people in residential care, and people living in military barracks be included in the population of concern? If so, is information about these marginalized and/or institutionalized populations included in the data available for the analysis? Is the focus on residents (including foreign citizens living in the jurisdiction), or citizens (including those living abroad), or enrolees (people registered as eligible for healthcare services under a health insurance plan)? More fundamentally, is the relevant general population the nation-state, a subnational population such as a province or county, or a supranational population such as a continent, a trade bloc, or indeed the entire globe? The latter is not as fanciful as it may appear. It is, for example, a common focus for global charities and international healthcare organizations.

A related choice is whether to simulate outcomes for the all-age general population or just one specific age cohort of the general population. For example, to evaluate a screening programme for people aged 50–60 one could simplify by just modelling lifetime outcomes for a single age cohort (e.g. people currently aged 50) or one could run everyone currently alive through the model. One might even consider more complex populations that change in size and composition over time depending on fertility and migration rates that may themselves be influenced by a decision—for example everyone currently alive plus everyone who would join the population through birth or migration during the time horizon of the policy evaluation. Somehow a judgment will have to be reached at the design stage of a study about each of these issues, which may be informed by the practical experience of researchers and then subsequently assessed by suitable sensitivity analyses.

4.1.4 Distributions between which equity-relevant populations?

Do concerns about unfair inequalities in the application under consideration focus on health differences between disease groups like the international classification of diseases (ICD) or social groups like socio-economic classes (SECs)? If the latter, then there are further decisions to make about the equity-relevant social groups. The acronym 'PROGRESS-Plus' (O'Neill et al., 2014) is a useful summary of common equity-relevant social group variables:

- Place of residence
- Race/ethnicity/culture/language
- Occupation
- Gender/sex
- Religion
- Education
- Socioeconomic status
- Social capital

with 'Plus' to remind us that many other groups may be equity-relevant, for example age groups, types of disability, adverse experiences, sexuality, and transgender status.

It is often important simultaneously to consider the distributional relationships between the equity-relevant variables and the outcome variable. Sometimes there is only one equity-relevant variable of interest, such as occupational class or a composite index of socioeconomic status based on several different markers of social disadvantage, such as household asset indicators or neighbourhood deprivation scores. If so, then one can use a bivariate approach showing the joint distribution between this variable and the outcome variable. If there are two or more different equity-relevant variables of distinct policy interest, however, a multivariate approach may be required. An appropriate way of presenting the distribution may then be an adjusted univariate distribution, which shows the distribution of the outcome variable after it has been adjusted to focus on 'unfair' variation associated with more than one equity-relevant characteristic.

Health expectancy at birth

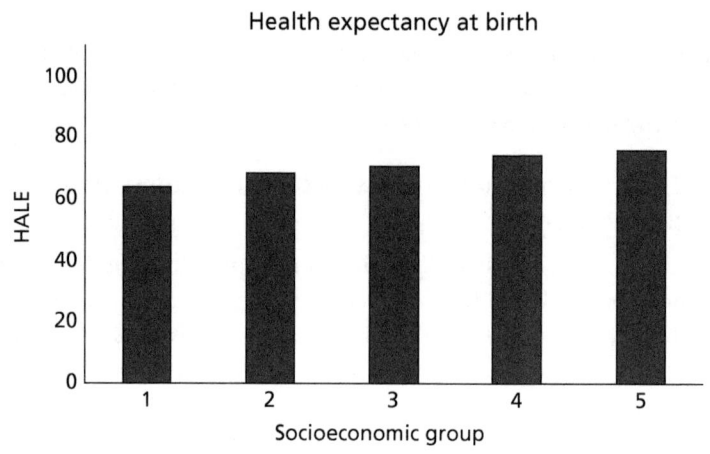

Figure 4.1 Group-level bivariate distribution.

Fig 4.1 illustrates a group-level bivariate distribution of health expectancy at birth by socioeconomic status group (five deprivation quintile groups) within the general population, with 1 being the most socially disadvantaged group. Fig 4.2 illustrates the corresponding group-level adjusted univariate distribution of health expectancy at birth by ten social subgroups based on two equity-relevant characteristics: socioeconomic status group (five deprivation quintile groups) and geographical location (north or south of England).

In Fig 4.1 the groups are ranked by social status, which exactly coincides with the ranking by health status. In Fig 4.2, however, the groups are ranked by health

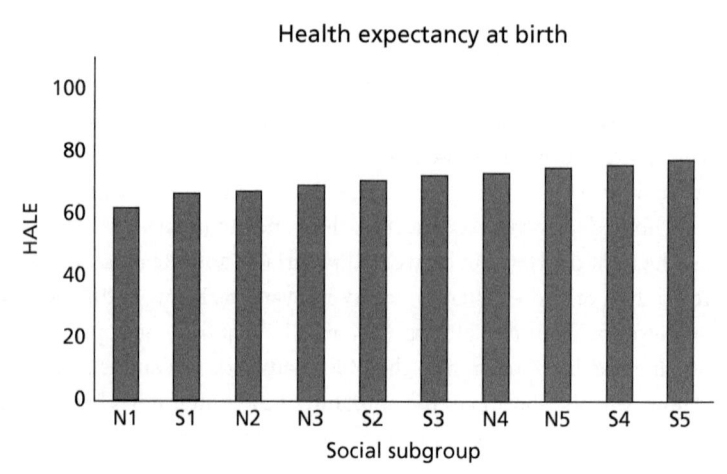

Figure 4.2 Group-level adjusted univariate distribution.

status. In this case, although the five-level deprivation ranking is preserved the ten-level ranking does not coincide with any obvious composite concept of social status rank. When there are several equity-relevant characteristics there are usually several ways of combining them to create a composite social status rank—for example a lexicographic ordering or a weighted sum of the ranks or scores for each component variable. In this example, one obvious approach would be a lexicographic ordering which treats deprivation as the primary social status variable and then, within the deprivation quintile groups, treats 'north' as having lower social status than 'south', since the north of England is generally less prosperous than the south. However, the health ranking does not coincide with this composite social ranking—for example people in deprivation group 2 living in the south (S2) have better health than people in deprivation group 3 living in the north (N3), despite being more deprived. The complexities involved in making such comparisons are a major topic of discussion in later chapters.

By way of comparison, Fig 4.3 shows the individual-level version of the adjusted univariate distribution in Fig 4.2. This is based on the same distribution but contains more information as it shows how the ten social subgroups vary in population size.

An adjusted univariate distribution is especially useful if one wants to allow for possible interactions between the characteristics under consideration. Looking separately at two different bivariate distributions (e.g. by deprivation and by geography) means that important interactions between the two different kinds of inequality may be missed and there is no overall measure of equity impact combining both kinds of inequality.

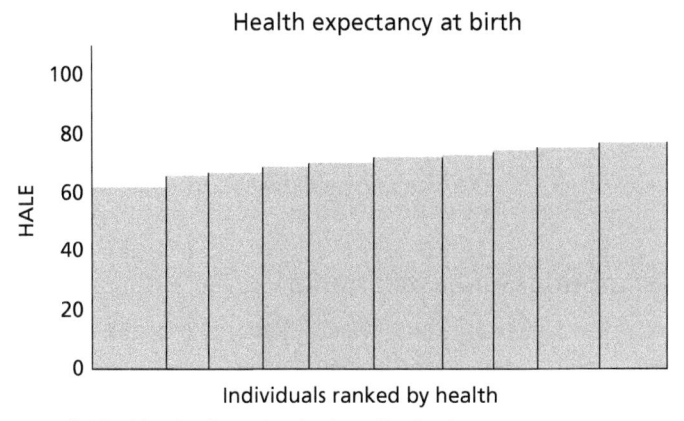

Figure 4.3 Individual-level adjusted univariate distribution.

Realised lifetime health (simulated)

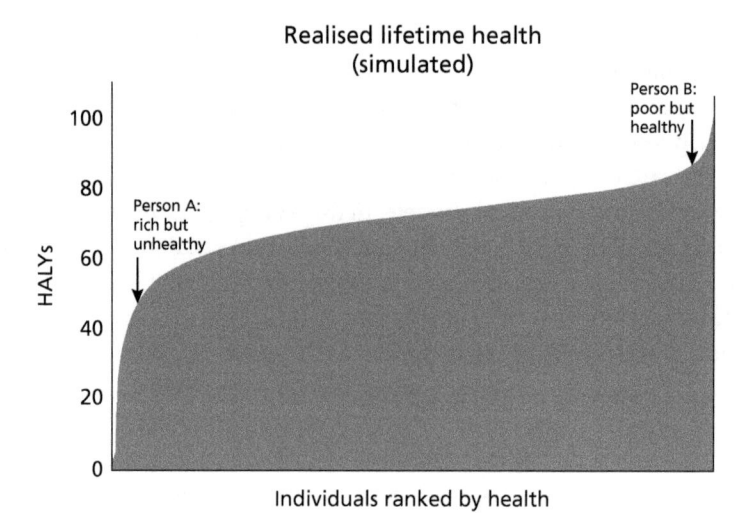

Figure 4.4 Individual-level univariate distribution showing 'overall' health variation.

Decision makers may also be concerned about individual-level inequality in realized health as well as inequality in expected health based on equity-relevant variables. For example, it may be considered unfair if an individual ultimately dies prematurely, even if they were expected to life a long and healthy life based on their social group, gender, and any other equity-relevant variables included in the analysis. Fig 4.4 shows an individual-level univariate distribution of realized lifetime health (i.e. health-adjusted age at death), ranked by health. It picks out two individuals, A and B, who confound the usual expectations of socioeconomic inequality in health—person A is rich but dies young, and person B is poor but dies old. There is an important debate in the population bioethics literature about inequality in expected health versus expected inequality in realized health—also known as the *ex ante* and *ex post* approaches (Adler, 2012; Fleurbaey & Voorhoeve, 2013)—and the related issue of group-level versus individual-level inequality (Asada et al., 2015; Eyal, 2018). In principle, it ought to be possible to conduct DCEA using simulated distributions of individual-level realized health of the kind shown in Fig 4.4. However, as discussed in Chapter 16 the data and methods for doing so are currently not well-developed.

4.1.5 Distributions adjusted how?

Just as not all inequality is inequity, not all differences in health, health services, and financial protection may be considered unfair. For example, it is not usually considered unfair for an 80-year old to have a much lower remaining life expectancy than a 20-year old (though the reverse may well be thought unfair).

To focus attention on unfair differences, we often need to adjust distributions for factors considered to represent fair sources of variation. When looking at inequality in health consequences between social groups, for example, we might want to adjust for differences in the age composition of those groups. This gives a focus on 'unfair' variation due to social status rather than 'fair' variation due to age. Or, when looking at inequality in health service utilization between social groups, one might want to adjust for differences in morbidity. This helps us focus on unfair variation in service use due to social status rather than fair variation due to differences in needs. Again, the implication is that the design stage of a study that uses concepts of fairness and unfairness should, in discussion with decision makers, nail their meanings as clearly as possible and certainly well enough to enable labelling of characteristics as the one or the other.

Some categories that might facilitate such a discussion include:

- Choice and responsibility: some inequalities that arise through choices made by responsible individuals may be regarded as fair (like the greater exposure to risk of people who engage in extreme sports).
- Luck: good and bad luck may be regarded as fortunate or unfortunate but not as unfair, even when luck creates inequalities.
- Preventability: inequalities that have no known means of being prevented may be regarded as fair, even though unfortunate.
- Treatability: inequalities that cannot be addressed by known healthcare technologies may be deemed fair, even though unfortunate, since there is nothing to be done about them.
- Compensatability: inequalities of one sort that are accompanied by inequalities of another sort might mitigate overall unfairness, as when males have shorter life expectancies but social advantages over females.

These ideas by no means amount to knock-down arguments and are at best pegs on which to hang discussions with decision-makers—vast philosophical literatures have been written about each. Such discussions might be enhanced by seeking information on public views among the relevant population and advice not only from philosophers about the value concepts but also from scientists about the determinants of health and the limited power of healthcare alone to make major impacts on some health distributions. Social value judgments about the fairness of health distributions will depend on factual beliefs about the complex causal pathways underlying the observed relationships (Deaton, 2013). Correlation does not imply causation, and associations between health and equity-relevant variables reflect a complex jumble of causal influences over the life-course—over time, for example, poor health can gradually cause poverty, just as poverty can gradually cause poor health. Detailed individual level longitudinal data will usually not be available to disentangle these historical causal pathways. However, there is by now a large body of multidisciplinary scientific theory and evidence about the social determinants of health over the life course. Decision makers may wish to seek expert advice about this literature when making value judgments about the fairness of health distributions, to reduce the risk of being led astray by erroneous factual beliefs. Some of these issues can be discussed and resolved as a matter of general methodological policy applicable to all DCEA studies used by a particular decision-making body (e.g. whether to focus on equity-relevant variables relating to social groups or disease groups or both) and some will require case-by-case discussion in the context of each topic.

4.1.6 Distributions observed when?

Various time-related issues need resolution at the design stage of a study. One concerns the time horizon over which decision impacts are measured. Does the 'post-decision' observation include impacts on health over the many decades of remaining life of the whole relevant population, or just the impacts likely to be realized during a shorter time horizon of policy interest (say the next five or ten years)? Should lifetime health be observed using information available at the start of life, the middle of life, or the end of life? When analysing unfair inequality in lifetime health by social group, it is usual to measure lifetime health as healthy life expectancy at birth. Another option is, however, to measure lifetime health from the date of onset of disease, which can be many years after birth. Whatever the choice is to be it needs to be settled at the design stage.

4.2 Evaluating equity impacts and trade-offs

The tools we introduce in this section are based on the 'value maximizing' way of thinking introduced in Chapter 2, which regards improving total population health and reducing unfair health inequality as policy objectives that can be traded off against one another to maximize social welfare. Another approach is to regard efficiency and equity as two distinct sets of considerations that occupy separate moral spaces and draw on categorically different ways of thinking. Equity can be thought of in terms of a duty to respect rights or to satisfy claims in proportion to strength—the 'moral rights' and 'fair shares' ways of thinking discussed in Chapter 2. It is hard, then, to see much sense in talk about 'trading off' equity and efficiency. The language of 'compromise' seems more appropriate. There are plainly other possibilities too, and we have not taken sides. The act of bringing equity and efficiency together to determine a 'grand optimum' versus a 'reasonable compromise' takes one along different paths. On the path to the grand optimum, trade-offs are identified and quantified in the analysis, as described in Part III of the book on 'Evaluating distributions'. The other path to reasonable compromise entails acceptance of efficiency and equity impacts that are not ideal but that nonetheless command widespread assent via the design of the decision-making process itself, who participates in it, and how discussions that balance different concerns have been organized and facilitated. Credibility of process replaces a specified rate of exchange between equity and efficiency. Either way, information about equity impacts and trade-offs can be a useful input to decision-making—though not the final word.

4.2.1 Types of equity metric: inequality indices and social welfare indices

Having established which aspects of inequality are to be considered inequitable in a study, we now turn to the main summary measures and the significant differences between them. There are two fundamental types of equity metric:

- Inequality indices
- Social welfare indices

Inequality indices compare distributions specifically in terms of inequality only, that is, the dispersion or variation of the outcome variable in the population. Social welfare indices compare distributions more generally in terms of both efficiency and equity, that is, the variation of the outcome variable and the total amount of the outcome. Inequality indices are useful for measuring equity impacts, whereas social welfare indices are useful for analysing trade-offs between equity and efficiency.

Some inequality indices are based on social welfare indices—for example the Atkinson index introduced below, the extended Gini index, generalized concentration index, and Kolm index described later in the methods chapters. However, there are also many useful inequality indices which are not based on social welfare indices—for example the slope and relative indices of inequality (Mackenbach & Kunst, 1997; Moreno-Betancur et al., 2015).

A useful graphical device for inequality measurement is the Lorenz curve developed by Max Lorenz (1880–1962), a US economist who used it to describe income inequalities. As used in health economics the Lorenz curve shows the cumulative percentage of health held by successive percentiles of the population. The percentage of individuals or households is plotted on the horizontal axis, the percentage of total HALYs on the vertical (Fig 4.5). A perfectly equal distribution, where each has the same number of HALYs, appears as a straight line called the line of equality. A completely unequal distribution, where one

[Figure 4.5: Lorenz curve showing cumulative % of health vs cumulative % of persons or households, with Line of equality, Area A, Area B, and Lorenz curve labeled.]

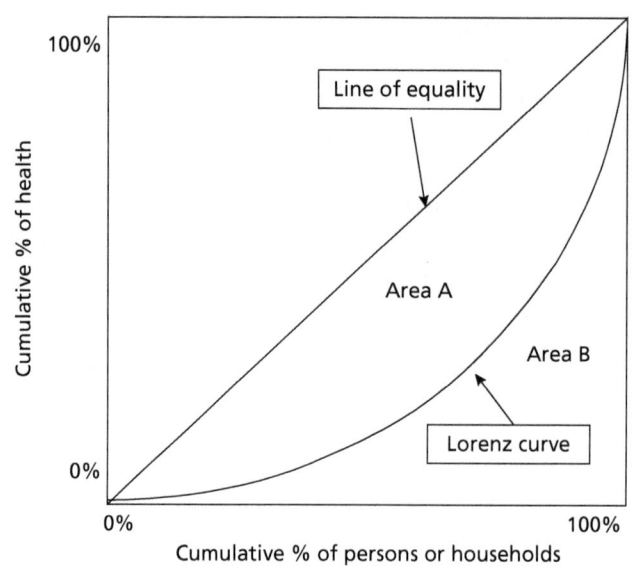

Figure 4.5 Lorenz curve.

person has all the health, appears as a mirror L shape. This is the line of perfect inequality.

A useful inequality measure directly based on the Lorenz curve is the Gini coefficient. This was developed by the Italian statistician Corrado Gini (1884–1965) as a measure of income inequality and has also been used to measure inequality in health and healthcare. The Gini coefficient is a number between 0 and 1, where 0 corresponds to perfect equality (everyone has the same health or healthcare) and 1 is perfect inequality (one person has all the health or healthcare). The Gini coefficient is related to the areas in a Lorenz diagram. Let the area between the line of perfect equality and Lorenz curve be A, and the area underneath the Lorenz curve be B, then the Gini coefficient is A/(A + B).

The social welfare function (SWF) approach introduces the idea of aversion to inequality explicitly. A simple SWF is this:

$$W_U = \sum_{i=1}^{N} h_i,$$

where W_U is social welfare, h_i is the health (measured in HALYs) of person i and N the number of people in the population. Social welfare is the sum across the population of all HALYs, implicitly assigning a unitary weight to each person. Implicitly, standard cost-effectiveness analysis uses this simple SWF.

The Atkinson SWF is:

$$W_A = \sum_{i=1}^{N} g(h_i)$$

$$g(h) = \frac{h^{1-\varepsilon}}{1-\varepsilon} \text{ for } 0 \leq \varepsilon \neq 1$$

$$g(h) = \ln(h) \text{ for } \varepsilon = 1$$

where ε is an equity parameter indicating the degree of aversion to health inequality. The value of ε is crucial. As ε approaches infinity, the SWF increasingly gives the least healthy person absolute priority—a view often loosely described as Rawlsian, after the American philosopher, John Rawls (Rawls, 1971).

The Atkinson social welfare index is an example of a level-dependent measure, where the priority given to improving the health or a person or group depends on their level of health. In philosophy this approach is known as 'prioritarianism', and can be interpreted either in terms of compassion for those with low levels of health or as form of pluralistic egalitarianism that pursues the twin goals of reducing health inequality and increasing total health (Otsuka & Voorhoeve, 2018). There are also rank-dependent indices which give priority to worse-off people depending on their health rank relative to others. The rank-dependent approach focuses on health ranks, whereas the level-dependent approach focuses on health levels. Both approaches give priority to people with a worse health level and hence a lower health rank—but in the level-dependent approach it matters how much worse. The level-dependent approach has the convenient property of being additively separable or subgroup decomposable. This means that one can look separately at different subgroups of the general population and measure the contribution to social welfare and inequality of each subgroup in isolation in ways that are directly comparable across the subgroups. This property means that equity and welfare impacts on the whole of society can be expressed as a function of equity and welfare impacts on its constituent parts—for example national equity impacts can be decomposed into local equity impacts by subnational region. The pros and cons of these different approaches for different purposes are taken up further in Chapters 12 and 13.

Social welfare indices indirectly imply equity weights for individuals and groups, depending on their existing health level or rank and the chosen inequality aversion parameter. Alternatively, one can apply direct equity weights to specific groups, such as patients needing end-of-life care or generally disadvantaged people. Direct equity weights allow greater flexibility to set weights in whatever specific pattern is preferred by decision makers, but lack a theoretical grounding in general ethical principles and are less generalizable across different types of equity concern and across different communities and cultures.

4.2.2 Ethical axioms for comparing distributions

How does one compare one distribution with another? How may one say whether one distribution is more, or less, unequal than other? Two fundamental and seemingly innocuous ethical axioms of social choice are the usual starting points for addressing these questions (Bleichrodt & Van Doorslaer, 2006):

- The principle of health monotonicity (Pareto principle)—if at least one person has more HALYs and no one has fewer, that is judged to be a better distribution.
- The principle of health transfers (Pigou-Dalton principle)—if HALYs are redistributed from a more healthy to a less healthy person, the distribution will be more equal provided the HALYs transferred do not exceed the initial difference in HALYs between them.

We owe the first of these principles to Vilfredo Pareto (1848–1923) and the second to Arthur Pigou (1877–1959) and former British Chancellor of the Exchequer Hugh Dalton (1887–1962). They were originally conceived in the context of inequalities of income and wealth (Cowell, 2011) but have been adapted to examine inequalities in health. The converse of the monotonicity principle is sometimes known as the 'no levelling down' principle: it is not good to reduce health inequality by harming someone's health without improving anyone's health.

Do your decision makers sign up to these value judgments? Would they add qualifications? Would they want further axioms? These two ideas underlie explicitly or implicitly most of the literature and the equity metrics used in this book and are much developed in later chapters; though it is possible to construct social welfare functions that violate both principles (Abasolo & Tsuchiya, 2013). For example, health poverty indices violate both principles since they are unconcerned with changes in health for people above the health poverty line (Cowell, 2011).

It is possible for one distribution of health to be more efficient than another but less equitable, that is, to improve total health but reduce health inequality. But it is also possible for one distribution to be both more efficient and equitable than another. There are also the possibilities that one distribution may be less efficient but more equitable than the other and, finally, one may be both less efficient and less equitable than the other. These four possibilities correspond to the four quadrants of the equity-efficiency impact plane introduced in Chapter 3.

It is not necessary to use formal approaches such as inequality indices, dominance analysis, and equity weighting. Analysts can present decision makers with a 'dashboard' of disaggregated distributional information and leave them to make their own informal assessment of equity impact. A dashboard needs careful design. If it is too comprehensive it may fail to summarize information in a way that decision makers can easily assimilate. In selecting what to include, analysts may slip in some of their own values at the expense of decision makers' values. Dashboard design, like DCEA design in general, is best done at the scoping stage of a study in collaboration with clients.

4.2.3 Summarizing equity impact using inequality indices

Inequality is a complex concept with many aspects that cannot all be captured in a single summary number. In what follows, we assume that appropriately adjusted distributions of lifetime health have been simulated under different decision-making scenarios. The task is now to summarize this distributional information using a suitable inequality index, for example to measure the degree of inequity in health levels in the baseline comparator situation, and after a new programme is implemented, and then to define equity impact as the difference.

Numerous inequality indices are available, including relative indices focusing on relative proportions, absolute indices focusing on absolute differences, attainment indices focusing on positive health outcomes (e.g. survival), and shortfall indices focusing on negative ill-health outcomes (e.g. mortality). Different indices can yield different conclusions about the direction on equity impact. For example, imagine everyone gains one HALY. This will have no effect on absolute inequality—absolute differences in health between people will remain the same. However, it may reduce relative inequality because it delivers a proportionately larger benefit to people with lower pre-existing levels of lifetime health. One HALY represents a 2% gain for someone with 50 expected HALYs, for example, but only a 1% gain for someone with a 100 expected HALYs. Hence the relative inequality impact may be positive (inequality-reducing) even though the absolute inequality impact is zero. Careful consideration and justification should therefore be given to the selection of a particular type of inequality index in a particular context, so that decision makers can be alerted to the fact that different indices can yield different directions and magnitudes of equity impact (Kjellsson et al., 2015).

Before producing an inequality index, it is worth graphing the relevant distributions to get a feel for the underlying patterns. This is worth doing even if the decision-making organization has pre-specified a standard reference case inequality index that you are obliged to use. For example, if the standard index presupposes a smoothly rising social gradient in health but your distribution is

U-shaped then there is a risk that using the standard index will suggest strange and spurious conclusions.

The next thing is to perform dominance tests to check two things: whether one distribution is unequivocally better than another for all groups (group-level Pareto dominance) and whether one distribution is unequivocally more equal than another according to any inequality index that respects the health transfers principle (group-level Lorenz dominance). Further dominance tests are also available to test whether one distribution is better than or more equal than another under almost any reasonable set of assumptions. These are discussed in Chapter 11.

Once this has been done, you can turn to specific inequality indices. As previously discussed, one key issue is whether to summarize the impact on inequality in health levels ('level egalitarian' concern), or inequality in the incremental health changes ('change egalitarian' concern), or both. The former requires calculating inequality indices for at least two distributions—the pre-decision distribution of lifetime health under the baseline scenario and the final post-decision distribution of lifetime health. The effect on inequality in levels is then the difference between the two. Calculating inequality in the incremental health changes, by contrast, only requires calculating an inequality index for one incremental distribution of net health benefits. The two approaches can yield different results. However, the results will be the same if an absolute index of inequality is used since the impact on inequality in health levels is then entirely determined by the absolute incremental health changes rather than the proportional changes relative to the baseline levels.

To summarize a bivariate distribution (Fig 4.1) we need a bivariate equity metric which measures the association between the health variable (the first variable) and the social status variable (the second variable)—for example a slope or concentration index of inequality. To summarize a univariate distribution (Figs 4.2, 4.3, and 4.4) we need a univariate equity metric which measures inequality only in the distribution of the health variable—for example a Gini or Atkinson index of inequality. However, it is possible to convert a univariate distribution into a bivariate distribution by treating health rank as if it were a separate variable indicating social status or unfair health advantage rank, as we illustrate in Chapter 7 by computing slope indices of inequality in lifetime health for adjusted univariate distributions of the kind illustrated in Fig 4.3. Conversions of this kind are straightforward when health and social rank coincide, as in Fig 4.1, though caution is required when they do not, as in Fig 4.3, and so the ranking variable cannot be interpreted as an independent measure of social status.

Levels of inequality are typically reported on a scale of 0–1, or 0–100%, though some indices of absolute inequality are reported as absolute differences on the same scale as the outcome variable. Due to the smaller magnitudes involved, it is often convenient to report changes in inequality in terms of hundredths of a percentage point. Equity impacts of a few hundredths of a percentage point may seem small when compared with net population total health impacts measured in thousands or millions of HALYs. Yet such impacts are not unimportant. Most health policy decisions involve investing small proportions of society's total economic wealth—usually a fraction of a percentage point—and hence cannot be expected to deliver more than a fraction of a percentage point reduction in health inequality. It can also be helpful to measure equity impacts in the same units as total health, for example in terms of equally-distributed equivalent HALYs. These are a form of equity-weighted HALYs that are comparable with the ordinary HALYs used to measure net population health impacts. Presenting efficiency and equity impacts on the same scale can make it easier for decision makers to assess the scale and importance of the equity impacts.

4.2.4 Thinking about equity-efficiency trade-offs

In many cases there is no need to analyse trade-offs between efficiency impact and equity impact. For example, the decision may lie in the 'win-win' or 'lose-lose' quadrant of the equity impact plane. Or dominance analysis may reveal that one decision is better than the alternative under almost any reasonable set of assumptions—for example it may be better for almost all groups, and just as good for the other groups. In other cases, it may be worth analysing equity or equity-efficiency trade-offs.

A health frontier diagram (see Fig 4.6) can be a helpful way of thinking about equity-efficiency trade-offs. This shows possible health outcomes for two social groups—disadvantaged group 1 (poor health prospects) and advantaged group 2 (better health prospects)—measured on the two axes. The 45° line of equality through the origin connects all distributions of equal health. Point B is the baseline distribution which is markedly unequal and presumptively inequitable. The space defined by the coordinates of B to the north east and bounded by the convex health frontier shows the possible additions to health for either group made possible by a new budget. It is convex because we assume that additional spending on either group is subject to diminishing marginal returns—the additions to health per additional dollar become smaller. Any point on or within the frontier can be reached through a suitable mix of health policies, holding constant wider government policies and social determinants of health outside the control of health policymakers. Points outside the frontier cannot be reached due to the limits of technology, scarce resources, and other constraints (Culyer & Wagstaff, 1993). Full equality of lifetime health lies beyond the health policy frontier, since healthcare policy is here assumed to be a

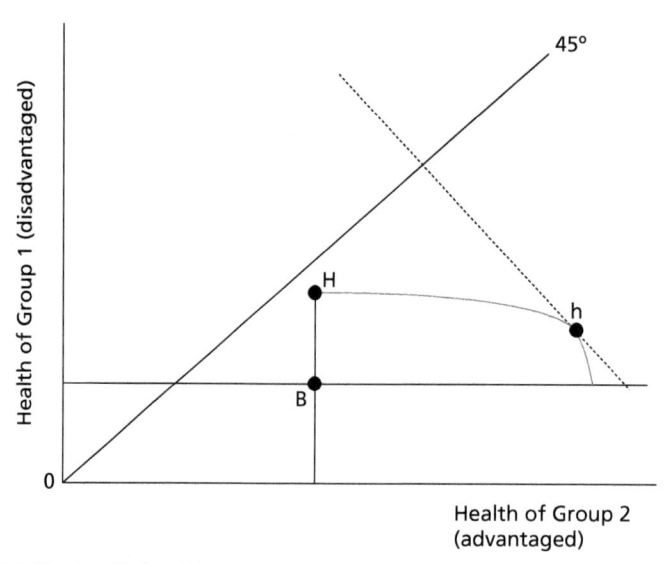

Figure 4.6 The health frontier.

relatively small contributor to overall health equity. This is usually the case with specific interventions for specific diseases. However, the line of equality might conceivably be within the attainable options in some cases—for example if the two groups were geographically defined but otherwise differed only in that the disadvantaged group were remote and hence more costly per HALY to treat.

Which is the best point to choose? There is a clear argument of group-level Pareto dominance for choosing a point on the frontier rather than one below it. For any point below the frontier there is always at least one point on it which is Pareto dominant. This equity-efficiency trade-off can be considered a 'no-brainer'. More difficult questions arise, however, when choosing between different points on the frontier. Two polar extreme equity principles are labelled H and h. The maximum health point, h, maximizes sum total health. This values a given rise or fall in the health of a member of either group the same, which is why the slope of the health policy frontier at this point is -1, as shown by the dotted line. The maximin point, H, maximizes the health of the least healthy group (the disadvantaged group).

In between these polar extreme positions there is an equity-efficiency trade-off. This trade-off can be analysed mathematically using a SWF that incorporates an inequality aversion parameter. Changing the value of this parameter can represent a wide range of ethical views, lying between the maximum health point, h, at one extreme to the maximin health point, H, at the other extreme.

The chosen point will depend on the degree of inequality aversion, and it will lie somewhere between h and H on the health frontier in Fig 4.6.

An implication of using the group level Pareto dominance criterion is that the indices we describe will never recommend the 'levelling down' of health to reduce health inequality. That is, they will not seek to reduce health differences by reducing the health of better-off groups without improving the health of worse-off groups.

4.3 Visualizing equity trade-offs

This section introduces two diagrammatic ways of presenting equity trade-offs in DCEA: the equity-weighted net health benefit plot and the social indifference curve in the equity-efficiency impact plane. The equity-weighted net health benefit plot shows the degree of inequity-aversion required to consider an option better than an alternative. The social indifference curve shows whether an option is better than the baseline comparator, given a specified level of inequality aversion or set of equity weights.

Each approach provides three key pieces of information for comparison with the baseline status quo:

- Net health benefit (or 'efficiency impact');
- Equity impact;
- Equity-weighted net health benefit (or 'social welfare impact').

All three pieces of information come in common units that are comparable with HALYs. These units can be referred to as equally distributed equivalent HALYs (EDE HALYs). There is then a simple arithmetical relationship between the three pieces of information: equity impact is the difference between equity-weighted net health benefit and net health benefit. Or, to put it another way, social welfare impact is the sum of efficiency impact plus equity impact. If equity-weighted net health benefit is positive then the option is better than the comparator—weighing up both net health benefit and health inequality impact—and otherwise not, setting aside wider considerations.

Fig 4.7 shows an equity-weighted net benefit plot comparing two hypothetical decision options X and Y against a baseline comparator.

Option X is cost-effective but equity-harming, whereas option Y is cost-ineffective but equity-improving. When concern for health inequality is zero—that is, when inequality aversion is zero at the y-axis intercept—option X is better than option Y. At this point, social welfare impact is defined purely in terms of total health benefit and so the most cost-effective option is considered best as in standard CEA. As concern for health inequality increases with the

Social welfare impact
(population level equity-weighted HALYs)

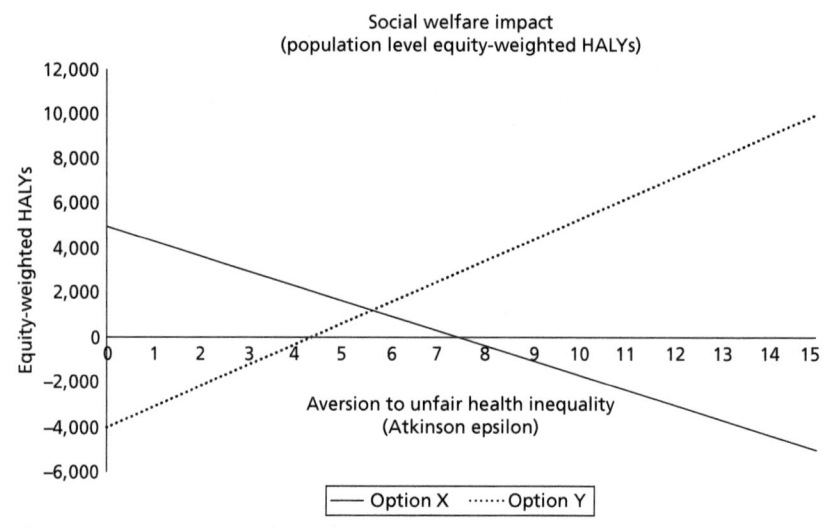

Figure 4.7 Equity-weighted net health benefit plot.

inequality aversion parameter value on the *x*-axis, however, option X starts to look worse (declining social welfare impact) whereas option Y starts to look better (increasing welfare impact). At parameter values above 4, Y is better than the comparator, and at parameter values above 6, Y is better than X. The size of the equity impact for any given level of inequality aversion can be read off the graph as the difference between equity-weighted net health benefit and net health benefit (the *y*-axis intercept).

Equity-weighted net benefit is standardized in a way that makes one unit of equity-weighted net benefit comparable to one standard unit of benefit (e.g. one HALY). One way to do this is using the idea of equitably distributed equivalent health (EDEH) in a conceptual experiment (see also Chapter 13). The decision maker is asked to imagine that unfair inequality in health between equity-relevant groups could be eliminated—but only at the cost of reducing total health. The population level EDEH is then the (lower) level of total health in a perfectly equal health distribution considered to be as good as the current unequal health distribution.

The appropriate inequality aversion parameter value is a matter for value judgment by the decision maker. Different parameter values may be appropriate in different contexts, and, for example, different parameter values may be appropriate in the context of different concepts of health (e.g. lifetime health versus future health, expected health versus realized health), different types of distribution (e.g. distributions of health levels versus incremental health changes), and different equity-relevant variables (e.g. distributions by disease group versus social group).

Using EDEH relies on there being sufficiently detailed information about the health distribution from which one can calculate inequality and social welfare indices. In many cases information is limited. For example, one may have information about only two groups—recipients of a programme and everyone else. In such cases, it is common to use direct equity weights, which give specific weights to specific recipients. It is then still possible to measure equity impact in HALY units, as explained in Chapter 14.

Fig 4.8 shows a social indifference curve in an equity-efficiency impact plane, where both equity and efficiency impact are measured in HALY equivalent units. A social indifference curve is a locus of points in the equity-efficiency impact plane considered equally as good as one another in terms of social welfare. If equity and efficiency impact are both measured in HALY equivalent units then equity indifference curves are straight lines at 135° to the origin like the one shown passing through the origin. All points on this social indifference line represent cases where equity impact plus efficiency impact equals zero. Equity-weighted net benefit is positive to the right of the indifference line and negative to the left. In other words, an option to the right of the social indifference line is better than the comparator, and an option to the left is worse.

Programme Y is a win-lose programme—it is cost-effective (positive efficiency impact) but harms equity (negative equity impact). To assess this equity trade-off, we need to choose equity weights. When equity weights are chosen to reflect strong concern for equity, the measured negative equity impact will be large—as shown by point Y^S in the diagram. By contrast, when equity weights are chosen to reflect weaker concern for equity, the measured negative equity impact will be smaller—as shown by point Y^W in the diagram. Whether the equity impact falls left or right of the social indifference line thus depends on the decision maker's strength of concern for equity. The analyst can then

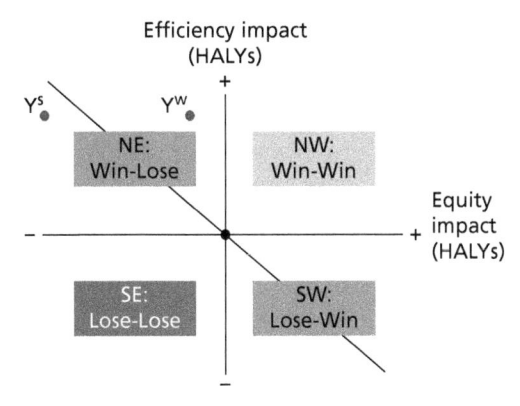

Figure 4.8 Social indifference curve in the equity-efficiency impact plane.

conduct sensitivity analysis to explore how far different equity weights lead to different recommendations.

4.4 Concluding comments

This chapter has introduced some of the most important ideas and techniques used in measuring and evaluating equity. They will be elaborated and applied in later chapters. Throughout it is important for the analyst to remember that he or she is unlikely to be the one accountable for any substantive social value judgments; that accountable role falls to decision makers. What the analyst can be held to account for is ability to convey to decision makers the often subtle ideas relating to both efficiency and equity, the options that lie open for them, some pros and cons, a 'way of thinking' about complex choices, and a set of practical tools for measuring and manipulating the variables in question.

Decision makers want headline findings about equity impacts and trade-offs to help them make sense of complicated technical data. However, they also want reassurance that they understand what the headline findings mean, what hidden assumptions and value judgments the findings may conceal, and how far the findings are robust. Therefore, they are likely to want a judiciously crafted 'dashboard' of information about the distributional breakdowns of interest, a clear statement of the underpinning assumptions and value judgments, and careful sensitivity analysis to understand how robust the findings are to alternative assumptions and value judgments.

4.5 Further reading

Kjellsson and colleagues provide a useful introduction to summary measures of health inequality and the value judgments underpinning them (2015) and Asada and colleagues provide useful advice on graphical communication of health inequalities (2017). Bellù and Liberati provide an easy-to-use online guide to calculating the Atkinson welfare index (2006). Adler and Cowell provide comprehensive and technically advanced treatments of social welfare and inequality indices, respectively (Adler, 2019; Cowell, 2011). These and other topics discussed in this chapter—including selecting distributional breakdowns and visualizing equity trade-offs—are also covered in more detail in the rest of the handbook.

References

Abasolo I. & Tsuchiya A. (2013). Is more health always better for society? Exploring public preferences that violate monotonicity. *Theory and Decision*, **74**, 539–563.

Adler M. (2012). *Well-being and Fair Distribution: Beyond Cost-benefit Analysis*. Oxford University Press, New York.

Adler M. (2019). *Measuring Social Welfare: an Introduction*. Oxford University Press, New York.

Asada Y., Abel H., Skedgel C., & Warner G. (2017). On effective graphic communication of health inequality: considerations for health policy researchers. *Milbank Quarterly*, 95, 801–835.

Asada Y., Hurley J., Norheim O., & Johri M. (2015). Unexplained health inequality—is it unfair? *International Journal for Equity in Health*, 14, 11.

Bellù L. & Liberati P. (2006). Policy impacts on inequality: welfare based measures of inequality: the Atkinson Index. EasyPol: online resource materials for policymaking. Food and Agricultural Organization of the United Nations, Rome.

http://www.fao.org/policy-support/resources/resources-details/en/c/848138/

Bleichrodt H. & Van Doorslaer E. (2006). A welfare economics foundation for health inequality measurement. *Journal of Health Economics*, 25, 945–957.

Cowell F. (2011). *Measuring Inequality*. Oxford University Press, New York.

Culyer A. & Wagstaff A. (1993). Equity and equality in health and healthcare. *Journal of Health Economics*, 12, 431–457.

Deaton A. (2013). What does the empirical evidence tell us about the injustice of health inequalities? *Inequalities in Health: Concepts, Measures, and Ethics*, 263–381.

Eyal N. (2018). Inequality in political philosophy and in epidemiology: a remarriage. *Journal of Applied Philosophy*, 35, 149–167.

Fleurbaey M. & Voorhoeve A. (2013). Decide as you would with full information! An argument against ex ante Pareto. In N. Eyal, S. Hurst, O. Norheim, D. Wikler. (eds), *Inequalities in Health: Concepts, Measures, And Ethics*. Oxford University Press, New York. pp. 113–128.

Kjellsson G., Gerdtham U., & Petrie D. (2015). Lies, damned lies, and health inequality measurements: understanding the value judgments. *Epidemiology*, 26, 673–680.

Mackenbach J. & Kunst A. (1997). Measuring the magnitude of socio-economic inequalities in health: an overview of available measures illustrated with two examples from Europe. *Social Science and Medicine*, 44, 757–771.

Moreno-Betancur M., Latouche A., Menvielle G., Kunst A., & Rey G. (2015). Relative index of inequality and slope index of inequality: a structured regression framework for estimation. *Epidemiology*, 26, 518–527.

O'Neill J., Tabish H., Welch V., Petticrew M., Pottie K., Clarke M., et al. (2014). Applying an equity lens to interventions: using PROGRESS ensures consideration of socially stratifying factors to illuminate inequities in health. *Journal of Clinical Epidemiology*, 67, 56–64.

Otsuka M. & Voorhoeve A. (2018). Equality versus priority. In S. Olsaretti (ed.), *The Oxford Handbook of Distributive Justice*. Oxford University Press, Oxford. pp. 65–85.

Rawls J. (1971). *A Theory of Justice*. Harvard University Press, Cambridge, MA.

Chapter 5

Introduction to the training exercises

Richard Cookson, James Love-Koh, Colin Angus, and James Lomas

Each methods chapter has an accompanying spreadsheet training exercise to give you hands-on practical experience in using the methods.[1] Seven of the exercises form a cumulative sequence relating to the example of nicotine replacement therapy (NRT) in England, and there are also two stand-alone exercises relating to other topics in other countries. This chapter explains how the exercises fit together, introduces the NRT example, and describes the policy questions addressed by the exercises.

5.1 Summary of the exercises

Fig 5.1 shows how the cumulative exercises on NRT fit together.

There are also two stand-alone exercises: exercise 6 on simulating baseline health by disease group, and exercise 10 on simulating distributions of financial risk protection.

Exercises 7–9, on simulating health distributions, show how to conduct distributional impact analysis by producing distributions of baseline health (pre-decision), health benefits, health opportunity costs, and final health (post-decision). Exercise 7 summarizes the baseline distribution of lifetime health in England in 2010 by social groups. Exercise 8 examines the distribution of health effects of two NRT programme funding options alongside the total costs. Exercise 9 examines the health opportunity costs of these options and shows how the various inputs can be brought together to compute net health equity impacts, produce the post-policy distribution of lifetime health, and plot the decision options in the equity-efficiency impact plane. Exercises 11–14

---

[1] The exercises are available at this website: https://www.york.ac.uk/che/research/equity/handbook

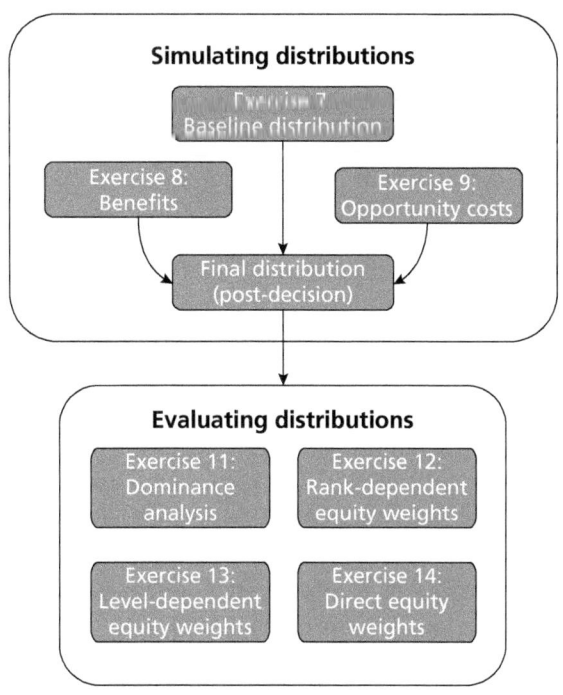

Figure 5.1 How the cumulative exercises fit together.

on evaluating health distributions then show how to evaluate the outputs of a distributional impact analysis and conduct equity-efficiency trade-off analysis using four different methods: dominance analysis, rank-dependent equity weights, level-dependent equity weights, and direct equity weights. Dominance analysis checks whether one option is better than another according to reasonably general ethical principles—for example group-level Pareto dominance asks whether at least one group is better-off and none worse-off. A 'win-win' option (better for both total health and health equity) is not necessarily Pareto dominant, so it is important to check. Rank-dependent and level-dependent equity weights compare distributions based on an equity parameter, reflecting degree of priority to less healthy people. Varying the equity parameter then systematically alters the indirect weights attached to specific groups depending on their health characteristics. Chapter 12 explains how to compare distributions using rank-dependent equity weights which give priority to worse-off people depending on their rank in the health distribution. Chapter 13 explains how to compare distributions using level-dependent equity weights, which give priority to worse-off people depending on their absolute level of health. Finally, Chapter 14 introduces direct equity weights for specific groups (e.g. patients needing end-of-life care, disadvantaged people). Direct equity weights allow greater flexibility than rank- or level-dependent equity weights, but at the cost of achieving less comprehensiveness and consistency.

5.2 The NRT example

5.2.1 Why NRT?

We have chosen an example that illustrates all the main steps in conducting distributional cost-effectiveness analysis (DCEA) for any healthcare or public health intervention. NRT, to help people stop smoking or chewing tobacco, is a classic example of a preventive healthcare intervention aimed at improving health and reducing health inequality. Across the globe, tobacco use generates a heavy disease burden that imposes costs on health services and falls disproportionately on disadvantaged communities, thus contributing to health inequality. In 2015, 11.5% of global deaths were attributable to smoking, and worldwide the age-standardized prevalence of smoking was 25% in men and 5.4% in women (Reitsma et al., 2017). Although smoking prevalence declined globally between 1990 and 2015, the number of smokers continued to rise as a result of demographic change (Ng et al., 2014). Tobacco control thus remains a substantial health policy problem worldwide, and the tobacco-related burden of disease continues to rise in low- and middle-income countries (LMICs) as existing smokers continue to age and fall ill (Reitsma et al., 2017).

New technologies such as e-cigarettes are starting to reduce the demand for NRT in England and some other high-income countries (Brown et al., 2014; Vardavas et al., 2014). However, publicly funded NRT remains an important component of tobacco control policies in high-income countries, and may in future become an important component in LMICs, few of which currently have any public funding of NRT (Piné-Abata et al., 2013). So, in years to come, health policymakers around the globe will face challenging questions about whether and how to invest in public funding of NRT and other tobacco control services—questions that raise important issues about equity as well as efficiency.

5.2.2 Three NRT policy options

The exercises ask you to imagine you are providing information to the National Health Service (NHS) in England in 2010. More specifically, the main decision-making organization is the NHS advisory body known as the National Institute for Health and Care Excellence (NICE), though the analysis is also designed to inform other organizations responsible for health sector decision-making in England.

You must help the NHS choose between three national policy options for public funding of NRT, allowing for their effects on private over-the-counter purchase of NRT:
1. No Public NRT: do not provide any public subsidy for NRT.
2. Universal NRT: offer free NRT to all smokers.
3. Proportional Universal NRT: Universal NRT with additional resources to encourage uptake in disadvantaged communities.

Standard cost-effectiveness studies show that NRT is highly cost-effective (Shahab, 2012), so there is little doubt that Universal NRT is better for total health than No Public NRT. However, there is less evidence about the additional costs and health benefits of investing additional resources to encourage uptake in disadvantaged communities—that is, the cost-effectiveness of Proportional Universal NRT versus Universal NRT. And standard cost-effective analysis (CEA) provides no evidence about the distributional implications of either option, or the potential trade-offs between cost-effectiveness and health inequality impact. If one ignores the additional cost, it may seem obvious that Proportional Universal NRT will increase total health and reduce health inequality compared with Universal NRT. However, if one allows for the health opportunity costs of this additional expenditure—and who bears those opportunity costs—there may potentially be trade-offs between improving total health and reducing health inequality. You will provide this information by putting together various components of DCEA in a cumulative sequence of training exercises.

In fact, the NHS implemented a centrally funded programme of Universal NRT in England during the 2000s (West et al., 2013). However, in 2013 funding for public health programmes, including preventive healthcare programmes of this kind, was subsequently reallocated and decentralized from the NHS budget to local government budgets, at which point some local areas started disinvesting from NRT and other smoking cessation services (Iacobucci, 2018). But you are not constrained by history: you are asked to imagine that you have been transported back in time to 2010, and that your task is to provide the NHS with equity-informative economic evaluation evidence that could influence national decision-making.

5.2.3 Assumptions about NRT delivery

NRT can be delivered in various forms, including chewing gum, transdermal patches, oral and nasal sprays, inhalers, and tablets/lozenges. NRT is effective with or without additional counselling, and approximately doubles the effect of whatever other actions a smoker takes when attempting to quit (Stead et al., 2012; Hartmann-Boyce et al., 2018).

To keep the exercise simple, we focus on delivering NRT simply and cheaply as a stand-alone service, rather than more intensively in combination with other therapies such as additional counselling or other stop smoking medications such as varenicline and the antidepressant bupropion. Combination therapy may increase quit rates, but any additional benefit appears to be small and there is doubt about the comparative effectiveness of more intensive smoking pharmacotherapies (Baker et al., 2016).

In common with most standard cost-effectiveness analyses, we also make the simplifying assumption of a constant unit cost of NRT delivery for writing and processing the prescription, including an allowance for the fixed overhead costs of staff, buildings, and facilities. In economic terms, we assume constant returns to scale and set aside economies of scale and scope associated with infrastructure investments in setting up local smoking cessation clinics and national teams to conduct evidence review, communication, and training around smoking cessation. We modify this assumption in one simple respect, by assuming a higher delivery cost in disadvantaged populations for the Proportional Universal NRT option. However, we do not undertake any explicit analysis of variation in overhead costs between clinics of different sizes in different geographical areas and with different levels of demand. How to analyse economies of scale and scope when evaluating infrastructure investments—often called 'health systems strengthening'—is an important but under-researched subject that we return to in Chapter 16.

5.2.4 Simple modelling approach

The exercises involve a simple 'table-based' decision tree model that can be implemented by anyone capable of using a spreadsheet, and does not require advanced modelling skills. The aim is to learn DCEA in a way that can be followed by anyone with a basic understanding of cost-effectiveness analysis and decision trees. The same basic concepts and methods can then be applied in the context of more advanced underpinning models—be they Markov models, microsimulation models, infectious disease transmission models, or whatever. We do not show you how to build and operate advanced decision analytical models, however, as other handbooks in this series cover those skills. Instead, we provide summary tables of data inputs and then show you how to manipulate them in a simple way to perform equity analyses.

5.2.5 Assumptions about key model inputs

- We focus on adult smokers aged 18 and over.
- We take the probability of quit success 12 months after receipt of NRT from a Cochrane systematic review (Stead et al., 2012).
- We apply a long-term relapse factor to allow for further relapse to smoking after 12 months.
- We estimate incremental health gains and healthcare cost saving per quitter by socioeconomic group (Love-Koh, 2020) using a modified version of the Markov model used by NICE to assess stop smoking services (Flack et al., 2007; Filby & Taylor, 2018).
- We use a weighted average NRT unit cost.
- We ignore the potential non-health benefits of tobacco use in terms of happiness or freedom, because such benefits are controversial and hard to measure (Levy et al., 2018) and because current methods of DCEA are unable to integrate equity in non-health benefits into the analysis, as discussed in Chapter 16.
- We allow for private purchase of NRT, and how this varies between the different public funding options.
- The distribution of health opportunity costs is taken from Love-Koh et al. (2020), which builds on the work of Claxton et al. (2015).

A final point is that we adopt an investment rather than a disinvestment perspective, by taking 'No Public NRT' as the baseline policy situation. In fact, the baseline situation in England in 2010 was 'Universal NRT'. Analytically, this is merely a presentational matter of shifting the origin of the equity impact plane—comparing option 1 against option 2 is mathematically equivalent to comparing option 2 against option 1. We use an investment perspective because this is the more usual case for health expenditure decisions and is more relevant to decision-making in LMICs which do not currently fund NRT. However, there is plenty of evidence from behavioural economics that individual judgments and behaviour are powerfully influenced by the baseline reference point—and so analytically equivalent comparisons may not be politically and psychologically equivalent (Kahneman, 2011). How far the biases and heuristics that influence individual and political decision-making should be incorporated into normative economic analysis is, however, a controversial issue.

5.3 Policy questions addressed by the exercises

5.3.1 Cumulative exercises relating to NRT

The NRT exercises build on one another cumulatively to provide a full DCEA analysis of the equity and efficiency impacts of NRT funding options and the corresponding equity-efficiency trade-offs. Reducing unfair inequality in lifetime health is an important equity objective for the English NHS, as discussed in Chapter 3. Do the various options for investing in NRT services reduce or increase unfair inequality in lifetime health in England, and if so by how much? We illustrate how to analyse this question, focusing on two different dimensions of 'unfair' inequality that interest policymakers in England: socioeconomic group (five groups based on neighbourhood deprivation) and geography (whether the individual lives in the north or south of England). This geographical variable is of interest because the north of England has a long history of social and economic disadvantage compared with the south, and there is a 'north-south divide' in the prevalence of smoking and other unhealthy behaviours and adverse health outcomes, even after adjusting for individual-level measures of socioeconomic status. We illustrate how to handle these two different equity-relevant variables simultaneously in the same equity analysis, though in principle any number and type of equity-relevant variable can be handled.

To give you a flavour of the findings, Fig 5.2 is an informal sketch of how the three options look in an equity-efficiency impact plane.

Both Universal Public NRT and Proportional Universal NRT are 'win-win' policies compared with No Public NRT—they both have a positive impact on

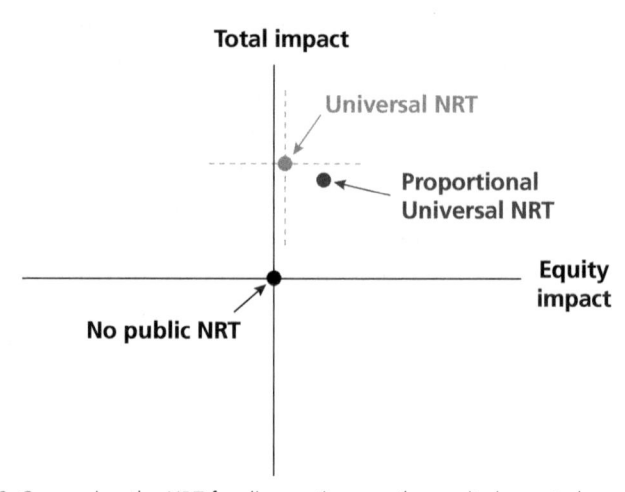

Figure 5.2 Comparing the NRT funding options on the equity impact plane.

total health and health equity (i.e. they improve total health and reduce unfair health inequality). They both lie in the north-east quadrant of the equity impact plane as defined by the solid axes going through the origin of No Public NRT. However, things are more complicated when we compare Proportional Universal NRT against Universal NRT, as illustrated by the dotted line alternative axes going through Universal NRT. These alternative axes reveal that Proportional Universal NRT harms total health but improves equity—that is, it is a 'lose-win' policy—compared with Universal NRT. There is therefore a trade-off between equity and efficiency, which can be analysed using equity weights.

5.3.2 Stand-alone exercises

The two stand-alone exercises are based on different topics in different countries. Exercise 6 looks at simulating baseline health by disease group and exercise 10 looks at simulating distributions of financial risk protection.

Decision makers may take the view that priority should be given to treating patients with more severe diseases. If so, they will need information on how severely ill different patient groups are, so that they can make comparisons in a systematic, evidence-informed manner based on consistent principles and evidence. Exercise 6 shows you how to compare baseline health between disease groups using various concepts of baseline health. The exercise does not examine smoking, which is a risk factor rather than a disease. The issue of severity is potentially relevant to the NRT example, however, as decision makers might take the view that smoking cessation is a low priority investment because smokers are not severely ill. Smoking can of course cause various severe illnesses in future—for example lung cancer, chronic obstructive pulmonary disease, heart disease, and stroke. But most smokers do not have those severe illnesses yet—they merely have a heightened risk of developing those illnesses later in life. So an important equity question is: how severely ill are smokers as a group compared with other patients who might benefit from healthcare expenditure? Answering these questions would require data not only on the burden of illness from smoking-related diseases, but also on how far smoking increases the risk of these diseases.

Exercise 10 focuses on financial protection from the risk of catastrophic healthcare expenditure, using an example from a low-income country—a tobacco tax in Lebanon. Financial risk protection is less relevant to the example of NRT in England, because England has a relatively generous system of universal health coverage and relatively few people face catastrophic risks of healthcare expenditure. However, it is directly relevant to LMICs without universal systems of healthcare coverage, where citizens face substantial and unequally distributed risks of hardship due to healthcare costs.

References

Baker T., Piper M., Stein J., Smith S., Bolt S., Fraser J., et al. (2016). Effects of nicotine patch vs varenicline vs combination nicotine replacement therapy on smoking cessation at 26 weeks: a randomized clinical trial. *Journal of the American Medical Association*, **315**, 371–379.

Brown J., West R., Beard E., Michie S., Shahab L., & McNeill A. (2014). Prevalence and characteristics of e-cigarette users in Great Britain: findings from a general population survey of smokers. *Addictive Behaviors*, **39**, 1120–1125.

Claxton K., Martin S., Soares M., Rice N., Spackman E., Hinde S., et al. (2015). Methods for the estimation of the National Institute for Health and Care Excellence cost-effectiveness threshold. *Health Technology Assessment*, **19**(14), 1–504. https://www.journalslibrary.nihr.ac.uk/hta/hta19140/#/abstract

Filby A. & Taylor M. (2018). NICE Modelling Report: Smoking Cessation Interventions and Services. https://www.nice.org.uk/guidance/ng92/evidence/

Flack S., Taylor M., & Trueman P. (2007). *Cost-effectiveness of Interventions for Smoking Cessation*. York Health Economics Consortium, York.

Hartmann-Boyce J., Chepkin S., Ye W., Bullen C., & Lancaster T. (2018). Nicotine replacement therapy versus control for smoking cessation. *Cochrane Database of Systematic Reviews*, **5**(5), CD000146.

Iacobucci G. (2018). Stop smoking services: BMJ analysis shows how councils are stubbing them out. *British Medical Journal*, 2018;362:k3649.

Kahneman (2011). *Thinking, Fast and Slow*. Macmillan, New York.

Levy H., Norton E., & Smith J. (2018). Tobacco regulation and cost-benefit analysis: how should we value foregone consumer surplus? *American Journal of Health Economics*, **4**, 1–25.

Love-Koh J., Cookson R., Claxton K., & Griffin S. (2020). Estimating social variation in the health effects of changes in health care. *Medical Decision Making*, https://doi.org/10.1177/0272989X20904360

Ng M., Freeman M., Fleming T., Robinson M., Dwyer-Lindgren L., Thomson B., et al. (2014). Smoking prevalence and cigarette consumption in 187 countries, 1980–2012. *Journal of the American Medical Association*, **311**, 183–192.

Piné-Abata H., McNeill A., Murray R., Bitton A., Rigotti N., & Raw M. (2013). A survey of tobacco dependence treatment services in 121 countries. *Addiction (Abingdon, England)*, **108**, 1476–1484.

Reitsma M., Fullman N., Ng M, Salama J., Abajobir A., Abate K., et al. (2017). Smoking prevalence and attributable disease burden in 195 countries and territories, 1990–2015: a systematic analysis from the Global Burden of Disease Study 2015. *Lancet*, **389**, 1885–1906.

Shahab L. (2012). Cost-effectiveness of pharmacotherapy for smoking cessation. National Centre for Smoking Cessation and Training. http://www.ncsct.co.uk/publication_Effectiveness_of_Smoking_Cessation_Services.php

Stead L., Perera R., Bullen C., Mant D., Hartmann-Boyce J., Cahill K., et al. (2012). Nicotine replacement therapy for smoking cessation. *Cochrane Database of Systematic Reviews,* **11**, CD000146.

Vardavas C., Filippidis F., & Agaku I. (2014). Determinants and prevalence of e-cigarette use throughout the European Union: a secondary analysis of 26,566 youth and adults from 27 countries. *Tobacco Control,* **24**(5), 442–448.

West R., May S., West M., Croghan E., & McEwen A. (2013). Performance of English stop smoking services in first 10 years: analysis of service monitoring data. *British Medical Journal,* 2013;347:f4921.

Part II
Simulating distributions

Chapter 6

Health by disease categories

Kjell Arne Johansson, Matthew M. Coates,
Jan-Magnus Økland, Aki Tsuchiya,
Gene Bukhman, Ole F. Norheim,
and Øystein Haaland

This chapter shows how to measure and compare the baseline health of disease groups using various concepts of health. The choice of health concept is an important value judgment for the decision maker, since different health concepts can have quite different equity implications about which disease group is worse-off in terms of health or has greater 'severity of illness'. We distinguish three main health concepts—current health, future health, and lifetime health—and show how each concept can be measured using three main metrics—absolute health achievement, absolute health shortfall, and relative health shortfall. The next chapter then shows how to measure and compare baseline health by social variables such as socioeconomic status, sex, and place of residence.

6.1 Concepts of health and severity

Severity of illness is often considered to be an important equity consideration in both clinical decision-making about individual patients and social decision-making about groups of patients (Otsuka & Voorhoeve, 2009; Norheim et al., 2014; World Health Organization, 2014). Patient-level priority setting—sometimes referred to as 'bedside rationing'—may include selecting whom to operate on and with what procedures, or deciding which patients to treat in specialized oncological or intensive care units with what type of treatment. Group-level priority setting can include public health decisions such as choosing to invest in nicotine replacement therapy for smoking versus subsidies for sport and physical activity, as well as healthcare decisions such as which medicines and treatments to fund for which patient groups. Patients with severe conditions can be given higher priority in decisions at all levels, but this chapter deals with decisions at the policy level.

When making decisions about the pricing and reimbursement of new medicines and devices, decision makers often have equity concerns about severity of illness as well as efficiency concerns about cost-effectiveness (Mirelman et al., 2012; Tanios et al., 2013). In low-income settings, for example, antipsychotics for schizophrenia may not be considered cost-effective. However, including drugs like risperidone and haloperidol on national essential drug lists may nevertheless be justified on the grounds that schizophrenia is an especially severe condition where quality of life is impaired from a young age. Both Norway (Ottersen et al., 2016) and the Netherlands (van de Wetering et al., 2013) use severity measurement methods as an input to healthcare priority setting decisions. This requires severity of illness to be quantified in a way that is consistent across conditions.

The term 'severity' has many meanings and exactly how it should be defined in a particular context is subject to value disagreement as well as a wide range of interpretations (Olsen, 2017; Barra et al., 2019). Urgency, for example, is a factor that can be conflated with severity. Urgency depends on the effectiveness of timely intervention. The earlier the treatment must be initiated to save a life or improve quality of life, the greater the urgency. However, this is not necessarily the same thing as severity, which depends on the burden of illness. Stroke is a good example of how urgency and severity may differ. With the recent introduction of thrombolysis and thrombectomy as treatment options for stroke, future health prospects for stroke patients have improved because these new treatments prolong life and improve quality of life—and in this sense severity of illness has been reduced. The urgency of treating stroke has, however, increased, as to be effective this treatment needs to be initiated within just a couple of hours after the onset of a stroke event. Patients are therefore, patients are now brought to hospital with ambulances for immediate stroke treatment. In the past, acetylsalicylic acid and rehabilitation were the only treatment options for stroke patients. In the emergency room, stroke patients were triaged as a non-urgent patient group because the timing of intervention did not influence the outcome much. The new stroke treatments illustrate how new interventions may influence urgency and severity in opposite directions. There is a critical time window for action to get optimal treatment effectiveness and, once that window passes, the same stroke patient is no longer an urgent case.

To help avoid this and other potential confusions relating to the term severity, we use the term *baseline health* by disease category in this chapter. Currently, there are three main schools of thought on how to measure baseline health by disease category, each focusing on: current health, health over future years, and health over the lifetime (see Fig 6.1).

CONCEPTS OF HEALTH AND SEVERITY | 107

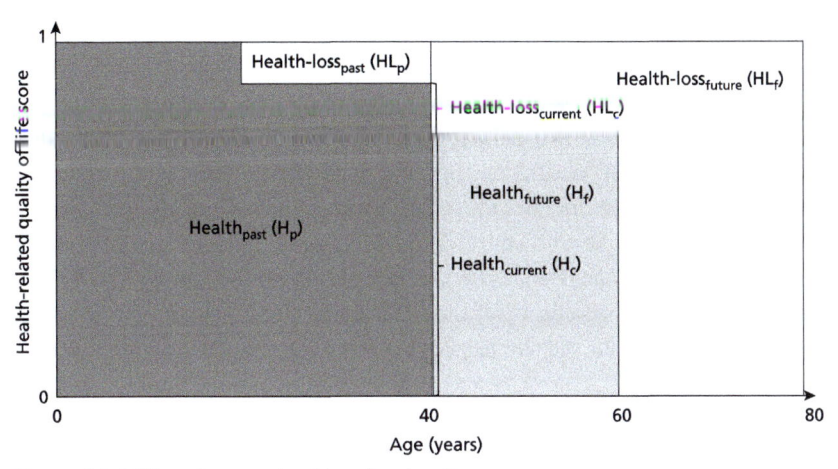

Figure 6.1 Different concepts of baseline health.
Note: this figure illustrates different concepts of baseline health for a patient who is currently aged 40 and who has had an existing condition since age 20. The patient has acquired another illness with an immediate impact on quality of life and is expected to live 20 years with the disease. Lifetime health is the sum of the two shaded boxes, that is, $H_p + H_f$. A fixed reference value of 80 is used as upper reference. The figure is adapted from similar diagrams by various authors (Lindemark et al., 2014; Olsen, 2017).

The first perspective, current health, assigns high weight to interventions that benefit groups with current discomforts or symptoms and diseases with high immediate mortality risk or symptoms that greatly reduce quality of life, independently of considerations of how long things may last (Nord, 1999). Patients with ruptured aortic aneurisms, for example, have poorer current health than patients in an early stage of breast cancer. The second perspective, future health, assigns higher weight to interventions that benefit groups with poor future health prospects after disease onset; and diseases with low future health—or, equivalently, high loss of future health compared with a reference norm—are considered worse, regardless of past health status (Scanlon, 2015; Olsen, 2017). Patients with pancreatic cancer, for example, have lower future health levels than patients with an uncomplicated radial fracture. The third perspective, lifetime health, incorporates past, current, and future health, and higher weight is assigned to interventions that benefit disease groups with low lifetime health or high loss of lifetime health compared with a reference norm (Parfit, 1990; Otsuka & Voorhoeve, 2009; Adler, 2011; Ottersen, 2013). Young patients with severe opioid addiction, for example, have lower lifetime health than older patients with dementia. Later chapters will explain equity methods for assigning higher weights to benefits to patient groups who are considered worse-off and how this ensures a more equal distribution of health. In this chapter we mainly focus on how to measure baseline health and illustrate how baseline measures of current, future, and lifetime health differ.

An overview of the baseline health terminology with examples of metrics used in this chapter is shown in Table 6.1. Each of the three main baseline health perspectives (current, future, and lifetime) can be combined with three different measurement principles (absolute health achievement, absolute health shortfall, and relative health shortfall), yielding nine different baseline health metrics. All of these can be measured using health-adjusted life years (HALYs), which can be either disability-adjusted life years (DALYs) or quality adjusted life years (QALYs). For the two perspectives that incorporate duration, future,

Table 6.1 Nine baseline health metrics

		TIME PERSPECTIVES		
		Current health	Future health	Lifetime health
MEASUREMENT PRINCIPLES	Absolute health achievement	$\underline{H_c}$ Health-related quality of life, pain scale, survival rate	$\underline{H_f}$ HALE from illness onset	$\underline{H_p + H_f}$ HALE from birth (includes past healthy life years and HALE from condition onset)
	Absolute health Shortfall	$\underline{HL_c}$ Disability weight (as used in DALY calculations), mortality rate	$\underline{HL_f}$ Shortfall in HALE from a reference, starting from illness onset	$\underline{HL_p + HL_f}$ Shortfall in HALE from a reference, starting from birth
	Relative health Shortfall	$\underline{HL_c/HL_c}$ Hazard ratio (as used in survival analysis): mortality rate for people with illness divided by mortality rate of comparable cohort without illness	$\underline{HL_f/(H_f + HL_f)}$ Proportional future shortfall: (shortfall in HALE from a reference, starting from illness onset) divided by (normal (average) HALE of people of same age and gender)	$(H_p + HL_f)/80$ Proportional lifetime shortfall: (shortfall in HALE, starting from birth) divided by (normal (average) HALE at birth)

Note:
HALE: healthy-adjusted life expectancy
DALY: disability-adjusted life years

and lifetime health calculations, health-adjusted life expectancy (HALE) is typically used—measured either from birth or from illness onset (Lindemark et al., 2014; Olsen, 2017). Details of these HALE calculations are presented later in the chapter. In the next section, we go into more detail on the three key baseline health perspectives and present how each of these concepts can be quantified.

6.1.1 Three time perspectives: current, future, and lifetime health

Current health is here defined as present pain or other disability, or mortality, measured by, for example, health-related quality of life or disability weights or crude short-term mortality. The current health perspective ignores expected future health deteriorations or improvements. Consider a case with two conditions, where condition A has high mortality and disability the first year, while the survivors go on to lead long and healthy lives. Condition B also has high mortality and disability the first year, but the mortality and disability remains high for the rest of their lives. The current perspective considers them equally unhealthy. One possible justification for restricting the focus to current health in the context of economic evaluation is to prevent double counting of future health in both the severity criterion and in the expected future treatment benefits (Nord, 1999).

The future health perspective broadens the current perspective by including expected future health. The reference time that future health is counted from may vary depending on the quantification goal, but common time points might be time of condition onset or time of a possible intervention. Metrics are typically based on life expectancy (LE), HALE, or DALYs lost compared with a reference norm. LE and HALE are expected health achievement measures and the DALY is a measure of shortfall. In the future health perspective, conditions A and B above with the same current mortality risk and disability will not have the same severity since the long-term sequelae of the latter are more serious.

The lifetime health perspective considers not only future health, but also past health, so that the focus becomes health over a lifetime from birth to death. Future health can be measured as described in the previous paragraph, whereas past health prior to the age of illness onset can be calculated using health-adjusted age (HAA)—that is, Health$_{past}$ in Fig 6.1—or disability-adjusted age (DAA)—that is, Health-loss$_{past}$ in Fig 6.1. One way to calculate HAA is simply to add together the average health quality weights for each year lived. In theory, it would also be possible to use data specific to the individuals under consideration, but such data are often not available. The sum of future and past health comprises lifetime health. Two illnesses may have similar average future HALE, but if one illness tends to occur at older ages it will have a larger average lifetime

HALE. Lifetime metrics are not age neutral as $age_a + LE(age_a)$ is typically an increasing function of age.

Reasonable people can disagree about the appropriate time perspective. For most purposes it is appropriate and convenient to use illness onset as the starting point for counting past health and future health expectations, and that is what we do in this chapter. However, earlier and later starting time points are possible, including the time of diagnosis and the time of decision. Which starting point to use may be worth considering, depending on the views of the relevant decision makers and stakeholders and the available data. Sometimes decision makers will want to assess the baseline health of risk factor groups—for example smokers or people with high blood pressure—rather than patient groups with a specific disease. When assessing future or lifetime health, that assessment needs to take into account how the risk factor influences the probability of future onset of various diseases, as well as current health based on current disease prevalence among the risk factor group.

People often have multiple disorders. Comorbidity may be a direct consequence of the primary condition (e.g. hepatitis C may be a consequence of injecting drug use disorder) or a consequence of treatment (e.g. sepsis may be a consequence of chemotherapy). Clustering of conditions can also be caused by genetic susceptibility and socioeconomic factors, where people with low levels of freedom, income, or education tend to have more difficulties changing health habits and therefore more often get multiple conditions. Policymakers may wish to estimate the independent contributions of each illness separately, but comorbidity complicates the analysis. Comorbidity may be handled in different ways and it is important to be explicit about this in the analysis when one calculates the baseline health of a particular condition.

6.1.2 Three measurement principles: absolute health achievement, absolute shortfall, and relative shortfall

Baseline health can be measured as absolute health achievement, absolute shortfall, or relative shortfall. Absolute health achievement represents the expected level of health achieved, currently, in the future, or over a lifetime. Lower health levels indicate lower baseline health. Consider the example in Table 6.2, where a person suffers condition C at the age of 20 and another person suffers condition D at the age of 70. Condition C has a future expected health level (H_f) of 7 if onset is at the age of 20 and H_f for condition D is 1 if onset is at age 70. Lifetime health levels ($H_p + H_f$) are 25 (18 + 7) and 56 (55 + 1), respectively. Person with condition D is the worse-off if measured by H_f and Person with condition C is the worse-off if measured by $H_p + H_f$.

Table 6.2 Fictional example comparing achievement and shortfall health metrics

Age of illness onset	HALE reference	Past health achievement	Future health achievement	Lifetime health achievement	Future health shortfall	Lifetime health shortfall	Relative future health shortfall	Relative lifetime health shortfall
		H_p	H_f	$H_p + H_f$	HL_f	$80 - (H_p + H_f)$	$HL_f/(80 - age)$	$(HL_p + HL_f)/80$
C 20	80	18	7	25	53	55	0.88	0.69
D 70	80	55	1	56	9	24	0.90	0.30

Note: This hypothetical example illustrates absolute achievement, shortfall, and relative shortfall health metrics for two persons that suffer condition C and D respectively starting at the ages of 20 and 70 respectively. HALE of 80 is used as lifetime reference.

Baseline health measured as absolute shortfall can be calculated from a fixed reference value or from a life table. For example, a priority-setting committee appointed by the Cabinet in Norway suggested using a fixed upper lifetime threshold of 80 HALYs to calculate absolute health shortfall in reimbursement decisions (Ottersen et al., 2016). Persons with condition C and D would then have experienced future absolute shortfalls (HL_f) of 53 (80-20-7) and 9 (80-70-1) HALYs and lifetime absolute shortfalls ($HL_p + HL_f$) of 55 (80-18-7) and 24 (80-55-1) HALYs. Notice that the future age-specific threshold is here calculated by the lifetime threshold of 80 minus current age. Alternatively, absolute shortfall can be calculated using a dynamic reference value by using age of disease onset and age specific HALE of the general population as an upper reference. A dynamic upper reference means that the HALE upper-reference varies according the age of disease onset, meaning that each age of onset has its unique upper HALE reference. A country specific liftable or a global reference table can be used, like the reference table used in Global Burden of Disease (GBD) studies (Global Burden of Disease Collaborative Network, 2017) constructed to estimate years of life lost (YLLs) (where the lowest age-specific mortality rates from all locations with populations > 5 million are used). With absolute shortfall metrics, rankings are the same as with absolute achievement levels and the person with condition C is worse-off.

Lastly, relative shortfall can be calculated as the proportion of future health loss by dividing shortfall in HALE by a standard HALE, either with a fixed reference value or a dynamic reference value based on individual characteristics, as is done in the Netherlands (Stolk et al., 2004; van de Wetering et al., 2013; Nord, 2015). In our example with a fixed HALE threshold of 80, person C would have a relative future shortfall of 88% ((80-20-7)/(80-20)), while person D would have a relative future shortfall of 90% ((80-70-1)/(80-70)). The relative shortfall metric gives a very different ranking from the other baseline health measures and person D is worse off. However, rankings reverse with relative lifetime shortfall. Person C would have a relative lifetime shortfall of 69% ((80-18-7)/80), while person D would have a relative lifetime shortfall of 30% ((80-55-1)/80).

6.2 Calculation methods and data inputs

This section describes how to calculate the health of a disease group according to the three perspectives described in Fig 6.1 and Table 6.1 and describes data needs for these analyses. The accompanying spreadsheet training exercise gives a practical example of how to calculate the nine different baseline health metrics. The results can either be presented separately alongside cost-effectiveness findings or used as the basis for equity weighting as described in later chapters. We also show how to compute the individual-level distribution of health within each disease category, as well as the group-level distribution of health between disease groups.

A set of key choices needs to be made when calculating baseline health, each of which will require consultation with the relevant decision makers. First, the time perspective (current health, future health, or lifetime health). Second, whether to use an absolute health level, absolute shortfall or relative shortfall measure of baseline health. Third, which specific disease category populations are to be compared. For example, if one calculates the baseline health of the population with acute lymphoblastic leukaemia (ALL), one may calculate baseline health for the whole ALL group, for only those with Philadelphia-chromosome-negative ALL, or for only children and adolescents. The target population for the intervention to be evaluated dictates for which population one calculates the baseline health.

We will now illustrate the application of health-adjusted age at death (HAAD) calculations (Johansson et al., 2020). HAAD is the number of years lived from birth to death, adjusted for health-related quality of life. From epidemiological and demographic data, we know the age specific incidence rates and population size in each age group. For each age group, we calculate future realized healthy life years from disease onset until death and add past health (health-adjusted age at disease onset, HAAD). In sum, this is realized lifetime health and is calculated for multiple conditions and in different country contexts. In our examples, we calculate HAAD based on the assumption that disease onset occurs in 2016, by using age specific incidence rates from the GBD 2016 data (2017). The conceptual framework for calculating HAAD is illustrated in Fig 6.2 (Johansson et al., 2020).

Three new concepts are introduced in Fig 6.2. First, period of increased mortality (PIM) is the period after onset of illness in which a person has increased risk of death. PIM can be temporary or lifelong, and excess mortality converges to background mortality after PIM. Second, period of increased disability (PID) is the period after onset of illness in which a person experiences increased disability. PID can also be temporary or lifelong, and excess disability converges on background disability after PID. Third, lifetime disease specific health-adjusted age at death ($HAAD_D$) measures past health and the future realized health that is expected. $HAAD_D$ can be summarized at an age group level ($HAAD_D$) or at an average level (across all age groups) for specific conditions. $iHAAD_D$ is a stochastic simulation of the individual's lifetime health based on the individual's age and sex at the point of illness onset. We run the stochastic simulation based on information that is in principle available at the point of illness onset, as if we

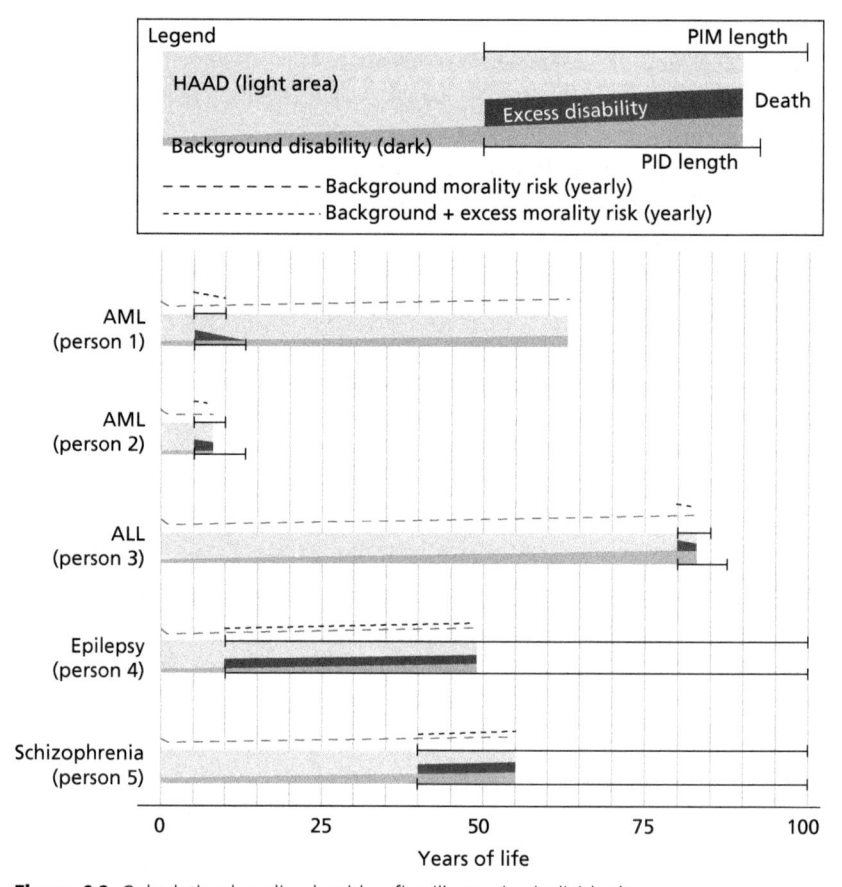

Figure 6.2 Calculating baseline health—five illustrative individuals.
Note: this figure illustrates realized lifetime health calculations (HAAD) for five individuals with different illnesses (AML, ALL, epilepsy, and schizophrenia). Onset of calculations are from birth and calculations end at the expected age of death for each person. Age of disease onset varies. Future health expectancies (with start at disease onset) reset the horizontal axis to 0 at onset and reach to the right of that point only. Each illness is illustrated with two set of y-axes, one for mortality (0 to 1) and one for disability (0 to 1). The dashed black line is background mortality risk from causes other than the disease, and the black dotted line is background mortality risk plus the excess risk of death caused by the disease. The medium dark grey area at the bottom is background health loss due to disability, dw, (here we use the average rate of disability in the general population), and the dark grey area is health loss caused by D (dw_D). The sum of the upper light grey area is disease-specific HAAD ($HAAD_D$) over a lifetime for each person. The top solid black line gives a period after the onset of disease when the person would be expected to have a period of increased mortality risk (PIM). The bottom line gives a similar period of increased disability (PID). Current and future health measures would only estimate the grey area from illness onset.

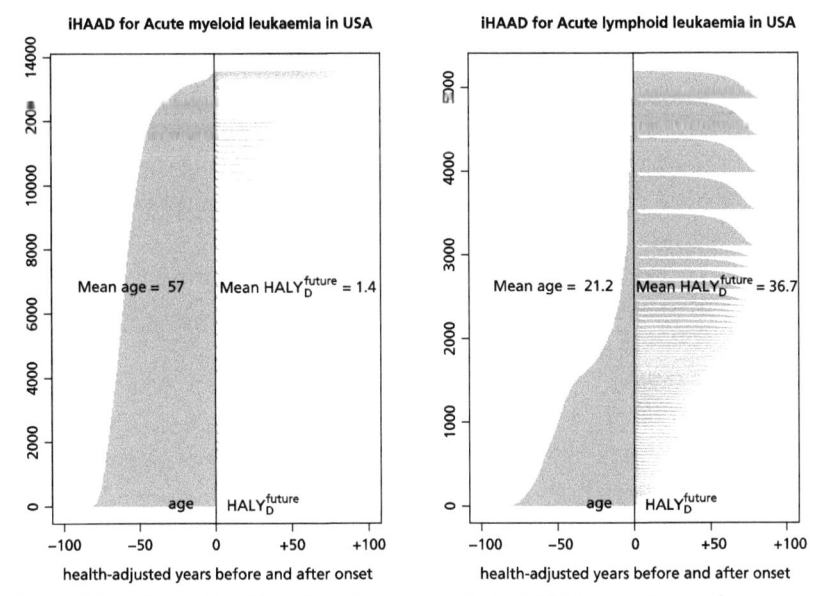

Figure 6.3 Individual health-adjusted age at death (iHAAD) for two types of cancer. Note: distribution of future health (realized health-adjusted life years with illness (HALY$_D^{future}$)) and past health (health-adjusted age) for acute lymphoblastic leukaemia (ALL) and acute myeloid leukaemia (AML), where illness onset is 2016 and the context is USA. The negative x-values are past health (health-adjusted age) and the positive x-values in the lower part of the figures are realized values of HALY$_D^{future}$ for each individual with ALL and AML.

were taking measurements from the point of illness onset. iHAAD is sensitive to the distribution of past and future health as opposed to the average HAAD.

6.2.1 Future health

Fig 6.3 shows expected distributions of past and future health for all individual patients in the USA that had incident cases of acute lymphoblastic leukaemia (ALL) and acute myeloid leukaemia (AML) in 2016. The x-axis shows health-adjusted years before and after disease onset, and 2016 is the year of illness onset. The y-axis shows individuals. Each is indicated with one bar, where individuals are ordered first by age of illness onset and then by expected age of death. We have used GBD data for age specific evidence on incidence rate, case fatality, and background mortality (GBD 2016 Disease and Injury Incidence and Prevalence Collaborators, 2017). Step-by-step details of the calculations, which also includes disability weights and adjustments for background mortality, can be seen in the exercise for this chapter.

The average expected future health level is very different for the two illnesses; AML has on average 1.4 years HALE from illness onset whereas ALL has on average 36.7 years HALE from illness onset. From a future health expectancy perspective, AML patients are therefore worse-off than ALL patients. When we look at the individual distribution of realised future health within the two disease groups, there are individuals in the ALL group with few future health-adjusted years, particularly the elderly. From a clinical point of view this is well known, as older patients with ALL get much smaller treatment benefits from current treatment protocols due to interactions between their greater background mortality risk and the biology of this illness. The scalloped shape of the ALL plot shows the variation in realized health-adjusted years for patients within the same age group of illness onset.

6.2.2 Lifetime health

As illustrated in Fig 6.3, the level of total realized lifetime health consists of two components: past health and future realized health:

$$\text{HAAD}(\text{age}) = \text{HAA}_{past} + \text{HALE}_{D}(\text{age}), \qquad (1)$$

where HAA_{past} is the health-adjusted age of the individual and HALE_{D} is the expected number of health-adjusted life years each individual has left to live at their respective age (future realized health). In our calculations, we are assuming population average health prior to illness onset and we adjust each past year before illness onset with background disability weights without the illness of interest (dw).

In Fig 6.4, the same individuals as in Fig 6.3 are now ranked in increasing order of realized lifetime health (HAAD). Looking at the distributions, there are individuals in the AML and ALL groups that have very low HAAD. In Fig 6.4, we have marked those with < 20 HAAD (T20) for AML or ALL in USA. Interestingly, the HAAD distribution looks different for the AML illness group (more equal) as compared to the ALL illness group (less equal).

In this example, the future and lifetime health perspectives yield very different severity rankings. Average lifetime health is almost identical for the two illnesses (HAAD for AML = 58.4 HALYs and HAAD for ALL = 57.9 HALYs). However, from the future health perspective, AML patients are much worse-off on average than ALL patients (AML = 1.6 HALYs and ALL = 37.7 HALYs).

6.2.3 Where can you get these data?

Estimates from GBD studies can be used to quantify baseline health by disease category. Table 6.3 shows the list of data and variables that are needed to calculate baseline health. However, calculations of baseline health by disease group are slightly different from the methods used for calculating disease burden in

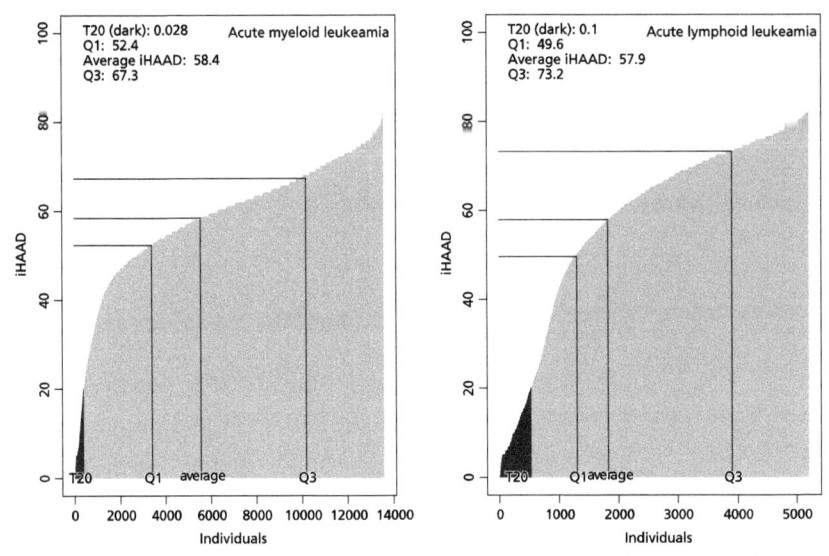

Figure 6.4 Distributions of health-adjusted age at death for individuals (iHAAD) with AML and ALL.
Note: distribution of realized lifetime health (individual health-adjusted age at death (iHAAD)) for new cases of AML (left) and ALL (right) in the USA in 2016, ranked in increasing order of realized lifetime health (HAAD).

GBD 2010 (and onwards). One key difference is that the GBD methods aim to measure total disease burden in the general population, yielding a higher burden for more prevalent diseases. We aim, however to measure baseline health for the average patient within each disease group, such that more common diseases are not automatically counted as being more 'severe' merely because more people are affected. The GBD study starts by estimating age- and sex-specific deaths from each cause for a given population in a specific year. Years of life lost (YLL) due to a given cause of death is an absolute gap measure, calculated from a life table, multiplying the number of deaths due to an illness by the expected future life years from the reference life table. Years lived with disability (YLDs) are calculated separately by creating estimates of prevalence of various disease sequelae for the current year (cross-sectional) and multiplying by corresponding disability weights. DALYs are the sum of YLLs and YLDs, therefore combining future health loss from mortality incidence in the current year and health loss from morbidity prevalence only in the current year. By contrast, baseline health metrics need to capture loss of health from both morbidity and mortality in individuals over the course of their lives. For GBD, the YLD and the YLL come (mostly) from different people (YLL from people who die in the

Table 6.3 Data and variables for calculating baseline health by disease group

Input variable	Description
PIM	*Period of increased mortality* From expert opinions. Number of years with increased mortality after illness onset. The rate at which mortality declines in the PIM is specific for each condition. For simplicity, PIM = 100 for chronic illnesses. PIM = 5 is used for ALL and AML.
PID	*Period of increased disability* From expert opinions. Number of years with increased disability after illness onset. The rate at which disability declines in the PID is specific for each condition. For simplicity, PID = 100 for chronic illnesses. We use PID = 5 for the leukaemias.
pop	*Population size, per 5-year age interval* From GBD 2016. Transformed to 1-year age intervals by distributing individuals evenly across the five years.
P_D	*Prevalence (per population) of illness per 5-year age interval* From GBD 2016. Assumed to be the same in all 1-year intervals.
I_D	*Incidence (per population) of illness per 5-year age interval* From GBD 2016. Assumed to be the same in all 1-year intervals.
M_D	*Illness specific probability of death per 5-year age interval, for total population* From GBD 2016 Assumed to be the same in all 1-year intervals.
q	*All cause probability of death per 5-year age interval, for total population (background mortality).* From GBD 2016. $q = M_{\text{All causes}}$ Assumed to be the same in all 1-year intervals.
YLD_D	*Years Lived with Disability of illness per 5-year age interval.* From GBD 2016. Assumed to be the same in all 1-year intervals.
Derived variables	**Description**
em_D	Excess mortality due to illness (case fatality rate). These are not given directly in GBD, but can be calculated using: $$em_D(\text{age}) = \frac{M_D(\text{age})}{P_D(\text{age})}$$ This is the extra risk of dying for individuals with illness that is caused directly by the illness itself. Note that this is different from M_D, which is the risk of dying from a particular illness for any individual in the population.

Table 6.3 Continued

Derived variables	Description
q_D	Probability of death due to illness and background mortality. These are not given directly in GBD, but can be calculated using: $q_D(\text{age}) = q(\text{age}) - M_D(\text{age}) + em_D(\text{age})$ Substituting em_D into q_D yields $q_D(\text{age}) = q(\text{age}) + M_D(\text{age})\left(\dfrac{1}{P_D(\text{age})} - 1\right)$ We can see from q_D that if $P_D=1$, meaning that all individuals in the population have a illness, q_D simply becomes q. This is also the case if there is no mortality from illness, so that $M_D = 0$.
q_D^{PIM}	During the period of increased probability of death due to illness, q_D is used for PIM years. After the period, q_D returns to q.
dw	Background disability weight without the illness of interest (1 is no disability and 0 is the highest disability). $dw = \dfrac{YLD_{\text{All causes}}}{100000}$.
dw_D	Disability weight due to the illness of interest (1 is no disability and 0 is the highest disability). $dw_D(\text{age}) = \dfrac{YLD_D(\text{age})}{P_D(\text{age})}$.
dw_D^{PID}	During the period of increased disability, the disability weight is: $dw_D^{PID} = 1 - \left(1 - \dfrac{\dfrac{YLD_{\text{All causes}}}{100000} - \dfrac{YLD_D}{100000}}{1 - \dfrac{YLD_D}{100000}}\right)(1 - dw_D)$. After the period, dw returns to that of the background population.

Note: The data source we used was the GBD 2016 study (GBD 2016 Disease and Injury Incidence and Prevalence Collaborators, 2017). Global, regional, and national incidence, prevalence, and years lived with disability for 328 diseases and injuries for 195 countries, 1990-2016: a systematic analysis for the Global Burden of Disease Study 2016. Lancet, 390, 1211-1259.

reference year; YLD from people with illness who survive the reference year). For our HAAD measure, both mortality and morbidity data belong to the same individual.

There are other sources of data for these calculations, depending on the population of interest. The analyst should be aware of limitations in the data that might compromise the results. In our examples, we have used average disability and mortality risk by causes of disease and disability with no explicit modelling of transitions between disease states. We did not have the inputs required to include dynamic transitions between health states. Additionally, there may be aspects to baseline health imperfectly captured by our inputs. The GBD study, for example, does not attribute deaths to schizophrenia. So, despite evidence that people affected with schizophrenia have shorter life expectancies through increased risk of death from other causes, using the GBD data only did not allow us to incorporate this evidence. Every data set and model will have trade-offs in complexity and generalizability that the analyst needs to be aware of when interpreting results.

6.3 Comparisons of baseline health by disease category

6.3.1 Baseline health across countries

In the previous section we have illustrated how current, future, and lifetime health can be calculated for ALL and AML in the USA. However, the country context can influence baseline health substantially. Suffering from ALL or AML in a low-income country, with poor coverage of cancer care and high background mortality risk from other conditions, can be much worse than suffering ALL or AML in a high-income country with universal coverage of the best cancer treatments available. Tables 6.4a, 6.4b, and 6.4c provide comparisons of health in four different countries for eleven conditions using all nine concepts of baseline health.

Epilepsy is an example of a disease for which new treatments have substantially changed baseline health in treated cases. In the 1950s, patients with epilepsy had extensive quality of life impairments due to frequent seizures. Some hospitals locked epileptic patients in cells to prevent injury during seizures. Now, with good anticonvulsants available, patients can easily be treated in an outpatient clinic and have normal lives. However, this is not the situation in all countries. Some low-income countries have very poor coverage of anticonvulsants, and this affects baseline health of epilepsy, both because of untreated disability and premature death. Fig 6.5 shows the distribution of lifetime health for epilepsy for patients in different settings. Epilepsy can leave individuals worse-off in all settings, but relatively more people are in the lower HAAD levels in Ethiopia and Haiti than any of the other settings. On average, epilepsy is much worse in Ethiopia (average HAAD 36.9) and Haiti (average HAAD 34.2) than in the USA (average HAAD 57.9) and Japan (average HAAD 62.9). These measures can also be affected by the age distribution of the populations, with younger populations having lower average HAAD because of younger average ages of disease onset.

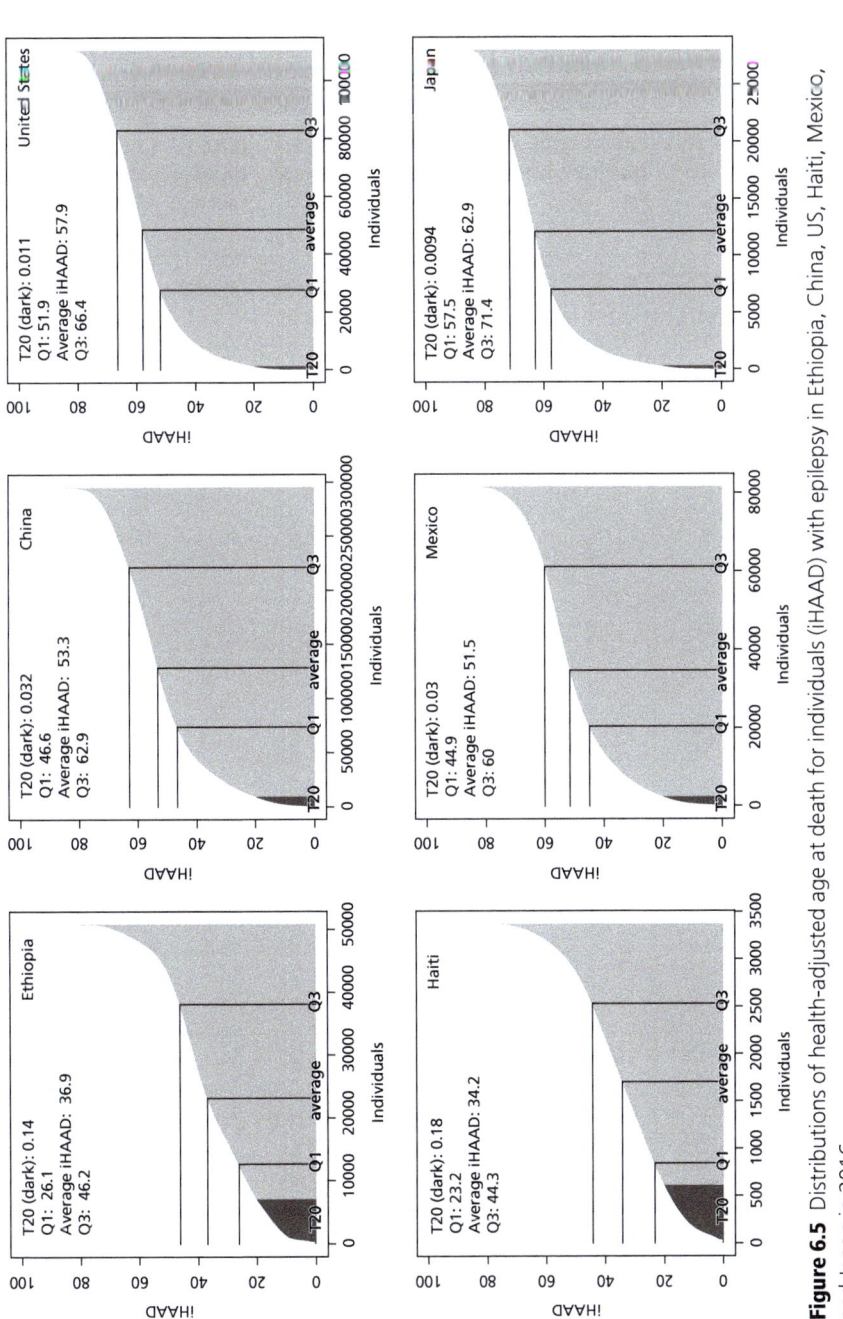

Figure 6.5 Distributions of health-adjusted age at death for individuals (iHAAD) with epilepsy in Ethiopia, China, US, Haiti, Mexico, and Japan in 2016.

HEALTH BY DISEASE CATEGORIES

Table 6.4 League table of baseline health by disease category in various countries and using current and future health metrics, conditions are rank ordered within each country by increasing future HALE

Condition	Current health			Future health		
	Case fatality rate	Disability weight	Hazard ratio	HALE future	HALE future shortfall	Realitive HALE future shortfall
Ethiopia						
Cervical cancer	0.21	0.24	18.6	8.6	10.6	0.54
Breast cancer	0.25	0.26	23.7	6.1	11.7	0.64
Acute lymphoid leukaemia	0.34	0.22	141	7.8	27.6	0.78
Acute myeloid leukaemia	0.79	0.31	247.3	1.2	28.2	0.97
Chronic kidney disease	<0.01	0.17	1.4	19.6	1	0.05
Alzheimer disease and other dementias	0.06	0.35	1.7	4.1	2.3	0.37
Epilepsy	0.01	0.44	3.2	23	23.9	0.5
Schizophrenia	<0.01	0.69	1	12.6	21.5	0.61
Tracheal, bronchus, and lung cancer	0.98	0.38	54.6	0.3	11.3	0.98
Ischaemic heart disease	0.06	0.21	3.9	18	0.5	0.03
Ischaemic stroke	0.05	0.3	2	9.6	5.2	0.38
Mexico						
Cervical cancer	0.13	0.23	23.3	14.8	9.1	0.38
Breast cancer	0.06	0.23	11.4	15.8	5	0.24
Acute lymphoid leukaemia	0.24	0.2	279.9	16.2	29.5	0.64
Acute myeloid leukaemia	0.66	0.29	431.6	2.8	32.7	0.93
Chronic kidney disease	0.01	0.2	2.1	16.5	1.8	0.1
Alzheimer disease and other dementias	0.06	0.36	1.8	4.9	2.8	0.35

Table 6.4 Continued

Condition	Current health			Future health		
	Case fatality rate	Disability weight	Hazard ratio	HALE future	HALE future shortfall	Realtive HALE future shortfall
Epilepsy	<0.01	0.35	3.2	32.4	17.1	0.34
Schizophrenia	<0.01	0.69	1	14.7	24.5	0.61
Tracheal, bronchus, and lung cancer	0.87	0.37	73.4	0.4	12.8	0.98
Ischaemic heart disease	0.08	0.23	4.8	18.4	0.6	0.03
Ischaemic stroke	0.02	0.27	2	12.1	4.4	0.27
USA						
Cervical cancer	0.09	0.24	16.7	17.4	6.5	0.27
Breast cancer	0.04	0.27	5.1	14	2.4	0.15
Acute lymphoid leukaemia	0.1	0.2	102.3	36.7	11.1	0.24
Acute myeloid leukaemia	0.66	0.38	112.7	1.4	14.3	0.93
Chronic kidney disease	<0.01	0.25	1.2	11.9	0.7	0.05
Alzheimer disease and other dementias	0.06	0.37	1.8	4.5	2.3	0.33
Epilepsy	<0.01	0.34	2.4	28.9	11.5	0.28
Schizophrenia	<0.01	0.69	1	15.6	25	0.59
Tracheal, bronchus, and lung cancer	0.46	0.34	32.6	1.5	10.4	0.84
Ischaemic heart disease	0.08	0.25	4	13.3	0.5	0.03
Ischaemic stroke	0.03	0.35	1.6	9	3.6	0.29
Japan+F40						
Cervical cancer	0.08	0.24	21.4	18.2	5.5	0.23

(*continued*)

Table 6.4 Continued

	Current health			Future health		
Condition	Case fatality rate	Disability weight	Hazard ratio	HALE future	HALE future shortfall	Realitive HALE future shortfall
Breast cancer	0.04	0.25	9.1	16.5	2.8	0.14
Acute lymphoid leukaemia	0.1	0.25	93.8	25.6	8.5	0.26
Acute myeloid leukaemia	0.46	0.36	118.7	2.1	13.1	0.87
Chronic kidney disease	<0.01	0.25	1.2	11	0.6	0.05
Alzheimer disease and other dementias	0.07	0.36	2	4.2	2.2	0.34
Epilepsy	<0.01	0.32	4.2	29.4	11.5	0.28
Schizophrenia	<0.01	0.69	1	15.1	24.7	0.61
Tracheal, bronchus, and lung cancer	0.38	0.34	30	1.9	8.4	0.8
Ischaemic heart disease	0.05	0.25	2.9	12.9	0.3	0.02
Ischaemic stroke	0.05	0.37	1.9	7.4	4	0.36

Note: HALE = health-adjusted life expectancy
Data from Global Burden of Disease Collaborative Network. (2017). Global Burden of Disease Study 2016 (GBD 2016) Reference Life Table. Seattle, United States: Institute for Health Metrics and Evaluation (IHME).

6.3.2 Baseline health league table

For decision-making purposes, presenting baseline health in league tables may be useful. Table 6.4 and 6.5 are baseline health league tables for cervical cancer, breast cancer, ALL, AML, chronic kidney failure, Alzheimer's disease, epilepsy, and schizophrenia for Ethiopia, Mexico, and Japan. All nine baseline health metrics in Table 6.1 are calculated: absolute health level, absolute health shortfall and relative shortfall calculations of current severity of illness, future severity of illness, and lifetime severity of illness. To calculate absolute and relative shortfall concepts, we use an upper reference for all countries based on the GBD 2016 reference life table (Global Burden of Disease Collaborative Network, 2017) with LE at birth of 86.6. Conditions

Table 6.5 League table of lifetime health by disease group in various countries, conditions are rank ordered within each country by increasing average HAAD

LIFETIME HEALTH

Condition	HAAD	HAAD shortfall	Relative HAAD shortfall	Age of disease onset	PIM	PID
ETHIOPIA						
Cervical cancer	54.7	31.9	0.37	50.9	5	5
Breast cancer	54.2	32.4	0.37	53.3	5	5
Acute lymphoid leukemia	35.4	51.2	0.59	30.3	5	5
Acute myeloid leukemia	35.9	50.7	0.59	38.3	5	5
Chronic kidney disease	64.7	21.9	0.25	49.9	100	100
Alzheimer disease and other dementias	69.6	17	0.2	74.6	100	100
Epilepsy	36.9	49.7	0.57	15	100	100
Schizophrenia	40.7	45.9	0.53	30.3	100	100
Tracheal, bronchus, and lung cancer	57.3	29.3	0.34	64	5	5
Ischemic heart disease	66.7	19.9	0.23	54.5	1	1
Ischemic stroke	62.9	23.7	0.27	59.8	100	100
MEXICO						
Cervical cancer	62	24.6	0.28	51.6	5	5
Breast cancer	66.6	20	0.23	55.8	5	5
Acute lymphoid leukemia	39.7	46.9	0.54	25.4	5	5
Acute myeloid leukemia	37.5	49.1	0.57	37.8	5	5
Chronic kidney disease	70.6	16	0.19	59.7	100	100

(continued)

Table 6.5 Continued

Condition	HAAD	HAAD shortfall	Relative HAAD shortfall	Age of disease onset	PIM	PID
LIFETIME HEALTH						
Alzheimer disease and other dementias	74	12.6	0.15	78.4	100	100
Epilepsy	51.5	35.1	0.41	20.5	100	100
Schizophrenia	44.5	42.1	0.49	31.7	100	100
Tracheal, bronchus, and lung cancer	61.2	25.4	0.29	67.8	5	5
Ischemic heart disease	72.7	13.9	0.16	60.6	1	1
Ischemic stroke	69	17.6	0.2	63.3	100	100
UNITED STATES						
Cervical cancer	64.1	22.5	0.26	52.2	5	5
Breast cancer	69.7	16.9	0.2	63.1	5	5
Acute lymphoid leukemia	57.9	28.7	0.33	23.6	5	5
Acute myeloid leukemia	58.4	28.2	0.33	64.9	5	5
Chronic kidney disease	72.7	13.9	0.16	69.5	100	100
Alzheimer disease and other dementias	73.5	13.1	0.15	80.2	100	100
Epilepsy	57.9	28.7	0.33	32.2	100	100
Schizophrenia	43.7	42.9	0.5	30.4	100	100
Tracheal, bronchus, and lung cancer	63	23.6	0.27	70.2	5	5
Ischemic heart disease	72.8	13.8	0.16	68.1	1	1
Ischemic stroke	70	16.6	0.19	69.9	100	100
JAPAN						

Table 6.5 Continued

LIFETIME HEALTH						
Condition	HAAD	HAAD shortfall	Relative HAAD shortfall	Age of disease onset	PIM	PID
Cervical cancer	69.7	16.9	0.19	57	5	5
Breast cancer	73	13.6	0.16	62.7	5	5
Acute lymphoid leukemia	66.8	19.8	0.23	45.9	5	5
Acute myeloid leukemia	63.6	23	0.27	68.9	5	5
Chronic kidney disease	76.8	9.8	0.11	74.1	100	100
Alzheimer disease and other dementias	76.9	9.7	0.11	83	100	100
Epilepsy	62.9	23.7	0.27	36.7	100	100
Schizophrenia	49	37.6	0.43	36.5	100	100
Tracheal, bronchus, and lung cancer	69.2	17.4	0.2	76	5	5
Ischemic heart disease	76.8	9.8	0.11	71.7	1	1
Ischemic stroke	73.6	13	0.15	74.7	100	100

Note: HAAD = health-adjusted age at death; PIM = Period of Increased Mortality due to illness; PID = Period of Increased Disability due to illness

Data from Global Burden of Disease Collaborative Network. (2017). Global Burden of Disease Study 2016 (GBD 2016) Reference Life Table. Seattle, United States: Institute for Health Metrics and Evaluation (IHME).

are rank ordered within each country by increasing future HALE in Table 6.4 and by lifetime HAAD in Table 6.5. The type of baseline health metric used in the analysis and the setting influences the rank order of conditions. With future HALE rank ordering, epilepsy is considered the most severe condition in Ethiopia, Mexico, and Japan and ALL is considered the most severe condition in USA. With lifetime HAAD, ALL is considered the most severe condition in Ethiopia and Mexico and schizophrenia is considered the most severe condition in USA and Japan.

6.4 Conclusion

In this chapter we have described nine different perspectives for comparing the baseline health of disease groups and we have shown how each perspective can be quantified. Which of these nine different health metrics is most useful depends on the values of decision makers in the specific decision-making context. Future absolute or relative shortfall health might be useful for a decision maker who is concerned only about current and future health and believes that past health is water under the bridge. Lifetime health might be more useful for a policymaker who believes that health comparisons at the group level should take into account the whole lifespan and that priority should be given to treating health conditions that are associated with least health from a complete life course perspective.

6.5 Further reading

Five readings are important to get a better understanding of severity, baseline health by disease categories, and such quantifications. Jan Abel Olsen gives a clear presentation of five equity principles (future health, future health losses, the proportion of future health lost, lifetime health losses, and lifetime health) (2017). In this chapter, Olsen discusses how these five metrics can be included quantitatively in policy decision-making and health economic evaluations. Barra et al. provide a nice literature review and an accessible philosophical analysis of how the severity concept has been used in the literature the last decades (2019). In addition, Barra et al. also present how severity has been applied in priority setting in Norway and Sweden. For a better understanding of the importance of lifetime health, we recommend Ottersen (2013). Ottersen provides a concise philosophical analysis of how the worse-off can be defined as those with the fewer lifetime quality-adjusted life years (QALYs). For more details on the HAAD methodology, we recommend Johansson et al. (2020). The philosopher Tim Scanlon presents philosophical arguments for the future health perspective in worse-off evaluations (Scanlon, 2015) and the text is accessible to non-philosophers.

References

Adler M. (2011). *Well-Being and Fair Distribution: Beyond Cost-Benefit Analysis.* Oxford University Press, New York.

Barra M., Broqvist M., Gustavsson E., Henriksson M., Juth N., Sandman L., et al. (2019). Severity as a priority setting criterion: setting a challenging research agenda. *Health Care Analysis*, 28, 25–44.

GBD 2016 Disease and Injury Incidence and Prevalence Collaborators (2017). Global, regional, and national incidence, prevalence, and years lived with disability for 328 diseases and injuries for 195 countries, 1990–2016: a systematic analysis for the Global Burden of Disease Study 2016. *Lancet,* **390**, 1211–1259.

Global Burden of Disease Collaborative Network (2017), *Global Burden of Disease Study 2016 (GBD 2016) Reference Life Table.* Institute for Health Metrics and Evaluation (IHME), Seattle.

Johansson K., Økland J.-M., Skaftun E., Buckhman G., Norheim O., Coates M., Haaland Ø.A. (2020). Estimating Health Adjusted Age at Death (HAAD). PLOS ONE. DOI: 10.1371/journal.pone.0235955.

Lindemark F., Norheim O., & Johansson K. (2014). Making use of equity sensitive QALYs: a case study on identifying the worse-off across diseases. *Cost Effective Resource Allocation,* **12**, 16.

Mirelman A., Mentzakis E., Kinter E., Paolucci F., Fordham R., Ozawa S., et al. (2012). Decision-making criteria among national policymakers in five countries: a discrete choice experiment eliciting relative preferences for equity and efficiency. *Value Health,* **15**, 534–539.

Nord E. (1999). *Cost-value Analysis in Health Care: Making Sense out of QALYs.* Cambridge University Press, Cambridge.

Nord E. (2015). Cost-value analysis of health interventions: introduction and update on methods and preference data. *PharmacoEconomics,* **33**, 89–95.

Norheim O., Baltussen R., Johri M., Chisholm D., Nord E., Brock D., et al. (2014). Guidance on priority setting in health care (GPS-Health): the inclusion of equity criteria not captured by cost-effectiveness analysis. *Cost Effective Resource Allocation,* **12**, 18.

Olsen J. (2017). Beyond cost-effectiveness: priority setting. In **J. Olsen** (ed.), *Principles in Health Economics and Policy.* Oxford Scholarship Online.

Otsuka M. & Voorhoeve A. (2009). Why it matters that some are worse-off than others: an argument against the priority view. *Philosophy & Public Affairs,* **37**, 171–199.

Ottersen T. (2013). Lifetime QALY prioritarianism in priority setting. *Journal of Medical Ethics,* **39**, 175–180.

Ottersen T., Forde R., Kakad M., Kjellevold A., Melberg H., Moen A., et al. (2016). A new proposal for priority setting in Norway: open and fair. *Health Policy,* **120**, 246–251.

Parfit D. (1995). Equality or priority (The Lindley Lecture, 1991). Lawrence, KS, University of Kansas, Kansas.

Scanlon T. (2015). Kamm on the disvalue of death. *Journal of Medical Ethics,* **41**, 490.

Stolk E., van Donselaar G., Brouwer W., & Busschbach J. (2004). Reconciliation of economic concerns and health policy: illustration of an equity adjustment procedure using proportional shortfall. *PharmacoEconomics,* **22**, 1097–1107.

Tanios N., Wagner M., Tony M., Baltussen R., van Til J., Rindress D., et al. (2013). Which criteria are considered in healthcare decisions? Insights from an international survey of policy and clinical decision makers. *International Journal of Technology Assessment in Health Care,* **29**, 456–465.

van de Wetering E., Stolk E., van Exel N., & Brouwer W. (2013). Balancing equity and efficiency in the Dutch basic benefits package using the principle of proportional shortfall. *European Journal of Health Economics,* **14**, 107–115.

World Health Organization (2014). Making fair choices on the path to universal health coverage. World Health Organization, Geneva.

Chapter 7

Health by social variables

James Love-Koh and Andrew Mirelman

This chapter explains how to estimate baseline distributions of lifetime health as inputs to distributional cost-effectiveness analysis (DCEA). It shows how the baseline distribution influences the assessment of equity impact and how the distribution of interest is defined by social value judgments about what constitutes unfair health inequality. A step-by-step guide to estimating a baseline distribution of health is provided, including analytical methods and appropriate sources of data, along with several practical examples demonstrating how baseline distributions have been produced in different settings.

7.1 Why baseline distributions are needed to assess relative inequality

Reducing the variation in lifetime health between social groups (the 'social distribution' of health) is a common equity objective. A baseline distribution provides a description of the health inequalities in a population prior to making a decision to allocate health resources. The impact of the decision on the baseline distribution can subsequently be evaluated, based on information about the incremental health effects and health opportunity costs. This allows an assessment of *how* equitable (or inequitable) the decision is, which will usually depend on the baseline level of unfair health inequality as well as the incremental changes.

A baseline health distribution is required to estimate the impact of an intervention on relative inequality. This is illustrated by the two scenarios shown in Fig 7.1. A common treatment effect is applied to two baseline health distribution scenarios with different levels of absolute and relative inequality. The change in health inequality is calculated as the difference in the equity gap (1) at baseline and (2) with the intervention. The change in absolute inequality is found to be identical in both scenarios, whereas a larger relative effect is found when baseline health is lower. The dependency of the equity impact on the baseline distribution of health extends to distributions with greater numbers of subgroups

Figure 7.1 Absolute and relative inequality for different baseline distributions.

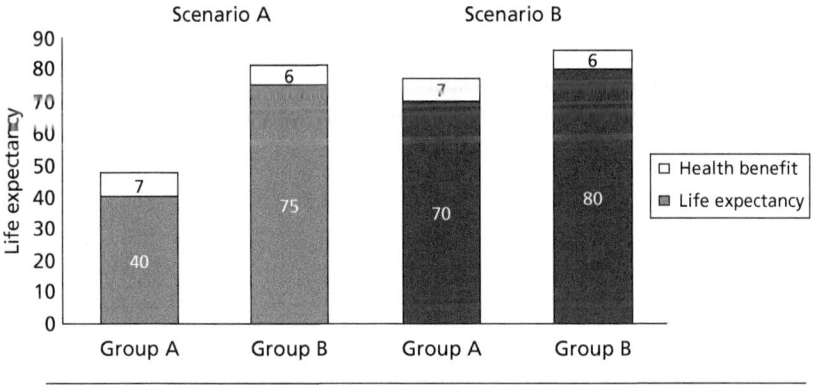

	Scenario A	Scenario B
Baseline		
Absolute inequality (gap)	35	10
Relative inequality (% diff)	88%	14%
Post-intervention		
Absolute inequality (gap)	35	9
Relative inequality (% diff)	72%	12%
Change		
Absolute inequality (gap)	−1	−1
Relative inequality (% diff)	−15%	−3%

(or individuals), as well as other relative inequality metrics, such as the Gini coefficient or the Atkinson index.

Reviews of health inequality measures (Kelly et al., 2007; Asada, 2010; Kjellsson et al., 2015) have acknowledged the advantages and disadvantages of both relative and absolute measures, concluding that best practice is usually to compute and report both types for completeness.

7.2 Health and determinants of health inequality

7.2.1 Lifetime health measures

The example in Fig 7.1 measures health in terms of life expectancy, a widely adopted health indicator because it can be relatively simply calculated from national mortality statistics. Although simple differences in life expectancy have been used to measure health inequalities and may be all that is possible in some situations (Mújica et al., 2014), quality-adjusted lifetime health measures will often be more useful in DCEA. Health-related quality of life (which for convenience we equate in this chapter with morbidity) would also be expected to vary across equity-relevant subgroups, so not accounting for it may result in an incomplete picture of inequalities.

One way to incorporate both quality and length of life is to use health-adjusted life years (HALYs). The most widely used HALY measures are quality-adjusted life years and disability-adjusted life years (DALYs). Both measures assume that all relevant components of health-related quality of life are adequately captured.

- QALYs are usually based on self-reported multi-attribute health questionnaires. Each specific combination of responses represents a health state, to which a pre-determined index value is assigned. The values are usually derived from preference elicitation studies in a representative sample of the relevant general population, and are anchored at 1 for full health and 0 for health states as bad as death or unconsciousness. Health-improving interventions will increase QALYs in the population.
- DALYs are based on the presence of one or more diseases or health conditions, defined using a standard clinical coding system such as the international classification of diseases (ICD). Each clinical code (or combination thereof) represents a health state, to which a pre-determined disability weight is assigned representing the loss of health-related quality of life relative to full health. The disability weights are sometimes based on expert opinion and sometimes on preference elicitation surveys in the relevant general population. An episode of severe diarrhoea, for example, has a disability weight (health loss) of 0.247 (Salomon et al., 2015). An intervention that improves health will reduce DALYs.

A simple illustration of the relationship between DALYs and QALYs is shown in Fig 7.2. These HALY measures have been used extensively in the economic evaluation of health interventions, as well as in population health measurement. The choice of measure used in the baseline distribution can therefore match the one used in economic evaluation: in high-income countries this is often the QALY, whilst in low- and middle-income settings, both are used and DALYs are preferred when there is a lack of QALY data. The process of estimating health-related quality of life weights and incorporating them in baseline distributions is described in the section 7.3.3 Health-adjusted life expectancy and age at death, later in this chapter.

7.2.2 Variable selection

In a distribution of 'pure' health inequality, individuals in a population can be ranked from least to most healthy based on their simulated lifetime health. The role of equity-relevant social characteristics need not be explored. The fundamental importance of health to well-being has been cited as a sufficient moral

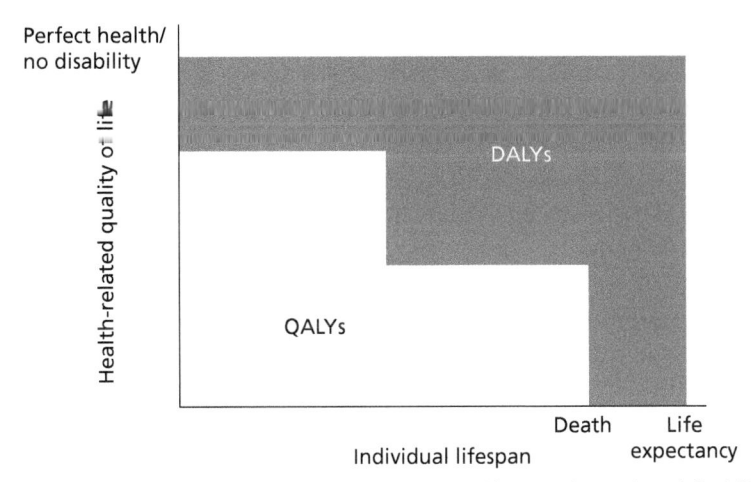

Figure 7.2 The relationship between quality-adjusted life years (QALYs) and disability-adjusted life years (DALYs).
Note: QALYs represent healthy years of health gained, whereas DALYs represent the gap between years lived in full health and years lived in less than full health. The health-related quality of life weights applied to health states can differ between the two measures.

condition for reducing 'pure' health inequalities of this type (Gakidou et al., 2000). These univariate distributions do not, however, provide a means of identifying those with the poorest health. Decision makers may therefore wish to examine how one or more equity-relevant social variables are associated with health inequalities. A fully comprehensive analysis of this kind would incorporate all the social variables relevant to equity, whether these are by ethnicity, socioeconomic status, geographical region, or others.

Estimating only the associations between sociodemographic characteristics and health can overlook the causal pathways that link them together, which are likely to be of interest to decision makers. For example, a gap of ten years in life expectancy between the richest and poorest in a country may be due to low income in childhood causing poor health in adulthood rather than poor health in childhood causing low income in adulthood. Unpicking these complex long-term causal relationships is empirically challenging, and so decision makers usually have to call on an analysis of the associations.

Deciding which causes of inequality are unfair is a question of value rather than of fact (it is *normative*). The normative basis for determining whether the association between health and a specific social factor is unfair is complex, requiring both the unpicking of the causal pathways and philosophical inquiry. However, the methods presented throughout this book are applicable given a variety of views about what 'unfairness' is, which is ultimately a matter of the value judgments made by decision makers. It is not necessary for analysts to take an a priori view about 'unfairness' (for a wide-ranging discussion on these value judgments, see Eyal et al., 2013).

Estimates of inequality by unfair factors may be biased by omitted yet fair sources of inequality. Consider a case in which inequality is estimated by one unfair factor, socioeconomic status, and fails to address a second 'fair' factor, age. If a larger proportion of the elderly (who have lower lifetime health) are in lower socioeconomic groups, then part of the observed inequality is in fact fair, as it is due to age and not socioeconomic status. A technique for removing fair sources of inequality from the baseline distribution is discussed in section 7.4.1.

The selection of equity-relevant variables for inclusion in any study of health distribution can also be limited by the availability of data. Each variable modelled has a multiplicative effect on the number of subgroups—for example the nine subgroups generated by two three-level variables expands to twenty-seven if we add a third. Large numbers of subgroups will place increasing demands on data required for parameterizing health distributions. However, in the absence of adequate data, alternative methods of including a variable can be explored—for example through expert opinion sought by a systematic and unbiased elicitation method.

7.3 Estimation

7.3.1 Types of health distribution

In this section, two ways of generating health distributions are described: *ex ante* health-adjusted life expectancy (HALE) and *ex post* health-adjusted age at death (HAAD). To illustrate, assume a simple case in which two social variables are being modelled: sex and a five-level measure of socioeconomic status. A distribution of HALE yields a set of age-based predictions of lifetime health for each of the ten subgroups and is most frequently reported as HALE at birth. Alternatively, a distribution of HAAD is estimated using a microsimulation approach, in which individuals are sampled one by one and allocated to a subgroup at the start of the simulation. Each then faces subgroup-specific mortality risks and health-related quality of life weights through their life course. The individual-level distribution of HAAD reflects within-group as well between-group inequalities. However, HAAD can be simulated with uncertainty only prior to death and is more computationally complex both to estimate and to combine with intervention treatment effects.

These measures of health are either period or cohort measures. Period measures use age-specific inputs at a fixed point in time, providing a snapshot of inequalities at a particular moment. Cohort measures model the lifetime health of a population born at a fixed point in time. The age-specific inputs used in this method can either be historical data for deceased cohorts (since their lifetime health is known) or be forecast for cohorts currently alive. Using cohort measures to address policy questions that affect the health of those currently alive (and whose future health is not known) will necessitate the use of technically complex forecasting methods that are beyond the scope of this chapter. We therefore focus the remainder of the chapter on calculating period measures of lifetime health.

Lifetime health, whether through HALE or HAAD measures, is estimated using two sets of inputs: mortality rates to predict length of life and health-related quality of life (or disability) weights to adjust for morbidity. Both inputs need to be specified by age and for each of the equity subgroups included in the analysis. HAAD distributions also require an estimate of the variability around both sets of inputs to reflect natural variations across individuals. Section 7.3.2 explains how mortality data are used to generate distributions of life expectancy and age at death. Section 7.3.3 shows how health-related quality of life data can be obtained and incorporated into these distributions.

7.3.2 Distributions of life expectancy and lifespan

7.3.2.1 Mortality data

The ideal form of mortality data required for estimating lifetime health is the crude mortality rate by single year of age for each subgroup. Data on population and number of deaths, if available, can also be used to calculate the standard error of a mortality rate. This measure of uncertainty can then be used in the techniques to account for uncertainty, covered in Chapter 15.

Crude all-cause mortality rates are frequently reported by age bands of five or ten years but may not be available for all equity-relevant subgroups. In such cases there may be additional data available to adjust the mortality data, such as evidence on mortality odds ratios that can be used as multipliers of some baseline level. An example of this is shown in Box 7.1, where the researchers estimated the HALE distribution by extrapolating from observed differences in life expectancy and prevalence, taken from multiple data sources for a country.

In many low- and middle-income countries, vital registration systems are underdeveloped (AbouZahr et al., 2015). When official mortality statistics at the aggregate country level are unavailable, modelled estimates can be used instead. A useful source is the periodically updated Global Burden of Disease study (Institute for Health Metrics and Evaluation, 2010), which has estimated the total years of life lost to and lived with disability for over 250 countries. Producing mortality estimates for equity-relevant subgroups is even more data

> **Box 7.1 Estimating a distribution of health for Ethiopia**
>
> In a paper in *Health Policy and Planning*, the authors constructed a baseline distribution of health in Ethiopia by socioeconomic group as an example of how an equity-informative economic evaluation could be conducted in the country (Dawkins et al., 2018). Here, the intervention of interest was rotavirus vaccination.
>
> In the absence of reliable census and vital statistics registries to provide a socioeconomic distribution of all-age all-cause mortality, the authors used Ethiopia's average health adjusted life expectancy (HALE) information from the readily available WHO Life Expectancy database (WHO, 2015). This was then adjusted for socioeconomic differences in mortality by using previously estimated differences in child mortality for Ethiopia (Tranvåg et al., 2013), on the assumption that child and adult patterns would be similar.
>
> Distributional information on morbidity represented another challenge. To make morbidity adjustments, data on the most important causes of illness were taken from the Ethiopian Demographic and Health Survey and combined with information from the Global Burden of Disease study (Institute for Health Metrics and Evaluation, 2010). An important limitation here was the lack of information on adult morbidity. The researchers, therefore, made several assumptions about the relationship between adult and child health.
>
> In the final step, the groups were ordered from least healthy to most healthy, adjusting for the size of the groups, to provide a baseline distribution of population health.

intensive and analysts should think carefully about ways that existing aggregate estimates can be adjusted. The transferability of information from individual studies or studies conducted in comparable settings should be assessed and analysts need to be transparent about assumptions made.

7.3.2.2 Life tables

Estimates of life expectancy are traditionally constructed using life tables. Life tables that incorporate current mortality and morbidity to generate an estimate of HALE can be useful for summarizing present inequalities. Life tables take the vectors of age-specific mortality and morbidity for each subgroup and perform a series of mathematical operations to provide estimates of age-specific HALE, of which HALE at birth is the most frequently reported.

Table 7.1 Key stages of Chiang II life table to calculate life expectancy

x	q_x	I_x	L_x	T_x	e_x
Age Interval	Probability of dying	Cohort surviving	Person years lived (current)	Person years lived (current + subsequent)	Life expectancy
$x = 1,...,z$	$\dfrac{n_x M_x}{1+(1-a_x)n_x M_x}$	$I_{x-1}(1-q_x)$	$n_x\left(I_{x+1}+\left(a_x\left(I_x - I_{x+1}\right)\right)\right)$	$\sum\limits_{x=x}^{z} L_x$	$\dfrac{T_x}{I_x}$

Note: n_x = number of years in the age interval; a_x = proportion of the age interval survived by those dying; M_x = mortality rate.

Ideally, a life table will use inputs by single year of age. Where data are not available to populate the table, a simplified 'abridged' version in age intervals can be used. Life tables also require specifying a parameter a_x for every interval x (where x = 1, ... ,z), which specifies the proportion of the interval survived by those who die during the interval. Although this can be empirically estimated, a standard assumption is that death occurs at the midpoint of the interval ($a_x = 0.5$ for all x).

Table 7.1 provides an overview of life table mathematics for the commonly used Chiang II method (Chiang, 1972). The table simulates a hypothetical cohort, a proportion of which dies during each interval. Using the proportion of the cohort alive at the end of each interval I_x, the number of life years lived in each interval L_x and the life expectancy at the start of the interval, e_x, can be calculated:

$$L_x = n_x \left(I_{x+1} + \left(a_x\left(I_x - I_{x+1}\right)\right)\right)$$

$$e_x = \sum_{x=x}^{x=z} \frac{L_x}{I_x}$$

where n_x is the number of years in the interval and z is the last interval. As e_x incorporates mortality information from all subsequent age intervals, HALE at birth (e_1) is a function of all mortality inputs and is therefore a comprehensive lifetime measure.

7.3.2.3 Microsimulation

Microsimulation can be used to model the distribution of individual lifespans. This approach, as shown in the disease-specific HAAD distributions covered in

Chapter 6, is more computationally demanding since each individual is simulated separately. This involves having the individual progress through successive periods of time, such as days, months, or years. The simulation procedure involves randomly selecting an individual with a specific set of equity-relevant characteristics, then simulating that individual's lifespan using subgroup-specific mortality risks. This process is then repeated until a sufficiently large sample has been generated. The probability that an individual with a given set of equity characteristics is selected is linked to underlying socio-demographics of the population.

The same mortality data used to populate the life tables (see section 7.3.2.2 on Life tables) can be used in the lifespan distribution. The principal difference is that the latter also embodies the variability within each group. The mortality risk for each cycle is instead defined as a random variable. The lifespan for each individual l_{ij} is calculated as:

$$l_{ij} = \sum_t D_{itj}$$

where D_{itj} represents the indicator variable that takes a value of 1 when individual i from subgroup j is alive in cycle t and 0 otherwise. Conditional on death having not already occurred, in each cycle $P(D_{itj} = 1)$ is determined by the age-specific probability of death for the relevant subgroup.

The random sampling of values during each cycle of each individual can lead to unstable estimates of inequality if the number of simulated individuals is too low. This is because statistical fluctuations from the random sampling process are more likely to bias results when the sample size is low. The number of simulations required for the output to stabilize is a function of input variance and model structure (for instance, cycle length). It is therefore advisable to check for stability. One way of doing this is by plotting summary statistics, such as the mean, for each cumulative simulation iteration and visually confirming the minimum required number of iterations.

7.3.3 Health-adjusted life expectancy and age at death

The next stage in the estimation procedure is to adjust estimates of life expectancy or lifespan for morbidity. The morbidity measure chosen should match the measure adopted in health economic evaluations undertaken in a particular setting.

7.3.3.1 Quality-adjusted life years

In many high-income countries, including the UK, Canada, Australia, and Japan, the QALY is the measure of choice (Rowen et al., 2017). Published health-related quality of life index values are typically estimated averages for all patients with a particular disease who have been recruited into a comparative effectiveness study. Such results are not directly useful for estimating social distributions of health, however, which need to reflect differences in average health between social subgroups.

A principal data source for estimating health-related quality of life weights by social subgroup are national health surveys such as the Health Survey for England or the Household, Income and Labour Dynamics in Australia. These annually or intermittently administer generic health questionnaires, such as the EQ-5D or SF-6D that can be used to generate quality of life weights. They have the added benefit of collecting demographic and socioeconomic data about individuals, and so allow the estimation of weights for a range of equity characteristics. A simple cross-tabulation of morbidity rates by age, sex, and other characteristics may produce unstable and unreliable estimates due to small numbers in some cells of the table, which means that random sampling error in small subgroups can get magnified by the small population denominator. Regression analysis can smooth out these random errors by borrowing strength from wider patterns in the data. Fig 7.3 shows how the predicted weights for

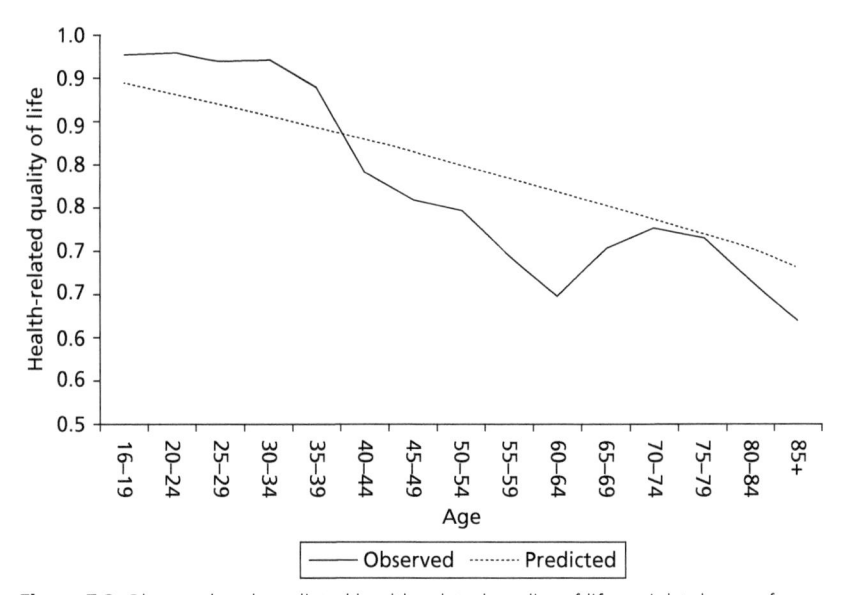

Figure 7.3 Observed and predicted health-related quality of life weights by age for an equity-relevant group.
Note: observed weights are estimated directly from survey responses, with the predicted weights estimated using regression analysis. The mean number of observations in age groups 65 and over (74) is considerably fewer than those in groups 64 and under (165).
Source: data from Love-Koh J., Asaria M., Cookson R., & Griffin S. (2015). The social distribution of health: estimating quality-adjusted life expectancy in England. *Value Health,* 18, 655–662.

one of the 180 subgroups (18 age, 5 socioeconomic, and 2 sexes) modelled by Love-Koh et al. (2015) removed the fluctuations of the observed scores caused by small numbers of respondents in older age groups.

7.3.3.2 Disability-adjusted life years

DALYs present a different challenge as they require prevalence estimates for a wide range of disabilities and conditions in order to establish a baseline distribution of health. Salomon et al. (2012) use prevalence data and weights on 1160 different diseases and conditions to calculate disability-adjusted life expectancy. However, obtaining data on all diseases by equity-relevant variables (other than age and sex) is not to be expected.

A practical alternative is to examine a subset of diseases that are likely to be the most influential determinants of the DALY weight for a subgroup. Disease burden statistics can be used to identify the largest causes of mortality and morbidity (GBD 2016 DALYs and HALE Collaborators, 2017), each of which can be mapped to a disability weight (Salomon et al., 2015). Distributions of prevalence for these diseases can be combined with the disability weights to calculate per capita DALYs (i.e. health loss) associated with each cause. These can then be summed over causes and subtracted from 1 to obtain a subgroup-specific morbidity weight. This process is illustrated in Table 7.2. Repeating this process over age bands will provide the required vector of age-specific morbidity weights.

7.3.3.3 Adjusting distributions of health for morbidity

The morbidity adjustment procedure for life tables is well established. When binary data are available on whether or not individuals have a limiting long-term illness, Sullivan's method (Sullivan, 1971) can be used to remove years of life lived in poor health to obtain disability-free life expectancy. A similar approach can also be employed using continuous measures of morbidity. As with the mortality data, a vector of age-specific morbidity weights is required for each subgroup. Three additional columns are added to the life table: first, the number of person years lived in an age interval L_x is multiplied by the corresponding morbidity weight u_x. The two subsequent operations of summing future intervals and dividing through by the surviving cohort are reapplied to obtain HALE Q_x:

$$Q_x = \sum_{x=x}^{x=z} \frac{L_x u_x}{I_x}$$

The life tables will now yield a vector of HALE estimates. Although HALE distributions can be configured to the first year of any age interval, HALE at birth is typically used to estimate baseline health distributions. Box 7.2 describes a HALE distribution estimated for England by Love-Koh et al. (2015).

Table 7.2 Calculating subgroup morbidity weights using disease prevalence distributions and disability-adjusted life year (DALY) weights

	Cause of disability			
	Stroke	Lower respiratory infections	Diarrhoeal diseases	COPD
Disability weight	0.309	0.217	0.17	0.092
Wealth quintile	**Prevalence**			
1 (lowest)	6.1%	1.0%	3.0%	24.0%
2	5.6%	0.7%	2.8%	20.0%
3	4.9%	0.5%	2.2%	18.0%
4	4.2%	0.2%	1.9%	17.0%
5 (highest)	4.1%	0.1%	0.8%	12.0%
	DALYs per capita			
1 (lowest)	0.0188	0.0031	0.0093	0.0742
2	0.0173	0.0022	0.0087	0.0618
3	0.0151	0.0015	0.0068	0.0556
4	0.0130	0.0006	0.0059	0.0525
5 (highest)	0.0127	0.0003	0.0025	0.0371

Wealth quintile	Overall DALYs per capita	Morbidity weight
1 (lowest)	0.105	0.895
2	0.090	0.910
3	0.079	0.921
4	0.072	0.928
5 (highest)	0.053	0.947

Note:

1. COPD = chronic obstructive pulmonary disease; DALYs = disability-adjusted life years

2. DALYs per capita are calculated as the disability weight multiplied by the prevalence, which are then summed over diseases to obtain average DALYs for each subgroup.

Box 7.2 Estimating a distribution of health for England

Love-Koh et al. (2015) estimated a baseline health distribution for England, composed of ten subgroups defined by sex and a five-level measure of socioeconomic deprivation. Mortality rates were obtained across eighteen five-year age bands for each of these ten subgroups and were incorporated into Chiang II life tables to estimate life expectancy at birth. The estimates were then adjusted for morbidity using quality-adjusted life year (QALY) weights. Linear regression analysis was conducted on EQ-5D questionnaire data from three years of a nationally representative health survey (n = 35,062).

Bivariate inequality was estimated for each equity variable: differences of 1 QALY between males and females and 11.87 QALYs between the top and bottom socioeconomic groups were found. When ranked in a univariate distribution, the difference between the least and most healthy groups was 12.9 QALYs. Morbidity adjustment made a substantial difference to the degree of inequality; quality-adjusted years of life lost to morbidity (QAYLL) over a lifetime ranged from 9 (females, lowest deprivation) to 13.9 (males, highest deprivation).

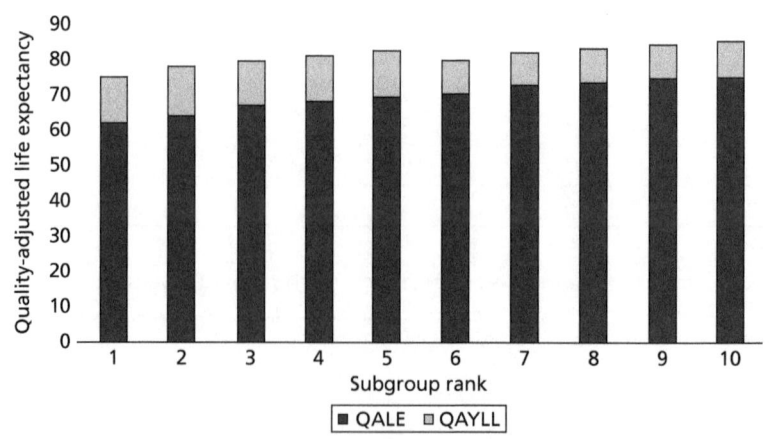

Figure 7.4 Quality-adjusted life expectancy and quality-adjusted years of life lost by sex and deprivation subgroups in England.
Source: data from Love-Koh J., Asaria M., Cookson R., & Griffin S. (2015). The social distribution of health: estimating quality-adjusted life expectancy in England. *Value Health*, 18(5), 655–662. https://doi: 10.1016/j.jval.2015.03.1784. Epub 2015 Apr 18.
Note: QALE = quality-adjusted life expectancy; QAYLL = quality-adjusted years of life lost

A similar procedure can be implemented when simulating *ex post* distributions of lifespan. Here, the indicator variable D_{itj} is multiplied by the morbidity weight u_{itj}. HAAD is then the sum over time of these products.

$$h_{ij} = \sum_t D_{itj} u_{itj}.$$

The within-group variation of u_{itj} can be captured by randomly drawing values from a probability distribution defined by a measure of the standard deviation (rather than standard error). An estimate of the standard deviation can be derived from health survey data. Although the normal distribution is a candidate distribution, this may (with a low probability) result in a value being drawn that lies outside the possible range (the range of quality of life weights using the original three-level version of the EQ-5D health questionnaire, for example, was -0.594 to 1). It has therefore been recommended to use the Beta distribution, which is bounded at [0,1] (Briggs et al., 2006). The Beta distribution has two parameters that determine the shape (α) and scale (β); these can be derived using an estimate of the mean μ and variance σ^2 using the following formulae:

$$\alpha = \mu \left(\frac{\mu(1-\mu)}{\sigma^2} - 1 \right)$$

$$\beta = \alpha \left(\frac{(1-\mu)}{\mu} \right)$$

7.3.4 Analysing and presenting distributions

This section explores useful ways of arranging and presenting distributions of health, as well as some basic summary metrics. More complex and computationally demanding metrics are covered in Chapters 11 and 12.

7.3.4.1 Bivariate and univariate distributions

The simplest way to represent a distribution of *ex ante* HALE is by plotting each equity variable against the corresponding estimate of HALE at birth to generate a series of bivariate distributions, as shown in Chapter 4. Simple illustrations such as these can provide decision makers with useful information about which characteristics are associated with the largest differences in health. A downside to analysing inequalities in this way comes when evaluating the expected impacts of new interventions, as before-and-after distributions would be required separately for each equity variable. This could make evaluating the overall inequality impact a cognitively demanding task as decision makers

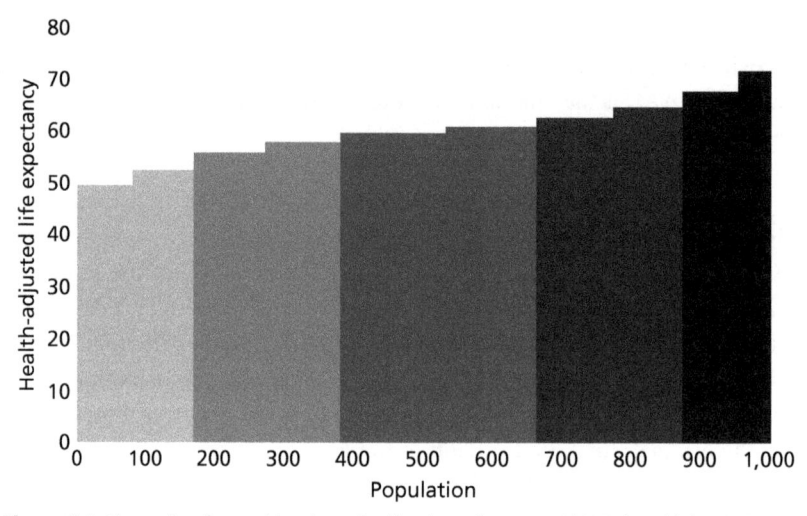

Figure 7.5 Example of a multivariate distribution of *ex ante* HALE, in which 1000 individuals belonging to ten subgroups are ranked in terms of health-adjusted life expectancy.

will be required to piece together a series of potentially different changes in inequality for each characteristic.

A useful solution to this issue is to combine the multivariate predictions of HALE into a single univariate distribution that reflects all sources of inequality simultaneously. This technique orders the whole population from least to most healthy, using population estimates for each subgroup to reflect their relative sizes in the overall distribution. Fig 7.5 demonstrates this for a population of 1000 divided into 10 unevenly-sized groups.

Although it is also possible to construct bivariate distributions of *ex post* HAAD using the characteristics of the individuals in a simulated sample, calculating summary statistics would negate the principal value of a HAAD distribution as within-group variation would be lost. A univariate distribution of HAAD can be easily constructed by ordering the sample from least to most healthy.

7.3.4.2 Inequality and health poverty analysis

The most basic measure that can be applied to HALE distributions is the gap between the most and least healthy individual or group (the top and bottom of the distribution, respectively). The absolute gap, like the relative gap is easy to compute but reflects only the extremes of the distribution. Denoting the HALE at birth for J ordered subgroups as $Q_1^1, Q_1^2, \ldots, Q_1^J$, the absolute gap is given as $Q_1^J - Q_1^1$, and the relative gap $Q_1^J / Q_1^1 - 1$.

An alternative approach that incorporates information across the entire distribution is to plot a line or curve of best fit through the data using an approach such as Ordinary Least Squares regression, which estimates the values that minimize the sum of the squared difference between observed and fitted data points. This is estimated by regressing HALE at birth Q_1^j on the fractional rank r_j of equity group j within a distribution[1] as follows:

$$Q_1^j = \beta_0 + \beta_1 r_j + \varepsilon_j,$$

where β_0 is a constant term and ε_j is the random error term. The slope of the line β_1 can be interpreted as the 'fitted' difference in HALE when moving from the lowest to highest group and is known as the slope index of inequality (SII). When we fit a particular line through the data, ε_j becomes observed error (or residual) $\hat{\varepsilon}_j$; the objective is therefore to find the values of β_0 and β_1 that minimize the sum of the squared residuals $\sum_{j=1}^{J} \hat{\varepsilon}_j^2$. These values can be derived analytically, yielding the following result for β_1:

$$\beta_1 = \frac{\frac{1}{J}\sum_{j=1}^{J}(Q_1^j - \bar{Q}_1^j)(r_j - \bar{r}_j)}{\frac{1}{J}\sum_{j=1}^{J}(r_j - \bar{r}_j)^2} = \frac{Cov(Q_1, r)}{Var(r)}$$

where $\bar{Q}_1^j$ and $\bar{r}_j$ are the means of HALE at birth and fractional rank, respectively. The slope index is an absolute measure of inequality as it is estimated on the same scale as the HALE. There are also ways of converting this into a relative index of inequality (RII), for example by dividing through by $\bar{Q}_1^j$. This RII is a measure of the percentage change when moving from the lowest to highest group; a RII value of 1.2, for instance, would indicate that HALE value in the highest group is 20% greater than the lowest. These are discussed in depth by Moreno-Betancur and colleagues (2015).

Gap statistics, slope, and relative indices of inequality can all be computed with basic data on mean outcomes and are easily interpretable. Each has its limitations however: gaps ignore data in the middle of the distribution and the SII and RII assume a linear relationship between the health outcome and the

---

[1] The fractional rank is the cumulative mid-point of the group within the distribution. For example if groups 1, 2, and 3 account for 10%, 20%, and 30% of the population, respectively, then the fractional ranks will be the following: Group 1: 0.1/2 = 0.05, Group 2: 0.1 + (0.2/2) = 0.2, Group 3: 0.1 + 0.2 + (0.3/2) = 0.45.

equity variable, though there are ways of addressing this, for example using power transforms. It is therefore good practice to calculate a range of equity metrics and visualizations to present to decision makers in order to provide a more complete picture of inequalities.

Inequalities in HAAD can be measured using the same simple methods described for the HALE distributions, using the simulated sample to calculate summary statistics such as the subgroup means. However, this does not exploit the richness of the individual-level data. Instead, approaches such as the social welfare analysis introduced in later chapters, as well as the SII and RII, can be estimated using the individual-level data. As there is more heterogeneity in individual HAAD than in group estimates of HALE, the magnitude of estimated inequality will also be greater.

HAAD distributions can also be used to measure the proportion of the population with health below a certain threshold level. Various measures of 'health poverty' can be constructed, using standard indices from the literature on income-related poverty, to investigate the three key dimensions of poverty (Jenkins and Lambert, 1997):

Incidence (H)—the number below the threshold (headcount)

Intensity (S)—the average distance below the threshold (shortfall)

Inequality (I)– the variation among those below the poverty threshold

Estimates of baseline health are required in health poverty analyses in order to determine whether the health effects of a programme push people above or below the health poverty line (and/or by how much). A lack of consensus on where to draw the health poverty line renders this issue a matter of social value judgment for decision makers. As health poverty indices are insensitive to changes in the health of those whose health lies above the health poverty line they are not susceptible to the 'levelling down' objection that is made to inequality indices that improve when the health of those at the top of the distribution is reduced. Social welfare indices that combine concern for health poverty with concern for total health (including improving the health of well-off people above the health poverty line) could theoretically address this issue and represents an interesting challenge for future research.

7.4 Further considerations

7.4.1 Adjusting for fair sources of inequality

Section 7.2.2 introduced the rationale for the additional methodological step of adjusting the distribution of health to reflect only unfair sources of inequality. This process is conditional on having defined adequately a set of social value judgments on fairness as well as having the requisite subgroup data on mortality and quality of life.

Regression analysis can once again be used, this time to estimate the statistical relationship between HALE (or HAAD) and any modelled equity characteristics. The principle behind this approach is that once the contribution of any fair sources of inequality to health is known, their effect can be removed from our estimates of overall inequality. The remaining inequality has been termed 'direct unfairness' (Fleurbaey and Schokkaert, 2009).

The procedure for modelling direct unfairness can be summarized in the following steps:

> Run an ordinary least squares regression of HALE on all equity-relevant (fair and unfair) characteristics. This provides a distribution of predicted HALE for all subgroups.
>
> Remove fair sources of inequality from the distribution by adjusting out the coefficients for the fair characteristics when predicting HALE for each subgroup. This involves fixing the values of the fair variables in the regression equation for all subgroups. For continuous variables the value is fixed to the mean, whereas, for discrete variables the value is fixed to a reference category. This effectively turns fair variables into additional constants in the regression equation.
>
> New predictions of HALE are then made for each of the subgroups based on this adjusted regression equation. In Table 7.3, for example, sex is considered a fair source of inequality, with 'male' being the reference category. Therefore, the predictions of HALE for females are the same as those for males in the corresponding subgroups (i.e. females and males in the same Indian subcontinent and index of multiple deprivation group).

7.4.2 Deriving additional distributions

Baseline health estimates can be used to derive a distribution for a second population with linked equity characteristics but a different socio-demographic structure. A local healthcare decision maker, for instance, might be interested in the health distribution for their area. However, the data required for estimating this distribution may be available only at the national level. In such cases, a national HALE distribution can be used to derive regional distributions, provided that region-specific demographic data are available and include equity-relevant characteristics. This technique is demonstrated in Table 7.4, where a region-specific health distribution is estimated by reweighting the national one according to local socioeconomic characteristics. A more uneven spread across income groups at the regional level is reflected in the higher estimate of health inequality.

7.5 Summary

This chapter has provided an overview of methods for producing baseline distributions of lifetime health by social variables. Estimating the baseline

Table 7.3 Fairness-adjusted health distribution by sex, ethnicity (% Indian subcontinent) and socioeconomic status (index of multiple deprivation)

Sex	% Indian subcontinent	Index of multiple Deprivation	Healthy life expectancy Unadjusted	Adjusted
Male	Q1–4	Q1	60.24	60.24
		Q2	66.63	66.63
		Q3	69.12	69.12
		Q4	70.52	70.52
		Q5	72.20	72.20
	Q5	Q1	60.24	60.24
		Q2	66.63	66.63
		Q3	69.13	69.13
		Q4	70.52	70.52
		Q5	72.21	72.21
Female	Q1–4	Q1	63.20	60.24
		Q2	69.24	66.63
		Q3	71.81	69.12
		Q4	73.16	70.52
		Q5	74.91	72.20
	Q5	Q1	63.20	60.24
		Q2	69.24	66.63
		Q3	71.82	69.13
		Q4	73.17	70.52
		Q5	74.91	72.21

Note: in the unadjusted distribution, all three characteristics are 'unfair' sources of inequality. The adjusted distribution removes the health inequality due to sex.

Source: Adapted from Asaria M. Distributional Cost-Effectiveness Analysis - A Tutorial. Med Decis Making. 2016 Jan; 36(1): 8–19.

Published online 2015 Apr 23. doi: 10.1177/0272989X15583266. Licensed under a Creative Commons 3.0 International Attribution.

distribution of health is useful when conducting DCEAs as it facilitates the estimation of equity impact in terms of a wide range of metrics, including relative inequality metrics and health poverty metrics.

We also illustrated a number of key challenges that arise when estimating the baseline distribution of lifetime health—including choice of health metric and equity-relevant variables. We demonstrated how to produce distributions of both *ex ante* HALE and *ex post* HAAD distributions. However, modelling

Table 7.4 Calculating regional inequalities from a national-level distribution

	Income level		
	Low	Middle	High
National HALE	50	60	70
Proportion (national)	0.35	0.35	0.3
Fractional rank (national)	0.175	0.525	0.85
SII (national)	29.6		
Proportion (regional)	0.20	0.20	0.6
Fractional rank (regional)	0.1	0.3	0.7
SII (regional)	32.1		

policy impacts on to individual-level distributions of *ex post* HAAD raises substantial methodological challenges, since one has to specify the variance and covariance for the conditional treatment effects by social group, in addition to the mean. Conducting equity-informative economic evaluation using *ex post* HAAD thus requires further methodological development, as is discussed further in Chapter 16.

The quantitative steps for estimating baseline health distributions have been described, along with a number of useful techniques and equations and types of required mortality and morbidity data. The direct unfairness method, which adjusts distributions to reflect only unfair inequality, is posited as a tool to understand inequities in baseline health distributions. The results can then be used in subsequent analytical stages of a DCEA.

7.6 Further reading

The technique for adjusting life expectancy to account for health-related quality of life was first proposed by Sullivan (1971). Subsequent studies have extended this original method to incorporate other types of health-related quality of life measures: Salomon et al. (2012) for DALYs and Love-Koh et al. (2015) for QALYs. Chiang (1972) provides a more technical treatment of the underlying life table methods that estimate life expectancy.

Health distributions can be analysed using an extensive range of inequality metrics. Two papers by Regidor (2004a, 2004b) provide a non-technical introduction to the field. The advantages and disadvantages of measures based on their characteristics (i.e. whether they are bounded or relative or absolute) are discussed by Kjellsson et al. (2015). Methods for adjusting health inequality measures to account for fair and unfair sources can be found in Fleurbaey and Schokkaert (2009).

References

AbouZahr C., De Savigny D., Mikkelsen L., Setel P., Lozano R., Nichols, E., et al. (2015). Civil registration and vital statistics: progress in the data revolution for counting and accountability. *Lancet,* **386**, 1373–1385. https://doi.org/10.1016/S0140-6736(15)60173-8

Asada Y. (2010). On the choice of absolute or relative inequality measures. *Milbank Quarterly,* **88**, 616–622. https://doi.org/10.1111/j.1468-0009.2010.00614.x

Asaria M., Griffin S., & Cookson R. (2015). Distributional cost-effectiveness analysis: a tutorial. *Medical Decision Making,* 1–12. https://doi.org/10.1177/0272989X15583266

Briggs A., Claxton K., & Sculpher M. (2006). *Decision Modelling for Health Economic Evaluation.* Oxford University Press, Oxford.

Chiang C. (1972). On constructing current life tables. *Journal of American Statistical Association,* **67**, 538–541.

Dawkins B., Mirelman A., Asaria M., Johansson K., & Cookson R. (2018). Distributional cost-effectiveness analysis in low- and middle-income countries: illustrative example of rotavirus vaccination in Ethiopia. *Health Policy and Planning,* **33**, 456–463.

Eyal N., Hurst S., Norheim O., & Wikler D. (eds) (2013). *Inequalities in Health: Concepts, Measures and Ethics.* Oxford University Press, Oxford.

Fleurbaey M. & Schokkaert E. (2009). Unfair inequalities in health and health care. *Journal of Health Economics,* **28**, 73–90. https://doi.org/10.1016/j.jhealeco.2008.07.016

Gakidou E., Murray C., & Frenk J. (2000). Defining and measuring health inequality: an approach based on the distribution of health expectancy. Bulletin. *World Health Organization,* **78**, 42–54.

GBD 2016 DALYs and HALE Collaborators (2017). Global, regional, and national disability-adjusted life-years (DALYs) for 333 diseases and injuries and healthy life expectancy (HALE) for 195 countries and territories, 1990–2016: a systematic analysis for the Global Burden of Disease Study 2016. *Lancet,* 1260–1344.

Institute for Health Metrics and Evaluation (2010). GBD Profile: Ethiopia. Global Burden of Disease Study. **Institute for Health Metrics and Evaluation, Seattle.**

Jenkins S. & Lambert P. (1997). Three 'I's of poverty curves, with an analysis of UK poverty trends. *Oxford Economic Papers,* **49**, 317–327.

Kelly M., Morgan A., Bonnefoy J., Butt J., & Bergmann V. (2007). *The Social Determinants of Health: Developing an Evidence Base for Political Action.* World Health Organization Commission on Social Determinants of Health. Universidad del Desarrollo, Chile and National Institute for Health and Clinical Excellence, UK.

Kjellsson G., Gerdtham U.-G., & Petrie D. (2015). Lies, damned lies, and health inequality measurements. *Epidemiology,* **26**, 673–680. DOI: 10.1097/EDE.0000000000000319

Love-Koh J., Asaria M., Cookson R., & Griffin S. (2015). The social distribution of health: estimating quality-adjusted life expectancy in England. *Value Health,* **18**, 655–662. https://doi.org/10.1016/j.jval.2015.03.1784

Moreno-Betancur M., Latouche A., Menvielle G., Kunst A., & Rey G. (2015). Relative index of inequality and slope index of inequality. *Epidemiology*, **26**, 518–527. https://doi.org/10.1097/EDE.0000000000000311

Mujica O., Vázquez E., Duarte E., Cortez-Escalante J., Molina J., & Barbosa da Silva J. (2014). Socioeconomic inequalities and mortality trends in BRICS, 1990–2010. *Bulletin. World Health Organization*, **92**, 405–412. https://doi.org/doi:10.2471/BLT.13.127977

Regidor E. (2004a). Measures of health inequalities: part 1. *Journal of Epidemioliogy and Community Health*, **58**, 858–861. https://doi.org/10.1136/jech.2003.015347

Regidor E. (2004b). Measures of health inequalities: part 2. *Journal of Epidemiology and Community Health*, **58**, 900–903. https://doi.org/10.1136/jech.2004.023036

Rowen D., Azzabi Zouraq I., Chevrou-Severac H., & van Hout B. (2017). International regulations and recommendations for utility data for health technology assessment. *Pharmacoeconomics*, **35**, 11–19. https://doi.org/10.1007/s40273-017-0544-y

Salomon J., Haagsma J., Davis A., de Noordhout C., Polinder S., Havelaar A., et al. (2015). Disability weights for the Global Burden of Disease 2013 study. *Lancet Global Health*, **3**, e712–e723. https://doi.org/10.1016/S2214-109X(15)00069-8

Salomon J., Wang H., Freeman M., Vos T., Flaxman A., Lopez A., et al. (2012). Healthy life expectancy for 187 countries, 1990–2010: a systematic analysis for the Global Burden Disease Study 2010. *Lancet*, **380**, 2144–2162. https://doi.org/10.1016/S0140-6736(12)61690-0

Sullivan D. (1971). A single index of mortality and morbidity. *HSMHA Health Reports*, **86**, 347–354.

Tranvåg E., Ali M., & Norheim O. (2013). Health inequalities in Ethiopia: modeling inequalities in length of life within and between population groups. *International Journal of Equity Health*, **12**, 52. https://doi.org/10.1186/1475-9276-12-52

World Health Organization (2015). *WHO Methods and Data Sources for Life Tables 1990–2015*. World Health Organization, Geneva.

Chapter 8

Costs and health effects

Colin Angus

This chapter addresses the question of how to model the lifetime costs and health effects of a health programme, while also considering how they are distributed across society. As in other chapters, we use lifetime health as an easily understood, widely used, measure of health over which decision makers are likely to want to minimize unfair inequalities, though other measures of health may be substituted if decision makers so desire. The conceptual framework and methods described in this chapter can readily be adapted to model the distribution of costs and effects across alternative time horizons. Similarly, we focus on modelling socioeconomic and geographic inequalities in health, but the same methods can be applied to other equity-relevant characteristics such as ethnicity or gender.

We introduce the concept of the 'staircase of inequality' to identify the stages at which differential costs and effects may arise for people with different equity-relevant characteristics and discuss the circumstances under which the steps on this staircase may differ, and how. We illustrate how to conceptualize this staircase for a given decision problem and address the key assumptions and data required to implement this approach, highlighting potential sources of this data and providing guidance for setting these parameters when evidence is scarce. We conclude with a discussion of several additional considerations that may be relevant when modelling distributions of health benefits.

8.1 The 'staircase of inequality'

The basic idea underlying our approach to modelling inequalities in the effects of healthcare can be traced back to 1971 when Julian Tudor-Hart posited the so-called inverse care law, according to which: 'The availability of good medical care tends to vary inversely with the need of the population served' (Tudor-Hart, 1971). Although Tudor-Hart was specifically referring to the quality of care provided in primary care settings, similar reflections have subsequently been made for many other aspects of healthcare and public health, for example the suggestion of an 'inverse prevention law' whereby those most in need of preventative measures, such as smoking cessation services, are the least likely to access them (Acheson, 1998). Concerns with inequality of access to health services may be particularly significant in countries that do not provide universal healthcare, or where there are physical or financial barriers that inhibit some individuals' ability to access care.

The ways in which health services are funded, organized, and delivered may introduce, exacerbate, or attenuate health inequalities in different ways and through different mechanisms. In the same way, the overall equity impact of a health programme can arise through the combination of many different processes. This potential multiplicity was formalized by Tugwell and colleagues as a 'staircase' effect (sometimes also referred to as a 'cascade') where inequalities in current health, access and adherence to care, and the efficacy of the care provided, can all act in combination to produce significant inequalities in the distribution of health benefits (Tugwell et al., 2006). Even though inequalities at each step in the staircase may be small, they can be compounded, leading to what is sometimes referred to as 'intervention generated inequality' (Lorenc et al., 2013). Tugwell and colleagues also suggested that it may be possible to take proactive steps to mitigate these effects by re-designing health programmes, for example by targeting care delivery or public information campaigns towards disadvantaged groups.

The *staircase of inequality* provides a framework for modelling the health inequality impacts of a health programme. This framework is flexible and can be adapted readily to model the impact of clinical interventions such as new treatments or health technologies, preventative interventions such as vaccination or screening programmes, and even behavioural interventions such as smoking cessation services. It can also be extended to model multiple interventions simultaneously, particularly where these may act at different steps on the staircase. Every programme will have its own staircase, depending on how it is delivered and used, but for every intervention or disease area the staircase will follow a common structure—illustrated in Fig 8.1.

8.1.1 Key steps on the staircase

8.1.1.1 Need

The first step concerns variation in the need for intervention in a particular population. Do some groups have a higher prevalence or severity of the health condition or levels of a behaviour that the intervention is targeted at? For socioeconomic status this is clear: there is a huge body of literature showing that lower socioeconomic status is associated with a greater prevalence of a

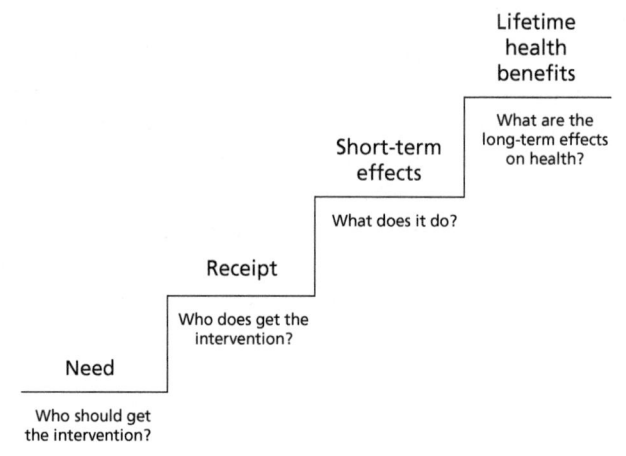

Figure 8.1 Overview of the staircase of inequality.

wide range of health conditions, higher levels of comorbidity and greater disease severity (Marmot et al., 2008). This means that socioeconomically disadvantaged individuals will be disproportionately represented among the target population for many health programmes. Other things equal, if all members of the target population were to benefit equally, then health programmes that disproportionately benefit socially disadvantaged individuals would tend to reduce socioeconomic inequality in health. However, other things may not be equal—inequalities arising at other steps on the staircase may work in the other direction, leaving it an open question whether the programme will increase or reduce social inequalities in health.

8.1.1.2 Receipt

The second step concerns inequality in those who actually receive the health service in question. This could arise from inequality of access to health services or variation in the extent to which different groups take up the offer of services such as screening or vaccination. Where interventions are not specifically targeted towards particular groups, or where receipt or uptake of the service relies on the individuals themselves, this step will tend to be skewed towards higher socioeconomic groups as they typically have greater access to health services and are more likely to participate in preventive programmes.

8.1.1.3 Short-term effects

The third step on the staircase concerns intervention effectiveness. Inequalities in effectiveness could arise from differences in disease severity, variation in adherence to medication or treatment regimens, or from differences in the extent to which behavioural interventions lead to changes in unhealthy behaviours. Inequalities could also arise from differences in rates of comorbid health conditions, or the clustering of several unhealthy behaviours, both of which may interact with other causes to steepen the staircase.

8.1.1.4 Lifetime health benefits

The final step concerns the translation of the short-term effects of the intervention into health benefits over lifetimes. This will often be driven by underlying inequalities in life expectancy and in general health. Other things equal, two people of the same age, but at opposite ends of the socioeconomic spectrum, may have substantially different remaining healthy life expectancies. Thus, an intervention which averts premature death may lead to a somewhat larger increase in expected lifetime health if the recipient is of higher socioeconomic status, as they can expect to live longer and in better health. There is evidence that the outcomes of healthcare are often worse in more disadvantaged populations (Cookson et al., 2016). In some cases, however, the opposite may be true. For example, greater severity of an illness or risk factor can mean greater capacity to benefit—a heavy smoker may stand to benefit more from quitting smoking than a light smoker.

8.1.2 Summary

The staircase framework allows the incorporation of inequalities that may arise at many different stages in the delivery and effects of an intervention in an integrated assessment of inequality impacts. By separating out the different steps on the staircase we can discover whether many small inequalities combine to produce a large overall inequality, even when no single aspect of the process is highly unequal on its own. The same principles can be applied equally to model the distributional impacts of new drugs, new clinical pathways, preventative interventions such as mosquito nets or vaccination programmes, and public health initiatives which target health behaviours, such as diet or physical activity. Staircases need not exhibit inequalities at each step. Nor is it necessary for all inequalities to run in the same direction. Unhealthy behaviours such as smoking are typically more prevalent in lower socioeconomic groups, representing a greater need for an intervention, although the same groups may be less likely to receive any intervention, and those who do receive it may find it less effective. Applying the staircase framework can thus help us to find out whether inequalities in different directions at different steps balance out, or whether large inequalities in one direction at some steps overwhelm small inequalities in the opposite direction at other steps.

8.2 Extending the staircase

8.2.1 Adding more steps

The four key steps in the staircase outlined in Fig 8.1 represent the most likely points at which inequality may be introduced into the costs and effects of an intervention on health. Occasionally one or more of these steps may itself comprise several intermediate steps. For example, inequalities of receipt of a vaccination programme in a rural area may be determined by a combination of inequalities in access to healthcare services and inequalities in willingness to receive the vaccine (e.g. some people may visit a doctor and face the choice of being vaccinated while others never visit the doctor and are never faced with the choice). These subsidiary gradients may be of different magnitudes or may, in some cases, run against each other. For example, lower socioeconomic groups in the UK are less likely to drink alcohol, and those who do drink consume less on average, yet they suffer substantially higher rates of alcohol-related health problems, a phenomenon known as the 'alcohol harm paradox'. In the case of interventions delivered in primary care, there may be inequalities in the use of or access to primary care services, which run in parallel to inequalities in intervention receipt among those who actually attend primary care. The four-step staircase should therefore be regarded as a starting point, which may be reduced by eliminating steps that are not necessary, or extended by adding further steps if the analysis requires it.

8.2.2 Introducing healthcare costs

When conducting a distributional cost-effectiveness analysis (DCEA), we are not only interested in modelling the distribution of health benefits from an intervention. As we shall see in Chapter 9, estimating the total incremental cost of the programme is crucial as this determines the health opportunity cost. When costs fall on third-party health budgets, rather being out-of-pocket costs for individual patients, it may not initially seem obvious why we should care about the distribution of those costs, that is, where and on whom money is actually spent to achieve health benefits. The health opportunity costs of reductions in third party budgets are imposed across the whole population served by the third-party payer irrespective of where the original costs were accrued. However, there are at least two reasons why we are interested in modelling the distribution of healthcare costs. The first and most important reason is to obtain a more accurate estimate of the total intervention cost, given there may be differences in delivery costs between different groups in the population. For example, delivering a vaccination programme in a rural area may cost more per person vaccinated than in a more densely populated, urban area. Future healthcare costs for population groups in poorer health or with higher levels of multimorbidity in older age may also be markedly higher. As a result, accounting for these gradients in cost may enable us to produce a more accurate estimate of the total cost of an intervention than if we were not modelling distributional effects at all, as is standard in many health economic models. In addition, as suggested above, while the distribution of costs borne by the healthcare sector itself may not be of particular interest to decision makers, the distribution of costs borne by other actors, including the public, may well be. For example, if more deprived groups typically live further from healthcare services and therefore incur additional time and financial costs in accessing care, this may be seen not only as an inequality in and of itself, but also as a factor which increases the inequality impact of any healthcare-based intervention. This issue, along with that of other costs borne by the individual, will be covered in depth in Chapter 10.

8.2.3 Delivery costs

Variations in programme delivery costs will be concentrated in the second step of the staircase, since this is the point at which interventions are actually delivered. The staircase approach ensures that differences between groups in total delivery costs which arise as a result of gradients in need or receipt are already captured. However, we should also consider whether, all else being equal, there are differences in the costs of delivering an intervention to individuals in different population groups. These differences might arise because the intervention being delivered may be slightly different, for example if more deprived groups are in poorer health and this requires a more intensive intervention, or if they are more likely to drop out of treatment early. Cost differentials might also arise because the intervention is the same, but delivery is more costly because the population is harder and therefore more expensive to reach. If an intervention is being delivered in primary care, additional costs might be incurred as part of outreach programmes to deliver the intervention to populations who do not have high levels of access to primary care services. These costs can arise as a result of trying to equalize delivery across all population groups, but can equally come from attempts to target interventions proactively at some groups in an effort to reduce inequalities. In the colorectal cancer screening example discussed in Box 8.1, the authors also looked at the cost-effectiveness of a 'targeted' programme where additional resources were spent to encourage more deprived groups to attend screening, finding that this improved cost-effectiveness while also reducing the inequality-increasing impacts of the policy overall.

> **Box 8.1 Modelling the distribution of health effects from a programme of colorectal cancer screening**
>
> In 2006, the UK launched a national programme of screening for colorectal cancer, through which all adults aged 60–74 were invited for a guaiac faecal occult blood test (gFOBT) to identify early signs of potential cancer. Asaria and colleagues used a staircase-based approach to model the distribution of health benefits arising from this programme across gender and quintile groups of deprivation. They identified a gradient in baseline health, with substantially greater quality-adjusted life expectancy at birth in the least deprived groups compared to the most deprived. They also identified an inequality in receipt, with a significantly larger proportion of the population accepting the invitation to screening from less deprived groups. They did not assume any gradient in either the short- or long-term impacts of the screening programme on health.
>
> After combining these gradients, the authors found a large inequality in the distribution of the health benefits of the screening programme. The least healthy quintile group in the population accrued just 4,000 QALYs, compared to 12,000 QALYs in the healthiest quintile group, meaning that just 10% of the benefits were experienced by the least well off 20% of the population. This programme therefore represented a classic example of intervention-generated inequality, whereby overall population health was improved, while at the same time inequality was increased.
>
> Source: Data from Miqdad Asaria, Susan Griffin, Richard Cookson, Sophie Whyte, and Paul Tappenden (2015). Distributional cost-effectiveness analysis of health care programmes—a methodological case study of the UK bowel cancer screening programme. *Health Economics*, 24(6), 742–754.

8.2.4 Downstream healthcare savings

Gradients in post-intervention costs may also manifest themselves at the third and fourth steps of the staircase. This may occur in the short term, for example where an intervention delivered in a hospital setting is more effective in some groups, reducing the required length of stay and therefore the associated costs. Alternatively, they may arise in the longer term, for example where there are substantial life expectancy differences between groups, when the cost of providing future healthcare—so-called 'survivor costs'—may vary widely. Gradients in either of these future costs may arise as a result of gradients in other steps in the staircase (e.g. differential efficacy of the intervention), or due to there being a gradient in the cost of providing future care, all else being equal.

8.3 Applying the staircase approach to a cost-effectiveness model

8.3.1 Designing the staircase

The process of model conceptualization is an important initial step in the development of any health economic model (Chilcott et al., 2010) and this is no different when the model incorporates equity considerations. The staircase framework fits neatly into the process described in the Drummond and colleagues 'blue book', forming an additional step where model developers consider what the relevant staircase might look like for the intervention they are evaluating and whether there are potential inequalities in any of these steps (Drummond et al., 2015). Collecting data on the scale of these inequalities can then take place alongside data collection for other aspects of the model.

8.3.2 Selecting the distributions of interest

Before beginning to collect data or to develop the model, it is important to identify the relevant distributions of interest. Part of this decision is selecting which equity-relevant characteristic(s) you want to model the distributional impacts over. Another decision is the choice of paradigm within which these impacts will be assessed. Are decision makers seeking to reduce unfair differences in the quality and outcomes of health service delivery within the specific subpopulation of programme recipients (e.g. a disease group or risk factor group), or to reduce inequality in health within the general population served by the decision-making organization? In many cases these will lead to the same conclusion, but not always. To illustrate the differences between these approaches, and why they matter, let us take the example of a smoking cessation intervention. A 2014 review concluded that smoking cessation programmes have a negative (harmful) equity impact on increasing socioeconomic inequalities, due to higher quit rates among more advantaged smokers (Hill et al., 2014). At the population level, however, the effect of such programmes on social inequalities in health will depend not only on the socioeconomic group average effects within the specific population of smokers, but also the distribution of smokers across the socioeconomic spectrum within the wider general population. If there are far more smokers in more deprived groups, then the total accumulated health gain may be larger than among the smaller number of smokers in less deprived groups. It is therefore entirely possible for an intervention to have a better individual outcome for those in less deprived groups compared to more deprived groups, while providing a larger overall benefit to the more deprived group.

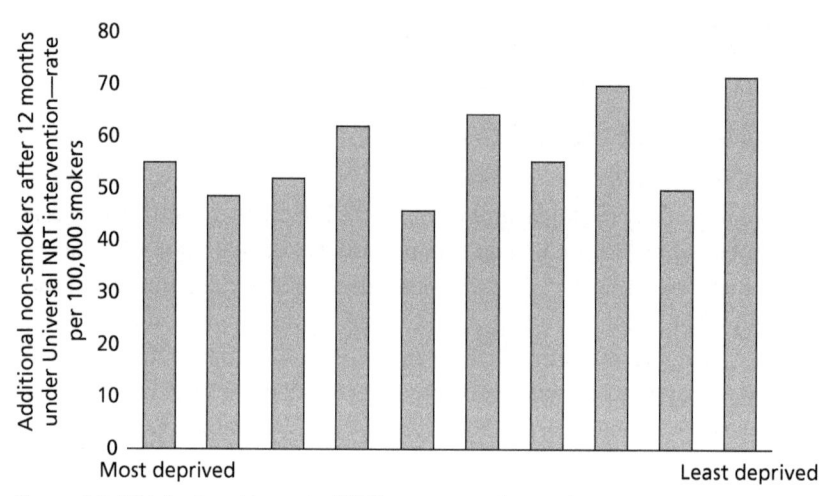

Figure 8.2 Distributional impact of NRT among smokers only.

Indeed, the nicotine replacement therapy (NRT) exercise discussed later in this chapter provides a clear example of this scenario. Fig 8.2 illustrates the modelled impact of the intervention on quit rates among smokers across ten socioeconomic groups. These results suggest that the intervention has the largest impact on smokers in the least deprived group.

This approach, however, does not account for the fact that there are considerably more smokers in the more deprived groups. Fig 8.3 shows the modelled impact of the intervention on quit rates per adult across the same groups. This change of denominator in the rate calculation has the effect of reversing the gradient, suggesting that the intervention may increase inequalities among smokers while reducing inequalities in the general population.

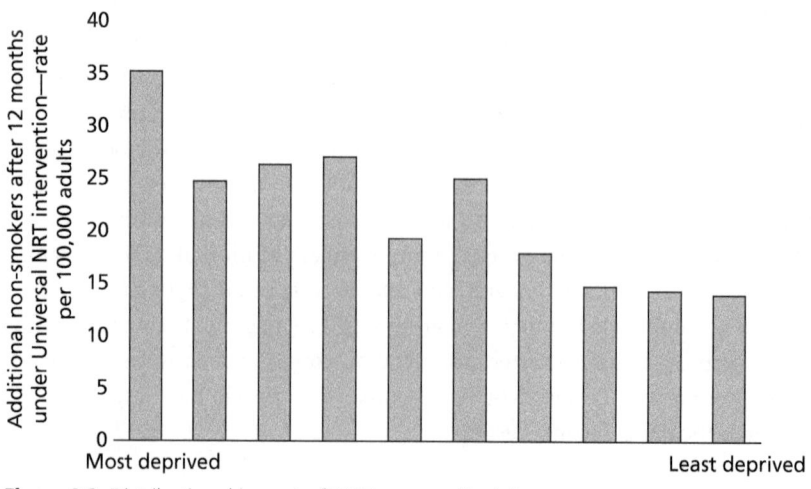

Figure 8.3 Distributional impact of NRT among all adults.

This situation is analogous to Rose's prevention paradox, which states that you can obtain larger population-level health impact from a large number of small individual level benefits than a small number of large benefits.

8.3.3 Building the staircase into the model

DCEA is an extension of cost-effectiveness analysis (CEA) which enlarges its scope without requiring any fundamental change in its methods or standards of good practice. As a result there will usually be little difference between the structure of a 'standard' cost-effectiveness model and a 'distributional' one, and the basic process of model building should follow the methods set out in the Briggs and colleagues 'green book' (Briggs et al., 2006). In essence, stratification by any equity-relevant characteristic is simply a form of subgroup analysis. There are, however, three differences that set equity informative models apart from 'standard' models. First, equity is usually a general population concept and so the subgroup differences are usually set in a wider general population context. Second, the stratification is based on equity-relevant characteristics of interest to decision makers—geography and socioeconomic status in the examples in this chapter. For models such as decision trees or Markov models, this will be implemented as several different models (or several runs of the same model using different input parameters), one for each level of the variable of interest (e.g. health decile groups), running in parallel. For more complex model structures such as Discrete Event Simulation or microsimulation models this may simply mean including the variable of interest in the model and modelling its interaction it with relevant probabilities and factors (e.g. times to events, or costs). A third difference is that an equity-informative model may include stratification of costs and effects at several explicit staircase steps. For example, a standard cost-effectiveness model for a primary care intervention may simply include a single parameter for the proportion of patients receiving the intervention in a specified timeframe. The equivalent equity-informative model may separately consider whether individuals are registered with a primary care practice, whether they actually attend it and whether, having attended it, they receive the intervention, as any of these steps may have their own inequality gradient.

When constructing any DCEA model it is therefore important that the model looks at costs and effects within the full population served by the decision-making organization, not just programme recipients, is stratified by the relevant equity-relevant characteristics, and explicitly includes all of the steps which you have identified as being relevant in your staircase.

8.3.4 Populating the staircase

Having designed the structure of your model, the next step is to populate it with data. In many respects this process will again be identical to that for a standard cost-effectiveness model. However, when searching for data on parameters related to the steps on the staircase, you additionally want these data to account for inequality gradients. In some cases, this information will already be available in the data you would typically have available—for example many population surveys routinely include information on sociodemographic variables. Routine data such as hospital records may also include such measures, or geographical data which can be mapped to them, for example patients' area of residence. An alternative approach is to identify external evidence on inequality gradients and combine this with unstratified data to populate the model. This should be done with some degree of caution, because combining data from multiple sources and studies may involve strong assumptions about the nature of those data. Typically, primary studies that do not report inequality gradients in their results will present a single population-level outcome, for example a measure of effect such as a relative risk. Let us call this effect RR_{Pop}. A further study may report an inequality gradient, for example, 'the effect of treatment X is 1.4 times greater in the most deprived group compared to the least deprived group'. If this study does not report the gradient across all intermediate socioeconomic groups then it will be necessary to assume a shape for the gradient. This assumption should be informed by all the available data, but in many cases, particularly where such data is scarce, the simplest assumption may be to assume that the relationship is linear, as illustrated in Fig 8.4. Note that we assume here that there are five strata in the equity-relevant characteristic; however, the approach is easily adapted to any number.

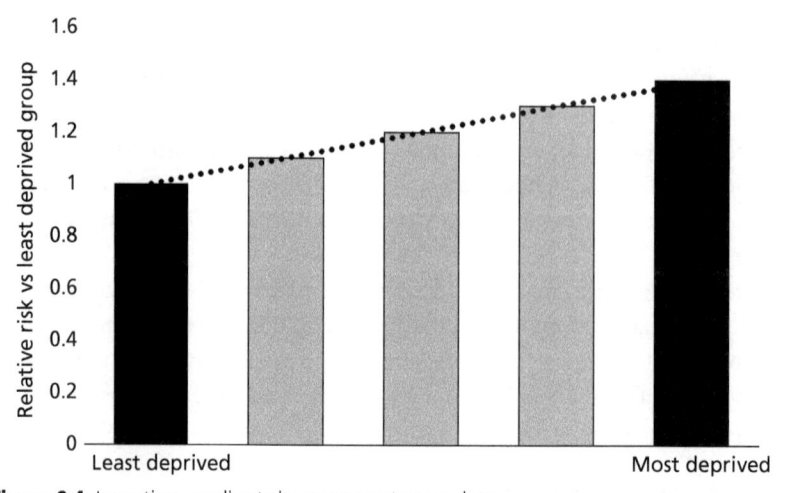

Figure 8.4 Imputing gradients in sparse outcome data.

We can then write the implied treatment effect for each group (RR_i) in terms of the least deprived group (RR_1) as follows:

$$RR_5 = 1.4 \times RR_1$$

$$RR_4 = 1.3 \times RR_1$$

$$RR_3 = 1.2 \times RR_1$$

$$RR_2 = 1.1 \times RR_1$$

But we know that the average of these effects must be the population effect, which we know, that is:

$$RR_{Pop} = \frac{RR_5 + RR_4 + RR_3 + RR_2 + RR_1}{5}$$

So we can simply substitute the first equations into the second and solve to identify RR_1 and put this back into the first equations to derive the treatment effect for each group. This approach assumes that the socioeconomic groups are of equal size, which will often be the case. However, the approach can easily be generalized when the populations of each group, denoted N_i, are unequal. The first set of equations then becomes:

$$RR_5 = 1.4 \times RR_1$$

$$RR_4 = \left(1.4 - \frac{N_5 + N_4}{2} \times \frac{1.4 - 1}{\frac{N_1}{2} + N_2 + N_3 + N_4 + \frac{N_5}{2}}\right) \times RR_1$$

$$RR_3 = \left(1.4 - \frac{N_5 + N_4 + N_3}{2} \times \frac{1.4 - 1}{\frac{N_1}{2} + N_2 + N_3 + N_4 + \frac{N_5}{2}}\right) \times RR_1$$

$$RR_2 = \left(1.4 - \frac{N_5 + N_4 + N_3 + N_2}{2} \times \frac{1.4 - 1}{\frac{N_1}{2} + N_2 + N_3 + N_4 + \frac{N_5}{2}}\right) \times RR_1$$

While the second equation becomes:

$$RR_{Pop} = \frac{RR_5 N_5 + RR_4 N_4 + RR_3 N_3 + RR_2 N_2 + RR_1 N_1}{N_5 + N_4 + N_3 + N_2 + N_1}$$

The same approach may also be followed in circumstances where data are available for all groups on the parameter of interest, but the group-level data are potentially unreliable due to small sample sizes, low data quality, or other issues of measurement. In such a situation, the group-level detail of the observed gradient may not be considered reliable, even if the overall pattern is. For example, data from a small survey may show that levels of some parameters increase as deprivation falls, but that this relationship is non-monotonic. If there is no compelling reason to believe that the true relationship is non-monotonic then it may be preferable to assume this arises from measurement error and impose a monotonic gradient on the parameter in the model. As with all aspects of model building, you may wish to seek input from clinicians and topic experts to determine the most appropriate assumptions to make in any given situation.

Throughout the process of selecting data to populate the staircase for any model, data should be selected using the same criteria as you would use for any other model parameters—looking across all relevant data sources and favouring results from the best available studies, undertaken in similar contexts to those of your current analysis and within a similar time frame. Box 8.2 highlights the range of data sources used to populate staircases in studies on low- and middle-income countries.

8.4 The example of NRT

We will now illustrate this process using the NRT example introduced in Chapter 5. The distribution of baseline health has been addressed in Chapter 7, but as the intervention is targeted at smokers, we also need to account for inequalities in smoking prevalence. In terms of receipt of the intervention, NRT is only used by smokers who are attempting to quit, so we need to consider potential inequalities in both quit attempts and also whether there is a gradient in the use of NRT among those who are trying to quit. There is also a potential gradient in cost, depending on whether smokers using NRT get this on prescription from their doctor or whether they buy it over the counter. When modelling success in quitting there may be gradients in terms of both short-term success and longer-term relapse into smoking. Finally, there may be difference in terms of the long-term health benefits and healthcare costs associated with quitting. Fig 8.5 illustrates the final conceptual staircase for NRT.

Having determined the steps in our staircase, we now turn to the data we can use to populate the model in order to estimate the distribution of lifetime health benefits and healthcare costs. Recall that we are looking at inequality across both quintile groups of socioeconomic deprivation and also geography, having split the country into north and south regions. It is worth noting that it is not

Box 8.2 Modelling the distributional impacts of tobacco taxes in low- and middle-income countries

Three recent studies have used an ECEA approach to estimate the distributional effects of increasing taxes on tobacco in China (Verguet et al., 2015), Lebanon (Salti et al., 2016), and Armenia (Postolovska et al., 2017). This approach requires the quantification of socioeconomic gradients in key areas such as smoking prevalence, health care usage, and income. Identifying suitable evidence to parameterize these gradients in LMIC countries can be challenging. However, these studies managed to use a range of sources to achieve this.

For China, Verguet et al. calculated gradients across income quintiles using data from international organizations such as the World Health Organization and the Asian Development Bank. In Lebanon, Salti et al. used a combination of national survey data and published research, although some of the survey data was over ten years old. Finally, for Armenia, Postolovska used data from national surveys, governmental performance reviews of the health sector, a report from the World Bank and data from a survey in Kyrgyzstan. Together these studies illustrate the breadth of evidence that can be used to populate the steps in the staircase of inequality.

Sources: Stéphane Verguet, Cindy Gavreau, Sujata Mishra, Mary MacLennan, Shane Murphy, Elizabeth D. Brouwer, et al. (2015) The consequences of tobacco tax on household health and finances in rich and poor smokers in China: an extended cost-effectiveness analysis. *Lancet Global Health*, 3(4), e206–216.

Nisreen Salti, Elizabeth Brouwer, and Stéphane Verguet (2016). The health, financial and distributional consequences of increases in the tobacco excise tax among smokers in Lebanon. *Social Science & Medicine*, 170, 161–169.

Iryna Postolovska, Rouselle F. Lavado, Gillian Tarr, and Stéphane Verguet (2017). Estimating the distributional impact of increasing taxes on tobacco products in Armenia: results from an extended cost-effectiveness analysis. World Bank, Washington, DC.

necessary, either in theory or in practice, that inequalities exist across both of these dimensions in every step in the staircase.

8.4.1 Need

Data on the baseline distribution of health was covered in Chapter 7. The proportion of the population falling into each deprivation/geography group is taken from national population estimates published by the Office of National Statistics (Office for National Statitics 2018). Data on the baseline prevalence of

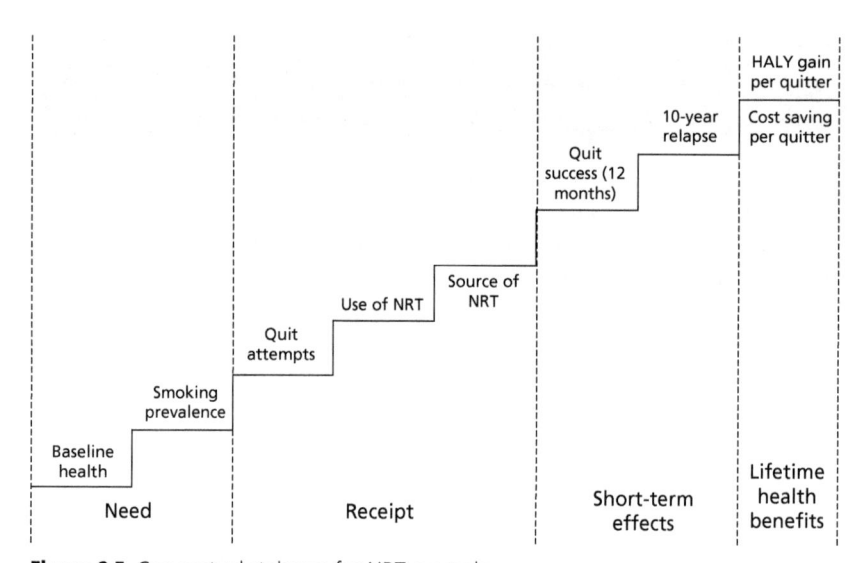

Figure 8.5 Conceptual staircase for NRT example.
Note: the text below the staircase indicates inequalities affecting costs only. Dashed lines represent the four key steps from Figure 8.1.

smoking by both deprivation and geography comes from the Smoking Toolkit Study, an individual-level survey, which has been collecting data on smoking status since 2007 (Fidler et al., 2011). Fig 8.6 shows the prevalence of smoking among adults in 2010 from this data, illustrating that there is a substantial socioeconomic gradient in smoking, with much higher rates of smoking in lower socioeconomic groups. At the same time, there is also a clear geographical north/south divide, with higher rates of smoking in the north, particularly in more deprived groups.

8.4.2 Receipt

Data on the proportion of smokers who had attempted to quit in the past year, stratified by socioeconomic status, is taken from the Smoking Toolkit Study. Estimates of the proportion of those attempting to quit who reported using any form of NRT comes from the same source. Although both of these measures show some variation between population groups, there is no consistent gradient across either measure.

8.4.3 Effects

An estimated 4% of smokers attempting to quit without any cessation aids succeed in still being smoke-free at 12 months (Hughes et al., 2004). We combine this figure with a socioeconomic gradient taken from Dobbie et al. (2015),

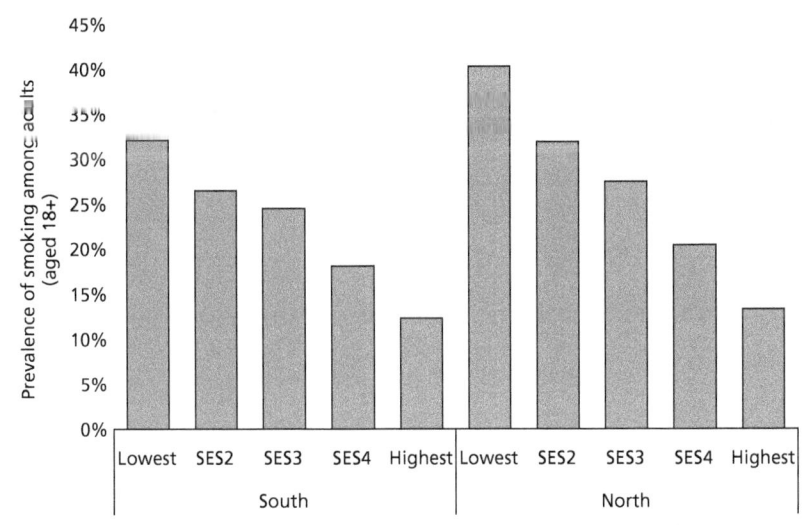

Figure 8.6 Geographical and socioeconomic variation in smoking prevalence in England in 2010.
Source: data from Fidler J., Shahab L., & West O. (2011). 'The Smoking Toolkit Study': A National Study of Smoking and Smoking Cessation in England. *BMC Public*.

using the method outlined above to give a successful quit rate rising from 3.2% in the most deprived group to 5.2% in the least deprived group. We take an estimate of the relative risk of 12-month abstinence for NRT versus control of 1.55 from the latest Cochrane review (Hartmann-Boyce et al., 2018), which does not suggest any evidence of this varying between different population subgroups. Note that this assumption, that the same relative risk applies to all socioeconomic groups, has the effect of increasing the slope of the socioeconomic gradient in absolute quit rates by a factor of 1.55, as illustrated in Fig 8.7. This may have an important bearing on the overall results of the model and, where the evidence to support such an assumption of constant relative effects is weak, may be an important assumption to test in sensitivity analyses on the final model. Finally, we incorporate evidence into the model of a long-term (ten-year) relapse rate of 37.1% based on a UK panel survey (Hawkins et al., 2010) which did not find any evidence of a socioeconomic gradient in this rate. We use ten-year abstinence as a proxy for lifetime abstinence, assuming those who relapse within ten years receive no health benefits from their period of abstinence.

8.4.4 Lifetime health benefits

Estimates of the total lifetime HALY gain for individuals who successfully gave up smoking and remained abstinent for at least ten years come from (Filby

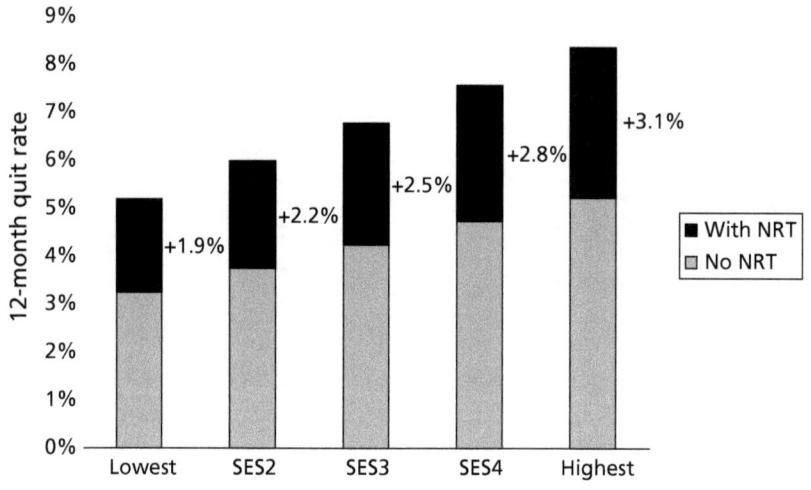

Figure 8.7 Socioeconomic gradients in smoking cessation rate with and without NRT. Source: data from Dobbie F., et al. 2015. Evaluating Long-Term Outcomes of NHS Stop Smoking Services (ELONS): a prospective cohort study. *Health Technology Assessment,* 19(95), 1–156. Hughes J., et al. (2004). Shape of the relapse curve and long-term abstinence among untreated smokers. Shape of the relapse curve and long-term abstinence among untreated smokers. *Addiction,* 99(1), 29–38. Boyce H., et al. (2018). Nicotine replacement therapy versus control for smoking cessation. *Cochrane Database of Systematic Reviews,* May 31; 5: CD000146. doi: 10.1002/14651858.CD000146.pub5.

and Taylor, 2018) and are illustrated in Fig 8.8. These figures show a U-shaped relationship with socioeconomic status, with those in the highest and lowest groups benefitting the most. This arises from conflicting gradients in life expectancy (being highest in the highest socioeconomic group) and prevalence of smoking-attributable disease (being highest in the lowest socioeconomic group). Note that the assumption that all successful quitters receive the same HALY gain is a strong one. A more refined approach would incorporate age into the model and consider future HALY gains as a function of the age at which you quit.

8.4.5 Healthcare costs

The cost of a single course of NRT is assumed to be £35.84 based on data from a recent UK trial (Essex et al., 2015) and this cost is assumed to be the same irrespective of whether it is being borne by the healthcare service or by private individuals. Estimates of the incremental healthcare cost saving for each long-term quitter compared to a continuing smoker are taken from Filby and Taylor (2018). As illustrated in Fig 8.9, these show a broadly inverse pattern to the incremental health gains in Fig 8.8.

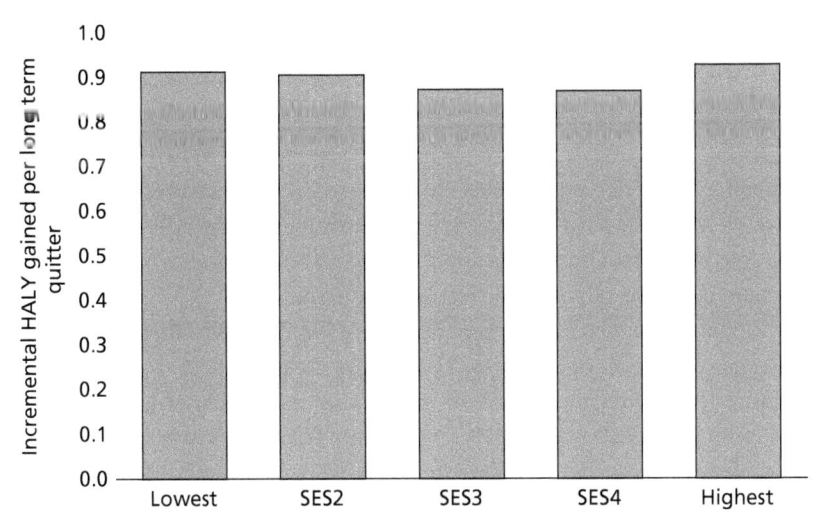

Figure 8.8 Socioeconomic gradients in lifetime health gains from smoking cessation.
Source: data from Filby A. & Taylor M. (2018). *National Institute for Healthcare and Excellence—Smoking Cessation Interventions and Services*. NICE.

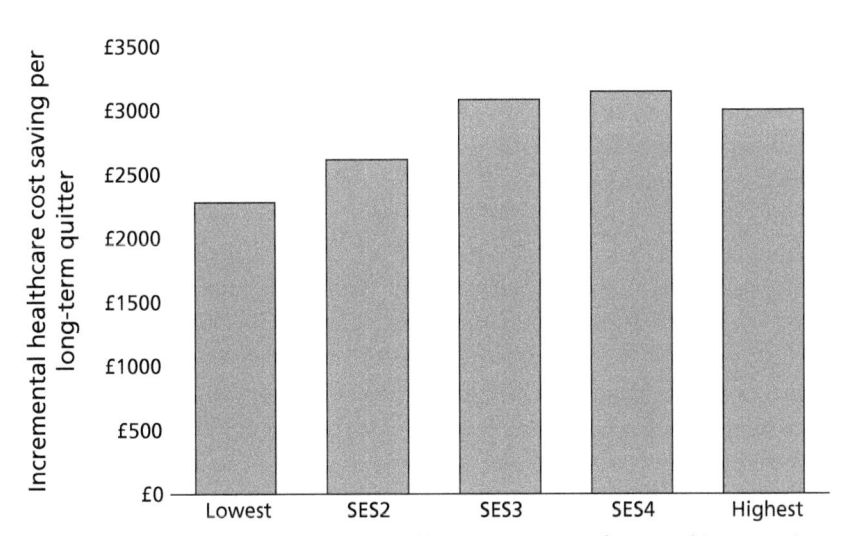

Figure 8.9 Socioeconomic gradient in healthcare cost savings from smoking cessation.
Source: data from Essex H., et al. (2015). Cost-effectiveness of nicotine patches for smoking cessation in pregnancy: a placebo randomized controlled trial (SNAP). *Nicotine & Tobacco Research*, 17(6), 636–642. Filby A. & Taylor M. (2018). *National Institute for Healthcare and Excellence—Smoking Cessation Interventions and Services*. NICE.

8.5 Conclusion

Adding the capability of answering questions of equity to a cost-effectiveness model may initially appear a daunting task. In this chapter, we have presented a simple, flexible framework—the 'staircase of inequality'—to help locate where inequalities may arise in the delivery and outcomes of an intervention. This new information can be used to augment existing modelling by estimating the distribution of benefits and costs across the population as well as producing better estimates of the overall cost-effectiveness of an intervention.

One of the strengths of this approach is that it can be applied to a diverse set of interventions, including those acting directly on current health, those acting directly on future health through prevention (e.g. vaccination/screening programmes), and those acting indirectly on health through health behaviours such as smoking or diet. Indeed, the same approach can be extended, with little additional effort, to model the distributional impacts on health of interventions that are not situated directly within the health sector, such as so-called 'sin taxes' on unhealthy foods or products such as tobacco or alcohol. However, one additional complexity in modelling behavioural public health interventions is that the relationship between the risky behaviour and health is often non-linear. As a result, models exploring the unequal impacts of behavioural interventions often require either microsimulations (where risk is calculated at the individual level) or stratification based on the level of unhealthy behaviour in addition to the 'unfair' characteristics.

The staircase framework presented here is flexible enough to be adapted to many modelling situations but is not without limitations. Perhaps the biggest limitation of the staircase approach is that it can be extremely data hungry. A full equity-informative cost-effectiveness model requires all the data required for a standard cost-effectiveness model, with some of the parameters further stratified across the 'unfair' parameters of interest and, potentially, additional steps included in the model. Such models will therefore typically require a greater number of assumptions than a standard model and there may be a greater degree of structural uncertainty in the model as a result. In some cases, it may not be possible to identify suitable data on the scale of some inequality gradients. Perhaps the simplest approach in such cases is to assume that there is no gradient, but test this assumption in a structural sensitivity analysis. In particular, it may be informative to undertake a form of threshold analysis: how steep would the gradient have to be in order to change your decision? To facilitate this, it may be helpful to include a single parameter representing the gradient, even if that is set to 0 in the base case analysis.

It is important to be aware that there is a possibility for bias in the availability of data around inequality gradients, for example where data exists only on gradients which slope in one direction, while data is missing on the gradients you might expect to run the other way. Where data is sparse like this it may be advisable to seek expert opinion or search for more qualitative literature which can inform some assumptions to 'fill in the blanks'.

A further consideration is the fact that inequality may not be constant over time. Throughout this handbook, we treat socioeconomic status as being time-invariant, although in reality there is always some degree of social mobility over the life course. This is further complicated by the idea that the relationship between deprivation and poor health is bidirectional: deprivation can lead to illness through poor diet, lower standards of living and worse access to healthcare, but poor health can equally drive people into deprivation—so-called 'downward social selection'. There is also some evidence to support the idea that inequality gradients in the individual steps in the staircase may themselves change over time. In an analysis of child health studies in Brazil, Victora and colleagues observed that public health interventions increased inequality in the short term, but narrowed them in the long term (Victora et al., 2000). They suggested that this may be because initial uptake was highest among higher socioeconomic groups, but that over time lower socioeconomic groups follow.

Finally, we have also not addressed the question of handling uncertainty using the staircase approach. This is because it is generally no different from handling uncertainty in a standard cost-effectiveness model, by parameterizing the uncertainty around the model inputs and drawing from those parameterizations in a series of probabilistic model runs—as described, for example, in Chapter 4 of the Briggs 'green book' (Briggs et al., 2006). However, there are some distinctive challenges to handling uncertainty in DCEA which are covered in Chapter 15.

8.6 Further reading

Tugwell and colleagues provide a helpful overview of the underlying concept of the staircase of inequality, including several illustrative examples (2006). Asaria and colleagues have produced a clearly set out tutorial which walks the reader through the bowel cancer screening analysis discussed in Box 8.1 (2016). The papers from Verguet and colleagues and Salti and colleagues provide valuable insight into the diversity of data sources which can be used to populate an equity-informative model, particularly in an LMIC setting (Verguet et al., 2015; Salti et al., 2016).

References

Acheson D. (1998). *Independent Inquiry into Inequalities in Health: Report.* The Stationery Office, London.

Asaria M., Griffin S., & Cookson R. (2016). Distributional cost-effectiveness analysis: a tutorial. *Medical Decision Making: an International Journal of the Society for Medical Decision Making,* **36**(1), 8–19.

Briggs, A., Sculpher M., & Claxton K. (2006). *Decision Modelling for Health Economic Evaluation.* Oxford University Press, New York.

Chilcott J., Tappenden P., Rawdin A., Johnson M., Kaltenthaler E., Paisley S., et al. (2010). Avoiding and identifying errors in health technology assessment models: qualitative study and methodological review. *Health Technology Assessment,* **14**(25):iii–iv, ix–xii, 1–107. doi: 10.3310/hta14250.

Cookson R., Propper C., Asaria M., & Raine R. (2016). Socio-economic inequalities in health care in England. *Fiscal Studies,* **37**(3–4), 371–403.

Dobbie F., Hiscock R., Leonardi-Bee J., Murray S., Shahab L., Aveyard P., et al. (2015). Evaluating long-term outcomes of NHS stop smoking services (ELONS): a prospective cohort study. *Health Technology Assessment,* **19**(95), 1–156.

Drummond M., Sculpher M., Claxton K., Stoddart G., & Torrance G. (2015). *Methods for the Economic Evaluation of Health Care Programmes.* Fourth Edition. Oxford University Press, New York.

Essex H., Parrott S., Wu Q., Li J., Cooper S., & Coleman T. (2015). Cost-effectiveness of nicotine patches for smoking cessation in pregnancy: a placebo randomized controlled trial (SNAP). *Nicotine & Tobacco Research,* **17**(6), 636–642.

Fidler J., Shahab L., & West O. (2011). 'The Smoking Toolkit Study': a national study of smoking and smoking cessation in England. *BioMed Central Public Health,* 11, 479.

Filby A. & Taylor M. (2018). *National Institute for Health and Care Excellence Smoking Cessation Interventions and Services.* York Health Economics Consortium, York.

Hartmann-Boyce J., Chepkin S., Ye W., Bullen C., & Lancaster T. (2018). Nicotine replacement therapy versus control for smoking cessation. *Cochrane Database of Systematic Reviews,* 5(5), CD000146.

Hawkins J., Hollingworth W., & Campbell R. (2010). Long-term smoking relapse: a study using the British household panel survey. *Nicotine & Tobacco Research,* **12**(12), 1228–1235.

Hill S., Amos A., Clifford D., & Platt S. (2014). Impact of tobacco control interventions on socioeconomic inequalities in smoking: review of the evidence. *Tobacco Control,* 23(e2), 89–97.

Hughes J., Keely J., & Naud S. (2004). Shape of the relapse curve and long-term abstinence among untreated smokers. *Addiction,* **99**(1), 29–38.

Lorenc T., Petticrew M., Welch V., & Tugwell P. (2013). What types of interventions generate inequalities? evidence from systematic reviews. *Journal of Epidemiology and Community Health,* **67**(2), 190–193.

Marmot M., Friel S., Bell R., Houweling T., Taylor S., and Commission on Social Determinants of Health (2008). Closing the gap in a generation: health equity through action on the social determinants of health. *Lancet (London, England),* **372**(9650), 1661–1666.

Office for National Statistics (2018). *Mid-2001 to Mid-2017 Detailed Time Series*. Office for National Statistics, Newport.

Postolovska I., Lavado R., Tarr G., & Verguet S. (2017). *Estimating the Distributional Impact of Increasing Taxes on Tobacco Products in Armenia*. World Bank, Washington, DC.

Salti N., Brouwer E., & Verguet S. (2016). The health, financial and distributional consequences of increases in the tobacco excise tax among smokers in Lebanon. *Social Science & Medicine*, 170, 161–169.

Tudor-Hart J. (1971). The Inverse Care Law. *Lancet*, 297(7696), 405–412.

Tugwell P., de Savigny D., Hawker G., & Robinson V. (2006). Applying clinical epidemiological methods to health equity: the equity effectiveness loop. *British Medical Journal*, 332(7537), 358–361.

Verguet S., Gauvreau C., Mishra S., MacLennan M., Murphy S., Brouwer E., et al. (2015). The consequences of tobacco tax on household health and finances in rich and poor smokers in China: an extended cost-effectiveness analysis. *Lancet Global Health*, 3(4), e206–216.

Victora G., Vaughan J., Barros F., Silva A., & Tomasi E. (2000). Explaining trends in inequities: evidence from Brazilian child health studies. *Lancet*, 356(9235), 1093–1098.

Chapter 9
Health opportunity costs
James Love-Koh

9.1 Introduction

This chapter introduces the concept of health opportunity cost and describes some approaches to quantifying both total health opportunity costs and their distribution. Non-health opportunity costs—such as forgone financial risk protection or forgone consumption, education, or employment benefits—are outside our brief for this chapter.

Accounting for opportunity costs is an essential component of economic evaluation and can have important distributional implications. A decision to use scarce resources one way rather than another usually benefits some people at the expense of others who would otherwise have benefited. Decision makers therefore need to consider the distribution of health opportunity costs as well as the distribution of health benefits. This challenge is a matter of horizontal equity: people with the same equity-relevant characteristics should receive the same priority, regardless of whether they bear health opportunity costs or receive health benefits.

However, estimating health opportunity cost distributions has demanding data needs. We therefore also describe ways of conducting scenario analysis through a range of plausible scenarios. These are characterized by their funding context (including insurance and donor-financed expenditure), the prevailing patterns of prevalence and utilization by equity-relevant variables, and whether evidence generated in similar settings can be borrowed and adapted.

9.1.1 What are opportunity costs?

An opportunity cost is defined as the value of a resource in its most highly valued alternative use. Opportunity costs are incurred whenever a decision is made to allocate scarce resources. The resources used in the provision of a health programme represent a lost opportunity to use them to do something else. When a health planner decides to fund a new health programme, the economic approach is to consider the benefits that could have been obtained by providing other services, some of which may even be of greater value.

The types of opportunity cost that should be considered in an economic evaluation depend upon the aspects of benefit that decision makers think are relevant to their decision. When evaluating a health programme, a major aspect of benefit is clearly health itself—for example as measured by quality-adjusted life years (QALYs) gained or disability-adjusted life years (DALYs) prevented. When economic evaluation is used to inform decisions aimed at improving population health, the opportunity costs therefore need to include forgone health—the health generated by the alternative use of resources that is forgone by introducing a new programme under consideration.

In practical terms, the greater the cost impact of a programme, the greater the amount of health can be produced through alternative means. These forgone benefits can be estimated empirically through a statistical analysis of the marginal productivity of the healthcare system—the relationship between health sector expenditure and health outcomes at the current margin. If a programme delivers more health benefits than could have been achieved with an alternative use of the same resources, population health increases and the programme can be regarded as cost-effective. When economic evaluation is used to inform decisions also aimed at improving health equity, the assessment needs to include information about equity in the distribution of health opportunity costs as well as health benefits.

9.1.2 Opportunity costs in distributional cost-effectiveness analysis

Health opportunity costs are an essential component of the net health benefit of a programme. Net health benefit (n) is defined as the difference between health benefits (h) and health opportunity costs:

$$n = h - \frac{c}{k}$$

where c is the cost of the programme and k is a measure of the rate at which costs are converted into forgone health. Net health benefit is similarly employed in equity-informative economic evaluation, but is estimated according to the equity-relevant variable, for example by socioeconomic status group indexed by j:

$$n_j = h_j - \frac{c}{k} p_j.$$

In this formulation, the health benefits for social group j (h_j) that were the subject of Chapter 8 are combined with the quantity $\frac{c}{k} p_j$, the proportion of opportunity costs expected to fall on the group. Most health systems include a substantial element of insurance and third-party payment, and individuals

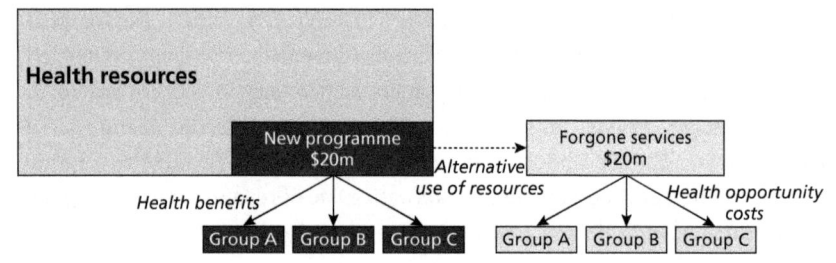

Figure 9.1 Independence of health opportunity cost distribution from the programme under evaluation.
Note: health resources are not necessarily fixed and can be altered (e.g. through insurance premiums or taxation).

rarely cover 100% of healthcare costs directly out of pocket. The proportion of the opportunity cost that falls on each group is therefore not determined by the proportion of the costs generated by each group. Instead, this proportion is determined by the distribution of the health benefits of the forgone activities that could otherwise have been funded by the third-party payers and individuals concerned. This means that the distribution of the health opportunity cost can often be estimated separately from the evaluation of any particular programme, and, once estimated, can be employed in all subsequent economic evaluations that impose costs on the same resource set. This relationship is illustrated in Fig 9.1, where the forgone services result in health opportunity costs falling on the same social groups (A, B, C) as those affected by the new programme, but not necessarily on the same disease (or patient) groups.

The distribution of the benefits of these forgone services depends on the decision-making context. This includes the source of funding (e.g. fixed health budget or increased taxation or insurance premiums), the perspective from which the study is being conducted (e.g. the range or scope of consequences to be considered), the behavioural responses of individuals and organizations to changes in their financial situation, the prevailing patterns of disease prevalence and service utilization in different population groups, and, of course, the meaning and empirical content given to 'health'.

In summary, in equity-informative evaluation there are two components to the health opportunity cost associated with a particular use of resources or budget: the magnitude of health opportunity costs (through the value of k) and their distribution by the equity relevant factor (P_j). The example in Box 9.1 illustrates why accounting for the distribution of opportunity cost is crucial in equity-informative evaluation and can have a potentially strong impact on health inequality impact assessment.

Box 9.1 Health opportunity costs in distributional cost-effectiveness analysis

The distribution of opportunity costs can potentially influence the magnitude and direction of the expected health inequality impact of a new programme. Suppose we are evaluating the effect of Treatment X on health inequalities between three equally-sized subgroups A, B, & C, who have respective baseline health-adjusted life expectancy of 60, 65, and 70. Treatment X benefits the least healthy groups more and may therefore reduce health inequalities. It is estimated that the incremental costs associated with funding Treatment X could have generated 12 health-adjusted life years (HALYs) had they been spent on other activities (see Table 9.1).

If we were to assume that this forgone health was distributed evenly, the distribution of net health benefit would still favour the least healthy in Group A and reduce the gap between A and C from 10 to 8 HALYs. However, suppose evidence shows that health opportunity costs fall disproportionately on Group A. The net health effects are now greater for most healthy group (Group C). This change in the distribution of opportunity cost means that the programme goes from reducing to increasing health inequalities.

Table 9.1 How the distribution of opportunity costs can influence the inequality impact of a hypothetical health programme

	Subgroup		
	A	B	C
A. Baseline health	60	65	70
B. Health benefits of Treatment X	8	7	6
C. Health opportunity cost	12 (across all subgroups)		
Opportunity costs (uniform assumption)			
D. Share of health opportunity cost	33%	33%	33%
E. Health opportunity cost (C x D)	4	4	4
F. Net effect (B-E)	4	3	2
G. Post-programme health (A+F)	64	68	72
Opportunity costs (with gradient)			
H. Share of health opportunity cost	50%	33%	17%
I. Health opportunity cost (C x H)	6	4	2
J. Net effect (B-I)	2	3	4
K. Post-programme health (A+J)	62	68	74

Note: all numbers are in terms of health-adjusted life years.

The notion of health opportunity costs is most typically associated with economic evaluation from a health sector perspective and publicly-funded healthcare. Economic evaluation has been used to inform decisions about which are the most valuable interventions by health technology assessment agencies and in health benefit package design. The method of analysis also applies to resource allocation decisions for other health-related budgets such as government-funded public health. Matters are more complex when dealing with systems of private or social insurance, which can be complicated by individual decisions on coverage and enrolment in insurance plans. However, health opportunity costs are still relevant since premiums cannot be raised indefinitely, changes in enrolment and coverage can have health effects, and both forgone private consumption and public expenditure outside the health sector can have health effects.

9.2 Estimating total opportunity costs

Estimating the magnitude and distribution of health opportunity cost requires an understanding of what health generating activities are forgone when a new programme is funded. Given this seemingly highly context-specific empirical question, early research into health opportunity cost involved interviewing healthcare purchasers to see what type of services were likely to be withdrawn (Appleby et al., 2009). If the services forgone are clearly identifiable, then the techniques described in Chapter 8 can be used to identify the distribution of health benefits from those forgone services (which are now forgone benefits). However, the authors of that study concluded that an implausibly large sample would be required to identify enough services at the fund/do not fund margin for decision makers to calculate what the health opportunity cost would be, noting as well that this margin would change over time.

An alternative approach is to model the statistical relationship between health outcomes and health expenditure using regression analysis. This method was pioneered in an analysis of two major disease areas in England by Martin and colleagues (2008), which was then extended to an analysis of the whole UK National Health Service (NHS) by Claxton and colleagues (2015). Similar analysis has been subsequently undertaken in both high-income (Vallejo-Torres et al., 2017; Edney et al., 2018) and low- and middle-income countries (LMICs) (Woods et al., 2016; Ochalek et al., 2018). The theory underlying this approach is the health production function for the health system. This charts the relationship between healthcare expenditure inputs and health outputs and is illustrated in Fig 9.2. The statistical analysis derives the elasticity of health with respect to expenditure—the change in health (Δh)

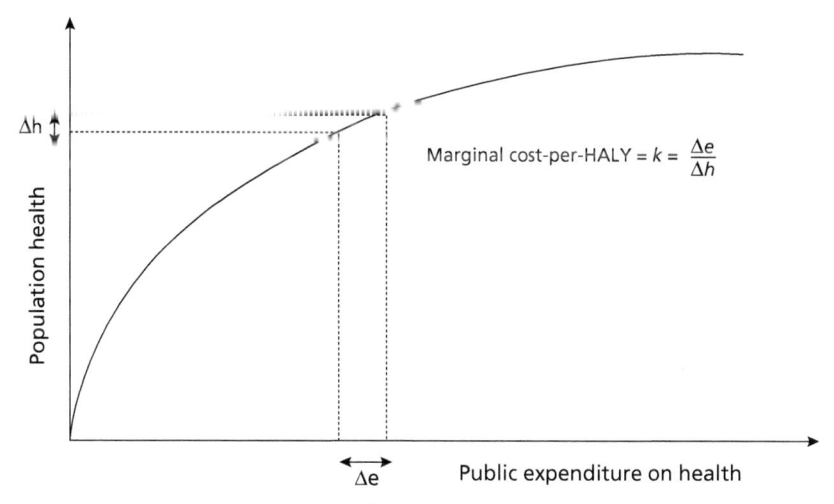

Figure 9.2 Health system production function.

[Figure shows axes: Population health (y-axis), Public expenditure on health (x-axis); a concave curve with marked Δh and Δe, and label: Marginal cost-per-HALY = $k = \frac{\Delta e}{\Delta h}$]

for a marginal change in health expenditure (Δe). As can be seen from the curvature of the production function in Fig 9.2, the rate of change in health depends on the current level of expenditure. The marginal productivity of the health system can be invoked as a measure of the opportunity cost when the total impact of the programme can be considered marginal with respect to the total amount of resource available. For programmes with non-marginal impacts, further research is needed as to how the elasticity changes with the level of expenditure.

This approach has produced estimates of health system marginal productivity using both within- and between-country data. Within-country analyses exploit variation between observation units (e.g. geographical districts) to estimate the statistical relationship between health outcomes and expenditure, so these data must contain observations for many units. Ideally the data set will have repeated measures over time to capture health outcomes temporally distant from delivery of the programmes and would be disaggregated by disease area so that heterogeneity in the production function can be modelled. In the absence of this type of data for within-country analysis, variation between countries might be exploited to estimate a common production function that would enable the imputation of country-level estimates. Table 9.2 lists five studies that estimated the marginal productivity of the health system up to mid-2018; more detailed descriptions of the methodological considerations and policy implications associated with this form of analysis can be found in Vallejo-Torres et al. (2016) and Thokala et al. (2018).

Table 9.2 Empirical studies estimating marginal productivity of health systems

Author (year)	Country	Data sets	Estimates of cost-per-HALY
Claxton et al. (2015)	England	Mortality and expenditure by 23 disease areas for 152 English regions. Morbidity adjustment from GBD data	£12,936
Lomas et al. (2018)	England	Same as Claxton et al.	£5389–£14,410
Ochalek et al. (2015)	123 LMICs	Cross-sectional and panel data on aggregate expenditure and mortality. GBD to adjust for country-level morbidity	From $3 (Nigeria) to $7,827 (Uruguay)
Vallejo-Torres et al. (2017)	Spain	HALE and expenditure estimates for 17 Spanish regions	€21,000–€24,000
Edney et al. (2018)	Australia	Expenditure, mortality & morbidity for 1389 Australian SLAs	AUD28,033

Note: HALY = Health-adjusted life year; GBD = Global Burden of Disease; LMICs = Low- and middle-income countries; HALE = Health-adjusted life expectancy; SLA = Statistical local area.

Once marginal productivity is estimated for a health budget (or particular set of health resources), the same health opportunity cost exchange rate k can be employed across all analyses. This is also the case for studies that estimate the marginal distribution of health opportunity cost. However, programmes that draw upon more than one source of funding from different sectors of government or industry with different objectives and constraints (e.g. separate public health and healthcare budgets) will require estimates of health opportunity cost for each sector.

Analysts undertaking an equity-informative evaluation should, in the first instance, try to identify existing studies of how health produced at the margin is distributed differently across subgroups (i.e. the health opportunity cost distribution) for the setting or budget of interest. If none are available, then published estimates of the marginal productivity for the healthcare system (i.e. the total health opportunity cost) can be used as the basis for disaggregation, with suitable scenario analysis to examine the implications of potential biases. Approaches to doing so are described in the following section.

In situations where neither total health opportunity cost estimates nor their distribution are available, several other options can be considered. In terms of accurately representing health opportunity costs in analyses, the optimal solution would be to conduct a bespoke analysis of a health system's productivity and distribution. Where this is not feasible, the next best alternatives are to elicit expert views or use plausibly comparable estimates from other settings or

Table 9.3 Calculating cost-per-health-adjusted life year (HALY) of disinvestment for two hypothetical programmes

	Programme X	Programme Y
Health resources		
A. Total expenditure	$5,000,000	
B. 1% change (A x 1%)	$50,000	
Programme impacts		
C. Per patient cost	$200	$300
D. Per patient HALYs	0.9	1.3
Disinvestment impact		
E. Proportion of disinvestment	0.4	0.6
F. Patients affected (E x B x 1/C)	100	100
G. Health forgone (F x D)	90	130
H. Cost-per-HALY lost	$227	

countries. If none of these options are available, then sensitivity and scenario analyses could be judiciously applied.

A value for k can theoretically be estimated if the likely displaced services are known. Culyer likens this to arranging services provided by a set of health resources from highest to lowest per person net health benefit on a bookshelf (Culyer, 2016), where the height and width of each 'book' are the respective health benefits and cost impact. In this scenario, the package of services is allocatively efficient (i.e. health is maximized) and the services with the lowest net benefits will be disinvested from first. Estimation of k based on disinvestment from two programmes is demonstrated in Table 9.3. Here, the incremental costs and health benefits of the two programmes are used to calculate how much health is forgone when a marginal change of 1% of the health budget is used to fund a new programme. The expected health loss for a given change in expenditure requires an estimate of the distribution of disinvestment over programmes (row E in Table 9.3).

9.3 Estimating distributions of opportunity costs

Estimating health opportunity costs through the marginal productivity of health systems provides two potential avenues for estimating health opportunity cost distributions: include equity-informative covariates in the statistical analyses of marginal productivity, or disaggregate the estimates of total health opportunity costs using information on the distribution of the marginal health outcomes according to equity-relevant characteristics.

9.3.1 Incorporating equity variables into statistical analysis of marginal productivity

The statistical analysis of marginal productivity is too complex to provide a step-by-step guide here. Several studies, for instance, use a mortality outcome in the regression analysis, requiring substantial additional modelling to account for quality of life effects (Claxton et al., 2015; Edney et al., 2018; Lomas et al., 2018; Ochalek et al., 2018). Techniques such as instrumental variables are also commonly used to reduce endogeneity bias, for which a range of validation statistical tests should be performed (Angrist et al., 1996). A technical discussion of these issues can be found in Gravelle & Backhouse (1987).

The distribution of health opportunity costs can be estimated using this framework by adding equity-relevant variables into the regression model, specifically an interaction term (or series of terms if the variable is categorical) between the equity variable and expenditure on health. This is then interpreted as the effect of the equity characteristic on the effect of expenditure on health.

Combining the independent effect of expenditure (α) with the equity group-specific effect (β_j) determines the change in health (Δh^j) for group j following a marginal change in expenditure ($\Delta e^{1\%}$). For example, a 1% change in expenditure yields the following health effect for group j:

$$\Delta h^j \mid \Delta e^{1\%} = 0.01 \times (\alpha + \beta_j) \times h^j$$

where h^j represents the health of group j (e.g. HALYs). The distribution of opportunity costs is obtained directly and can be expressed as the share of the total health opportunity cost borne by each group:

$$p_j = \frac{\Delta h^j \mid \Delta e^{1\%}}{\Sigma_j \Delta h^j \mid \Delta e^{1\%}}$$

Directly incorporating equity into the statistical estimation of opportunity costs places extra demands on the available data. First, there must exist a data set that provides a link between expenditure, health outcomes, and equity relevant characteristics. Second, the number of observations needs to be large enough to accommodate the additional covariates, particularly if the equity variable is categorical and requires the addition of several dummy variables. An analysis of the distribution over five socioeconomic subgroups, for example, when combined with the 152 geographical areas used by Claxton et al. (2015), would be based on approximately 30 observations per subgroup, significantly reducing statistical power. Conversely, the sample of nearly 1400 areas used in the analysis by Edney and colleagues (2018) would be much better placed to accommodate the use of additional covariates.

Another important consideration is that the equity variables should be carefully selected to align with the analysis units. If these units are geographical areas, for instance, then area-level socioeconomic measures, such as the Index of Multiple Deprivation in England, can be used. In all cases the interpretation of the results should match the unit of analysis and the level of disaggregation of the data, and the temptation to infer individual-level effects from group level estimation should be resisted. If the unit of analysis represents large, socioeconomically heterogeneous populations, then socioeconomic variation in outcomes will not be appropriately captured.

9.3.2 Using within-country estimates of marginal productivity

A more pragmatic approach is to disaggregate the marginal unit of health indirectly. As noted previously, attempts to directly observe whose health services are affected following expenditure changes have been found to be infeasible. Instead, secondary data can sometimes be used to identify variables as proxies. At the simplest (and crudest) level, healthcare utilization could act as this proxy variable—for example the total number of healthcare appointments or episodes or days, potentially weighted for cost or case-mix or quality. The share of total utilization for each subgroup would here be used as the estimate of the share of opportunity cost p_j. This entails three central assumptions:

(1) A unit of utilization generates the same health regardless of where it takes place in the health system (e.g. by provider type, disease category, geographical location).

(2) A unit of utilization generates the same health regardless of the social characteristics of the recipient.

(3) The social distribution of services affected at the margin is the same as the average social distribution across the health system.

The extent to which assumption (2) influences any estimates will be revealed only when further empirical work has been conducted on the link between healthcare inputs and health outputs by social group. It is likely that more affluent groups are generally more effective at producing health from any given healthcare input, due to fewer co-morbidities and greater ability to invest additional time and resources in recovery, care coordination, and prevention (Cookson et al., 2016). However, a potentially countervailing factor is that affluent patients may

Table 9.4 Share of marginal unit of health opportunity cost by disease area for England

Disease area	Proportion of opportunity cost	Disease area	Proportion of opportunity cost
Total	100%	Infectious diseases	2.0%
Respiratory	30%	Hearing	1.8%
Neurological	14%	Genitourinary	1.4%
Circulatory	14%	Dental	0.9%
Mental health	12%	Vision	0.5%
Endocrine	7.8%	Skin	0.3%
Gastrointestinal	5.7%	Poisoning	0.1%
Cancers & tumours	3.4%	Learning disability	0.1%
Musculoskeletal	3.0%	Healthy individuals	0.1%
Blood disorders	2.8%	Maternity & neonate	0.1%

Source: Data from Claxton, K., Martin, S., Soares, M., Rice, N., Spackman, E., Hinde, S., Devlin, N., Smith, P.C., Sculpher, M.. Methods for the estimation of the National Institute for Health and Care Excellence cost-effectiveness threshold. Health Technol. Assess. (Rockv). 2015. 19, 1–504. https://doi.org/10.3310/hta19140

tend to seek healthcare when they are less severely ill, thereby reducing the potential health benefit obtained from healthcare utilization.

Our ability to relax assumptions (1) and (3) depends on how marginal productivity is estimated in the original study. They can be partially addressed if marginal productivity is estimated separately by disease area and summed to obtain an aggregate health effect. This would provide the share of the overall health opportunity cost falling on each disease area (p_d). Table 9.4 shows these quantities for the UK NHS from Claxton et al. (2015). The social distribution of utilization for each disease area can then be used to split the disease-specific shares. Summing over diseases yields the share of overall health effect:

$$p_j = \sum_d p_{dj} = \sum_j p_d x_{dj}$$

where x_{dj} is the share of the disease-specific effect attributable to subgroup j. Two advantages of this approach are that a unit of utilization now produces differential health effects based on the disease area, and the disease-specific effects are directly linked to marginal changes in expenditure.

The key challenge that arises is to identify the data source(s) from which to estimate the social distribution of disease. Since the opportunity costs will fall on users of the displaced services, utilization statistics would be an appropriate

Table 9.5 Ongoing (as of 2019) household surveys in low- and middle-income countries (LMICs) with information on health, healthcare, and equity-relevant characteristics

Data set	Relevant variables	Description
WHO Study on global ageing and adult health	Healthcare utilization, household assets	Longitudinal study of six LMICs, total sample size 40,000
Demographic and health surveys	Disease prevalence, healthcare utilization, wealth, education	Household survey programme covering nearly 100 LMICs. Sample sizes range from 4000 to 15,000.
Global burden of disease	Disease prevalence & incidence, region (selected countries)	Comprehensive database of epidemiological levels and trends. Covering 195 countries and 350 diseases.
Multiple indicator cluster surveys	Disease prevalence, household assets, education level	Household survey programme covering over 100 LMICs, with focus on child and maternal health. Average sample size of 11,000.
Stepwise Approach to Surveillance Surveys	Disease & risk factor prevalence, household income, and education	National & subnational household surveys of over 100 LMICs, with focus on non-communicable diseases. Sample sizes range from 1000 to 10,000.
Country-specific household surveys	Typically: healthcare utilization, assets, or wealth,	Examples include the Malawian Integrated Household Survey, the Brazilian National Household Sample Survey, and the Indonesian Family Life Survey

choice if they cover sufficient activity within the disease area. Social distributions from hospital data, for example, might be more appropriate for cancer services than for mental health, where treatment can take place in out-of-hospital community centres. Household surveys with health components can often provide a source of additional, sometimes more reliable, source of data on disease prevalence and utilization by equity-relevant variables. Examples of these types of surveys with data for LMICs are provided in Table 9.5.

Where utilization data are not available, distributions of incidence or prevalence can provide an acceptable alternative. The limitations of using these types of data must also be acknowledged, however. Prevalence will capture changes in the social distribution of disease over time, although incidence will likely be sufficient for many acute conditions. However, neither will reflect differences in healthcare-seeking behaviour between social groups. If the set of resources include programmes for which individual agency is a factor, then a prevalence measure will overestimate the share of opportunity cost for any groups (e.g. low socioeconomic status groups) who are less likely to use services.

Box 9.2 describes how Love-Koh et al. (2020) used the approach described above to estimate the distribution of health opportunity costs in England. Both incidence and utilization data are combined with the disease-specific opportunity cost shares shown in Table 9.6.

Box 9.2 Distribution of health opportunity costs in England

Claxton et al. (2015) conducted a study estimating marginal productivity for the UK NHS, deriving a value of k, the exchange rate between financial costs and health opportunity costs. Love-Koh et al. (2020) used their results to explore how these health opportunity costs were distributed by subgroups based on age, socioeconomic status, and sex.

The marginal unit of health opportunity cost estimated by Claxton and colleagues was comprised of health effects from 23 different disease areas. Global Burden of Disease data on disease incidence was used to apportion the disease-specific shares to age and sex groups. For example, 29.7% of health produced at the margin is produced in the respiratory illness disease area. As 6.1% of incident respiratory disease occurs in females aged 30–44, they calculate the share of the overall health opportunity cost for this subgroup to be 29.67% x 6.1% = 1.81%.

These quantities were combined with the socioeconomic distribution for age, sex, and disease category (from administrative hospital data) to obtain the proportion of health opportunity cost by age, sex, socioeconomic status, and disease. For the subgroup of females aged 30–44 with respiratory illness, the calculation is shown in the table below.

Table 9.6 Share of respiratory illness hospital care utilization of 30–44 year-old females by socioeconomic group

	Socioeconomic group					
	1	2	3	4	5	Total
Share of utilization	26.8%	22.8%	21.9%	15.4%	13.1%	100%
Share of overall health opportunity cost	0.48%	0.41%	0.40%	0.28%	0.24%	1.81%

Note: socioeconomic group 1 = lowest, 5 = highest.

Source: Love-Koh J., Cookson R., Claxton K., & Griffin S. (2020). Estimating social variation in the health effects of changes in healthcare expenditure. *Medical Decision Making*, 40(2), 170–182.

These calculations are repeated for each of the age, sex, and disease subgroups. Summing over disease areas yields the distribution of health opportunity costs by the three social characteristics of age, sex, and socioeconomic status. The distribution by sex and socioeconomic status is presented in Table 9.7.

Distribution of health opportunity costs in England *(continued)*

Table 9.7 Estimates of health opportunity costs by sex and socioeconomic group for England

Group	Socioeconomic group					Total
	1	2	3	4	5	
Female	14.0%	11.9%	11.8%	8.7%	7.5%	54%
Male	12.4%	10.0%	10.0%	7.3%	6.4%	46%
Overall	*26.4%*	*21.9%*	*21.8%*	*16.0%*	*13.9%*	*100%*

Source: Love-Koh J., Cookson R., Claxton K., & Griffin S. (2020). Estimating social variation in the health effects of changes in healthcare expenditure. *Medical Decision Making*, 40(2), 170–182.

9.3.2.1 Using between-country estimates of marginal productivity

Due to their demanding data requirements, it may not be possible to conduct within-country marginal productivity studies for every setting. Information on marginal productivity for a wide range of countries can alternatively be sourced from between-country studies of marginal productivity. Such studies have adopted a similar approach to the within-country analyses: regression analysis is used to estimate the statistical relationship between mortality and health expenditures, and a series of adjustments are subsequently performed to incorporate the effects on morbidity.

Ochalek and colleagues identify the four key stages in this approach (Ochalek et al., 2015). The econometric analysis provides the elasticity of mortality with respect to public expenditure on health for each country, from which a survival (i.e. length of life) effect can be obtained. Morbidity effects can then be extrapolated from the mortality effects or estimated directly through an additional econometric analysis. Combining the survival and morbidity effects provides the health effects from expenditure changes in terms of HALYs.

The between-country approach can potentially be used to estimate disease-specific shares of the marginal health effect by including disease-specific mortality as the outcome variable in the regression analysis. The social distribution of disease can then be used to disaggregate this portion of the marginal effect using the methods described in the previous section. However, undertaking this for an exhaustive list of diseases covering all health expenditure will likely not be feasible, as it would require cross-country mortality data for each cause. This means that the contribution of (at least) a subset of diseases to the overall marginal health effect will not be available.

One way to disaggregate these effects is to use an approach based on benefit incidence analysis (BIA). BIA quantifies the average distribution of benefits from government-provided (or subsidized) health services, where 'benefit' is usually defined as financial value in terms of cost-weighted utilization (McIntyre and Ataguba, 2011). The output of a BIA is the distribution of average cost-weighted health service utilization across social groups. The utilization data are typically sourced from national health surveys that also contain a broad range of respondents' socioeconomic information.

The BIA approach combines benefits across different types of health services. Benefits (b_j) are calculated as the average annual utilization (u_{jq}) for an equity-relevant group (j) and service type (q) multiplied by the average unit cost (c_q) minus the average cost of user fees (f_{jq}), summed across service types:

$$b_j = \sum_q \left(u_{jq} c_q - f_{jq} \right)$$

The share of marginal opportunity cost for each group can be obtained from a BIA by making two strong assumptions: (1) that cost-weighted utilization is an accurate proxy for health benefit (i.e. more costly services deliver greater health benefit) and (2) that marginal utilization is the same as average utilization. The share for each group p_j would then equal $\dfrac{b_j}{\sum_j b_j}$. An example of a benefit distribution estimated for Malawi by Mangham (2006) is shown in Fig 9.3. Contrary to the example of England, this shows higher utilization amongst the higher socioeconomic groups. The output of a BIA represents an improvement over unweighted utilization count data and can be a useful alternative for data-poor LMICs, with appropriate allowance for the two strong assumptions required.

Marginal benefit incidence analysis (MBIA) provides an extension to conventional average BIA that estimates this marginal distribution directly. MBIA

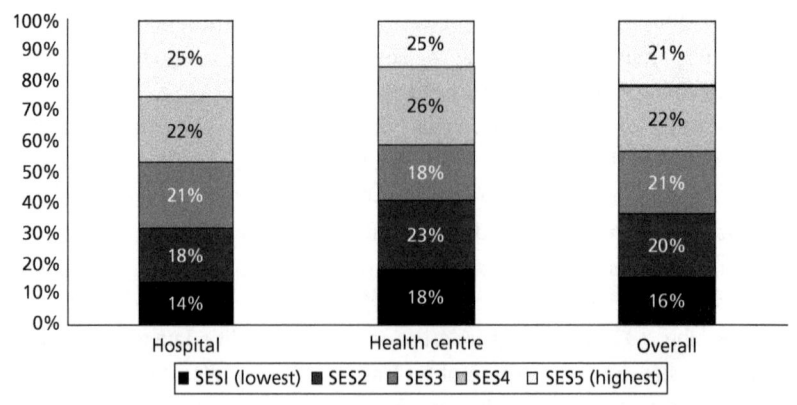

Figure 9.3 Benefit incidence analysis of Malawian government health expenditure. Source: data from Mangham L. (2006). Who benefits from public spending on health care in Malawi? An application of Benefit Incidence Analysis to the Health Sector. *Malawi Medical Journal*, 18(2), 60–65.

estimates the statistical relationship between benefit incidence (for each equity-relevant group) and public health expenditures using the same type of regression framework adopted in the marginal productivity analyses discussed previously.

Few applications of MBIA have been conducted in the health sector, due to the demanding data requirements and complex estimation procedure alluded to previously. However, the limited available evidence does indicate differences between the average and marginal distributions of benefits. Kruse and colleagues find that increasing public healthcare expenditures in Indonesia benefited low income groups more substantially than a traditional average BIA would suggest; the bottom socioeconomic quartile received 23% of the benefits in the traditional BIA versus 25% in the MBIA (Kruse et al., 2012). Conversely the shares of the top quartile group dropped from 24% in the BIA to 21% in the MBIA. Where available, then, MBIA data are preferable to conventional average BIA data as a basis for assessing the marginal distribution of health opportunity costs.

9.4 Further considerations

9.4.1 Insurance and donor-financed healthcare

We have so far seen how empirical studies of health system marginal productivity can provide estimates of health opportunity costs, on the assumption of an exogenous government health budget. This framework may require modification in the case of insurance-based systems in which healthcare is financed from a pool of premiums paid by the insurer's policyholders and in which the budget can be considered endogenous, that is, under the control of the insurer.

In such cases, an insurer can of course choose to fund a new programme by displacing previously funded services, imposing opportunity costs on the recipients of displaced services in the manner we have discussed throughout this chapter. However, the insurer can instead choose to raise premiums to cover the new costs, which would affect the enrolment decisions of a subset of policyholders. If so, some patients may switch to coverage plans with lower coverage and lower premiums, whilst in private systems without mandatory coverage they could disenroll from insurance entirely.

Although quantifying the distribution of opportunity costs in such cases is a challenge that has yet to be addressed, preliminary work has been undertaken into estimating the total health opportunity costs associated with enrolment decisions. The model proposed by Vanness (2017) for a private insurance market uses the elasticity of enrolment with respect to premium price to determine the number of people disenrolling. Data on the age distribution of those disenrolling is combined with the associated morbidity and mortality decrements to estimate the overall health loss. Future research can extend this framework to account for more complicated scenarios, including employer-provided or social insurance.

Another type of health budget hitherto not discussed is that of non-governmental organizations (NGOs) and global health partnerships, which often fund large programmes of care operating in LMICs using overseas development aid money and private philanthropy (McCoy et al., 2009). Although some of these organizations may choose to pool part of their budget with government expenditures in 'basket funds', a significant proportion remains at their discretion. This discretionary budget is analogous to a single-payer health system, in which health opportunity costs can arise whenever a new programme is funded.

Estimating the marginal productivity of NGO expenditure through the statistical methods outlined in section 9.2 is possible, although no studies have done so at the time of writing. However, a number of additional factors are also present that increase the complexity. First, identifying exogenous instrumental variables when estimating an independent effect of donor expenditure on health outcomes in the regression model poses a significant challenge. Second, for multinational donors the health opportunity costs from funding a programme in one country may fall on the population of another country. Third, NGO budgets may face greater constraints in terms of workforce and facilities. Fourth, changes to NGO expenditure may create spillover effects for the government healthcare system. For example, they may create parallel supply chains and service delivery that reduces the effectiveness of existing government-funded activities.

9.4.2 Scenario analysis

The techniques for estimating of the size and distribution of health opportunity costs presented in this chapter can produce approximations of varying degrees of accuracy and bias. Since health opportunity cost estimates are a potentially influential determinant of the distribution of net benefit, scenario analysis around them is recommended to test the robustness of any estimated equity impact.

The selection of alternative scenarios necessitates a qualitative judgment regarding data sources. For example, using social prevalence data to disaggregate health opportunity costs ignores the possibility that lower socioeconomic groups may be less likely to utilize health services, and so may overestimate differences. Differences in utilization, meanwhile, can result from unequal access to treatments or differences between groups in the propensity to change behaviour. Expert judgment can be sought to ascertain whether these factors are likely to be present and what type of scenario analysis would therefore be appropriate. For example, a conservative scenario analysis could re-estimate results using a uniform distribution or a pro-rich distribution of health opportunity costs, depending on the expected degree of bias.

Scenario analysis will also be required in the absence of any estimates on the health opportunity cost distribution. These scenarios should be informed, at the very least, by some theoretical or qualitative understanding of the social

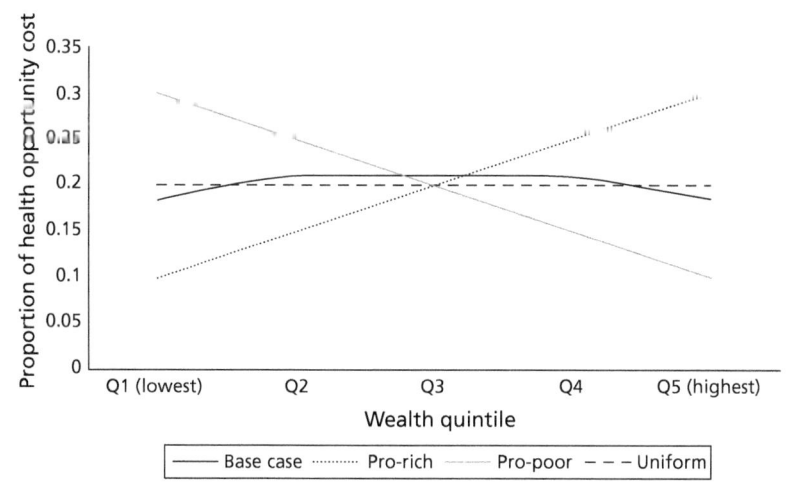

Figure 9.4 Scenario analysis of health opportunity costs over wealth quintile groups. Source: data from Dawkins B., et al. (2018). Distributional cost-effectiveness analysis in low- and middle-income countries: illustrative example of rotavirus vaccination in Ethiopia. *Health Policy and Planning*, 33(3), 456–463.

characteristics of health service users. For example, in an evaluation of rotavirus vaccination in Ethiopia by Dawkins and colleagues, a base case distribution over wealth quintile groups was an inverted U-shape, which was based on assumptions that the richest and poorest groups utilized less public healthcare services. For the poorest group this was due to the presence of user fees, whilst for the highest group it was assumed that private healthcare was more regularly sought. This scenario and the others tested by the authors in their study is shown in Fig 9.4.

9.4.3 Beyond health opportunity costs

Our attention in this chapter has focused exclusively on health opportunity costs. However, the benefits of many health programmes are wider than their impacts on health—they may also improve individual capabilities like independence or freedom, or provide consumption benefits due to greater economic productivity. In order not to bias economic evaluation in favour of new programmes, if additional aspects of benefit are included on the benefit side, they should also be reflected on the opportunity cost side.

The additional aspects of benefit may also be of interest from an equity perspective if their distribution is of social concern. In the case of consumption benefits, for example, this would mean accounting for the forgone economic output and household production due to ill-health suffered by individuals who would otherwise have benefited from the displaced services and identifying how this differs by social characteristics. This represents an important empirical challenge for future research.

9.5 Summary

This chapter provided an overview of health opportunity costs in equity-informative economic evaluation. The size of the health 'loss' imposed by a programme is determined by an exchange rate between costs and health forgone. The exchange rate can be determined from statistical analysis of health expenditure and health outcomes, and a number of these marginal productivity studies have emerged since 2015.

How health opportunity costs are distributed is a more challenging issue. The general guidance provided in this chapter is a summarized in Fig. 9.5. Social distributions of healthcare utilization and disease prevalence or incidence can be used to provide a crude initial benchmark. However, these average

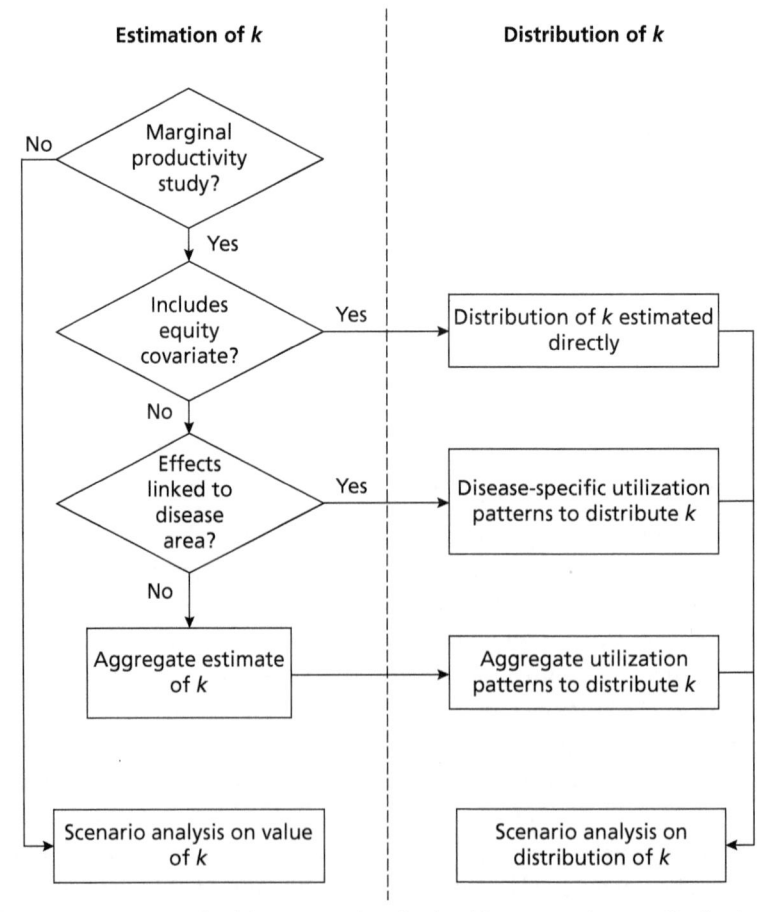

Figure 9.5 Summary of guidance on estimating health opportunity cost distributions using marginal productivity analysis.
Note: Disease prevalence or incidence statistics can be used to disaggregate health effects where healthcare utilization data are unavailable.

distributions may differ from the distribution at the margin, where incremental funding decisions are made. It may be possible to obtain a distribution of marginal health benefit, however, if suitable outputs are available from an original marginal productivity analysis.

Between-country studies of marginal productivity provide total health opportunity cost estimates for a wide range of countries and can be disaggregated using the techniques of benefit incidence analysis. However, given that estimating health opportunity cost distributions is a highly complex empirical problem, extensive scenario and sensitivity analysis should be conducted to validate the robustness of equity-informative economic evaluations. Later chapters will demonstrate how to use these distributions of opportunity cost to evaluate programmes, and the appropriate weighting of opportunity costs alongside benefits is discussed extensively in Chapter 14.

9.6 Further reading

The literature on health opportunity costs is closely linked with the literature on the 'cost-effectiveness threshold'—a benchmark cost-per-HALY ratio against which new treatments are compared. Vallejo-Torres et al. (2016), Culyer (2016), and Thokala et al. (2018) discuss the relationship between thresholds and health opportunity costs, what each represents, and how they can inform decision-making.

A landmark empirical analysis of health opportunity costs for use in economic evaluation is Claxton et al. (2015). Other studies have adapted this approach to different settings, including Vallejo-Torres et al. (2017) for Spain and Edney et al. (2018) for Australia. Ochalek et al. (2018) have produced estimates for 97 countries, including many LMICs, using a cross-country analysis. An analysis of the social distribution of health opportunity cost in England is given by Love-Koh et al. (2020).

References

Angrist J., Imbens G., & Rubin D. (1996). Identification of causal effects using instrumental variables. *Journal of American Statistical Association*, 91, 444–455. https://doi.org/10.1080/01621459.1996.10476902

Appleby J., Devlin N., Parkin D., Buxton M., & Chalkidou K. (2009). Searching for cost effectiveness thresholds in the NHS. *Health Policy (New York)*, 91, 239–245. https://doi.org/10.1016/j.healthpol.2008.12.010

Claxton K., Martin S., Soares M., Rice N., Spackman E., Hinde S., et al. (2015). Methods for the estimation of the National Institute for Health and Care Excellence cost-effectiveness threshold. *Health Technology Assessment (Rockville)*, 19, 1–504. https://doi.org/10.3310/hta19140

Cookson R., Propper C., Asaria M., & Raine R. (2016). Socioeconomic inequalities in health care in England. *Fiscal Studies*, 37, 371–403.

Culyer A. (2016). Cost-effectiveness thresholds in health care: a bookshelf guide to their meaning and use. *Health Economic Policy and Law*, 11, 415–432. https://doi.org/10.1017/s1744133116000049

Dawkins B., Mirelman A., Asaria M., Johansson K., & Cookson R. (2018). Distributional cost-effectiveness analysis in low- and middle-income countries: illustrative example of rotavirus vaccination in Ethiopia. *Health Policy Planning*, 33, 456–463.

Edney L., Haji Ali Afzali H., Cheng T., & Karnon J. (2018). Estimating the reference incremental cost-effectiveness ratio for the Australian health system. *Pharmacoeconomics*, 36, 239–252. https://doi.org/10.1007/s40273-017-0585-2

Gravelle H. & Backhouse M. (1987). International cross-section analysis of the determination of mortality. *Social Science Medicine*, 25, 427–441.

Kruse I., Pradhan M., & Sparrow R. (2012). Marginal benefit incidence of public health spending: evidence from Indonesian sub-national data. *Journal of Health Economics*, 31, 147–157. https://doi.org/10.1016/j.jhealeco.2011.09.003

Lomas J., Martin S., & Claxton K. (2018). *Estimating the Marginal Productivity of the English National Health Service from 2003/4 to 2012/13* (CHE Research Paper No. 158). Centre for Health Economics, York.

Love-Koh J., Cookson R., Claxton K., & Griffin S. (2020). Estimating social variation in the health effects of changes in health care. *Medical Decision Making*, 40(2), 170–182. https://doi.org/10.1177/0272989X20904360

Mangham L. (2006). Who benefits from public spending on health care in Malawi? An application of benefit incidence analysis to the health sector. *Malawi Medical Journal*, 18, 60–65.

Martin S., Rice N., & Smith P. (2008). Does health care spending improve health outcomes? Evidence from English programme budgeting data. *Journal of Health Economics*, 27, 826–842. https://doi.org/10.1016/j.jhealeco.2007.12.002

McCoy D., Chand S., & Sridhar D. (2009). Global health funding: how much, where it comes from and where it goes. *Health Policy Planning*, 24, 407–417. https://doi.org/10.1093/heapol/czp026

McIntyre D. & Ataguba J. (2011). How to do (or not to do) ... a benefit incidence analysis. *Health Policy Planning*, 26, 174–182. https://doi.org/10.1093/heapol/czq031

Ochalek J., Lomas J., & Claxton K. (2015). *Cost per DALY Averted Thresholds for Low- and Middle-Income Countries: Evidence from Cross Country Data* (CHE Research Paper No. 122). Centre for Health Economics, York. https://doi.org/10.1128/MCB.00849-10

Ochalek J., Lomas J., & Claxton K. (2018). Estimating health opportunity costs in low- and middle-income countries: a novel approach and evidence from cross-country data. *British Medical Journal of Global Health*, 3, e000964. https://doi.org/10.1136/bmjgh-2018-000964

Thokala P., Ochalek J., Leech A., & Tong T. (2018). Cost-effectiveness thresholds: the past, the present and the future. *Pharmacoeconomics*, 36, 509–522. https://doi.org/10.1007/s40273-017-0606-1

Vallejo-Torres L., García-Lorenzo B., Castilla I., Valcárcel-Nazco C., García-Pérez L., Linertová R., et al. (2016). On the estimation of the cost-effectiveness threshold: why, what, how? *Value Health*, 19, 558–566. https://doi.org/10.1016/j.jval.2016.02.020

Vallejo-Torres L., García-Lorenzo B., & Serrano-Aguilar P. (2017). Estimating a cost-effectiveness threshold for the Spanish NHS. *Health Economics*, 1–16. https://doi.org/10.1002/hec.3633

Vanness D. (2017). Deriving an opportunity cost-based threshold for CEA in the United States, in: *International Health Economics Association Boston Congress*. pp. 1–11.

Woods B., Revill P., Sculpher M., & Claxton K. (2016). Country-level cost-effectiveness thresholds: initial estimates and the need for further research. *Value Health*, 19, 929–935. https://doi.org/10.1016/j.jval.2016.02.017

Chapter 10

Financial protection

Andrew Mirelman and Richard Cookson

This chapter shows how to use distributional cost-effectiveness analysis (DCEA) to analyse the impacts of healthcare and public health decisions on equity in the distribution of financial protection from out-of-pocket (OOP) healthcare costs. Accompanying the text is a step-by-step spreadsheet training exercise based on a previously published study of a potential tobacco tax increase in Lebanon. Throughout, we point out limitations of existing methods and data sources and discuss areas for future research.

The basic analysing steps for analysing impacts on equity in financial protection are similar to those for analysing equity impacts in health—that is, one needs to analyse the baseline distribution (pre-decision), the effects, the opportunity costs, and the final distribution (post-decision). However, different data and methods are required because at each step one is measuring distributions of financial protection rather than distributions of health.

In line with the existing literature on this topic, we focus on financial protection from private OOP expenditure on healthcare that exposes people to financial hardship and threatens living standards (WHO, 2020). Financial protection in this sense is often an important concern for decision makers responsible for healthcare financing and delivery. This may be especially true in countries where many people lack healthcare insurance, so are exposed to serious financial risks if they fall ill and need costly medical treatment (Smith, 2013).

People also face broader health-related threats to living standards, including insurance premium cost increases due to illness ('pre-existing conditions'), lost earnings due to illness, lost household production due to illness and any consequent costs of long-term care, and consumption costs of acquiring harmful addictions to tobacco, alcohol, illicit drugs, gambling, and other unhealthy behaviours. If decision makers so desire, and with the appropriate data, it is possible both to incorporate these broader financial protection consequences in CEA and to analyse the distribution of such consequences in DCEA.

10.1 Background

Providing financial protection against OOP healthcare expenditure is a fundamental objective of health systems and decision makers are often interested in financial protection outcomes as well as health outcomes (WHO, 2000). The WHO Health Systems Building Blocks framework lists financial protection as a key outcome of a health system and the Sustainable Development Goals (SDGs) list financial protection as a key indicator of Universal Health Coverage (WHO, 2007; United Nations, 2018).

Many low- and middle-income countries (LMICs) lack pre-paid pooling mechanisms that address the financial risks of illness, and direct OOP expenditure remains a major source of healthcare payments (Musgrove, 2004). As a result, large portions of the population are exposed to financial insecurity due to the risk of facing OOP payments that are uncertain in their size and timing and can take up a large proportion of household income (Moreno-Serra et al., 2013). Providing insurance, or other pooled and pre-paid financing for healthcare, can reduce this financial insecurity as well as improve access to beneficial health services and thereby improve health outcomes. Within countries, socially and economically disadvantaged individuals typically face greater risks of financial harm, because they are more likely to fall ill, less likely to have health insurance, and less able to pay a large and unexpected bill for receiving healthcare. Decision makers thus often have important concerns about equity in the distribution of financial protection, as well as about efficiency in terms of increasing average levels of financial protection. There is a growing empirical literature on the financial protection impacts of health interventions in LMICs, and studies that present financial protection effects alongside costs and health effects are known as 'extended cost-effectiveness analysis' (ECEA) studies (Verguet et al., 2016, 2015).

10.2 Baseline financial protection

There are two main ways of measuring financial protection: using a threshold hardship indicator or a continuous measure of welfare loss. The former provides a binary indicator of whether a household's level of OOP healthcare expenditure is considered to impose hardship. The latter provides a continuous measure of the welfare loss to a household from OOP financial risk, based on willingness to pay for insurance (Wagstaff, 2018). In principle, the latter is more informative since it captures the value of protection from different degrees of hardship from different levels of OOP cost, rather than collapsing everything down to a simple binary indicator. However, measures of welfare loss require more data and are harder to explain to decision makers in a simple, intuitive way. Given that threshold hardship measures are more commonly used, we focus on them in this chapter.

When assessing financial hardship, it is not enough to measure the average OOP cost faced by a household, or the probability of facing a given absolute level of OOP cost. The same absolute OOP cost might impose severe hardship on a poor household while making a negligible difference to the material living standards of a wealthy household. To convert a measure of OOP cost into a measure of financial hardship, therefore, an adjustment needs to be made for a household's ability to pay.

There are two main ways of constructing a threshold hardship indicator—the 'catastrophic expenditure' approach and the 'impoverishing expenditure' approach. Both are based on a normative threshold set by the decision maker to indicate whether financial effects from healthcare expenditure are considered disruptive to a household's standard of living. To calculate the incidence of catastrophic expenditure, the proportion of household expenditure taken up by OOP costs is compared to a threshold proportion considered to be catastrophic. By contrast, the incidence of impoverishing expenditure is calculated by estimating household expenditure in two different states—with and without the OOP expenditure—compared with a poverty line (i.e. the absolute level of expenditure considered to represent poverty). The OOP cost is considered 'impoverishing' if it pushes a household across the poverty line.

Threshold hardship indicators can examine the incidence of hardship in terms of the absolute headcount of people incurring it, or in terms of the relative proportion of the general population suffering hardship. Hardship indicators can also examine the intensity of hardship as the average distance between actual and threshold expenditure among those suffering hardship—also knowns as the 'overshoot'. In the catastrophic expenditure approach, intensity is measured as an expenditure proportion—that is, how far households are pushed above the catastrophic expenditure threshold—while in the case of impoverishing expenditure, intensity is measured in terms of absolute expenditure—that is, how far households are pushed below the poverty line.

Both incidence and intensity measures can be broken down by equity-relevant variables (such as income, geography, ethnicity, and gender) to assess distributional impacts. The baseline distribution of financial protection by equity-relevant variables will depend on structural features of the healthcare financing system, as well as wider demographic, social, and economic factors that influence population health and wealth (McPake, 2018). For example, inequalities in financial protection between the rich and the poor are generally smaller in health systems that are publicly financed and free at the point of care (e.g. the UK National Health Service), than in health systems that feature more cost sharing.

10.2.1 Catastrophic health expenditure

A threshold hardship measure assesses OOP expenditure on healthcare as a proportion of the household budget (Wagstaff & Doorslaer, 2003; O'Donnell et al., 2007; Wagstaff et al., 2018a, 2018b). Depending on data availability and reliability, the household budget can be measured in terms of income, consumption, or expenditure. In LMIC settings, for example, the budget is usually measured as non-food expenditure, whereas in HIC settings disposable income is often used (Cylus et al., 2018), as discussed later.

Catastrophic health expenditure is calculated by estimating OOP health expenditure as a fraction of household expenditure, and comparing this to a threshold that is deemed catastrophic (Demery, 2003). OOP health expenditure is usually defined as expenditure directly related to accessing and using healthcare, including travel costs, as well as direct medical expenditure such as fees to healthcare providers. The total OOP expenditure T_i for a household i is deemed catastrophic if it exceeds a threshold proportion z of a household's expenditure x_i (Wagstaff & Doorslaer, 2003). An indicator of whether or not a household incurs catastrophic expenditure, E_i, is defined equal to 1 if $T_i/x_i > z$. The headcount of the number of households incurring catastrophic payments, H_{cata}, is then computed as $\left(\sum_{i=1}^{n} \frac{E_i}{n}\right) \times 100$ where n is the total number of households.

In addition to the incidence or headcount measure of catastrophic expenditure, the intensity of catastrophic expenditure, or overshoot, is the amount by which the OOP expenditure share of the household budget exceeds the catastrophic threshold. Here, the overshoot O_i is defined as $E_i((T_i/x_i) - z)$. Then, the mean positive overshoot MPO is computed as $\sum_{i=1}^{n} O_i / \sum_{i=1}^{n} E_i$. The mean catastrophic payment overshoot O then reflects both the incidence and intensity of catastrophic payment and is defined as $O = H_{cata} \times MPO$.

The estimation of the total household budget (the denominator) when assessing catastrophe needs careful consideration. It is customary to use a measure of disposable income, which typically provides a more accurate picture of real differences in living standards than total expenditure or income. However, the appropriate approach may depend on the setting and data availability. For example, in HICs it is customary to use disposable household income after taxes, transfers, and housing costs are deducted and equivalized for household composition. In LMICs, by contrast, accurate data on disposable income are rarely available so it is customary to use non-food expenditure, which is available from household surveys (O'Donnell et al., 2007).

Another analytical choice when using a threshold measure is to decide what level is considered catastrophic. This is ultimately a matter of normative judgment for the decision maker. There is no universally accepted figure, and analysts should investigate local conventions, discuss this with decision makers, and be transparent. In a 2003 report on health systems performance assessment, for example, the World Health Organization used a threshold of 40% of non-food expenditure, noting that historical estimates at the time typically ranged from 5% to 20% of total household income (Ke Xu et al., 2003). A more recent global study of catastrophic health expenditure used thresholds of 10% and 25% of total household expenditure, which are also used for indicators listed in the Sustainable Development Goals (Wagstaff et al., 2018b). Any doubts about the threshold used to determine catastrophe should be tested through consultation with decision makers and sensitivity analyses should be conducted.

10.2.2 Impoverishing health expenditure

The other threshold measure for assessing financial burden is called impoverishing health expenditure. Here again a social value judgment is involved, and the same issues arise as before for catastrophic health expenditure. The impact on impoverishment is assessed as whether OOP health expenditure shifts a household across a poverty line. To calculate the incidence of households who fall into poverty due to OOP healthcare expenditure, one first needs to estimate the total number of households above the poverty line and then estimate how many of them are impoverished after incurring OOP expenditure.

To calculate this, one begins with an indicator P_i^{pre} for household i defined as 1 if consumption:

$$x_i < z_{pov}^{pre}$$

where z_{pov}^{pre} is the pre-payment threshold of poverty. Next, the pre-payment poverty headcount is calculated as:

$$H_{pov}^{pre} = \sum_{i=1}^{n} P_i^{pre} / n$$

Doing the same for the post-payment period gives H_{pov}^{post} and the impact on the poverty headcount is a simple subtraction:

$$PI^H = H_{pov}^{post} - H_{pov}^{pre}$$

The intensity, or poverty gap may also be of interest. A household's position relative to the poverty line in the pre-payment period is defined as:

$$g_i^{pre} = x_i - z_{pov}^{pre} \quad \text{if } P_i^{pre} = 1$$

The average pre-payment gap G_{pov}^{pre} is then $\sum_{i=1}^{n} g_i^{pre}/n$, and the normalized pre-payment poverty gap is:

$$NG_{pov}^{pre} = G_{pov}^{pre} / z_{pov}^{pre}$$

Doing the same gap calculations for the post-payment period then gives the impact for the poverty gap and normalized poverty gap as:

$$PI^{G} = G_{pov}^{post} - G_{pov}^{pre} \quad \text{and} \quad PI^{NG} = NG_{pov}^{post} - NG_{pov}^{pre}$$

The equations for poverty headcount do not account for those who are already in poverty prior to OOP expenditure, so it is advisable to use poverty gap measures when one is interested in impoverishing health expenditure. The choice of which poverty line to use is often decided within a country or determined using global estimates such as those provided by the World Bank (e.g. at $1.90/day in 2018). There are many definitions of poverty, such as those based on subsistence, basic needs, relative deprivation, wealth, time poverty, and multidimensional poverty (UNECE, 2017). Whichever poverty line is chosen, it should be made transparent, tested in sensitivity analysis, and discussed with relevant decision makers.

10.2.3 Applying weights to the distribution

Catastrophic and impoverishing expenditure measures can be made 'distribution-sensitive' by accounting for different priorities that decision makers may want according to another variable or to different subgroups. For instance, a system of weights could be derived where those at the lower end of the income distribution receive a higher weight than those at the upper end. One approach for doing this is to plot the cumulative share of households exceeding the catastrophic threshold E_i (y-axis) against the cumulative share of the sample ranked by pre-payment income (x-axis). Twice the area between these two curves then gives the concentration index C_E, which is a value between -1 and 1. Then, using the rank of the person in the distribution r_i, the weighting function is defined as: $w_i = 2 \times \dfrac{N+1-r_i}{N}$ for N persons. The weighted headcount formula becomes:

$$W_{cata}^{E} = \sum_{i=1}^{n} w_i \frac{E_i}{n}$$

which means that the weighted headcount can be conveniently calculated using the formula:

$$W_{cata}^{E} = H_{cata}(1 - C_E)$$

A regressive concentration index for catastrophic payments will be negative, so in that case the headcount ratio will be inflated to indicate that the problem is worse for the poor. This will be the other way around for a progressive distribution of catastrophic payments. A similar approach can be used for catastrophic overshoot, denoting the concentration index for overshoot as C_O. A weighted version of catastrophic overshoot is given by the formula:

$$W_{cata}^{O} = O_i(1 - C_O)$$

The concentration index is just one weighting system that can be used. Without using explicit weights, measures already have implicit weighting since they count any person or household that exceeds a given catastrophic or impoverishment threshold equally. Whether and how weights are applied is a matter for discussion with decision makers.

There may be distributional issues implicit in the choice of a catastrophic or impoverishing threshold that is used. For example, the use of a threshold proportional to income to determine catastrophe will be problematic if the poor spend a higher proportion on non-discretionary items (Moreno-Serra et al., 2013). One proposed solution to this issue is to have a variable threshold of catastrophe that is progressive, such that catastrophe for poorer households is lower than it is for richer households (Ataguba, 2012).

10.3 The distribution of financial protection effects

The distribution of financial protection effects can be analysed using the 'Staircase of Inequality' framework introduced in Chapter 8. Fig 10.1 shows the same staircase as the diagram in Chapter 8 except new text (in red) has been added where paying for and receiving health services may influence both the short-term and long-term costs incurred by individuals and households.[1]

---

[1] There may also be interactions between health and financial protection effects at each step. For instance, on the 'receipt' step there may be those who are too poor to afford care who will trade-off an increased health risk for a short-term decrease in financial risk from not having to incur healthcare costs. In the long term, however, the increased health risk may lead to hardship and impoverishment.

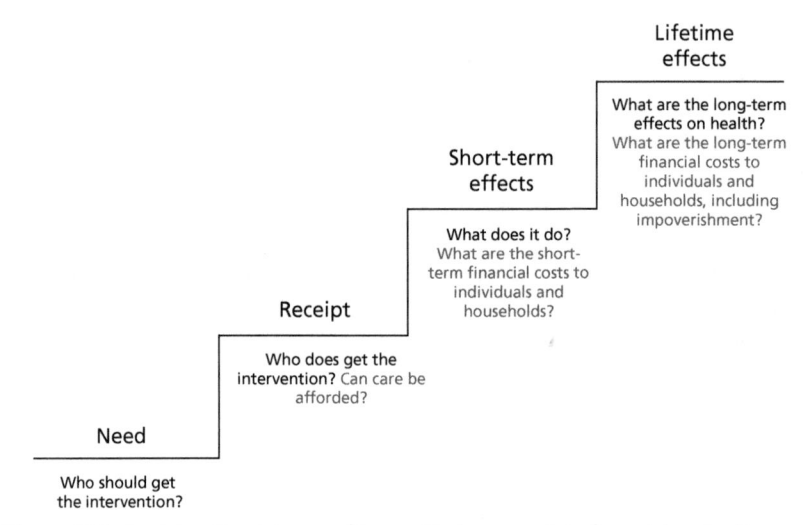

Figure 10.1 Applying the staircase of inequality framework to financial protection effects.

Staircase levels (bottom to top):
- **Need** — Who should get the intervention?
- **Receipt** — Who does get the intervention? Can care be afforded?
- **Short-term effects** — What does it do? What are the short-term financial costs to individuals and households?
- **Lifetime effects** — What are the long-term effects on health? What are the long-term financial costs to individuals and households, including impoverishment?

This staircase can be applied to preventive public health policies as well as healthcare coverage decisions about which treatments to fund at what level of co-payment. We illustrate below, with our example of a tobacco tax in Lebanon. At the need stage, we model baseline differences in the prevalence of smoking, smoking-related illness, health care utilization, and insurance coverage to cover the costs of treatment for smoking-related illness; at the receipt stage we model differences in behavioural responses to the tax (i.e. how far smokers reduce consumption and who quits altogether); and at the short- and long-term effect stages we model differences in effects on smoking-related illness and catastrophic OOP expenditure on treatment for smoking-related illness.

10.4 The distribution of financial protection opportunity costs

Chapter 9 focused on simulating distributions of health opportunity costs. However, there are also opportunity costs related to financial protection. Given a finite health budget, additional expenditure on one set of treatments with financial protection benefits will divert (or 'crowd out') coverage of other treatments with financial protection benefits. For example, if care for diabetes is added to a health benefit package that already includes basic surgery, it is unlikely that the surgical interventions will cease to be covered.

Something must give, and unless the budget is expanded to cover the additional service costs, opportunity costs might take the form of longer waiting times for other treatments and, in rarer cases, involve the removal of less cost-effective interventions from the benefits package of the insurance scheme.

Opportunity costs are a concern because they also may pose financial burdens on households. The net financial protection benefits after allowing for opportunity costs may differ from the gross financial protection benefit. Assessing financial protection opportunity costs, however, is not straightforward and will depend on many factors related to the health system and an individual's ability (or preference) to pay for services privately. Furthermore, those who bear the brunt of the financial protection opportunity costs may differ from those who gain the largest financial protection benefits. For example, since the poor have greater difficulty paying any given level of OOP healthcare cost, they face higher opportunity costs of forgone healthcare coverage in terms of financial protection than the rich (Skinner et al., 2018).

Data for addressing this concern are likely limited; however, one at least needs to consider potential financial protection opportunity costs and how they could vary by equity-relevant subgroups. If appropriate, one should even conduct sensitivity analysis under alternative assumptions. In some cases, financial protection opportunity costs will be less relevant. For example, in the referenced tobacco tax example the costs of the tax fall on household budgets rather than on public healthcare budgets. Even here, however, there may be indirect effects on financial protection from OOP expenditure insofar as households can choose to spend their income on private healthcare insurance.

Given the difficulties of accounting for the opportunity costs of financial protection impacts, it may not be possible to do this in an evidence-informed manner. However, it is important to acknowledge this as a limitation of the analysis and to make an attempt to avoid under- or overcounting of opportunity costs. The difficulties may also be handled as sensitivity analysis to test the robustness of the conclusions of a particular study in response to changing assumptions about the size and incidence of opportunity costs.

10.5 Illustrative example: a tobacco tax in Lebanon

In this section we illustrate how financial protection impacts can be analysed, using the example of a large (50%) tobacco tax increase in Lebanon (Salti et al., 2016). The spreadsheet exercise accompanying this chapter takes you through this analysis in more detail.

The exercise assesses the distributional impacts of the tobacco tax in terms of financial protection. In this case we do not consider opportunity costs of financial protection from healthcare costs, since we assume that the opportunity costs fall entirely on taxation, rather than displacing coverage of other health services from within the healthcare budget. The distribution of opportunity costs is instead examined by looking at the distribution of the cost of taxation to private consumption.

In this exercise, we focus exclusively on the OOP costs from smoking-related healthcare expenditure. However, concerns about the OOP costs of healthcare for smoking-related illnesses may also be accompanied by concerns about the potentially regressive nature of tobacco taxes—poorer groups have the potential to bear a larger financial burden from increased tobacco consumption costs either in absolute or in relative terms. These concerns could be examined through a separate analysis of tax burdens.

Fig 10.2 shows the equity staircase concept applied to the tobacco tax example.

There are income group differences along the entire staircase, including differences in the prevalence of smoking and smoking-related illness, the price elasticity of demand (i.e. how smokers respond to tobacco tax increases in terms of reducing purchasing), the utilization of healthcare services, and the coverage of OOP costs by insurance. In each case, the distributions typically favour richer groups who have lower rates of smoking, utilize care more often, and who pay a lower fraction of healthcare costs OOP due to better insurance coverage. The price elasticity of demand is expected to be higher in the poorer groups who will be more responsive to a price increase of tobacco.

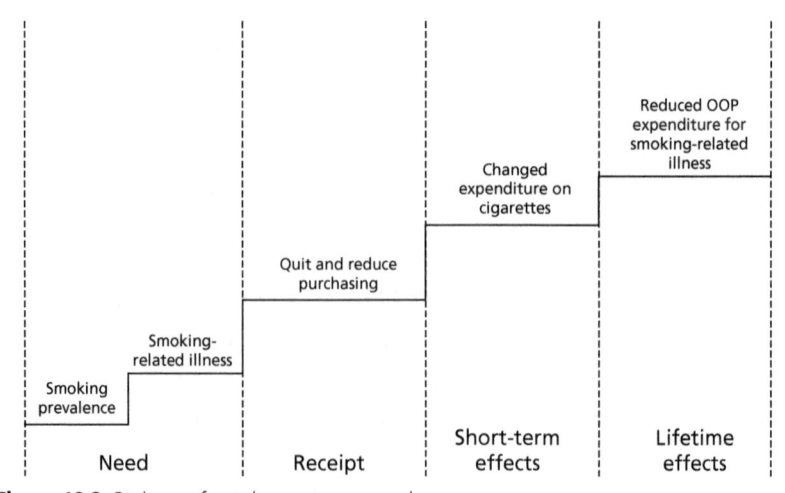

Figure 10.2 Staircase for tobacco tax example.

Fig 10.3 shows the levels of catastrophic health expenditure in the baseline scenario for both smokers and non-smokers. The baseline figures are estimated using country-level data for the prevalence of smoking, healthcare utilization, prevalence of smoking-related illness, and the costs incurred as a proportion of household expenditure. For each piece of information, this information is collected disaggregated by wealth quintile. One sees that smokers have a higher level of catastrophic health expenditure that comes from having higher risks of poor health. The poorer income groups also have higher prevalence of catastrophic health expenditure, and the wealthiest group is seen to have no catastrophic health expenditure at all.

The effect of the policy comes from a 50% increase in the post-tax retail price of cigarettes. This is compared with a scenario of 'no price increase' of tobacco. We simplify by assuming that the tax has a perfect 100% pass-through to consumers. That is, the consumers will see the full 50% price increase, and none of

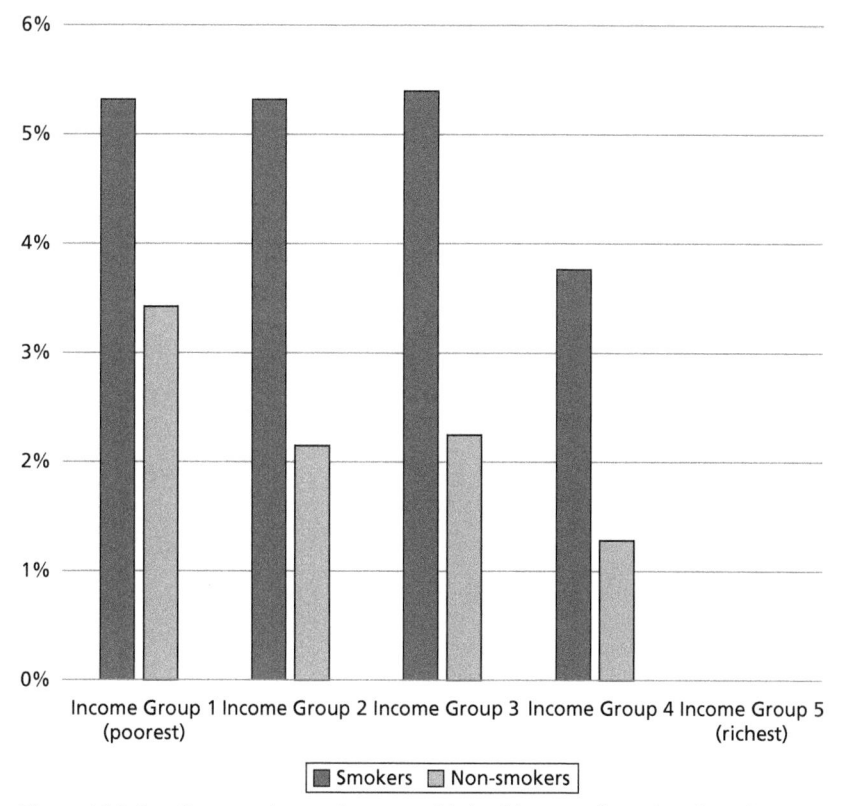

Figure 10.3 Baseline prevalence of catastrophic health expenditure for all smoking-related illness.

the tax will be absorbed by producers. The effect of the tax is modelled using estimated price elasticities of participation, representing the percentage change in the prevalence of smoking in response to a one per cent change in price. Since poorer smokers are expected to be more responsive to changes in price, they have larger (in absolute terms) price elasticities. The elasticity figures are shown in Fig 10.4.

The −0.16 elasticity among the poorest group, for example, means that a 50% increase in price leads to a 50 * −0.16 = 8% decrease in the prevalence of smoking in that group. The threshold for catastrophic healthcare expenditure is assumed to be 10% of equivalent annual household income. We find that the proportion of households incurring catastrophic payment falls from about 20% in the status quo scenario, to about 18% after the tax is imposed. This difference is not distributed evenly. As Fig 10.5 shows, more of this benefit goes to the poorest group. In fact, the richest group sees no financial protection benefit from the tax since they never incur catastrophic healthcare costs in either scenario—the richest group is insured against high-cost forms of care and has sufficient income to cover OOP healthcare costs.

There are many sources of uncertainty in this analysis, and many potentially contestable value judgments, the implications of which can be summarized and explored in various ways as discussed in Chapter 15.

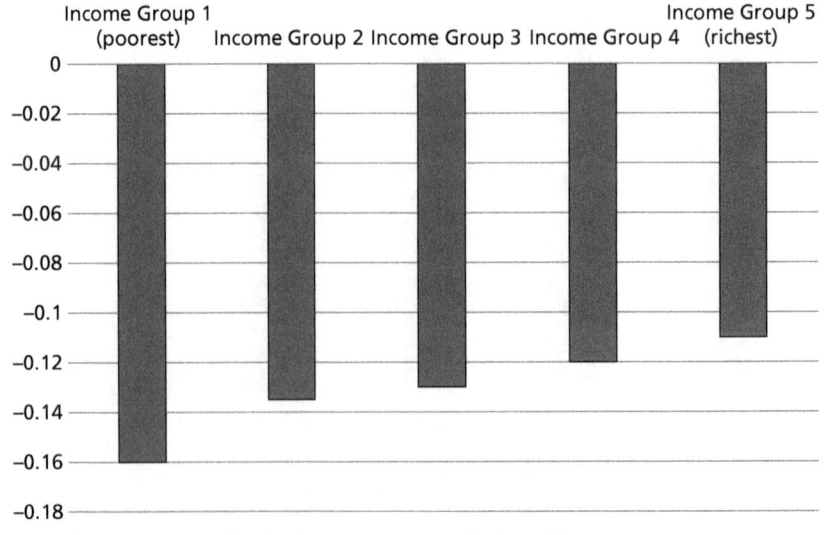

Figure 10.4 Elasticity of participation (or quitting) of smoking.

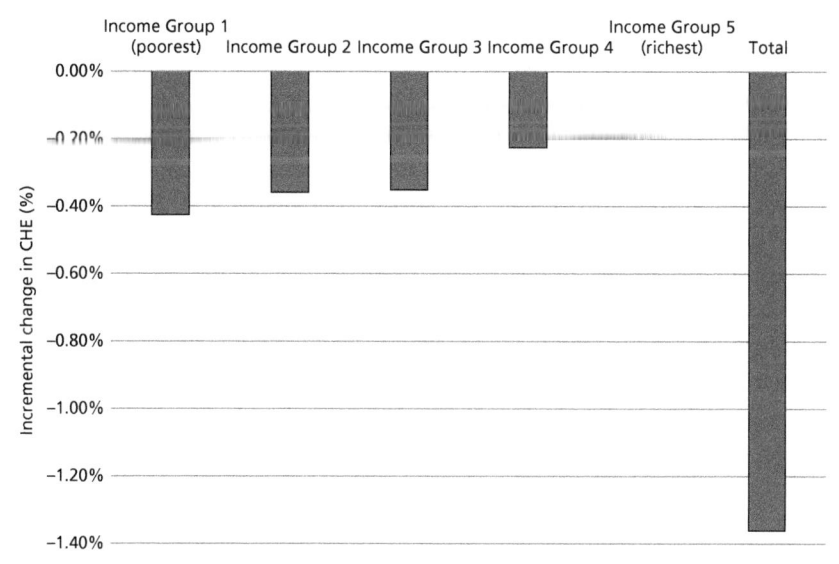

Figure 10.5. Catastrophic health expenditure impact by expenditure quintile group.

10.6 Discussion

Financial protection impacts differ from health impacts and may also have different distributional patterns. Analysing distributional impacts on financial protection is conceptually similar to analysing distributional impacts on health, though requires different outcome measures and data sources. Some of the same basic steps are required, with a need to understand the baseline distribution, the distribution of effects and the distribution of opportunity costs, and the same underpinning decision model can be used as the basis for analysing both health effects and financial protection effects.

The standard approach we have described in this chapter is the use of household budget-related threshold metrics of catastrophic and impoverishing OOP expenditure. These metrics are simple and intuitive and can provide useful information to decision makers. However, they are also subject to a number of limitations (Moreno-Serra et al., 2013; Flores and O'Donnell, 2016). One is that they do not identify lack of financial protection among people who cannot afford to use health services and hence report low or no healthcare spending (Moreno-Serra et al., 2011). More generally, they do not capture the negative impacts of financial insecurity for those who are exposed to risk of catastrophic health expenditure but do not actually incur such expenditure (Pradhan and Prescott, 2002; Saksena et al., 2014). Another limitation is that application of the same proportional budget threshold to all households may tend to overestimate financial hardship among rich households and underestimate hardship among poor households who spend a higher proportion of their income on basic necessities such as food, shelter, and utilities (Cylus et al., 2018). Another limitation is the focus on financial protection from OOP healthcare expenditure only. In some contexts, decision makers may also be interested in protecting people from broader financial risks of illness—for example costs of increased healthcare insurance, productivity costs of illness through loss of earnings and household production, and consumption costs of unhealthy addictions such as tobacco, alcohol, illicit drugs, and gambling (McIntyre et al. 2006). In principle these wider costs can be included in a broader measure of financial protection—the challenge is finding suitable data sources for these broader cost measurements and applying the staircase of inequality to create distributions thereof. A fourth limitation is that measures of the impoverishing impact of OOP healthcare expenditure typically take a descriptive approach rather than conducting causal analysis of the relevant counterfactual—so it is not really known whether OOP expenditure caused households to become poor (Flores et al., 2008).

There are therefore many exciting challenges for future research in this area, to develop new metrics of financial protection, along with more careful methods of causal inference, and apply them in ways that provide more useful information to decision makers (Wagstaff and Eozenou, 2014; Flores and O'Donnell, 2016).

10.7 Further reading

O'Donnell and colleagues provide an important training resource on measuring health equity, which includes useful chapters on measuring catastrophic and impoverishing expenditure with practical tips about household survey data sources and programming code (O'Donnell et al., 2007). Verguet and colleagues provide a useful tutorial on extended cost-effectiveness analysis and how financial protection effects can be integrated into economic evaluations (Verguet et al., 2016). McIntyre and colleagues lay out a framework for understanding financial protection from OOP healthcare expenditure and the impacts it can have on people's lives (McIntyre et al., 2006). Moreno-Serra and colleagues and Cylus and colleagues describe the limitations of standard measures of financial protection (Moreno-Serra et al. 2011: Cylus et al., 2018). Flores and O'Donnell give a more advanced reading on developing new financial protection metrics (Flores and O'Donnell, 2016).

References

Ataguba J. (2012). Reassessing catastrophic health-care payments with a Nigerian case study. *Health Economic Policy and Law, 7*, 309–326. https://doi.org/10.1017/S1744133110000356

Cylus J., Thomson S., & Evetovits T. (2018). Catastrophic health spending in Europe: equity and policy implications of different calculation methods. *Bulletin World Health Organization, 96*, 599–609. https://doi.org/10.2471/BLT.18.209031

Demery L. (2003). Analyzing the incidence of public spending, in: **F. Bourguignon** & **L. Silva** (eds), *The Impact of Economic Policies on Poverty and Income Distribution*. World Bank, Washington, DC. pp. 41–68.

Flores G., Krishnakumar J., O'Donnell O., & Van Doorslaer E. (2008). Coping with health-care costs: implications for the measurement of catastrophic expenditures and poverty. *Health Economics, 17*, 1393–1412. https://doi.org/10.1002/hec.1338

Flores G. & O'Donnell O. (2016). Catastrophic medical expenditure risk. *Journal of Health Economics, 46*, 1–15. https://doi.org/10.1016/J.JHEALECO.2016.01.004

Xu K., Evans D., Kawabata K., Zeramdini R., Klavus J., & Murray C. (2003). Understanding household catastrophic health expenditures: a multi-country analysis, in: **D. Evans** & **C. Murray** (eds), *Health Systems Performance Assessment : Debates, Methods and Empiricism*. World Health Organization, Geneva. pp. 565–572.

McIntyre D., Thiede M., Dahlgren G., & Whitehead M. (2006). What are the economic consequences for households of illness and of paying for health care in low- and middle-income country contexts? *Social Science Medicine, 62*, 858–865. https://doi.org/10.1016/J.SOCSCIMED.2005.07.001

McPake B. (2018). Crunching health expenditure numbers: important but treacherous terrain. *Lancet Global Health, 6*, e124–e125. https://doi.org/10.1016/S2214-109X(18)30007-X

Moreno-Serra R., Millett C., & Smith P. (2011). Towards improved measurement of financial protection in health. *PLoS Medicine, 8*. https://doi.org/10.1371/journal.pmed.1001087

Moreno-Serra R., Thomson S., & Xu, K. (2013). Measuring and comparing financial protection, in: **I. Papanicolas** & **P. Smith** (eds), Health systems performance comparison: an agenda for policy, information and research. Open University Press, Maidenhead, UK. pp. 223–254.

Musgrove P. (2004). Basic Patterns in National Health Expenditure, in: *Health Economics in Development*. World Bank, Washington, DC. pp. 375–400.

O'Donnell O., van Doorslaer E., Wagstaff A., & Lindelow M. (2007). Analyzing *Health Equity Using Household Survey Data*. World Bank, Washington, DC. https://doi.org/10.1596/978-0-8213-6933-3

Pradhan M. & Prescott N. (2002). Social risk management options for medical care in Indonesia. *Health Economics, 11*, 431–446. https://doi.org/10.1002/hec.689

Saksena P., Hsu J., & Evans D. (2014). Financial risk protection and universal health coverage: evidence and measurement challenges. *PLoS Medicine, 11*, e1001701. https://doi.org/10.1371/journal.pmed.1001701

Salti N., Brouwer E., & Verguet S. (2016). The health, financial and distributional consequences of increases in the tobacco excise tax among smokers in Lebanon. *Social Science Medicine*, **170**, 161–169. https://doi.org/10.1016/j.socscimed.2016.10.020

Skinner J., **Chalkidou K.,** & **Jamison D.** (2018). *Valuing Protection against Health-Related Financial Risks* (No. 9). Benefit-Cost Analysis Reference Case Guidance Project, Harvard University, Cambridge, MA.

Smith P. (2013). Incorporating financial protection into decision rules for publicly financed healthcare treatments. *Health Economics*, **22**, 180–193. https://doi.org/10.1002/hec.2774

United Nations Economic Commission for Europe (2017). *Guide on Poverty Measurement, in: Conference on European Statisticians*. United Nations Economic Commission for Europe, Yerevan, Armenia. p. 216.

United Nations (2018). Sustainable Development Goals Knowledge Platform https://sustainabledevelopment.un.org/

Verguet S., Kim J., & Jamison D. (2016). Extended cost-effectiveness analysis for health policy assessment: a tutorial. *Pharmacoeconomics*, **34**, 913–923. https://doi.org/10.1007/s40273-016-0414-z

Verguet S., Laxminarayan R., & Jamison, D. (2015). Universal public finance of tuberculosis treatment in India: an extended cost-effectiveness analysis. *Health Economics*, **24**, 318–332. https://doi.org/10.1002/hec.3019

Wagstaff A. (2018). *Catastrophic Medical Expenditures: Reflections on Three Issues (No. WPS8651), Policy Research Working Paper*. World Bank, Washington, DC.

Wagstaff A. & Doorslaer E. van (2003). Catastrophe and impoverishment in paying for health care: with applications to Vietnam 1993–1998. *Health Economics*, **12**, 921–933. https://doi.org/10.1002/hec.776

Wagstaff A. & Eozenou P. (2014). *CATA meets IMPOV: a Unified Approach to Measuring Financial Protection in Health (No. WPS6861), World Bank Policy Research Working Paper*. World Bank, Washington, DC.

Wagstaff A., Flores G., Hsu J., Smitz M.-F., Chepynoga K., Buisman L., et al. (2018a). Progress on catastrophic health spending in 133 countries: a retrospective observational study. *Lancet Global Health*, **6**, e169–179. https://doi.org/10.1016/S2214-109X(17)30429-1

Wagstaff A., Flores G., Smitz M.-F., Hsu J., Chepynoga K., & Eozenou P. (2018b). Progress on impoverishing health spending in 122 countries: a retrospective observational study. *Lancet Global Health*, **6**, e180–192. https://doi.org/10.1016/S2214-109X(17)30486-2

World Health Organization (2007). *Everybody's Business: Strengthening Health Systems to Improve Health Outcomes. WHO's Framework for Action*. **World Health Organization**, Geneva.

World Health Organization (2000). *The World Health Report 2000*. **World Health Organization**, Geneva.

World Health Organization (2020) Financial Protection https://www.who.int/health_financing/topics/financial-protection/en/

Part III
Evaluating distributions

Chapter 11
Dominance analysis
Owen O'Donnell and Tom Van Ourti

This is the first of four chapters concerned with the evaluation of health distributions. The methods presented in these chapters can help decision makers to evaluate, compare, and order health distributions on the basis of explicit, consistent, and contestable ethical principles, rather than rely on intuitive judgments that are opaque, potentially inconsistent, and not easily challenged. It takes four chapters to cover the material because the exercise is inherently normative and raises complex and controversial ethical issues. Opinions differ about equity: an ethical principle can be supported by some and legitimately disputed by others. There are many principles to choose from. And those that find favour may be incompatible, giving rise to difficult trade-offs. Conducting this normative analysis in a careful, explicit, and systematic manner can help to shed light and remove heat. The methods in these four chapters focus on evaluating distributions of health—a future challenge is evaluating multidimensional distributions of health and non-health outcomes, such as income, as well as information about the distribution of health.

Assume that, as an analyst, you are tasked with advising an equity-sensitive decision maker contemplating whether to implement a treatment or prevention programme. The decision will rest, at least in part, on comparison between the distribution of health that would be generated by the programme with the distribution achieved without it. Following the methods presented in Chapters 7–9, you simulate these distributions. You must now convey the information contained in them to the decision maker. Presenting the raw distributions will be overwhelming if the data are at the individual level or are aggregated to any more than a few groups. Even if the decision maker comprehends the data and realizes, for example, that the choice is between one distribution that offers better average health and another with less inequality, they may find it difficult to make this trade-off. Whatever they decide implies judgment about the value attached to equity relative to efficiency.

In this chapter, we explain how to establish whether one health distribution is dominant; that is, whether it is unambiguously preferred according to general ethical principles. The next three chapters then address the question of how to handle situations where these principles provide insufficient guidance, leaving more than one option on the table and controversial ethical trade-offs to consider.

Initially, in section 11.1, we assume only that the decision maker prefers one person to enjoy better health if no one else suffers worse health and that they prefer less inequality for a given average level of health. These two principles—attributed to Pareto and Pigou-Dalton respectively—are sometimes sufficient to order distributions from the most to least preferred. In section 11.2, we show that when they are not, additional assumptions about where in the distribution the decision maker is most averse to inequality may be enough to determine the preferred order. For example, there may be greater concern about differences in health at the bottom of the distribution between the most severely ill.

In sections 11.1 and 11.2, we assume that all differences in health between individuals are inequitable. The decision maker is presumed to be averse to health inequality whatever its source. They are considering, for example, whether to use available resources to improve the health of the most severely ill a little or to obtain a larger health gain for the less severely ill. Characteristics of patients other than their health are considered irrelevant to the decision. In section 11.3, we relax this assumption and consider how to balance pursuit of efficiency in maximizing total health with the reduction in *unfair* health inequality, which might be considered to be that associated with socioeconomic status (SES). This is the problem tackled in many applications of distributional cost-effectiveness analysis (DCEA). It often involves focusing on differences in health between large population groups distinguished by equity-relevant characteristics, such as area deprivation score, where variation in health across individuals within each group is ignored or considered ethically unobjectionable.

11.1 How far can Pareto and Pigou-Dalton take us?

We use a simple stylized example to illustrate the extent to which various ethical principles can determine an ordering of health distributions from most to least preferred. Table 11.1 shows the distribution of lifetime health-adjusted life years (HALYs) over a population of three individuals under five mutually exclusive policy regimes, corresponding to the implementation of different treatment or prevention programmes. Some other concept of health could be used, so long as the basic unit of health is measured on a cardinal and interpersonally comparable scale suitable for cost-effectiveness analysis and the calculation of

Table 11.1 Stylized HALY distributions generated by hypothetical policies

	Programme					
Individual	A	B	C	D	E	F
1	20	30	20	35	26	26
2	40	45	45	40	46	46
3	60	60	70	72	69	81
Mean	40	45	45	49	47	51
Gini	0.2222	0.1481	0.2469	0.1678	0.2033	0.2397

Note: the Gini index measures relative inequality capturing the size of health ratios, not differences. It is 0 if everyone has the same health and 1 if one person has all the health.

total health benefits. Let programme A represent the baseline. Chapters 6 and 7 explain how to simulate the respective baseline distribution. The distribution consistent with each of the programmes B–F is obtained by starting from the baseline, adding the simulated distribution of health benefits from the programme (Chapter 7) and netting out the simulated distribution of health opportunity costs (Chapter 8). Having simulated these distributions, the task is to help a decision maker choose between them in accordance with their ethical principles.

Consider the choice between A and B. If programme B is implemented, individuals 1 and 2 gain HALYs, while individual 3 is unaffected. Assume that all individuals prefer to have more HALYs and the decision maker respects this. Provided the decision maker also adheres to the *Pareto principle*—if at least one person is made better off and no one is worse-off, then social welfare rises—they prefer to implement B rather than remain with the status quo A.[1]

Programme B raises mean health and reduces health inequality. It is in the win-win quadrant of the equity-efficiency impact plane (Fig 11.1).[2] There is no conflict between equity and efficiency in this case. Even when there is, the

---

[1] More accurately, B is preferred to A by any decision maker with preferences that satisfy *monotonicity*, that is, their welfare improves when the HALYs of any individual increase. The Pareto principle, which is defined with respect to utilities not HALYs or health, is equivalent to monotonicity if each person's utility is an increasing function only of their own HALYs—they do not care about the HALYs of others (Amiel & Cowell, 1994). We will assume this equivalence throughout.

[2] The programme that is Pareto preferred always has a higher y-ordinate in the equity-efficiency impact plane, which shows mean health. However, the policy with a higher y-ordinate is not necessarily Pareto preferred.

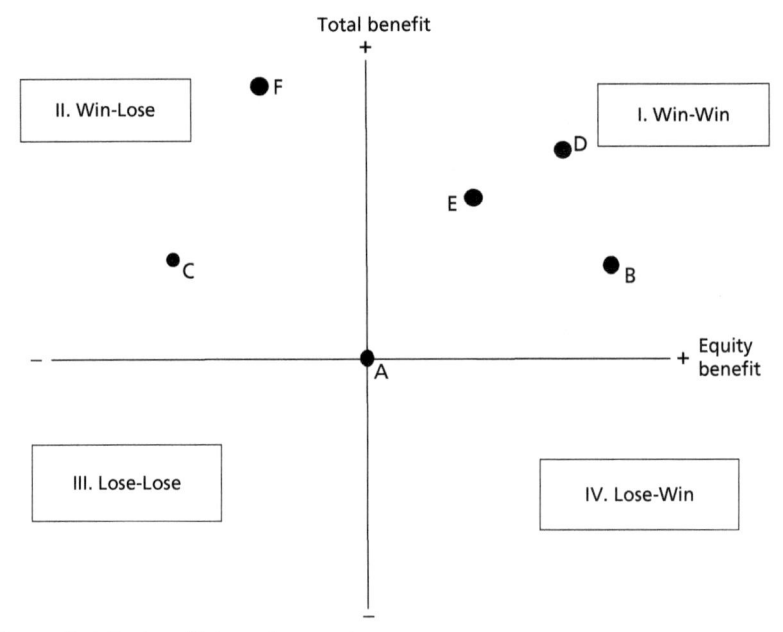

Figure 11.1 Equity-efficiency impact plane.

Pareto principle is sometimes sufficient to identify the preferred policy. For example, compare the status quo A with the health distribution generated by C, which is in the win-lose quadrant (it benefits the two healthier individuals without harming the least healthy and so increases inequality), and yet it is preferred to A by any decision maker who respects this principle.

Not only are B and C Pareto preferred to A, the cumulative distributions generated by these programmes, F_B and F_C, both first order stochastically dominate the distribution obtained with A, F_A.[3] That is, compared with A, programmes B and C result in a smaller (or equal) proportion of individuals with HALYs below any given value. If the decision maker prefers to minimize the fraction of the population with health that falls short of some value (whatever it is), then they will prefer a first order stochastically dominating distribution. In this example, both Pareto and *first order stochastic dominance* (FOSD) establish a

---

[3] $F_x(h) = P(H \leq h)$ is the cumulative distribution under programme x, where H refers to the random variable (HALYs) and h is a particular value of this variable. First order stochastic dominance of F_x over F_z: $F_x \succ_{FSD} F_z$ iff $F_x(h_j) \leq F_z(h_j) \forall h_j = \{h_1, h_2, \ldots, h_k\}$ and $F_x \neq F_z$.

For example, $F_B \succ_{FSD} F_A$ because

$F_B(20) = 0 < F_A(20) = 1/3$, $F_B(40) = 1/3 < F_A(40) = 2/3$ and $F_B(60) = 3/3 = F_A(60) = 3/3$.

preference for B and C over A. This consistency does not always hold. If in addition to Pareto the decision maker's preferences are assumed to respect the *anonymity principle*, then FOSD can be used to order a greater number of distributions than is achieved with the imposition of Pareto alone. Anonymity requires indifference to the identity of who is healthy and who is not, such that social welfare remains constant when health is switched between individuals or groups (Amiel & Cowell, 1994).[4] This is not uncontentious. It would be violated, for example, if the decision maker preferred to avoid ill-health being concentrated among the poor. We will return to such preferences in section 11.3.

There is no FOSD between the distributions generated by B and C.[5] This is because the healthiest individual enjoys better health with C but the unhealthiest is better off with B. Invoking anonymity and switching health between individuals under either intervention does not change this. The Pareto and anonymity principles are not sufficient to identify the preferred distribution. A preference for equality is. The programmes generate the same mean level of health, they are equally cost-effective, but inequality is unambiguously greater under C. The difference in inequality can be a tie breaker in such situations. Provided the decision maker is averse to inequality, they will select B over C.[6]

A preference for equality is represented by the *Pigou-Dalton transfer principle* (Dalton, 1920; Pigou, 1952), which is known as the *principle of health transfers* in the domain of health (Bleichrodt & van Doorslaer, 2006). This maintains that redistribution of a quantity of health from one person to another less healthy person is preferred, provided the positions of those individuals in the health distribution are not reversed.[7] Obviously, health cannot be transferred directly between individuals. However, through the selection of programmes

---

[4] Consider a perturbation of the status quo distribution, such that the HALYs of individuals 2 and 3 are switched while individual 1 continues to get 20 HALYs. Call this A'. This distribution is first order stochastically dominated by the distribution arising from B. Intervention B is not preferred to A' by the Pareto principle because individual 2 is worse-off under B. However, B is preferred to A by Pareto, and by the anonymity principle the decision maker is indifferent to the distributions generated by A and A'. Hence, with both Pareto (strictly, monotonicity) and anonymity, B is preferred to A', which is the same ordering produced by FOSD.

[5] $F_B(20) = 0 < F_C(20) = 1/3$, $F_B(45) = 2/3 = F_C(45) = 2/3$ and $F_B(60) = 3/3 > F_C(60) = 2/3$.

[6] Note that if C resulted in greater mean health than B, then C could be preferred to B despite the former being win-lose and the latter being win-win relative to A in the equity-efficiency impact plane.

[7] *Principle of health transfers (PHT)*: if F_x can be obtained from F_z by a transfer of health $\delta > 0$ from an individual with health $h+k$ to an individual with health h, then $F_x \succ F_z$ if $k > 0$ and $\delta < k/2$, and $F_z \succ F_x$ if $k < 0$, where $\succ$ indicates 'socially preferred to'.

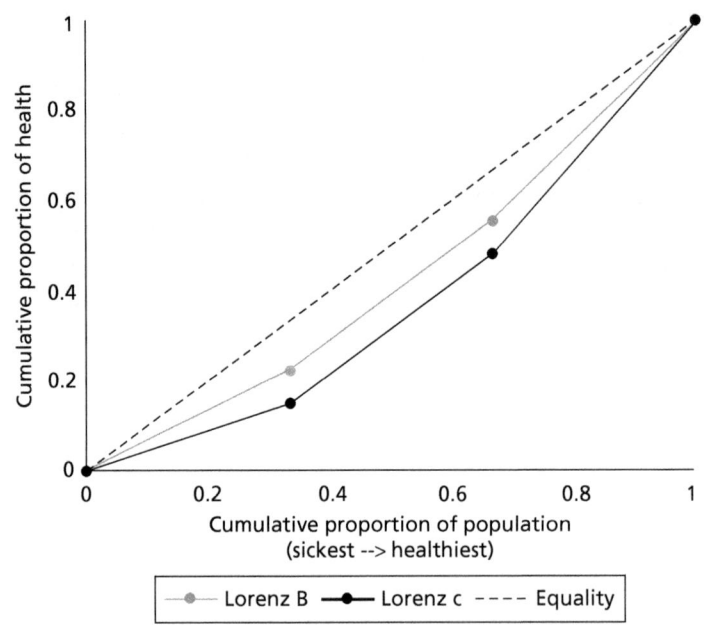

Figure 11.2 Lorenz curves for programmes B and C.

there is indirect shifting of the distribution of health across (groups of) individuals. Allocating resources to the treatment of cancers at the cost of treatment being unavailable to correct mild hearing loss can be thought of as redistributing health from individuals with a slight health problem to those with a major health problem.

The principle of health transfers, if accepted, provides normative justification for using *Lorenz dominance* to order health distributions that have the same mean. The Lorenz curve traces the cumulative proportion of health in a population against the cumulative proportion of the population ranked from the least to the most healthy.[8] Fig 11.2 shows the Lorenz curves for the HALY distributions arising from programmes B and C. The Lorenz curve for B is unambiguously closer to the diagonal, which represents perfect equality; indicating less inequality with B. That is, the distribution F_B Lorenz dominates the distribution F_C.[9] Therefore, given that the two distributions have the same mean,

---

[8] Define $p = F(h)$, $f(x) = F'(x)$ and $\mu = \int x f(x) dx$. The Lorenz curve is:

$$L(p) = \frac{1}{\mu}\int_0^h x f(x) dx, \quad 0 < p < 1 \text{ (Lambert, 1993).}$$

[9] Lorenz dominance (LD): $F_B \succ_{LD} F_C$ iff $L_B(p) \geq L_C(p) \; \forall p \in [0,1]$ and $L_B \neq L_C$.

F_B can be obtained from F_C by a Pigou-Dalton (inequality decreasing) transfer of HALYs: starting from F_C, the transfer of 10 HALYs from individual 3 to the less healthy individual 1 gives F_B. Consequently, B is preferred to C by the principle of health transfers. In general, if two distributions have the same mean and one Lorenz dominates the other, then the dominating distribution is preferred by any decision maker who adheres to that principle. If greater equity is taken as synonymous with reduced relative inequality, then Lorenz dominance provides a useful check on whether a programme lies in the equity-improving side of the equity-efficiency impact plane irrespective of how relative inequality is measured.

If there is no Lorenz dominance but the means differ, then Pareto, anonymity, and the principle of health transfers can sometimes still be sufficient to order distributions. Consider the choice between B and D. There is neither FOSD nor Lorenz dominance between the respective distributions (see Table 11.1 and Fig 11.3a). There is, however, *generalized Lorenz dominance* (GL dominance), and this allows the distributions to be ordered in terms of welfare without invoking any additional ethical principle. The GL curve is simply the Lorenz curve scaled by the mean. It traces the cumulative mean of health against the cumulative proportion of the population ranked from the least to the most healthy. Fig 11.3b shows that the GL curve of distribution F_D is always above or equal to the GL curve of F_B : F_D GL dominates F_B.[10]

If a distribution F_x GL dominates another distribution F_z, then Pigou-Dalton inequality decreasing transfers can always be applied to the latter to produce a distribution that is Pareto dominated by F_x.[11] Provided the decision maker's preferences are also consistent,[12] Pareto, anonymity, and the principle of health transfers are then sufficient to establish a preference for the GL dominating distribution (Shorrocks, 1983). This is a powerful result that allows programmes that appear to have conflicting implications for equity

---

[10] The GL curve is the Lorenz curve scaled by the mean: $GL(p) = \mu L(p)$. Generalized Lorenz Dominance (GLD): $GL_D(p) \geq GL_B(p) \ \forall p \in [0,1]$ and $GL_D \neq GL_B$. This is equivalent to second order stochastic dominance (Shorrocks, 1983).

[11] In the example, starting from F_B, transferring 5 HALYs from individual 2 to individual 1 results in a distribution, say $F_{B'}$, that is preferred to F_B by PHT. Compared with $F_{B'}$, individuals 1 and 2 get the same number of HALYs in F_D, while individual 3 gets more. Hence, F_D is preferred to $F_{B'}$ by Pareto.

[12] More precisely, what is required is that preferences are *transitive*: $F_v \succ F_z$ and $F_x \succ F_v \Rightarrow F_x \succ F_z$.

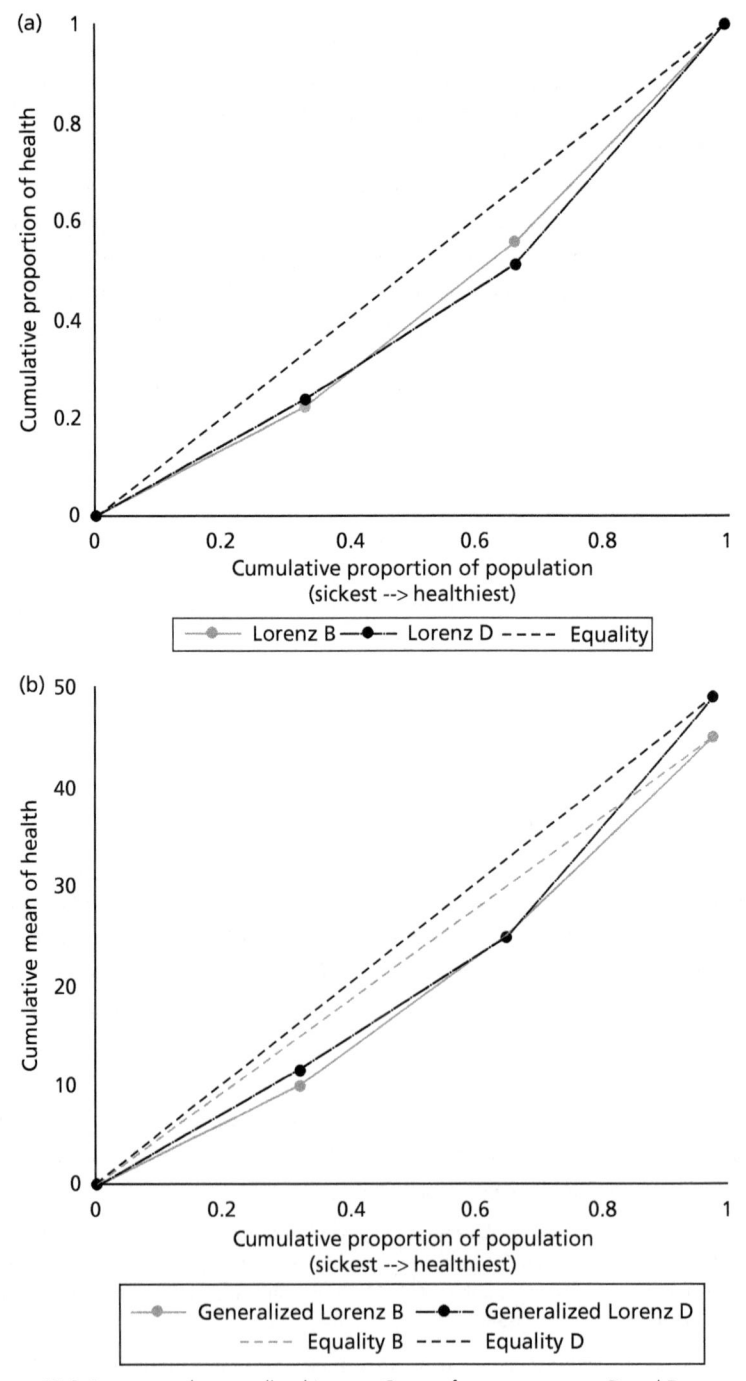

Figure 11.3 Lorenz and generalized Lorenz Curves for programmes B and D.

and efficiency to be compared and ordered on the basis of criteria that may appeal to the ethics of many decision makers. It allows evaluation of northwesterly movements in the equity-efficiency impact plane. Such movements can potentially be preferred (in accordance with the three stated principles) to a movement in the north-easterly direction.[13] However, GL dominance makes it possible to trade-off equity against efficiency only to a limited extent. Implicitly, efficiency is prioritized over equity. For a distribution to be GL dominant, it must have a higher mean. It is impossible for a more equal distribution with a lower mean to be GL dominant. A south-easterly movement in the equity impact plane can therefore never be preferred according to this criterion.

The choice between B and E provides an example in which one distribution (F_E) has both a higher mean and greater inequality. In this case, unlike the comparison between B and D, the least healthy individual is better off with the programme that generates the lower mean (B), while the healthiest individual is better off with the programme that produces the higher mean. As a result, the GL curves cross (Fig 11.4),[14] so there can be no GL dominance. Pareto, anonymity, and the principle of health transfers provide an insufficient ethical basis for choosing between B and E. Some additional normative judgment must be made.

One option is to follow the approach taken in Chapters 12 and 13. That is, to evaluate each distribution by passing it through a particular social welfare function (SWF) to get a quantitative measure of the welfare (and inequality) generated. Comparing the measures between the two programmes identifies which one would be preferred by a decision maker who, in addition to adhering to the general principles of Pareto, anonymity, and health transfers, is assumed to be averse to inequality to some precisely specified degree that is represented by the chosen functional form and parameter values of the SWF. The main disadvantage of this approach is that it requires a quantitative specification of the decision-maker's degree of inequality aversion, rather than just a qualitative commitment to a general ethical principle. Decision makers

---

[13] Because B does not Lorenz dominate D, inequality is not unambiguously lower in B; it is not lower using any measure consistent with PHT. But the area between the Lorenz curve and the line of equality (Fig 10.3a) appears smaller for B indicating less relative inequality, which is confirmed by a smaller Gini index (Table 10.1). Hence, we position D to the left of B in Fig. 10.1. An intervention positioned even further to the left entering the win-lose quadrant (relative to A) could also be preferred to B.

[14] However, B Lorenz dominates E. There is greater relative inequality with E by any measure consistent with PHT.

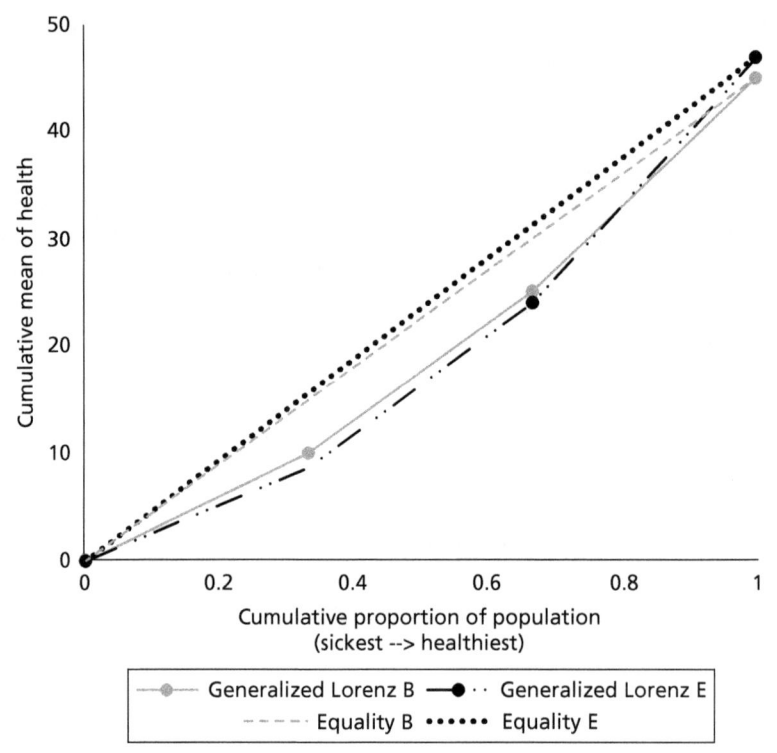

Figure 11.4 Generalized Lorenz curves for interventions B and E.

may not have precisely defined views about health inequality aversion and may be reluctant to be pinned down to a specific numerical value that might set an awkward precedent for future decisions. Eliciting the intensity of the decision maker's distaste for inequality may be difficult and, in the absence of GL dominance, the welfare ordering of programmes is not invariant to the value assumed. Nonetheless, sensitivity analysis may be able to establish that the ordering only changes at extreme values of inequality aversion that the decision maker is able to reject.

11.2 Higher order GL dominance

An alternative way forward is to invoke ethical principles that are more restrictive than the principle of health transfers but are still reasonably general, stopping short of imposing a particular form of the SWF and a precise value for the degree of inequality aversion. The approach we describe, which is proposed by Aaberge et al. (2019), can provide a welfare ordering of distributions

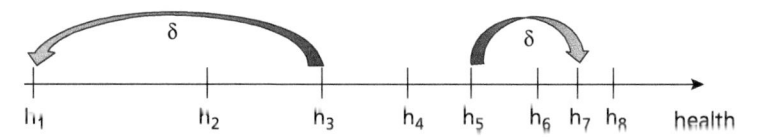

Figure 11.5 Illustration of downside positional transfer sensitivity.
Note: h_8 is the healthiest individual or group.

consistent with decision-maker preferences that are representable by the family of rank-dependent SWFs (Weymark, 1981; Yaari, 1987, 1988).[15] The general form of the SWF must be restricted to capture broad attitudes to inequality, but attention need not be limited to a particular functional form and a specific parameterization of it.

The principle of *downside positional transfer sensitivity* (DPTS) (Mehran, 1976; Zoli, 1999) represents the view that inequalities in health matter more when they are experienced at the bottom of the distribution than the top—in the same way that income inequality between the poor and the desperately poor may arouse greater concern than income inequality between rich and super rich. According to DPTS, a transfer of health from one person to a less healthy person reduces inequality to a greater extent, and so raises social welfare more, when the transfer occurs further down the distribution.[16] Fig 11.5 (Makdissi & Yazbeck, 2014) illustrates a transfer of an amount δ of health from the third least healthy person in the distribution, which is assumed to be left-skewed, to the least healthy person. Consistent with the principle of health transfers, this reduces health inequality and raises welfare. The same transfer is made from the fifth least healthy person to the seventh least healthy person. By the same principle, this will increase inequality and reduce welfare. Note that both transfers occur between individuals who are two ranks apart in the distribution. According to DPTS, the combination of these two transfers between individuals separated by the same number of ranks will reduce inequality and raise welfare. The welfare increasing transfer that occurs towards the bottom of the distribution dominates the welfare depleting transfer that occurs further up the distribution.

---

[15] A rank-dependent SWF delivers a weighted average of health with weights that decrease as rank rises from the sickest to the healthiest person.

[16] *Downside positional transfer sensitivity*: if an amount of health (δ) is transferred up the distribution from a person at rank p_k to a healthier person at rank $p_{k+\gamma}$ $(\gamma > 0)$, the same amount of health is transferred down the distribution from a person at $p_{j+\gamma}$ to a sicker person at p_j, and $p_k > p_j$, then welfare rises (inequality falls).

This principle may be ethically appealing to decision makers. Its usefulness derives from its close connection with *second order generalized Lorenz dominance* (SOGLD). GL dominance is established through comparison of cumulative means. To establish SOGLD, one compares *weighted* cumulative means using weights that decrease linearly as rank rises from the least to most healthy (Aaberge et al., 2019).[17] This weighting scheme implies greater sensitivity to inequality at the bottom of the distribution, which gives the connection with DPTS.[18] If some distribution, F_x, GL dominates another, F_z, at the second order, then F_x will be preferred to F_z by any decision maker with rank-dependent preferences who adheres to DPTS (Aaberge et al., 2019). This provides normative justification for ordering distributions using SOGLD.

The left panel of Table 11.2 shows y-ordinates of the GL curve for the distributions generated by programmes B and E (and for another programme F that we will come to shortly). Comparison confirms Fig 11.4: the GL curves for B and E cross. The middle panel shows, for each distribution, the y-ordinates (height) of the second order GL curve, which is simply the cumulative mean of the GL curve. Since the height of the respective curve for B lies everywhere above that for E, the distribution generated by B GL dominates at the second order.[19] Hence, B is preferred by any decision maker who accepts DPTS.

Now consider programme F, which compared with E results in the same number of HALYs for the two least healthy individuals but generates many more HALYs for the healthiest individual (Table 11.1). Comparing B with F, there is no GL dominance at either the first or the second order (Table 11.2). Pareto, anonymity, the

---

[17] A distribution F_w second order GL dominates another distribution F_z if $GL_x^2(p) \geq GL_z^2(p)$ $\forall p \in [0,1]$ and $GL_x^2 \neq GL_z^2$, where $GL^2(p) = \int_0^p GL(t)dt = \int_0^p (p-t)F^{-1}(t)dt$. The healthiest individual up to the quantile (p) being evaluated gets the least weight $(p-t)$ and the difference in weights given to any two individuals is equal to the difference in their fractional ranks. Second order GL dominance is equivalent to third order inverse stochastic dominance (Aaberge et al., 2019).

[18] This weighting scheme does not imply imposition of a specific value for the degree of inequality aversion. There is no quantification of welfare. Rank-dependence and DPTS are the only restrictions on preferences that must be made to infer the welfare ordering of distributions from a finding of second order GL dominance. This is analogous to PHT being sufficient (given equal means) to infer a welfare ordering from first order GL dominance.

[19] We do not consider statistical inference since the distributions that are evaluated and compared are presumed to be simulated. If the methods presented here were used with estimated distributions, then inference would be needed. See Aaberge et al. (2019) for the appropriate tests.

Table 11.2 Orders of generalized Lorenz curves for three distributions

	First order			Second order			Third order		
Individual	B	E	F	B	E	F	B	E	F
1	10	8.67	8.67	3.33	2.89	2.89	1.11	0.96	0.96
2	25	24	24	11.67	10.89	10.89	5.00	4.59	4.59
3	45	47	51	26.67	26.56	27.89	13.89	13.44	13.89

Note: the table shows the y-ordinates (height) of orders of GL curves.

principle of health transfers, and DPTS are not sufficient to establish which of B and F is preferred. The greater sensitivity to inequality at the bottom of the distribution that is implied by DPTS is not sufficient for the advantage B gives to the least healthy individuals to outweigh the very strong advantage F gives to the healthiest individual. Some ethical judgment beyond DPTS must be invoked to justify a choice between the programmes.

If the decision maker is even more sensitive to inequality at the bottom of the distribution than is implied by DPTS, then this can be taken into account through imposition of the principle of second order DPTS. This states that a *pair* of transfers that reduce inequality at the bottom of the distribution outweigh a pair of transfers of equal magnitude that raise inequality further up the distribution.[20] Fig 11.6 illustrates a transfer δ from the second least healthy to the least healthy person and an equally sized transfer from the third to the fourth least healthy person (Makdissi & Yazbeck, 2014). Since the difference in ranks of the donor and recipient is the same for each transfer, the net effect is a fall in inequality and a rise in welfare by the principle of DPTS. By the same principle, the two transfers that occur further up the distribution raise inequality and lower welfare. According to second order DPTS, the net effect of the two pairs of transfers is a fall in inequality and a rise in welfare. There is even greater concern about inequality at the bottom compared with the top than is the case with DPTS.

---

[20] *Second order downside positional transfer sensitivity*:

1. If an amount of health (δ) is transferred up the distribution from a person at rank p_k to a healthier person at rank $p_{k+\gamma}$ ($\gamma > 0$), the same amount of health is transferred down the distribution from a person at $p_{j+\gamma}$ to a sicker person at p_j, and $p_k > p_j$, and
2. An amount δ is transferred up the distribution from a person at rank p_m to a healthier person at rank $p_{m+\gamma}$, the same amount of health is transferred down the distribution from a person at $p_{n+\gamma}$ to a sicker person at p_n, with $p_n > p_m$ and $p_m > p_k$, then welfare rises (inequality falls).

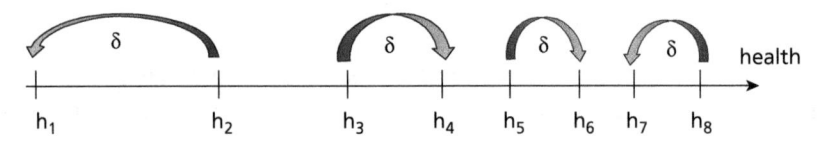

Figure 11.6 Illustration of second order downside positional transfer sensitivity.
Note: h_8 is the healthiest individual or group.

The usefulness of this principle again derives from its connection with GL dominance. If a distribution F_x GL dominates another F_z at the third order, then F_x is preferred to F_z by any decision maker with rank-dependent preferences who adheres to second order DPTS (Aaberge et al., 2019). GL dominance at the third order is again established by comparing weighted cumulative means of health, but now with weights that decrease at a diminishing rate as rank rises from the least to most healthy.[21] This non-linearity ensures that even greater weight is placed on the bottom of the distribution compared with SOGLD.

The right panel of Table 11.2 shows, for each distribution, the y-ordinates of the third order GL curve, which is simply the cumulative mean of the respective second order curve. Since the height of the curve for B is always greater or equal to that for F, the distribution generated by intervention B is GL dominant at the third order. Hence, B is preferred by any decision maker with preferences consistent with rank-dependence and second order DPTS.

GL dominance at higher orders continues to be equivalent to the preference ordering of a decision maker who adheres to respectively higher orders of DPTS (and rank dependence). Hence, the procedure can continue until dominance at some order is found. The decision maker must then be encouraged to consider whether the ethics represented by DPTS at the respective order are acceptable. Successively higher orders of DPTS place increasing relative weight on inequality to the disadvantage of the least healthy individuals. At the extreme, we arrive at a Rawlsian scenario in which weight is placed only on the least healthy person.

11.3 Unfair health inequality

11.3.1 Two approaches

The transfer principles discussed in the previous sections capture aversion to all health inequality irrespective of how it is generated and who suffers

---

[21] A distribution F_x GL dominates at order i another distribution F_z if: $GL_x^i(p) \geq GL_z^i(p)$ $\forall p \in [0,1]$ and $GL_x^i \neq GL_z^i$, where $GL^i(p) = \int_0^p GL^{i-1}(t)dt$ $= \frac{1}{(i-1)!}\int_0^p (p-t)^{i-1} F^{-1}(t)dt, i = 2,3,...$

the health disadvantage. This is founded on the anonymity principle that health is the only characteristic relevant to prioritizing treatment. Equity informative health economic evaluation based on this principle therefore addresses socioeconomic differences in health, as well as racial, gender, geographic, and other socially dimensioned inequalities in health, only indirectly.

Relaxing the anonymity principle requires taking a position on what sources of health inequality are considered unfair, and which are accepted as fair (see Chapters 2–4). Presume the dimension(s) of health inequality that offend the decision maker's ethics have already been determined. How can you now identify the intervention that generates the preferred health distribution consistent with this specific inequality aversion?

One approach is to simulate, for each programme, the distribution of health that is considered by the decision maker to be unfair. This multivariate approach results in adjusted univariate distributions of health. The technical apparatus set out in sections 11.1–11.2 can then be used to evaluate, compare, and order these distributions. This would involve ranking individuals by predictions of lifetime health that are purged of any variation generated by 'equity-irrelevant' variables. Application of this approach involves crossing the philosophical minefield surrounding the definition of unfair health inequality (charted in Chapters 2 and 4). There is a risk that value judgments imposed in the estimation and simulation exercise are not transparent and, therefore, not subject to full scrutiny. Further, application requires rising to the not insubstantial empirical challenge of identifying variation in health attributable to determinants that are considered to be unfair sources of health inequality.[22]

An alternative, which we describe in this section, is to make a bivariate extension of the rank-dependent approach by ranking individuals according to a single equity-relevant variable, such as an indicator of SES, to which health should not be related if the distribution of health is to be considered fair. Equity principles are then explicitly defined in terms of aversion to health transfers between individuals ranked by that equity-relevant variable, rather than by health. This imposes strong value judgments: all health differences along the distribution of the chosen equity-relevant variable are considered unfair and

---

[22] Besides standard statistical problems of endogeneity, reverse causality, and measurement error, if 'fair' and 'unfair' determinants of health interact, then they cannot be separated in a way that is consistent with all ethical principles that many would find appealing (Fleurbaey & Schokkaert, 2009). Further, one must decide whether health differences that happen by chance, which are included in the error of any statistical model used to purge the health distribution of fair inequalities, are to be counted as fair or unfair.

any other sources of unfair health inequality are ignored. The approach cannot accommodate preferences of a decision maker who is averse to differences in health between individuals who are distinguished by more than one equity-relevant variable.[23]

The approach is feasible provided the equity-relevant variable is at least ordinal, such that individuals can be ranked (and possibly grouped) by it. If it is perfectly correlated with health, so ranking by it corresponds to ranking by health, then there is no difference from the univariate approach of sections 11.1–11.2. This is a plausible scenario in many applications of DCEA that use grouped data. For example, mean health will often rise monotonically from lower to higher ranked socioeconomic groups. However, if it is possible to work with simulations of lifetime health based on additional equity-relevant variables, then perfect correlation of health and SES is not plausible: many poor individuals experience better health than many rich individuals.

In what follows, we will use 'income' as shorthand for 'equity-relevant variable', and we will assume that either the marginal distribution of this variable is exogenous—that is, invariant across the programmes under evaluation—or that the decision maker is indifferent to this distribution.

11.3.2 Pareto and Pigou-Dalton again

If a programme reduces health at least at one point in the income distribution, then the Pareto principle is insufficient to establish whether the programme is welfare improving. It may still be possible to obtain a welfare ordering by relying on the *principle of income-related health transfers* (PIRHT), which states that a transfer of health from one person to a poorer person, provided it has no impact on the average level of health, reduces income-related health inequality and raises social welfare from the perspective of a decision maker who is averse to such inequality (Bleichrodt & van Doorslaer, 2006).[24]

---

[23] It would be possible to rank by a composite index that is a weighted combination of all variables considered to be equity-relevant. Construction of such an index would require the imposition of value judgments (reflected in the weights) about the relative extent to which variables are considered equity relevant. Use of the index would require representation of ethical principles through the desirability of transfers between individuals ranked by the composite measure.

[24] *Principle of income-related health transfers* (PIRHT): let $F_{H,Y}^{j}$ be the joint health-income distribution generated by programme $j = x, z$. If $F_{H,Y}^{x}$ can be obtained from $F_{H,Y}^{z}$ by a transfer of health $\delta > 0$ from an individual with income $y + k$ to an individual with income y, then $F_{H,L}^{x} \succ F_{H,Y}^{z}$ if $k>0$, and $F_{H,L}^{z} \succ F_{H,Y}^{x}$ if $k<0$.

Reconsider the policy choices presented in Table 11.1, but now in light of information that individuals 1, 2, and 3 are the middle-income, poorest, and richest respectively. Starting from C, a transfer of ten HALYs from the richest to the middle-income person gives the distribution resulting from B and would be approved by any decision maker who accepts the PIRHT. So, B is preferred to C by that principle. In combination with Pareto, PIRHT is sometimes sufficient to order distributions with unequal means. For example, starting from C, a transfer of one HALY from the richest to the poorest, which is welfare improving by PIRHT, plus a gain of six HALYs to the middle-income individual, which is welfare improving by Pareto, gives the distribution generated by E. So, E is preferred to C.

More generally, you can determine whether Pareto and PIRHT are sufficient to order distributions by checking for *generalized concentration curve dominance*. The generalized concentration curve (GCC) is analogous to the GL curve, with the one difference that individuals are ranked along the *x*-axis by income (from poorest to richest), rather than health. So, GCC traces the cumulative mean of health along quantiles of the distribution of income.[25] If one GCC is always above or equal to another, then it dominates.[26] For example, in Fig 11.7 the distribution produced by E GCC dominates that arising from C. The dominating distribution is preferred by any decision maker who respects Pareto, PIRHT, and a partial anonymity principle that income is the only characteristic relevant to determining the social welfare attached to a person's health.[27]

11.3.3 Higher order generalized concentration curve dominance

If GCCs intersect, you can invoke an analogous DPTS principle as an ethical basis for using dominance at some higher order to identify the socially preferred distribution. According to this principle, a difference in health between a poor and a very poor person is of greater concern than the same difference

---

[25] The generalized concentration curve is defined, $GC(q) = \int_0^q h(u)du$, where $h(q) = E\left[H|Y = G^{-1}(q)\right]$ is the conditional expectation of health at income quantile $q = G(y)$ of the marginal distribution of income $G(y)$.

[26] Generalized concentration curve dominance: $GC_x(q) \geq GC_z(q)\ \forall q \in [0,1]$ and $GC_x \neq GC_z$.

[27] Income-related relative health inequality can be assessed using the concentration curve, $C(q) = GC(q)/\mu$. Concentration curve dominance is defined analogously to generalized concentration curve dominance.

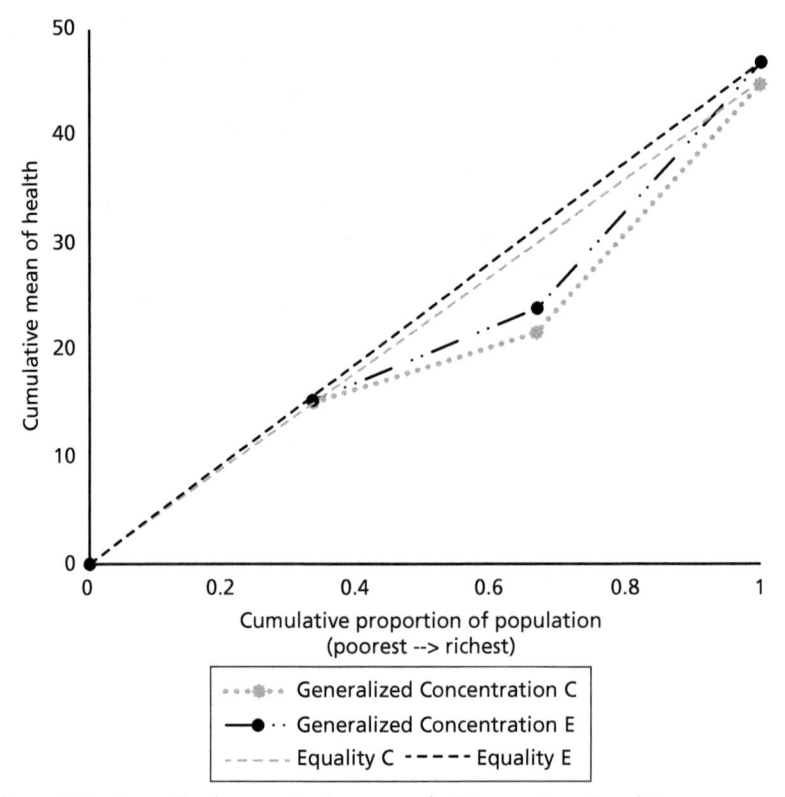

Figure 11.7 Generalized concentration curves for interventions C and E.

between a merely rich and a very rich person.[28] A decision maker with rank-dependent preferences consistent with this principle will prefer a distribution that GCC dominates at the second order (defined as the third order by Makdissi and Yazbeck (2014)).[29] As in the univariate case, you can proceed to test dominance at higher orders on the basis of successively higher order DPTS principles

---

[28] Bivariate DPTS: if an amount of health is transferred up the income distribution from an individual at income rank q_k to a richer person at rank $q_{k+\gamma}$ $(\gamma > 0)$, the same amount of health is transferred down the income distribution from an individual at $q_{j+\gamma}$ to a poorer person at q_j, and $q_k > q_j$, then income-related health inequality falls and welfare rises (Makdissi & Yazbeck, 2014).

[29] Aaberge (2009) labels the cumulative proportion of a variable ranked by itself, the first order Lorenz curve, while Makdissi and Mussard (2008) label the cumulative proportion of a variable ranked by another variable, the second order concentration curve. To maintain consistency within this chapter, we adopt Aaberge's labelling of orders. You should

that put increasing relative weight on inequality to the disadvantage of the poorest individuals.[30]

11.3.4 Group level analysis

Simulations often give mean health across individuals grouped by an equity-relevant variable, which we continue to label 'income'. With this information, you could weight the health of each group by its population size and proceed as in the previous two subsections. Provided each group is homogeneous in terms of income, then this group level analysis is founded on the same ethical principles cited in the previous two subsections. It is not necessary to assume homogeneity of health within each group because the decision maker is assumed to be averse only to health inequality associated with income. Within-group health inequality is of no concern. Of course, this is a strong assumption. On top of concern about income-poor individuals experiencing worse health, for example, there may be a preference to direct resources to the most severely ill among the poor.[31]

If there is heterogeneity in income within each group, and the simulation cannot capture this, then the transfer principles must be made stronger. You would need to assume that when health is transferred from a group that is richer, on average, to a group that is poorer, inequality falls and welfare rises. In the presence of within-group heterogeneity in both income and health that is not modelled, such a transfer could, in theory, correspond to taking health from a poorer and less healthy person and giving it to a richer and healthier person. Most decision makers would probably not judge this to reduce inequality. It has to be assumed that the decision maker is prepared to accept that allocating resources on the basis of simulated group averages will result in infringement of equity preferences specified over individual outcomes. The extent of such

---

keep this in mind when consulting papers on concentration curve dominance (Makdissi & Mussard, 2008; Makdissi & Yazbeck, 2014; Khaled et al., 2018).

[30] Define the GCC at order σ, $GC^\sigma(q) = \int_0^q GC^{\sigma-1}(u)du$, $\sigma \in [2,3,...]$. The second order curve (GC^2) is simply the cumulative mean of the GCC. Define generalized σ-concentration curve dominance of distribution w over z: $GC_w^\sigma(q) \geq GC_z^\sigma(q)$ $\forall q \in [0,1]$ and $GC_w^\sigma \neq GC_z^\sigma$. If this holds, then w generates greater welfare than z using any rank-dependent SWF that satisfies restrictions consistent with bivariate DPTS at order σ-1 (Makdissi & Yazbeck, 2014).

[31] It is possible to allow for two-dimensional equity preferences within the rank-dependent approach by defining weights that are a function of rank in the SES distribution and using these to weight a concave function of health that captures aversion to pure health inequality. See Bleichrodt et al. (2005) and Makdissi and Yazbeck (2016).

infringement can be limited by disaggregating groups and so reducing the heterogeneity within them. The appropriate degree of disaggregation is not exclusively a matter of data availability in terms of how many risk factors can be used to predict lifetime health outcomes. There are also social value judgments to be made by the decision maker about which risk factors count as 'unfair' or 'equity-relevant' sources of individual level variation. If a risk factor is not considered an unfair source of variation then the appropriate approach is to remove the influence of this risk factor through standardization. For example, health outcomes are often standardized for age, reflecting a value judgment that age is not an unfair source of variation in health.

11.4 Conclusion

We have presented an approach to making equity-sensitive choices between programmes that uses dominance analysis to order the resulting heath distributions on the basis of minimally constraining, abstract ethical principles. The recommended procedure is summarized in Figs 11.8 and 11.9. These figures represent the case in which the decision maker is potentially averse to all health inequality. Modifications required for application to unfair health inequality are given in endnotes.

First, consider whether the decision-making authority accepts the Pareto principle. If not, this and the following two chapters do not provide tools that can usefully inform the decision. But in this case, even standard health economic evaluation may not be considered unhelpful. If Pareto is thought to be acceptable, then consider whether the same holds for anonymity. Is health the only characteristic relevant to the allocation of healthcare resources?[32] If the answer is negative because the decision maker is concerned about health inequality in relation to some equity-relevant variable, such as SES, then the bivariate extension to dominance analysis, based on GCC and bivariate transfer principles discussed in section 11.3, may be used to order distributions. Alternatively, one may use the multivariate approach based on applying dominance analysis to an adjusted univariate distribution of health that only includes variation predicted by the equity-relevant variables. This is the approach used in exercise 11, which examines an adjusted distribution of lifetime

---

[32] If attention were restricted to unfair health inequality, then the question would be whether health predicted on the basis of unfair determinants is the only characteristic considered relevant. If the bivariate approach of sections 11.3.2–11.3.3 were followed, then you would ask whether there is one unfair determinant that is considered to be the only relevant characteristic.

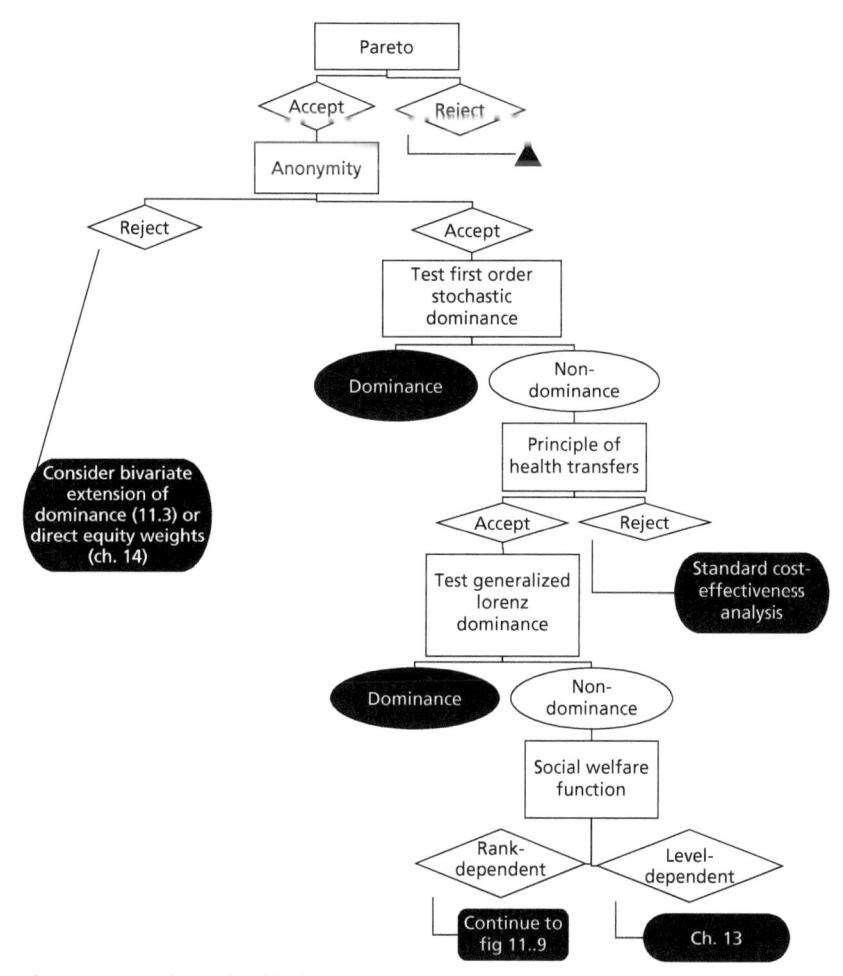

Figure 11.8 Ordering health distributions using stochastic dominance.

health based on two equity-relevant variables: SES and geography. When there is only one equity-relevant variable, and when this variable is monotonically related to health, then the multivariate approach is equivalent to the bivariate approach. Finally, if anonymity is rejected because the allocation of resources to specific groups is considered critical to equity, then application of direct equity weights to these groups, as explained in Chapter 14, may be the best way forward.

If both Pareto and anonymity are considered acceptable, then test (pairwise) for FOSD. If this is found, then a preference ordering is established. In the likely case that there is no FOSD, then ask whether the principle of health transfers (PHT) appeals to the decision maker.[33] A negative answer again renders the methods presented in this and the following two chapters impotent. A standard health economic evaluation that assumes indifference to inequality is sufficient. If PHT is accepted, you should check for GL dominance.[34] If dominance is found, all well and good. You can make a recommendation to any decision maker who prefers more health to less, and less health inequality to more. If there is no GL dominance, then consider whether a level-dependent or a rank-dependent SWF provides the more reasonable representation of the decision maker's preferences. In both cases, the decision maker is considered to prefer the option that would emerge from maximization of the weighted sum of (transformed) health. With level dependence, the weights (implicitly) depend only on the level of health and decline as health improves. If this is seen as a good representation of the decision maker's preferences, then the approach taken in Chapter 13 can be followed. With rank dependence, the weights depend only on health rank and decline in moving from the least to the most healthy. If this is more appealing, continue to Fig 11.9.

Now consider whether the decision maker is also likely to accept the principle of DPTS, which implies greater sensitivity to inequality toward the bottom of the health distribution. If yes, then test for second order GL dominance. If dominance is found, then a welfare ordering is obtained without making any assumption about the decision maker's precise degree of inequality aversion beyond the range implied by DPTS. Otherwise, continue to consider the ethical appeal of sequentially higher orders of DPTS. If each is believed consistent with the decision maker's ethics, then test for GL dominance at the respective order. If dominance is not found up to an order of DPTS that is considered the limit of the decision maker's concern for the least healthy, then you may want to specify a particular form of a rank-dependent SWF along with a parameterization of it that reflects a specific degree of inequality aversion (subject to satisfying the order of DPTS) and is considered consistent with the decision maker's preferences. This step, which is explained in the next chapter, will deliver an ordering of the interventions that is not robust to the precise degree of inequality aversion specified. The extent of sensitivity to the chosen parameter values should be tested.

---

[33] With the bivariate approach, you would need to consider whether the principle of income-related health transfers is consistent with the ethics of the decision maker.

[34] Concentration curve dominance in the bivariate case.

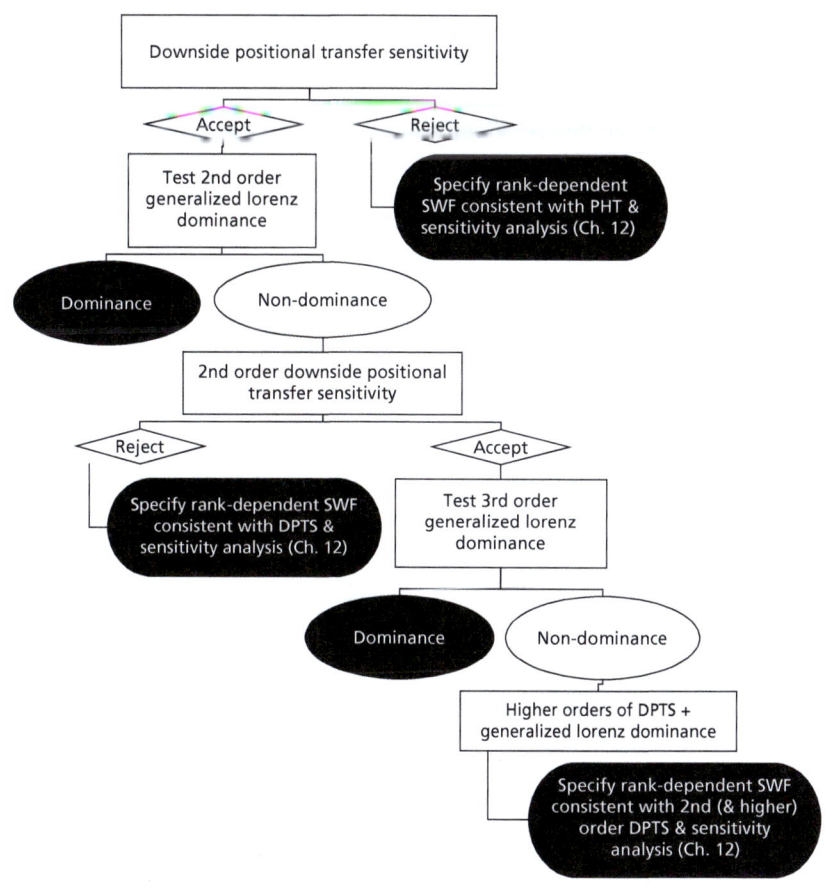

Figure 11.9 Ordering health distributions using higher order generalized Lorenz dominance.

11.6 Further reading

For an introduction to welfare economics covering Pareto, transfer principles, SWFs, and cost-benefit analysis, see Johansson (1991). The welfare foundations of rank-dependent health inequality measures are set out in Bleichrodt and van Doorslaer (2006), who establish that the principle of health transfers is the critical ethic of such measures. The use of Lorenz dominance to establish a welfare ordering of distributions based on the ethical principle of DPTS is proposed in Aaberge (2009) and further developed in Aaberge et al. (2019). For the application of these principles to the measurement of health inequality, see Makdissi and Yazbeck (2014).

References

Aaberge R. (2009). Ranking intersecting Lorenz curves. *Social Choice and Welfare*, 33, 235–259.

Aaberge R., Havnes T., & Mogstad M. (2019). *Ranking Intersecting Distribution Functions*. University of Chicago, Mimeo. https://sites.google.com/site/magnemogstad/home/publications

Amiel Y. & Cowell F. (1994). Monotonicity, dominance and the Pareto principle. *Economics Letters*, 45(4), 447–450.

Bleichrodt H., Doctor J., & Stolk E. (2005). A nonparametric elicitation of the equity-efficiency trade-off in cost-utility analysis. *Journal of Health Economics*, 24, 655–678.

Bleichrodt H. & van Doorslaer E. (2006). A welfare economics foundation for health inequality measurement. *Journal of Health Economics*, 25, 945–957.

Dalton H. (1920). The measurement of the inequality of incomes. *Economic Journal*, 30, 348–361.

Fleurbaey M. & Schokkaert E. (2009). Unfair inequalities in health and health care. *Journal of Health Economics*, 28, 73–90.

Johansson P. (1991). *An Introduction to Modern Welfare Economics*. Cambridge University Press, Cambridge. doi:10.1017/CBO9780511582417.

Khaled M, Makdissi P. & Yazbeck M. (2018). Income-related health transfers principles and orderings of joint distributions of income and health. *Journal of Health Economics*, 57, 315–331.

Lambert P. (1993). *The Distribution and Redistribution of Income: a Mathematical Analysis*. Second edition. Manchester University Press, Manchester.

Makdissi P. & Mussard S. (2008). Analyzing the impact of indirect tax reforms on rank dependant social welfare functions: a positional dominance approach. *Social Choice and Welfare*, 30, 385–399.

Makdissi P. & Yazbeck M. (2014). Measuring socioeconomic health inequalities in presence of multiple categorical information. *Journal of Health Economics*, 34, 84–95.

Makdissi P. & Yazbeck M. (2016). Avoiding blindness to health status in health achievement and health inequality measurement. *Social Science and Medicine*, 171, 39–47.

Mehran F. (1976). Linear measures of income inequality. *Econometrica*, 44, 805–809.

Pigou A. (1952). *The Economics of Welfare*. Fourth edition. Macmillan, London.

Shorrocks A. (1983). Ranking income distributions. *Economica*, 50, 3–17.

Weymark J. (1981). Generalized Gini inequality indices. *Mathematical Social Sciences*, 1, 409–430.

Yaari M. (1987). The dual theory of choice under risk. *Econometrica*, 55, 99–115.

Yaari M. (1988). A controversial proposal concerning inequality measurement. *Journal of Economic Theory*, 44, 381–397.

Zoli C. (1999). Intersecting generalized Lorenz curves and the Gini index. *Social Choice and Welfare*, 16, 183–196.

Chapter 12

Rank-dependent equity weights

Owen O'Donnell and Tom Van Ourti

The previous chapter showed that dominance analysis can sometimes establish the ordering of health distributions from the most to least preferred without assuming anything about the decision maker's values other than consistency with reasonably general and lucid ethical principles. But this is not always the case. No distribution may dominate. If there is dominance, it may be achieved only by invoking complicated supplementary principles that are difficult for non-specialists to comprehend, challenge, and communicate to others for the purpose of holding decision makers accountable. Or dominance may be obtained only through reliance on an extreme principle approaching the Rawlsian maximin that may be found unappealing because it focuses on the health of the worst-off group and almost entirely ignores the health of everyone else. In these situations, it may be useful to order distributions by a quantitative measure predicated on assumptions about the specific nature and degree of the decision maker's aversion to inequality. Without dominance, the ordering will not be invariant to the specific values of the equity weights chosen to aggregate health across individuals, but the degree of sensitivity can be tested.

Even when dominance can be established on the basis of general, transparent, and acceptable (to decision makers) ethical principles, a quantitative measure of the welfare (and inequality) generated by each distribution may still be attractive. Standard health economic evaluation is based on the cost per health-adjusted life year (HALY) metric. It can be made sensitive to equity by comparing the number of HALYs generated by each programme with a 'penalty' imposed to adjust for any resulting inequality. Since this merely involves an adjustment to the standard metric, it may be more appealing than the less familiar dominance analysis.

This chapter explains how to obtain and compare inequality penalized measures of population health outcomes. We restrict attention to methods consistent with the representation of a decision maker's preferences through the family of rank-dependent social welfare functions (SWFs). That is, the equity weight placed on an individual's health depends only on the rank of that individual in the distribution of health. The next chapter explains how to pursue the same objective using prioritarian SWFs that implicitly determine equity weights by the health level, rather than the rank, of each individual. Chapter 14 dispenses with the SWF apparatus and so allows greater flexibility in setting equity weights in relation to health and other characteristics, but at the cost of being less comprehensive, which leaves scope for inconsistent application of weights across decisions.

The next section notes that the transfer principles that provide the normative foundation for dominance analysis also imply restrictions on rank-dependent equity weights. These weights therefore allow a variety of equity concerns to be incorporated into economic evaluation. Section 12.2 gives examples of application using one particular family of rank-dependent SWFs. Section 12.3 makes clear how rank-dependent weights differ from the level-dependent weights used in the next chapter, and notes strengths and weaknesses of each method. Section 12.4 shows how the rank-dependent approach is easily extended to allow for aversion to health inequality in a specific dimension, such as socioeconomic status.

12.1 Rank-dependent equity weights, transfer principles, and dominance

If the decision maker puts health distributions into a preferred order as if applying a certain set of rules,[1] then those 'social preferences' can be represented by the family of rank-dependent SWFs (Weymark, 1981; Yaari, 1987, 1988). These functions define social welfare as a weighted sum of health levels, with the weight given to each individual being dependent only on their position in the health distribution.[2] Aversion to inequality can be incorporated by giving more weight to the less healthy.

Bleichrodt et al. (2004) proposed using this class of social welfare functions to evaluate and compare HALY distributions. This *rank-dependent HALY model* offers a general framework for incorporating a variety of equity concerns into health economic evaluation in a coherent way.[3] To respect the *Pareto*

---

[1] The preferences must be continuous, transitive, complete, and satisfy the dual independence axiom, which we define in note 15.

[2] Rank-dependent SWFs take the form $W_\omega(F) = \int_0^1 \omega'(p) F^{-1}(p) dp$, where F is the cumulative distribution function of health, $F^{-1}(p)$ is its p-quantile and $\omega'(p)$ is a weight function—the derivate of a function of the ranks—specified to ensure the preferences conform to various ethical principles.

[3] Bleichrodt et al. (2004) call it the rank-dependent quality-adjusted life year (QALY) model. We use HALY for consistency with the other chapters in this book.

principle, all the weights must be non-negative, such that welfare rises if one person's health improves and no one's health deteriorates.[4] If the weights are restricted to be constant and sum to 1, then we get the utilitarian SWF according to which welfare depends only on mean health.[5] This is the basis for standard economic evaluation that is insensitive to inequality. Consistency with the *principle of health transfers* (PHT)—a transfer of health from one individual to a less healthy individual raises welfare—requires that the weights decrease as one moves up the health distribution from the least to the most healthy.[6] Consistency with the *principle of downside positional transfer sensitivity* (DPTS)—greater aversion to inequality at the bottom of the distribution than at the top (see Chapter 11)—requires that the weights decrease at a diminishing rate as one moves up the distribution (Aaberge, 2009; Aaberge et al., 2019).[7]

Pareto, PHT, and DPTS, therefore, provide normative justification for restrictions imposed on the equity weights of a rank-dependent SWF. They also provide the ethical foundation for dominance analysis. If the generalized Lorenz (GL) curve of one health distribution dominates that of another at the second order, then the dominating distribution is preferred by any decision maker who adheres to DPTS (as well as Pareto and PHT) (see Chapter 11). It follows that the dominating distribution will also generate greater welfare when both are evaluated using any rank-dependent SWF with weights that, consistent with DPTS, decrease at a diminishing rate (and also satisfy the restrictions required for consistency with Pareto and PHT).[8] If second order GL dominance is found, then you can rest assured that the specific values chosen for the equity weights

---

[4] For the SWF given in note 2 to satisfy the Pareto principle, the weighting function must be restricted such that $\omega'(p) \geq 0 \ \forall p \in [0,1]$.

[5] The utilitarian SWF is obtained from that given in note 2 with the restriction, $\omega'(p) = 1 \ \forall p$. The model also nests the Rawls' maximin SWF, which is obtained by giving a non-zero weight to the least healthy individual only.

[6] $\omega''(p) \leq 0 \ \forall p$.

[7] $\omega'''(p) \geq 0 \ \forall p$.

[8] Aaberge et al. (2019), drawing on Aaberge (2009), prove the following equivalence:

$GL_x^2(p) \geq GL_z^2(p) \ \forall p \in [0,1]$ and $GL_x^2 \neq GL_z^2$
$\Leftrightarrow W_\omega(F_x) \geq W_\omega(F_z) \ \forall \ \omega(p)$ with $\omega'''(p) \geq 0 \ \forall p$
$\Leftrightarrow W_\omega(F_x) \geq W_\omega(F_z) \ \forall$ rank-dependent W_ω satisfying DPTS
with preferences also restricted to satisfy $\omega'(p) \geq 0$, $\omega''(p) \leq 0 \ \forall p$ and $\omega'(1) = \omega(0) = 0$, $\omega(1) = 1$.

See Chapter 11 note 16 for the definition of DPTS and note 17 for the definition of $GL_x^2(p)$.

will not change the preference ordering obtained from a rank-dependent SWF, provided the aforementioned restrictions on the weights are satisfied.

Correspondences between restrictions on the equity weights of a rank-dependent SWF and the ethics represented by transfer principles, and between those principles and GL dominance, extend to higher orders of DPTS and GL dominance.[9] If GL dominance is found at some particular order, then a rank-dependent SWF will give the same ranking of the distributions as the dominance test irrespective of the precise functional form and inequality aversion parameter chosen, provided the equity weights are restricted to decrease on moving from less to more healthy individuals in a way that is consistent with a corresponding transfer principle, for example decreasing at a diminishing rate for second-order DPTS. The transfer principle makes explicit, and therefore open to scrutiny, the ethical value judgment underpinning the welfare ordering obtained.

12.2 Quantification of welfare and inequality

The equity weights can be scaled to ensure that the quantification of welfare that comes out of the rank-dependent SWF lies between zero and mean health.[10] If health is equally distributed, then welfare reaches its upper bound at the mean. Otherwise, welfare falls short of this maximum. The welfare function gives the *equally distributed equivalent health* (EDEH): the level of health that if it were equally distributed would generate the same welfare as is obtained from the actual (unequal) distribution. That is, $W_\omega = (1 - I_\omega)\mu$, where W_ω is social welfare, μ is mean health, and I_ω is a rank-dependent measure of relative inequality, such as the Gini coefficient, that lies between 0 (no inequality) and 1 (extreme inequality—one person has all the health). The EDEH welfare index is equal to mean health less the cost of inequality, $I_\omega \mu$. Multiplying a measure of relative inequality by mean health converts it into a measure of absolute inequality on the same scale that is used to measure health. This gives the cost of inequality

---

[9] If $\omega'''(p) \leq 0 \, \forall p$, then second order DPTS is satisfied (see Chapter 11 note 20). Consequently, using results given in Chapter 11, if distribution F_x generalized Lorenz dominates F_z at the third order, then F_x will be ordered above F_z by any rank-dependent SWF with a weight function that satisfies $\omega''''(p) \leq 0 \, \forall p$, plus the restrictions on the first three derivatives required for Pareto, PHT, and DPTS. Alternating signs of each derivative of the weight function ensures satisfaction of successively higher orders of DPTS.

[10] This requires setting $\omega(0) = \omega'(1) = 0$ and $\omega(1) = 1$.

expressed in units of health, which can be thought of as a social welfare penalty of inequality.

Quantification of welfare (and inequality) requires specification of exactly how the equity weights differ along the health distribution. If the health of the individual at a particular quantile p is given the weight $\eta(1-p)^{\eta-1}$ with $\eta \geq 1$, and weighted health is averaged over all individuals, then we get the extended Gini welfare function (Donaldson and Weymark, 1980; Yitzhaki 1983).[11] The restriction on the value of the inequality aversion parameter η ensures that all weights are positive and so the Pareto principle is satisfied. With $\eta = 1$, there is no concern about inequality, everyone's health is weighted equally and welfare is equal to mean health. At $\eta > 1$, there is aversion to inequality, the PHT is satisfied and welfare will be less than mean health if there is any inequality. GL dominance implies the welfare ordering that will be found from applying the extended Gini SWF with $\eta > 1$. If one health distribution generalized Lorenz dominates another distribution, then passing both distributions through the extended Gini SWF will reveal that the dominating distribution generates the greater quantity of welfare providing $\eta > 1$, irrespective of the precise value chosen above 1. Inference cannot be made from the welfare ordering obtained from application of the extended Gini SWF to dominance, however. Using $\eta = 1.5$, this SWF may quantify the welfare generated by distribution X to be greater than that produced by distribution Y, but the welfare ordering could be reversed at some other value of $\eta > 1$. Even if the welfare ordering were to remain consistent at all values of $\eta > 1$, GL dominance may still not hold since the ordering could change if some other type of (rank-dependent) SWF were used. Dominance, when it is found, is a much stronger result than can be obtained from application of the extended Gini, or any other, social welfare function.

To be consistent with DPTS, it is necessary to set $\eta > 2$. If there is second-order GL dominance, then the welfare ordering obtained from application of the extended Gini SWF will remain the same irrespective of the value chosen for η provided it is greater than 2. With $\eta = 2$, the relative inequality measure, I_ω, is the Gini index (of inequality) and the measure of absolute inequality (μI_ω) is the generalized Gini index. Consequently, these popular inequality indices do not satisfy DPTS. Setting $\eta > 3$ ensures consistency with second

---

[11] The extended Gini welfare function is $W_\omega(F) = \int_0^1 \eta(1-p)^{\eta-1} F^{-1}(p) dp, \eta \geq 1$ where $F^{-1}(p)$ and p are defined in note 2.

Table 12.1 Welfare and inequality generated by hypothetical programmes

	Programme					
	A	B	C	D	E	F
Relative inequality						
$\eta = 1$	0.0000	0.0000	0.0000	0.0000	0.0000	0.0000
$\eta = 2$	0.2222	0.1481	0.2469	0.1678	0.2033	0.2397
$\eta = 3$	0.3333	0.2222	0.3704	0.2313	0.3026	0.3486
Absolute inequality						
$\eta = 1$	0.00	0.00	0.00	0.00	0.00	0.00
$\eta = 2$	8.89	6.67	11.11	8.22	9.56	12.22
$\eta = 3$	13.33	10.00	16.67	11.33	14.22	17.78
EDEH welfare						
$\eta = 1$	40.00	45.00	45.00	49.00	47.00	51.00
$\eta = 2$	31.11	38.33	33.89	40.78	37.44	38.78
$\eta = 3$	26.67	35.00	28.33	37.67	32.78	33.22

Notes: table shows the extended Gini index of relative inequality (I_ω), the extended generalized Gini index of absolute inequality ($I_\omega\mu$), and the extended Gini measure of welfare (EDEH, $W_\omega = (1-I_\omega)\mu$) for the stylized health distributions presented in the previous chapter in Table 11.1.

order DPTS—even greater concern about inequality toward the bottom of the distribution (see Chapter 11).

Using the extended Gini welfare function, Table 12.1 shows measures of relative inequality, absolute inequality, and EDEH at three values of the inequality aversion parameter (η) for the stylized distributions generated by the different programmes introduced in the previous chapter (Table 11.1). With $\eta = 1$, both measures of inequality are zero and the EDEH is equal to mean health because there is no aversion to inequality and so no welfare cost arising from it. As the inequality aversion parameter is increased, both measures of inequality increase for all programmes, as they must. Irrespective of the degree of inequality aversion among the values considered, the ordering of programmes from more to less relative inequality is always $C > F > A > E > D > B$. Because of the differences in mean health, however, the ranking in terms of greater to less absolute inequality differs: $F > C > E > A > D > B$. The larger mean under F and E raises the welfare costs of the (relative) inequality experienced with these programmes relative to C and A respectively.

With no aversion to inequality, the preference ordering (based on EDEH) is $F \succ D \succ E \succ C \sim B \succ A$.[12] Programme F is most preferred because it generates the highest mean health, while A is least preferred because it gives the lowest mean. C and B are valued equally because they have the same mean. When the inequality aversion parameter is raised to 2, which corresponds to adherence to PHT but not DPTS (there is aversion to inequality but it is not greater at the bottom of the distribution), the preference ordering changes to $D \succ F \succ B \succ E \succ C \succ A$. Policy F is no longer preferred to D because the greater inequality with F imposes a larger welfare penalty. B shifts up the preference ordering because it has the smallest welfare cost from inequality. Raising the inequality aversion parameter to 3 produces another reordering: $D \succ B \succ F \succ E \succ C \succ A$. F drops below B because it is penalized even more for the high degree of inequality it generates.

Some of the welfare orderings observed from Table 12.1 are predictable from the dominance analysis conducted in Chapter 11. It is established there that: (1) B and C both first order stochastically dominate A, (2) D generalized Lorenz dominates B, and (3) B generalized Lorenz dominates C.[13] Hence, $D \succ B \succ C \succ A$ for any $\eta > 1$. This is confirmed in Fig 12.1, which plots the EDEH against η for each policy. The figure also illustrates that there is no GL dominance between B and E. With positive but lower inequality aversion ($\eta < 1.6$), E generates more welfare than B. At higher degrees of inequality aversion, the preference ordering is reversed. At all $\eta > 2$, which implies that DPTS is satisfied (greater aversion to inequality at the bottom of the distribution), $B \succ E$. This confirms the result given in Chapter 11: B second order generalized Lorenz dominates E, and so B is preferred by any decision maker who accepts DPTS. In Chapter 11, we noted that adherence to the ethics represented by DPTS is insufficient to determine which of B and F is preferred, since there is no second order GLD. This can also be seen in the figure. With inequality aversion slightly in excess of $\eta = 2$, such that DPTS holds marginally, the welfare generated by F is just above that produced by B. However, as the inequality aversion parameter increases toward 2.5 the welfare rankings are reversed. The welfare advantage of B over F then widens as η increases. Given that B generalized Lorenz dominates F at the third order, we know that at any $\eta > 3$, which

---

[12] $\succ$ and $\sim$ indicate 'preferred to' and 'indifferent to' respectively.

[13] Actually, it is observed in Chapter 11 that B Lorenz dominates C, but since they both generate the same mean, this implies generalized Lorenz dominance.

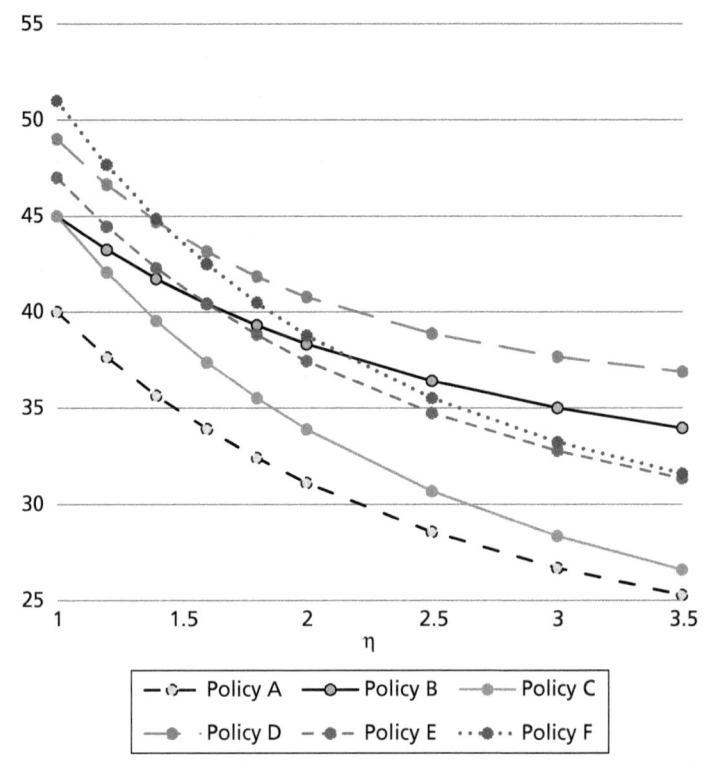

Figure 12.1 Equally distributed equivalent health against inequality aversion (η)—extended Gini SWF.

is sufficient to satisfy second order DPTS, there will be a preference for B over F, and this is apparent in the figure.

These examples are intended to clarify the correspondences that exist between transfer principles, restrictions on rank-dependent equity weights, and dominance. They should not be interpreted as implying that testing sensitivity of welfare orderings obtained from the extended Gini welfare function with respect to its inequality aversion parameter η fully substitutes for dominance analysis. The latter is more general. Dominance establishes a preference ordering using any rank-dependent SWF (restricted to satisfy certain transfer principles), not only using the extended Gini function.

12.3 Comparison with level-dependent equity weights

Rank-dependent SWFs represent a decision maker's preferred ordering of distributions as if it were obtained from comparing weighted sums of individual health levels. Aversion to inequality is captured directly by giving greater weight to less healthy individuals. Level-dependent or prioritarian SWFs, which are used to make the equity-efficiency trade-off described in the next chapter, take an unweighted sum of the social welfare generated by individual health, rather than a weighted sum of the individual levels of health. Aversion to inequality is captured indirectly by making each individual's contribution to social welfare a concave function of their health level. This social value of individual health increases with health at a diminishing rate and so ensures greater social value is attached to marginal gains in health experienced by the less healthy.[14] While the differences between the two families of SWF may appear technical, they correspond to different ethical principles that potentially have important consequences for the welfare ordering of distributions and, consequently, the prioritization of programmes.[15] When a rank-dependent SWF is used to order distributions, it is implicitly assumed that the decision maker is concerned about the number of people in poor health more than the severity of the health problems those people experience (Bleichrodt et al., 2008; Aaberge et al., 2019). Consequently, greater priority is given to the least healthy individuals when their number is larger, but not when their health is lower. Relative to the allocation made by an equity-insensitive decision maker, maximization of a rank-dependent SWF can result in more resources being directed to treatment of the most severe disease when its prevalence increases but not when its severity

---

[14] A prioritarian SWF can be obtained from the rank-dependent variety we present in note 2 by setting all weights to 1 $(\omega'(p)=1 \; \forall p)$ and replacing $h(p) = F^{-1}(p)$ with $g(h)$, $g'(h) \geq 0$, $g''(h) \leq 0 \; \forall h$. One could use a weighting function to explicitly represent aversion to inequality and a concave health transformation function to allow for diminishing marginal social welfare from health to obtain a hybrid rank-dependent prioritarian SWF: $W_\omega(F) = \int_0^1 \omega'(p) g(h(p)) dp$ (Bleichrodt et al., 2005).

[15] The first three of the assumptions about decision-maker preferences listed in note 1 must hold for those preferences to be represented by a SWF, irrespective of whether it is the rank-dependent or prioritarian variety. In addition, the *independence axiom* must hold for a prioritarian SWF to give welfare orderings consistent with decision-maker preferences. This requires that the preference ordering of two health distributions be invariant with respect to the mixing of population shares given health levels: Let F_x, F_z and F_v be distributions, and $\alpha \in [0,1]$. $F_x \succeq F_z \Rightarrow (\alpha F_x(h) + (1-\alpha) F_v(h)) \succeq (\alpha F_z(h) + (1-\alpha) F_v(h))$.

In contrast, the *dual independent axiom* (Yaari, 1987) that is necessary for a rank-dependent SWF to give a welfare ordering consistent with decision-maker preferences requires that the ordering be invariant with respect to mixing of health levels given population shares:

$$F_x \succeq F_z \Rightarrow \left(\alpha F_x^{-1}(h) + (1-\alpha) F_v^{-1}(h)\right)^{-1} \succeq \left(\alpha F_z^{-1}(h) + (1-\alpha) F_v^{-1}(h)\right).$$

worsens (Bleichrodt et al., 2008). In contrast, adoption of a prioritarian SWF implies the value judgment that the level of health of those in poor health is more important than their number. Maximization of this type of function will result in giving more resources to treatment of the most severe disease when its severity worsens, but the response to an increase in its prevalence is the same as that of an equity-insensitive decision maker (Bleichrodt et al., 2008). There can be ethical objections to the implications of each family of welfare functions for the prioritization of resources. Which of the two positions is considered to be more acceptable is evidently a matter to be discussed with the decision makers in a particular situation.

The downside of making economic evaluation sensitive to equity, irrespective of whether this is done using rank or level-dependent weights, is that if application is made to a series of choices in an uncoordinated fashion (each evaluation is conducted in isolation from the others), then the set of interventions selected can, in aggregate, result in a health distribution that is Pareto dominated by an alternative that is feasible given the resource constraint (Bleichrodt et al., 2004). Essentially, no allowance is made for the possibility that inequality generated by one intervention may be offset by inequality in the opposite direction generated by another.[16] The likelihood of obtaining a Pareto inferior outcome from uncoordinated choices will vary from case to case. It could be that it is quite unlikely in most circumstances. But it can only be avoided entirely if equity concerns are ignored by adoption of a utilitarian SWF. Use of a rank-dependent SWF at least ensures that it does not arise when conducting evaluations of interventions that are equity neutral, in the sense that they do not change the ranking (and so the equity weights) of individuals in the health distribution (Bleichrodt et al., 2004). Uncoordinated application of a prioritarian SWF to a series of such interventions could produce a Pareto inferior outcome.

This advantage of the rank-dependent approach comes at a cost. The evaluation must be conducted using the distribution of health over the full population. Those unaffected by the programme being evaluated cannot be ignored. Doing so would change the health distribution ranks, and so the weights, of

---

[16] Consider a population of two identical individuals. One choice is between an intervention that generates an additional 9 HALY for each individual and another that gives 20 HALY to individual A and 0 to individual B. Aversion to inequality may lead the decision maker to select the former intervention. A second choice is between an intervention that also produces 9 HALY for each individual and another that gives 20 HALY to individual B and 0 HALY to individual A. Another inequality averse decision maker may also opt for the intervention that gives an equal number of HALY to each person. In aggregate, both individuals gain 18 HALY. If the decision makers had selected the interventions favoured by equity insensitive evaluations, each individual would have gained 20 HALY.

those impacted by the programme, which could affect the outcome of the evaluation. This lack of *separability* greatly increases the information that must be gathered to conduct an evaluation based on a rank dependent SWF (Adler, 2019). Separability of the prioritarian SWF can in theory be an important advantage of that approach. It means that you can ignore all individuals unaffected by the programme being evaluated. However, this comparative advantage is lost if, as is often the case, the evaluation is conducted using grouped data at a high level of aggregation, since all groups are likely to be affected by the programme and so all of them must be considered irrespective of whether a rank or level-dependent SWF is used. Furthermore, even with disaggregated or individual level analysis the advantage arising from the separability of level-dependence is lost if health opportunity costs are spread across the whole population rather than being confined to the specific population of programme recipients. Nevertheless, the separability of the level-dependent approach does offer the advantage of subgroup decomposability. This means, for example, that national welfare can be expressed as a function of welfare within each subnational region, allowing subgroup decomposition of the contribution of each region to the overall national impact on equity and welfare.

12.4 Aversion to socioeconomic-related health inequality

Aversion to health inequality in relation to an equity-relevant variable such as socioeconomic status is easily handled with the rank-dependent approach simply by ranking according to that variable. For shorthand, let us refer to the characteristic as 'income', although it could be any social variable along which health should not vary if equity is to be achieved. The only restriction is that it must be measured on (at least) an ordinal scale. Rank-dependent welfare is still a weighted sum of health, only now the equity weights are determined by position in the income distribution.[17] The weights are again restricted to be non-negative (to satisfy Pareto) and to sum to 1 (to ensure that welfare has an EDEH interpretation).[18] Consistency with the *principle of income-related*

---

[17] The SWF now takes the general form: $W_v(F_{H,Y}) = \int_0^1 v'(q)h(q)dq$, where $F_{H,Y}$ is the joint distribution of health (H) and 'income' (Y) (again used as shorthand for any (at least) ordinal variable that defines the dimension in which health inequality is assessed), and $h(q)$ is the conditional expectation of health at income quantile q and $v'(q)$ is the weight function.

[18] The restrictions on the weight function are: $v'(q) \geq 0 \ \forall q \in [0,1]$, $v(0) = v'(1) = 0$ and $v(1) = 1$.

health transfers (PIRHT)—a transfer of health from a richer to a poorer individual raises welfare (see Chapter 11, note 24)—requires that the weights decrease moving up the income distribution to richer individuals.[19] If there is generalized concentration curve (GCC) dominance of one distribution over another, then the dominating distribution is preferred by any decision maker who accepts Pareto and PIRHT. And that distribution will be evaluated to generate more welfare by any rank-dependent SWF with restrictions on the equity weights to ensure compliance with those two ethical principles.

Consistency with the bivariate variant of DPTS—greater aversion to health inequality at the bottom of the income distribution than at the top (see Chapter 11, note 28)—requires that while moving up the income distribution the equity weights decrease at a diminishing rate.[20] If there is second order GCC dominance of one distribution over another, then the dominating distribution is preferred by any decision maker who accepts Pareto, PIRHT, and bivariate DPTS. Any rank-dependent SWF with equity weights restricted to ensure consistency with these three ethical principles will evaluate the dominating distribution as generating more welfare. As in the univariate case, these correspondences between ethical principles and restrictions on the equity weights of a rank-dependent SWF, and between welfare orderings obtained from that function and dominance continue to hold at higher orders of DPTS and dominance.[21]

With appropriate scaling of the weights (v) (see note 18), the welfare function returns the level of health that, if it were equally distributed across individuals with different incomes, would generate the same welfare as the actual distribution of health that varies with income. That is, the equally distributed

---

[19] $v"(q) \leq 0 \ \forall q$.

[20] The restrictions on the weighting function that are required for consistency with first and second order bivariate DPTS are respectively $v'''(q) \geq 0$ and $v''''(q) \leq 0 \ \forall q$.

[21] See Chapter 11, note 30, for definition of the generalized σ-concentration curve, GC^σ and of GCC dominance at order σ. The correspondence between GCC dominance at order σ and the preference ordering obtained from a bivariate rank-dependent SWF is as follows:

$GC_x^\sigma(q) \geq GC_z^\sigma(q) \ \forall q \in [0,1]$ and $GC_x^\sigma \neq GC_z^\sigma \Rightarrow W_v(F_{H,Y}^x) \geq W_v(F_{H,Y}^z)$ for all $W_v(\ )$ that satisfy:

1. $v'(q) \geq 0, \ v"(q) \leq 0 \ \forall q \in [0,1]$ for $\sigma \geq 1$,
2. $v'''(q) \geq 0 \ \forall q \in [0,1]$ for $\sigma \geq 2$,
3. $v''''(q) \leq 0 \ \forall q \in [0,1]$ for $\sigma \geq 3$ (Makdissi and Yazbeck, 2014).

Note that σ in our notation is σ-1 in Makdissi and Yazbeck. See Chapter 11, note 29.

by income equivalent health (EDIEH): $W_v = (1 - I_v)\mu$, where I_v is a rank-dependent measure of income-related relative health inequality and $I_v \mu$ is the absolute counterpart to such inequality and captures its welfare cost. If the joint distribution of health and income that arises from one programme (x) concentration curve dominates that generated by another programme (z), health increases with income in both cases (such that $I_v^j > 0$, $j = x, z$) and the welfare function respects PIRHT, then relative inequality will be lower with x ($I_v^x < I_v^z$) and, if mean health is the same, welfare will be greater with this intervention ($W_v^x > W_v^z$).[22]

As in the univariate case, to quantify such differences in welfare and inequality you need to specify precisely how the equity weights vary along the income distribution. Specifying the weight for the individual at quantile q of that distribution as $v(1-q)^{v-1}$, with $v \geq 1$, gives measures analogous to those obtained from the extended Gini family of SWF defined over a univariate distribution (Wagstaff, 2002). The restriction on the sign and magnitude of v ensures that the Pareto and PIRHT principles are satisfied. For bivariate DPTS, you need $v > 2$ and for second order DPTS you need $v > 3$. With $v = 2$, relative and absolute income-related health inequality are measured by the concentration index and generalized concentration index respectively (Kakwani et al., 1997), and so these popular measures do not satisfy bivariate DPTS.[23]

---

[22] The σ-concentration curve, C^σ, is the respective generalized curve divided by mean health. Concentration curve dominance at order $\sigma \geq 1$ is defined as: $C_x^\sigma(q) \geq C_z^\sigma(q) \ \forall q \in [0,1]$ and $C_x^\sigma \neq C_z^\sigma$. This implies: $I_v(F_{H,Y}^x) \leq I_v(F_{H,Y}^z)$ for all $I_v(\ )$ that satisfy the restrictions on the weighting function given in 1–3 of the previous note (Makdissi and Yazbeck, 2014). We assume that health is increasing, on average, with income rank, such that $I_v(F_{HY}^j) > 0$. If the health-income relationship has the opposite sign, then the concentration curve will lie above the line of equality and concentration curve dominance of F_{HY}^x over F_{HY}^z implies greater income-related relative health inequality to the advantage of the poor, $I_v(F_{HY}^x) < I_v(F_{HY}^z) < 0$.

[23] The concentration index (CI) is twice the area between the concentration curve and the diagonal, and the generalized concentration index (GCI) is twice the area between the GCC and the line of equality. The CI and GCI (=$\mu \times$CI) are closely related to the relative index of inequality (RII) and slope index of inequality (SII) that are commonly used in epidemiology to measure relative and absolute socioeconomic-related health inequality respectively: RII=CI/2Var(q) and SII=GCI/2Var(q), where Var(q) is the variance of the rank, which approaches 1/12 in large samples. Hence, RII and SII also do not satisfy bivariate DPTS.

With this specification, welfare is in theory maximized when there is the greatest degree of health inequality, provided it is to the advantage of the poor $(I_\upsilon < 0)$. It is hard to imagine how a health programme could generate a negative correlation between income and health, as the normal positive correlation is one of the most robust and pervasive relationships in the whole of social science. Nevertheless, this hypothetical implication would strike many as normatively inappropriate. Erreygers et al. (2012) propose an alternative specification of equity weights that avoids this implication by allowing symmetrical aversion to deviations (in either direction) from the health of the person with median income.[24]

12.5 **Conclusion**

Distributional cost-effectiveness analysis involves first simulating the distributions of health (net of health opportunity costs) generated by the prevention or treatment options under consideration, which requires identification of the health outcome of interest to the decision maker and selection of any equity-relevant variables in relation to which its distribution is to be described. It then involves evaluating and ranking these distributions according to the ethics of the decision maker—potentially including their willingness to trade off the maximization of average health against the minimization of health inequality.

This chapter has presented an approach to establishing a social welfare ordering over health distributions that is consistent with, and complementary to, the dominance analysis set out in Chapter 11. When dominance is found, you can measure welfare and inequality using the methods presented here and know that the ordering of distributions will be consistent with that established by the dominance analysis, provided the parameterization of the welfare function respects the appropriate restrictions. The quantities obtained will vary with the chosen functional form and inequality aversion parameter, but the welfare ranking will be preserved. When dominance is not found, you can add assumptions about the decision maker's specific degree of inequality aversion that go beyond transfer principles, or, even better, elicit this parameter, and so order distributions by measures of welfare. In this case, sensitivity analysis should be

---

[24] The weights are defined by: $1 - \beta 2^{\beta-2} \left[(q-0.5)^2\right]^{\frac{\beta-2}{2}} (q-0.5), \beta > 1$. Restricting $\beta > 2$ leads to a focus on the extremities of the distribution—the richest and poorest. Khaled et al. (2018) identify the positional transfer sensitivities that correspond to the ethical principles advocated by Erreygers et al. (2012) and show how to order health distributions consistent with these principles.

conducted to test the extent to which the ordering is dependent on the functional form and parameter values chosen for the welfare function.

The measures of welfare and inequality presented in this chapter and the next share some assumptions about the decision maker's social preferences concerning equity and efficiency in the distribution of health, but there are important differences. One is whether the decision maker is concerned more about the proportion of the population that is in poor health (the position assumed in this chapter) or the severity of illness suffered by those in poor health (the stance assumed in the next chapter). Decision makers should be consulted to establish which ethical position is most consistent with their principles. If this cannot be done, or if the results of consultation are inconclusive—which is not unlikely—then sensitivity analysis across the approaches should be conducted. In all cases, good practice requires that the analyst is explicit about the normative principles underlying the analysis, particularly when these value judgments rest merely on what the analyst considers appropriate.

12.6 Further reading

For an excellent introduction to SWFs and an argument for their greater use in decision-making, see Adler (2019). Bleichrodt et al. (2004) set out a coherent framework for incorporating equity into health economic evaluation in the form of the rank-dependent HALY (QALY) model. Bleichrodt et al. (2008) show the implications for healthcare resource allocation of taking account of equity using either a rank-dependent or a level-dependent welfare function. The relationships between extended Gini function inequality aversion parameter, transfer principles, and dominance are shown in Aaberge et al. (2019). For welfare functions that are sensitive to both mean health and health inequality, see Wagstaff (2002), Erreygers et al. (2012), and Makdissi and Yazbeck (2016).

References

Aaberge R. (2009). Ranking intersecting Lorenz curves. *Social Choice and Welfare*, **33**, 235–259.

Aaberge R., Havnes T., & Mogstad M. (2019). *Ranking Intersecting Distribution Functions*. University of Chicago, Mimeo. https://sites.google.com/site/magnemogstad/home/publications

Adler M. (2019). *Measuring Social Welfare: an Introduction*. Oxford University Press, Oxford.

Bleichrodt H., Diecidue E., & Quiggin J. (2004). Equity weights and the allocation of health care: the rank-dependent QALY model. *Journal of Health Economics*, **23**, 157–171.

Bleichrodt H., Doctor J., & Stolk E. (2005). A nonparametric elicitation of the equity-efficiency trade-off in cost-utility analysis. *Journal of Health Economics*, **24**, 655–678.

Bleichrodt H. & van Doorslaer E. (2006). A welfare economics foundation for health inequality measurement. *Journal of Health Economics*, 25, 945–957.

Bleichrodt H., Crainich D., & Eeckhoudt L. (2008). Aversion to health inequalities and priority setting in health care. *Journal of Health Economics*, 27, 1594–1604.

Donaldson D. & Weymark J. (1980). A single parameter generalization of the Gini indices of inequality. *Journal of Economic Theory*, 22, 67–86.

Erreygers G., Clarke P., & and Van Ourti T. (2012). Mirror, mirror, on the wall, who is this land is the fairest of all? Distributional sensitivity in the measurement of socioeconomic inequality in health, *Journal of Health Economics*, 31, 257–270.

Kakwani N., Wagstaff A., & Van Doorslaer E. (1997). Socioeconomic inequalities in health: measurement, computation and statistical inference. *Journal of Econometrics*, 77, 87–104.

Khaled M., Makdissi P., & Yazbeck M. (2018). Income-related health transfers principles and orderings of joint distributions of income and health. *Journal of Health Economics*, 57, 315–331.

Makdissi P. & Yazbeck M. (2014). Measuring socioeconomic health inequalities in presence of multiple categorical information. *Journal of Health Economics*, 34, 84–95.

Makdissi P. & Yazbeck M. (2016). Avoiding blindness to health status in health achievement and health inequality measurement, *Social Science and Medicine*, 171, 39–47.

Wagstaff A. (2002). Inequality aversion, health inequalities and health achievement, *Journal of Health Economics*, 21, 627–641.

Weymark J. (1981). Generalized Gini inequality indices. *Mathematical Social Sciences*, 1, 409–430.

Yaari M. (1987) The dual theory of choice under risk. *Econometrica*, 55, 99–115.

Yaari M. (1988) A controversial proposal concerning inequality measurement. *Journal of Economic Theory*, 44, 381–397.

Yitzhaki S. (1983). On an extension of the Gini index. *International Economic Review*, 24, 617–628.

Chapter 13
Level-dependent equity weights

Ole F. Norheim, Miqdad Asaria,
Kjell Arne Johansson, Trygve Ottersen, and
Aki Tsuchiya

The previous chapter explained how you can use rank-dependent social welfare functions (SWFs) to evaluate health distributions in a manner that is founded on explicit, challengeable, and consistent ethical principles. This chapter explains how you can do this using level-dependent SWFs. A level-dependent SWF uses information about the absolute level of health—for example a health-adjusted life expectancy (HALE) at birth of 62—and weights health gains for one person or group relative to another as a function of their respective health levels. By contrast, a rank-dependent SWF weights health gains as a function of the ranking within the full population distribution of health—for example a HALE of 62 might be the second lowest ranked subgroup in order of health, depending on the health levels of all other subgroups in the population. A level-dependent SWF is also called a prioritarian SWF (Adler, 2012, 2019). A level-dependent SWF gives priority to the worse-off based on their absolute level of health compared with others, whereas a rank-dependent SWF gives priority to the worse-off based on their relative position in the health distribution compared with others.

The aim of this chapter is to describe level-dependent SWFs and how they can be used to conduct equity-efficiency trade-off analysis. We show how this is done with a numerical inequality aversion parameter within a level-dependent health-related SWF—a level-dependent equity parameter, for short.[1] The basic prioritarian principle is a specific value judgment about giving priority to those who are worse-off based on their absolute level of health. This can be consistent with many different sets of weights, which vary according to the chosen equity

---

[1] In the income inequality literature this is usually called an 'inequality aversion' parameter. We sometimes use the shorter phrase 'equity parameter' because in DCEA the focus is usually on 'unfair' inequality associated with equity-relevant characteristics, rather than 'pure' inequality between individuals.

parameter. We show how level-dependent equity parameters can be used to perform a systematic sensitivity analysis of how different degrees of concern for the worse-off have different policy implications.

The chapter is organized as follows. Section 13.1 introduces the rationale for level-dependent SWFs and explains some differences between classical utilitarian and prioritarian SWFs. Social value judgments over distributions are important characteristics of social welfare and a SWF is therefore inherently a normative evaluation tool (as is the utilitarian SWF). The section also explains the role of equity weights in the analysis. The basic intuition throughout is that there will be some set of weights assignable to people that make it worthwhile to accept a certain loss of average population health in order to achieve greater equality in health. In section 13.2 we explain how measures of health inequality or inequity can be derived from level-dependent SWFs. Section 13.3 discusses social value judgments about health distributions and how these can be captured in an equity parameter and further used to explore equity-efficiency trade-offs between maximizing health and reducing unfair health inequalities. The basic idea is to use information about a social decision maker's aversion to unfair inequality and make a level-dependent transformation of individual health that displays decreasing marginal social value. Together with information about the existing distribution of health, this then indirectly implies a specific set of equity weights. In section 13.4 we explain equity-efficiency trade-off analysis step by step: how to choose the appropriate SWF; choice of inequality aversion parameter; data inputs needed; how to estimate results and plot them on the equity impact plane; and finally, how to perform sensitivity analysis with different values of the inequality aversion parameter. Section 13.5 compares level-dependent and rank-dependent SWFs and how to choose between them for a particular evaluation. The last section concludes.

13.1 **Level-dependent SWFs explained**

In this section we introduce one attractive level-dependent SWF that has been applied to health distributions, Atkinson's SWF, which focuses on total health and relative inequality in health (Anand et al., 2001; Johansson & Norheim, 2011; Norheim, 2013; Asaria et al., 2015, 2016). Box 13.1 describes an analysis from a UK study that used Atkinson's SWF.

To understand the structure of such an analysis, consider a simple example, based on Table 11.1 in Chapter 11.

Fig 13.1 shows the distribution of lifetime health over a population with three individuals under three alternative programmes that cost the same. Programme A is the status quo. With programme B, individual 1, who is the worst off, will gain 10 HALYs, individual 2 will gain 5 HALYs, and individual 3

LEVEL-DEPENDENT SWFS EXPLAINED | 255

> **Box 13.1 Empirical example (Asaria et al., 2015)**
>
> A methodological case study of the UK bowel cancer screening programme compared two redesign policy options: (1) the introduction of an enhanced targeted reminder aimed at increasing screening uptake in deprived and ethnically diverse neighbourhoods, and (2) the introduction of a basic universal reminder aimed at increasing screening uptake across the whole population. One key result was that the first option would reduce inequities in health, but with loss of total net health gains. The second option would yield higher health gains, but not significantly reduce inequity in outcomes. By using a social welfare function approach, Asaria et al. were able to analyse the trade-off between improving total health gain and reducing inequities in health. The targeted reminder would achieve higher social welfare than the alternative policy with a sufficiently high concern of the worse-off (or aversion to inequality).
>
> Data from Asaria, Griffin, Cookson, Whyte, & Tappenden (2015). Distributional cost-effectiveness analysis of health care programmes--a methodological case study of the UK Bowel Cancer Screening Programme. Health Econ, 24, 742-754.

who is the best off will gain nothing. With programme C, individual 1 will gain nothing, individual 2 will gain 5 HALYs, and individual 3 will gain 10 HALYs. A utilitarian SWF (see below) yields the same net sum of health effects under B and C (15 additional HALYs), and hence they deliver the same gain in social welfare. A utilitarian decision maker will be indifferent between B and C. The

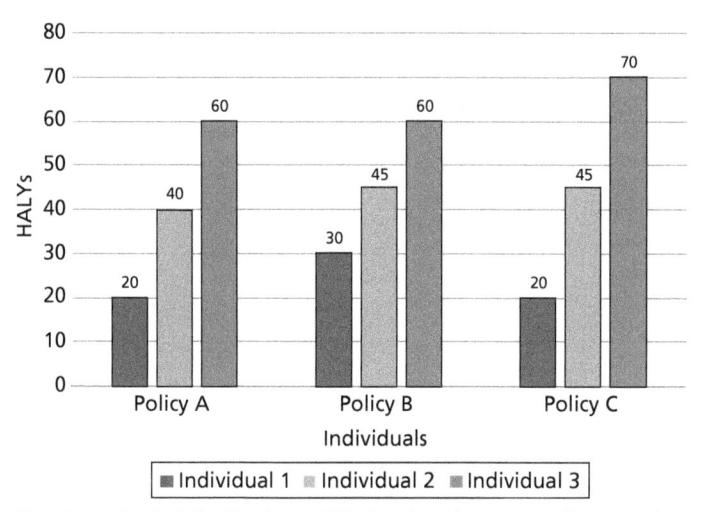

Figure 13.1 Hypothetical distributions of lifetime health generated by two alternative policies (B and C)—compared to A.

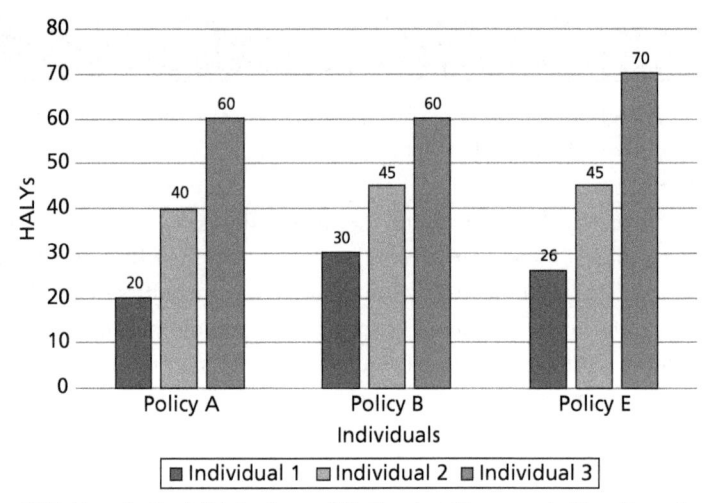

Figure 13.2 Hypothetical distributions of lifetime health generated by alternative policies (B and E)—compared to A.

baseline inequality in health levels by itself is irrelevant information for a utilitarian decision maker: only the total net health effects compared with the status quo baseline situation under programme A matter for assessing gains in social welfare.[2]

In a level-dependent SWF, more weight is given to health gains for the worse-off—in this case individual 1. The total health gain is the same in B and C, so a level-dependent SWF will rank B over C since more weight is given to gains to individual 1. This is straightforward.

Now compare distribution B and E (Fig 13.2). Under programme E, individual 1 will gain 6 HALYs, individual 2 will gain 5 HALYs, and individual 3 will gain 10 HALYs, totalling 21 HALYs. In this case, a utilitarian SWF will rank E over B, since the net sum of health is larger under E compared to B. This is also straightforward.

---

[2] We assume the health gains are measured in a way that reflects a full and final accounting of the individual value of health. In other words, if h denotes the individual's health profile (or, more precisely, a large vector of numbers representing the probabilities of many different possible multi-dimensional health states occurring in many different periods of time over the course of a whole life) and $u(h)$ denotes the value to the individual of that health profile, then we assume HALYs represent $u(h)$ (= individual value). As explained in Chapter 2 on principles of health equity, HALYs can be interpreted in many different ways—for example some people interpret them as the individual's own preferences for health, whereas others interpret them as a measure of health benefit reflecting general population average value judgments about the individual value of different health states.

How a level-dependent SWF will rank the two distributions is, however, not so straightforward. It depends on the weights assigned to gains for the worse-off. Intuitively, decision makers would rank B over E if their aversion to inequality is sufficiently high: the weight given to gains to individual 1 relative to gains to individual 3 needs to be large enough to cancel out the fact that the health gain to individual 1 is smaller than the health gain to individual 3. If aversion to inequality is low, then the weight given to individual 1 relative to individual 3 will not be enough to overcome the difference in health gain, and the decision maker will rank E over B. In what follows, we make explicit this equity-efficiency trade-off and formalize it.

First, we turn to the theoretical basis for this type of analysis and we start with the normative choice of SWFs (Anand et al., 2001; Anand, 2002; Bleichrodt & van Doorslaer, 2006; Adler, 2019). A health maximizing utilitarian SWF is the simple sum of individual health gains:

$$W_u = \sum_{i=1}^{N} h_i,$$

where W_u is social welfare, h_i is the health) of individual *I*, and N the number of people in the population. In principle, health could be measured on any cardinal scale that can be added up, and could represent current health, future health, or lifetime health. To fix ideas, however, we can think of health as lifetime health measured in terms of health-adjusted life expectancy at birth. Implicitly, standard cost-effectiveness analysis uses such a SWF—it simply adds up individual net health gains (i.e. health gains minus health opportunity costs) to yield net population health gain, implicitly assigning a unitary weight to each.

The level-dependent (prioritarian) SWF is a sum of transformed individual health levels representing each individual's contribution to social welfare. Individual health is transformed into the corresponding social welfare contribution using a concave function, meaning that extra weight is given to health gains to people who are worse-off in terms of health. In its more general form, prioritarianism is a consequentialist ethical theory that evaluates outcomes by the transformed sum total of individual well-being, with more weight given to well-being gains for the worse-off relative to the better off (Parfit, 1997, 2002). Prioritarianism has a single objective: to maximize the sum total of well-being values adjusted so as to give 'priority' (a larger weight) to the worse-off. The ethical justification for assigning extra weight is simply that the more worse-off a person is, the more important it is, morally speaking, to help that person. In this chapter we are concerned with gains and distribution of lifetime health and define the worse-off as those with less lifetime health.[3] In practice, we

---

[3] Other ways of defining the worse-off are discussed in Chapter 6.

often speak of two objectives—increasing total health and reducing health inequality—which philosophers call a 'pluralist egalitarian' view (Otsuka & Voorhoeve, 2018). In cases where there is a distributive conflict between the two objectives, a trade-off must be made. If a choice requires a trade-off between priority to the worse-off and total health, a level-dependent SWF will integrate both concerns by using an 'inequality aversion' parameter that makes this trade-off explicit. The SWF can rank options if the decision maker is willing to specify a value, or by sensitivity analysis if they are willing to specify a *range* of reasonable values.

The level-dependent SWF can be written as:

$$W = \sum_{i=1}^{N} g(h_i),$$

where N = total population size, and $g(h_i)$ is a strictly increasing and strictly concave transformation function of health.

The transformation of health into social welfare is what distinguishes this SWF from the utilitarian SWF. The Atkinson, isoelastic transformation function can be written as:

$$g(h) = \frac{h^{1-\varepsilon}}{1-\varepsilon}$$

with $\varepsilon > 0$, ε is an equity parameter indicating the degree of aversion to health inequality. In the special case of $\varepsilon = 1$, $g(h) = \log h$. With $\varepsilon = 0$, the SWF becomes utilitarian. Fig 13.3 illustrates how the transformation function works.

The form of the transformation function (left panel in Fig 13.3) reflects the relative sensitivity to transfers at different levels of health and is a direct reflection of impartial societal value judgments. Note that the marginal social value of a change in health (HALY) decreases with increasing health (right panel in Fig 13.3), and this satisfies the Pigou-Dalton condition ((Bleichrodt & van Doorslaer, 2006), see also Chapter 11).[4]

The concept of 'equally distributed equivalent' (EDE) is key to understanding the Atkinson SWF (Atkinson, 1970). Atkinson introduced EDE as the social welfare of a given income in a population that takes both its total and

---

[4] With Atkinson's transformation function, this works well for lifetime health above 10–20 HALYs (which is very often the case). When lifetime health approaches zero, the marginal value approaches infinity. This is not realistic and may restrict the use of this SWF for low levels of lifetime health. One example would be comparisons involving diseases associated with under-five mortality in low-income countries.

LEVEL-DEPENDENT SWFS EXPLAINED | 259

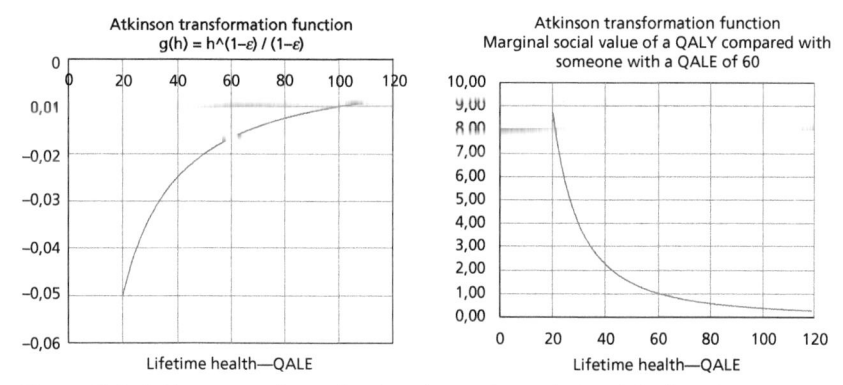

Figure 13.3 Atkinson transformation function and marginal social value of a HALY.
Note: the left panel shows the transformation function for a value of (= 2), the right panel shows the corresponding marginal social value of a HALY compared with a HALY to someone with a lifetime health of 60.

distribution into account. The EDE is the level of income that if equally distributed would generate the same level of social welfare as that generated by the actual distribution of income. The EDEH of a given distribution is the level of health per person which, if equally distributed, would give the same level of social welfare as the original distribution. The value of ε is crucial. As ε approaches infinity, the SWF approaches the 'Rawlsian SWF' that assigns absolute priority to the worst off (as illustrated in Fig 13.4).

In this figure, the upper panel shows one actual distribution of lifetime health for five quintiles. The average is 69 HALYs. Imagine a utilitarian SWF with $\varepsilon = 0$. This would mean that the upper panel and the left-hand panel represent distributions that achieve the same level of social welfare. Alternatively, imagine a Rawlsian SWF, with ε approaching infinity. This would mean that the upper panel and the right-hand panel represent distributions that achieve the same level of social welfare. In other words, a given distribution (in the upper panel) can be equally good as a uniform distribution at 69 or another uniform distribution at 62, depending on the equity parameter.

EDEH is ordinally equivalent to the Atkinson index of social welfare—that is, it ranks HALY distributions in the same order. It can be written as follows:

$$EDEH = \left(\frac{1}{N} \Sigma h_i^{1-\varepsilon} \right)^{\frac{1}{1-\varepsilon}}.$$

EDEH expresses the level of social welfare represented by an Atkinson SWF on the same scale as individual health.

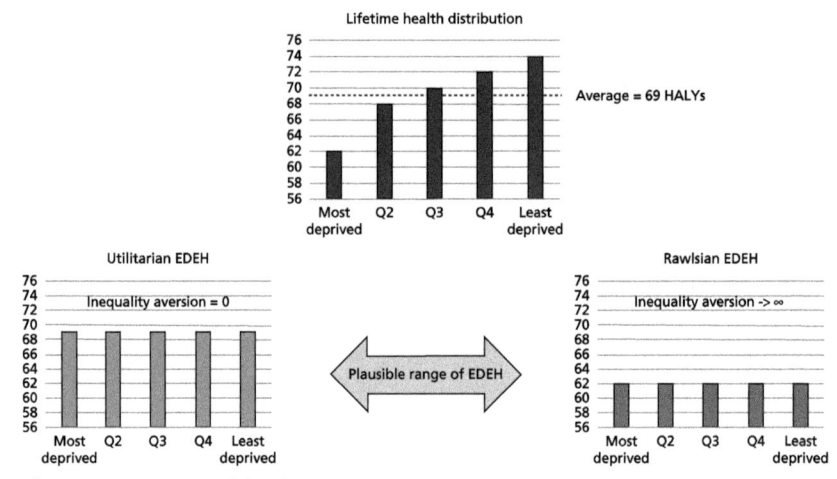

Figure 13.4 EDEH explained.

Note: the left panel shows inequality aversion = 0 and the right panel shows inequality aversion → infinity.

There are several variants of the level-dependent social welfare function. We have so far discussed Atkinson's SWF applied to distributions of health. Let us now briefly compare it to the Kolm-Pollak SWF (Kolm, 1976; Asaria et al., 2016). The Kolm-Pollak SWF can be written as follows:

$$\sum_{i=1}^{N} g(h_i) = -\sum_{i=1}^{N} e^{-\alpha h_i},$$

where α is the aversion to inequality parameter. The ordinally equivalent Kolm-Pollak EDEH form is written as:

$$EDEH = \left(\frac{1}{\alpha}\right)\log\left(\frac{1}{n}\sum_{i=1}^{N} e^{-\alpha h_i}\right)$$

The most important difference between the two is that the Atkinson EDEH is concerned with relative inequality and the Kolm-Pollak EDHE is concerned with absolute inequality in lifetime health. Compare distributions in Programme X and Y in Fig 13.5.

The baseline levels (shaded dark grey) are the same in X and Y. In distribution X, each individual gets another 10 HALYs. In distribution Y, each individual gets another 30 HALYs. Absolute differences between the resulting levels of health (10 HALYs) are the same between individuals in X and Y, while the relative differences are not (in distribution X, individuals 2 and 3 have 33% and 67% more health than individual 1; in distribution Y, the gaps are 20% and 40% respectively). For a given α, the Kolm-Pollak index of inequality will be the same in the two distributions, while Atkinson's index of inequality would be different. Another way to

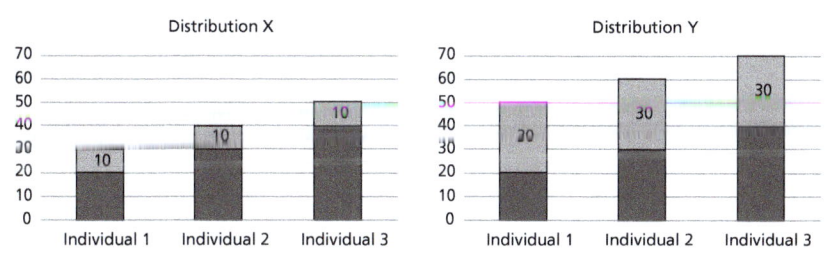

Figure 13.5 Illustration of two distributions with the same absolute inequality, but different relative inequality.

put it is that the Atkinson index satisfies the axiom of scale invariance: any equal proportional change in each individual's level of health should not change the measure of inequality. In the measurement of income inequality, scale invariance is often seen as a desirable property. Others, including Atkinson, have argued that scale invariance may not be the right property of a health inequality index (Atkinson, 2013). Since age at death has an upper limit of, say, about 120 years, decision makers may be more concerned about absolute inequalities than relative. If the analyst is concerned with absolute inequality, the Kolm-Pollak index may be appropriate. However, the Kolm-Pollak index is rarely used and most analysts seem to be most concerned with relative inequalities (for discussions about relative and absolute inequality in health see Gakidou et al., 2000; Harper et al., 2010). Whether decision makers in general think absolute or relative inequality is most important is unfortunately not known. In the absence of any reason for presuming one thing rather than another, some attempt to elicit actual decision makers' views in any specific application seems desirable.

The Kolm-Pollak SWF transformation function can be written as follows:

$$g(h_i) = -e^{-\alpha h_i}$$

The form of the function is illustrated in Fig 13.6.

We see from the right-hand panel in the figure that the marginal social value of a HALY difference is decreasing as health increases, and—unlike the Atkinson function—the marginal value does not approach infinity as health approaches zero. Hence, the Kolm-Pollak function may be useful in analyses involving diseases associated with child mortality.

13.2 Measures of inequality in health derived from SWFs

A level-dependent SWF can be represented as the combination of aggregate health and an inequality metric applied to the distribution of health (Sen, 1997). An abbreviated form of EDEH can then be written as:

$$\text{EDEH} = \mu * (1 - \text{Inequality})$$

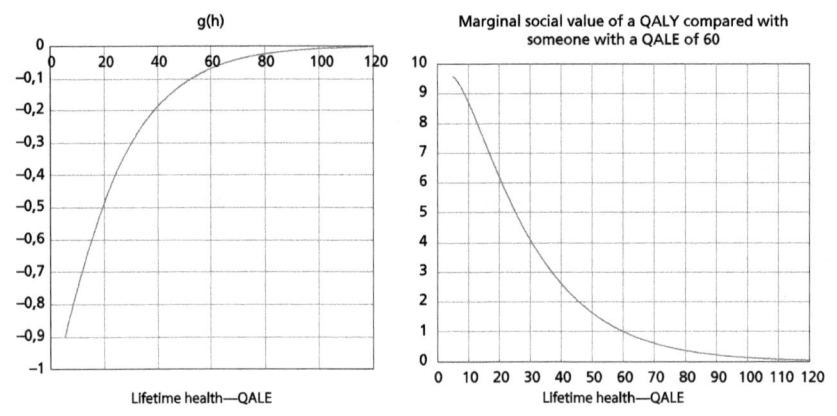

Figure 13.6 Kolm-Pollak transformation function and marginal value of a HALY. Note: the left panel shows the function for a given value of (= 0.025); the right panel shows the marginal social value of a HALY difference compared with someone with a HALE of 60.

where μ is mean health in the population and 'Inequality' is a measure of inequality or inequity in health. For absolute measures, such as Kolm-Pollak, the abbreviated form is: EDEH = μ–K(α). It is easy to see that if health is distributed equally, EDEH equals mean health in the population. For an equal distribution, EDEH = μ holds by definition, regardless of the aversion for inequality. If there is inequality (measured on a scale from 0–1, where zero is no inequality), the level of welfare is discounted according to the level of inequality and the disvalue assigned to this level of inequality. A distribution with high mean health and high health inequality thus can have lower social welfare than a distribution with lower mean health and lower health inequality if inequality aversion is sufficiently strong.

Atkinson index of inequality A(ε), where 0 represents no inequality and 1 represents full inequality, can be written as follows:[5]

$$A(\varepsilon) = 1 - \frac{EDEH}{\mu}$$

The abbreviated form allows a convenient split between equity and health impact and these two objectives can be represented on the equity impact plane. The split also helps us perform trade-off analysis between health maximization and equity.

---

[5] For absolute inequality measures, such as Kolm-Pollak, we get: $K(\alpha) = 1 - \dfrac{EDEH}{\mu}$

13.3 Aversion to unfair inequality in health

Before moving to the trade-off analysis, more needs to be said about the inequality aversion parameter. The level-dependent SWF forces the analyst to be explicit about social value judgments: the weights to be assigned to transfers from the better off to the worse-off or vice versa. As we have seen, when $\varepsilon = 0$, the SWF becomes 'utilitarian'. As ε approaches infinity, the SWF approaches the 'Rawlsian SWF' that would assign all weight to the worst-off. When Atkinson's SWF is used for evaluation of income distributions, analysts typically use a range of ε from 0 to 4 (Anand et al., 2001). Social preferences over health distributions are far less explored, although there is a growing literature where aversion to inequality in health has been empirically explored (Lindholm & Rosen, 1998; Dolan, 2003; Tsuchiya & Dolan, 2005, 2007; Dolan et al., 2008; Dolan & Tsuchiya, 2009; Baker et al., 2010; Lancsar et al., 2011; Bansback et al., 2012; Edlin et al., 2012; Norman et al., 2013; Petrou et al., 2013; Shah et al., 2014, 2015; Robson et al., 2017; Rowen et al., 2016a, 2016b; Ali et al., 2017; Cookson et al., 2018). Most of these studies ask members of the public about aversion to unfair health inequalities associated with socioeconomic status. Few studies ask decision makers or compare their preferences to the general public (Lindholm & Rosen, 1998; Tsuchiya & Dolan, 2007). Only a few studies ask about aversion to 'pure' inequality in health (Dolan et al., 2008; Dolan & Tsuchiya, 2012; Ottersen et al., 2014). As a general pattern, the degree of inequality aversion identified in these studies tends to be weaker (albeit still inequality averse) compared to those found in studies that focus on inequalities in health across socioeconomic groups (Costa-Font & Cowell, 2019).[6]

Results vary and this may be due to different survey methodologies, countries, and settings. Some are also based on convenience samples and cannot be seen as representative. Yet, these preliminary findings may indicate that aversion to health inequalities are stronger than for income inequalities. Aversion to health inequalities associated with socioeconomic status may also be stronger than aversion to pure health inequalities. The range for Atkinson's ε varies from 1.4 to more than 10 in this sample of surveys, indicating that the range of values for the inequality aversion parameter is wide. More empirical studies with standardized methods are clearly warranted (Costa-Font & Cowell, 2019).

If the analyst has credible evidence on a social decision maker's aversion to inequality in the form of a specific value or range of ε, the level-dependent SWF

---

[6] More work is also needed to distinguish clearly between studies measuring aversion to inequality from a perspective of (1) individual self-interest, (2) veil of ignorance, and (3) impartiality.

can be directly applied to the analysis of health distributions. If not, an alternative is to do sensitivity analysis over a wider range of values. This is the topic we explore in the next section.

13.4 Equity-efficiency trade-off analysis in practice: sensitivity analysis

We now have enough background and tools to explore how distributions of health can be ordered according to a level-dependent social welfare function. First, we show the result from such an analysis for the simple three-person example illustrated in Fig 13.2. Next, we outline a stepwise procedure for a trade-off analysis with data from the nicotine replacement therapy (NRT) exercise.

Returning to Fig 13.2, recall that we compared two policies (B and E) where one had higher impact on health than the other, while the latter reduced health inequality more than the former. The question is: for what values of ε would a level-dependent SWF rank E over B and for what values would it rank B over E? By using EDEH as a measure of social welfare, we can plot social welfare from different distributions as a function of the inequality aversion parameter ε (Fig 13.7).

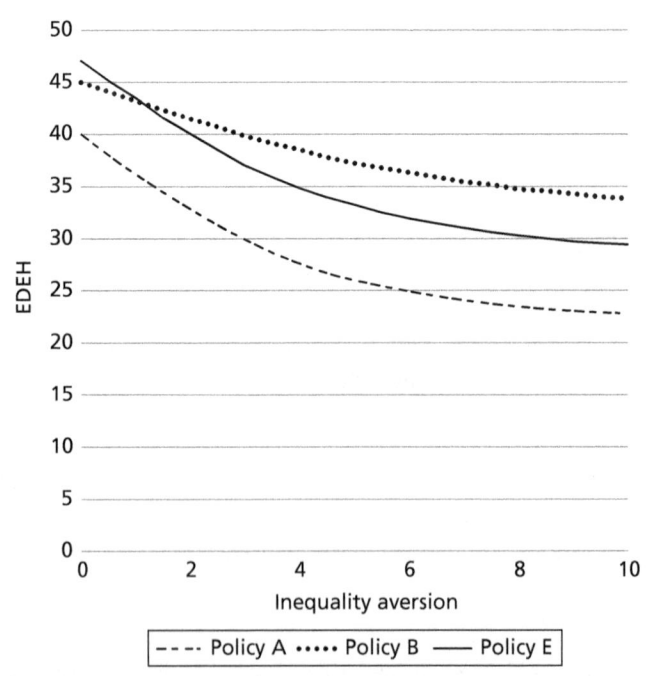

Figure 13.7 Social welfare from different health distributions (A, B, and E) as a function of aversion to inequality (range 0 to 10).

We see from Fig 13.7 that both B and E are ranked above the baseline (Programme A), while E is ranked over B when ε is low, below approximately 1.3, and B is ranked over E when ε is higher, for all values above 1.3.

One implication to draw from this example is that the conclusion is quite clear if we believe the social decision maker has a moderate to high aversion to inequality. Programme B is ranked above E in terms of EDEH when there is high aversion to inequality. A more definitive conclusion is not possible without better information on a reasonable range of ε for the social decision maker.

Next, let us turn to the NRT exercise. Recall that we compare two programmes, Universal NRT and Proportional NRT, to no publicly financed NRT (status quo). Net health impact from the two policies on ten groups is illustrated in Fig 13.8. Again, the task is how to rank the two policies. Universal NRT has higher health impact than Proportional Universal NRT, while the latter has higher equity impact.

This example uses reported data and results for groups defined by geography and socioeconomic status. To do our analysis with the data at hand, we must make three simplifying assumptions:

1. Our analytical focus is on health-related well-being.
2. If we have the data, it is always preferable to estimate health-related well-being from individual data. In this case we do not have individual data, only

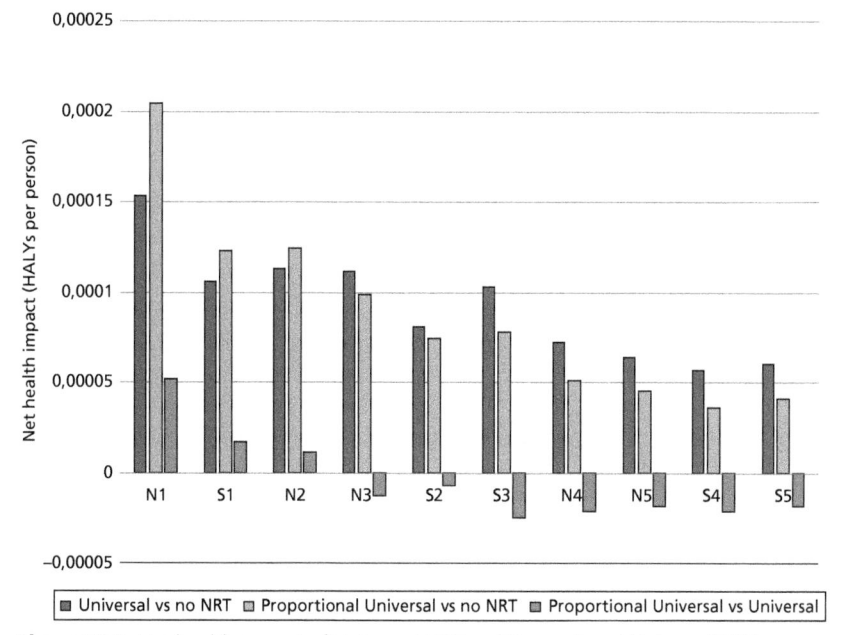

Figure 13.8 Net health impact of Universal NRT and Proportional Universal NRT versus no NRT for ten social groups, ranked by health.

data grouped by socioeconomic status and area of living. We also know the number of people in each group. We must assume, and this is a strong assumption, that all individuals in each group have the same baseline health and the same health increment. We therefore disregard within-group inequalities.

3. Finally, level-dependent SWFs are by definition concerned with pure health distributions (univariate analysis), regardless of cause or association (bivariate or multivariate analysis). With the data at hand, we have only grouped data based on non-health characteristics. No other inequality is observed or modelled. To overcome this limitation, we identify the worse-off by ranking groups from lowest to highest lifetime health, disregarding within-group inequalities. In this simplified univariate analysis we necessarily underestimate overall actual inequalities in lifetime health.

We now explain a stepwise procedure for trade-off analysis using a level-dependent SWF. The task is to order policies according to their impact on total health and health distribution.

13.4.1 Step 1: choose data input

One advantage of level-dependent SWFs is that they do not require more information than is typically available in a standard economic evaluation: baseline levels of health and incremental health. Information on levels of health are often available since it is needed to calculate incremental health gains in most models. If the lifetime health perspective is chosen, though, some additional modelling of the baseline may be needed. Table 13.1 illustrates typical data needs for evaluating distributions, based on the NRT exercise.

In this example, we are interested in lifetime health and health expectations. One single intervention will typically not substantially change life expectation in large groups. The average health impact in each group is therefore small, while actual benefits for some individuals may be large. The direction of change is therefore key.

13.4.2 Step 2: choose social welfare function

The main choices are Atkinson's SWF as an attractive example of level-dependent SWFs the Kolm-Pollak SWF if absolute inequality is of key concern. If the analyst is *only* interested socioeconomic health inequality, bivariate or multivariate equity metrics should be chosen (as discussed in Chapters 11 and 12).

Table 13.1 Example of data needs: population size and HALE under the different programme options (based on the NRT exercise)

Subgroups	Population size	No NRT (HALE)	Universal (HALE)	Proportional Universal (HALE)
1	7279927	61.925214	61.925367	61.925418
2	3959316	65.953455	65.953561	65.953577
3	5050982	66.816952	66.817065	66.817076
4	4616011	68.975036	68.975148	68.975135
5	6331048	70.344928	70.345009	70.345002
6	6474305	72.213544	72.213647	72.213622
7	4701015	72.648215	72.648287	72.648266
8	4159448	74.561156	74.561220	74.561201
9	6194904	75.597859	75.597916	75.597895
10	6501111	77.323144	77.323204	77.323185
Average HALE		70.626197	70.626290	70.626287

13.4.3 Step 3: choose inequality aversion parameter (ε) or range of ε

The sensible procedure here, in the absence of information about the kind of inequality aversion actually felt by decision makers will be to choose a reasonable range of values for ε. We suggest as a rule of thumb to start with a range between 0 and 20 and reduce the range if high values do not change the ranking. Yet another, possibly more politically demanding, procedure would be to conduct in-project experiments designed to elicit the relevant features of decision makers' values.

13.4.4 Step 4: estimate net health benefit and equity impact

Calculating net health benefits is straightforward and follows standard methods, where incremental health gain equals total health gains for the choice option in question minus total health from the alternative programme or the baseline (or status quo).

To calculate equity impact, choose the appropriate measure of equality. If the Atkinson framework is chosen, first calculate EDEH for the policies being

Table 13.2 Health distributions summarized as average HALE, A(ε), and EDEH for the NRT example (ε = 5)

	No NRT	Universal	Proportional Universal
Average HALE	70.626197	70.626290	70.626287
A(ε) (bigger is worse)	0.0122070	0.0122068	0.0122067
EDEH (bigger is better)	69.7640611	69.7641664	69.7641719

compared and then calculate inequality by using: $A(\varepsilon) = 1 - \frac{EDEH}{\mu}$. Equity impact is calculated as the difference in A(ε) between the policies being compared

Use a reasonable range of values for ε and choose a plausible value for presentation of your main result. Table 13.2 illustrates results for health impact per person, A(ε) and EDEH using data from Table 13.1. Here we have used: ε = 5.

Table 13.2 shows that Proportional Universal is better than Universal (has a bigger EDEH) under this assumption; the differences appear small but would be larger if we reported EDEH at general population rather than individual level.

13.4.5 Step 5: plot results on equity impact plane

Results on net health impact and net equity benefit can also be plotted on the equity impact plane and are useful for understanding whether there is a trade-off between net health impact and net equity benefit, and the magnitude of potential impacts. It is also useful (in later steps) for communication with decision makers. To avoid information overload, it is convenient to choose a reasonable value for ε.[7] Testing out different values of ε is also helpful.

For the NRT example, net health and equity impact is calculated directly from Table 13.2 (below), see Fig 13.9.

13.4.6 Step 6: perform ethical sensitivity analysis by using different values of ε

Finally, calculate EDEH for the options in question by using a wide range of reasonable values (e.g. between 0 and 15 or higher) for the inequality aversion parameter and plot results in a graph (as in Fig 13.10).

---

[7] For communication purposes, two graphs with different inequality aversion parameters (one low and one high) may also be produced.

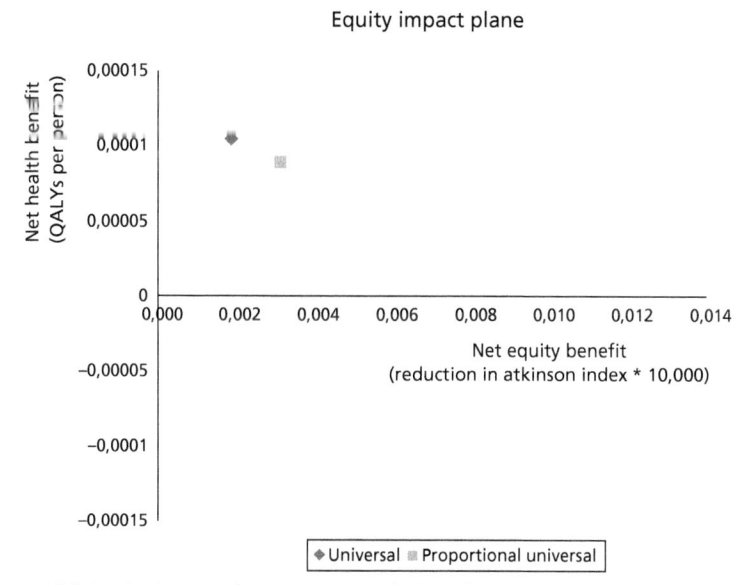

EQUITY-EFFICIENCY TRADE-OFF ANALYSIS IN PRACTICE: SENSITIVITY ANALYSIS | 269

Figure 13.9 Equity impact plane, NRT example ($\varepsilon = 5$).
Note: in this analysis, net health impact and net equity benefit of Universal NRT and Proportional Universal NRT is compared to No NRT (baseline).

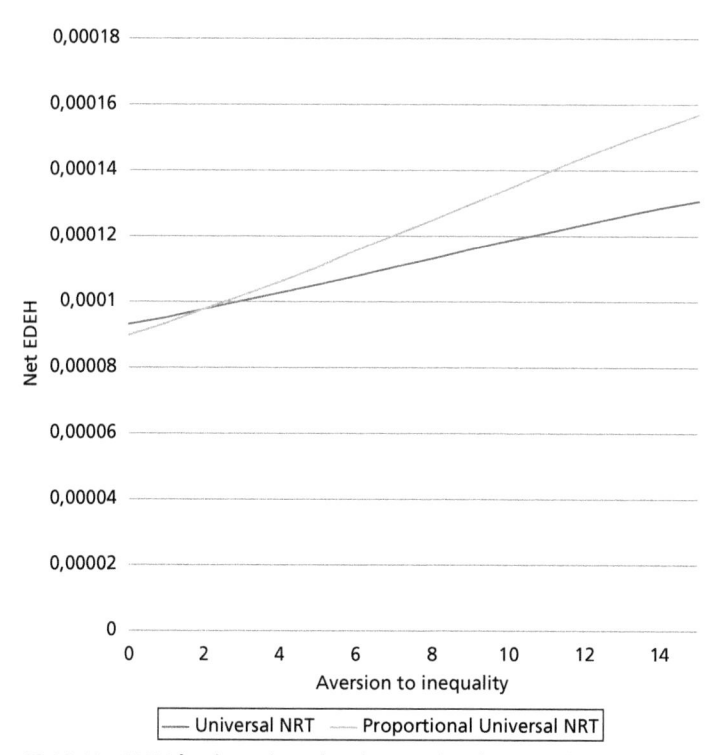

Figure 13.10 Net EDEH for the Universal and Proportional Universal NRT programme compared to no NRT as a function of different values of inequality aversion ($\varepsilon = 0$ to 15).

We see from the graph that net EDEH is highest for the Proportional Universal NRT programme if aversion to inequality is higher than about 2.2. Other forms of sensitivity analysis for other types of input where there is uncertainty are also possible and often necessary.

13.5 Comparison with rank-dependent SWFs

There are many similarities between level- and rank-dependent SWFs. Differences in practical implications may be few and the two types of analysis will often provide similar results. With respect to dominance ordering, there is little difference.

Both level and rank-dependent SWFs are consistent with Generalized Lorenz (GL) dominance. In cases where GL dominance provides only a partial ordering of health distributions, both level- and rank-dependent SWFs are ways of completing the GL partial ordering. Both types of SWFs provide complete orderings that rank one distribution over another when the GL partial ordering leaves them non-comparable. The key point is that both types of SWFs are within the broader class of Paretian, Pigou-Dalton respecting SWFs (Bleichrodt & van Doorslaer, 2006; Adler, 2019).

One pragmatic advantage with a level-dependent SWF is that it relies only on available data from standard economic evaluations: baseline levels of health and incremental health. Analysis is quite straightforward and does not require additional data on personal characteristics like income or area of living. However, if the study needs only to deal with bivariate or multivariate equity analysis (e.g. health inequality by personal characteristics such as income, or a combination of income and education), the rank-dependent SWFs could be chosen (Wolfson & Rowe, 2001). The level-dependent SWFs (Atkinson and Kolm-Pollak) are inherently univariate.

It is important to remember that rank-dependent SWFs do not satisfy the axiom of separability. Suppose the health of separate individuals in a population can be represented by a vector. Separability means that the ranking of the vectors is independent of the well-being levels of the unaffected individuals. SWFs that capture a concern for relative rank violate the separability axiom, while level-dependent SWFs satisfy the separability axiom. Evaluations using rank-dependent SWFs must include data on the distribution of health over the whole population. Since rank may also affect members of the population that are unaffected by the intervention in question, weights may also change and hence evaluation of distributions is not independent of non-affected individuals. This type of analysis can be quite data hungry.

13.6 Conclusion

In this chapter we have described how to conduct equity-efficiency trade-off analysis using an inequality aversion parameter within a level-dependent health-related social welfare function. We have also noted that standard CEA does not avoid these thorny value judgments: it simply makes a very specific value judgment that decision makers do not care about health inequality at all. If a decision maker, or the analysts, care about health inequality, this can be captured by standard measures of health (in)equity, such as the Gini or the Concentration Index and a rank-dependent SWF. This chapter has discussed level-dependent SWFs that are compatible with the ethical framework of prioritarianism. The basic prioritarian principle is compatible with different value judgments about how much priority to give to the worse-off. Level-dependent SWFs can be used to order different distributions of health following from different decisions. Even if the analyst does not know how much weight to assign to the worse-off, we have shown how equity parameters can be used consistently and systematically to perform a sensitivity analysis of how different degrees of concern for the worse-off imply different sets of equity weights for different people and can have different policy implications. Equity-efficiency trade-off analysis does not replace the need for decision makers to exercise their own judgment and wrestle with thorny ethical issues, but it can provide a helpful framework for thinking about the issues and useful analytical insight to inform their choices.

13.7 Further reading

Adler provides a useful introduction to level-dependent social welfare functions (2019). Asaria and colleagues provide an example of how level-dependent equity weights can be used in practice in distributional cost-effectiveness analysis (2015). Parfit is the classic statement of the general prioritarian view in ethics (1997). Ottersen sets out the prioritarian view as applied to lifetime health (2013).

References

Adler M. (2012). *Well-Being and Fair Distribution: Beyond Cost-Benefit Analysis*. Oxford University Press, New York.

Adler M. (2019*). Measuring Social Welfare: An Introduction*. Oxford University Press, New York.

Ali S., Tsuchiya A., Asaria M., & Cookson R. (2017). How robust are value judgments of health inequality aversion? Testing for framing and cognitive effects. *Medical Decision Making*, 37, 635–646.

Anand S. (2002). The concern for equity in health. *Journal of Epidemiology and Community Health*, 56, 485–487.

Anand S., Diderichsen F., Evans T., Shkolnikov V., & Wirth M. (2001). Measuring disparities in health: methods and indicators. In T. Evans, M. Whitehead, F. Diderichsen, A. Bhuiya, & M. Wirth (eds), *Challenging Inequities in Health: from Ethics to Action*. Oxford University Press, Oxford. pp. 49–67.

Asaria S., Griffin S., & Cookson R. (2016). Distributional cost-effectiveness analysis: a tutorial. *Medical Decision Making*, 36, 8–19.

Asaria M., Griffin S., Cookson R., Whyte S., & Tappenden P. (2015). Distributional cost-effectiveness analysis of health care programmes—a methodological case study of the UK Bowel Cancer Screening Programme. *Health Economics*, 24, 742–754.

Atkinson A. (1970). On the measurement of inequality. *Journal of Economic Theory*, II, 244–263.

Atkinson A. (2013). Health inequality, health inequity and health spending. In N. Eyal, S. Hurst, O.F. Norheim, & D. Wikler (eds), *Inequalities in Health: Ethics and Measurement*. Oxford University Press, New York.

Baker R., Bateman I., Donaldson C., Jones-Lee M., Lancsar E., Loomes G., et al. (2010). Weighting and valuing quality-adjusted life-years using stated preference methods: preliminary results from the Social Value of a QALY Project. *Health Technology Assessment*, 14, 1–162.

Bansback N., Brazier J., Tsuchiya A., & Anis A. (2012). Using a discrete choice experiment to estimate health state utility values. *Journal of Health Economics*, 31, 306–318.

Bleichrodt H. & van Doorslaer E. (2006). A welfare economics foundation for health inequality measurement. *Journal of Health Economics*, 25, 945–957.

Cookson R., Ali S., Tsuchiya A., & Asaria M. (2018). E-learning and health inequality aversion: a questionnaire experiment. *Health Economics*, 27(11), 1754–1771.

Costa-Font J. & Cowell F. (2019). Incorporating inequality aversion in health-care priority setting. *Social Justice Research*, 32, 172–185.

Dolan P. (2003). Fairness in health: what the public thinks. In A. Oliver (ed.), *Health Care Priority Setting. Implications for Health Inequalities. Proceedings From a Meeting of the Health Equity Network*. Nuffield Trust, London.

Dolan P., Edlin R., & Tsuchiya A. (2008). The relative societal value of health gains to different beneficiaries. Discussion Paper. HEDS Discussion Paper 08/12.

Dolan P. & Tsuchiya A. (2009). The social welfare function and individual responsibility: some theoretical issues and empirical evidence. *Journal of Health Economics*, 28, 210–220.

Dolan P. & Tsuchiya A. (2012). It is the lifetime that matters: public preferences over maximising health and reducing inequalities in health. *Journal of Medical Ethics*, 38, 571–753.

Edlin R., Tsuchiya A., & Dolan P. (2012). Public preferences for responsibility versus public preferences for reducing inequalities. *Health Economics*, 21, 1416–1426.

Gakidou E., Murray C., & Frenk J. (2000). Defining and measuring health inequality: an approach based on the distribution of health expectancy. *Bulletin of World Health Organization*, 78, 42–54.

Harper S., King N., Meersman S., Reichman M., Breen N., & Lynch J. (2010). Implicit value judgments in the measurement of health inequalities. *Milbank Quarterly,* **88**, 4–29.

Johansson K. & Norheim O. (2011). Problems with prioritization: exploring ethical solutions to inequalities in HIV care. *American Journal of Bioethics,* **11**, 32–40.

Kolm S.-C. (1976). Unequal inequalities. *Journal of Economic Theory,* **12**, 416–442.

Lancsar E., Wildman J., Donaldson C., Ryan M., & Baker R. (2011). Deriving distributional weights for QALYs through discrete choice experiments. *Journal Health Economcs,* **30**, 466–478.

Lindholm L. & Rosen M. (1998). On the measurement of the nation's equity adjusted health. *Health Economics,* 7, 621–628.

Norheim O. (2013). Atkinson's index applied to health: can measures of economic inequality help us understand trade-offs in health care priority setting? In **N. Eyal**, **S. Hurst**, **O.F. Norheim**, & **D. Wikler** (eds), *Inequalities in Health: Ethics and Measurement.* Oxford University Press, New York. pp. 214–230.

Norman R., Hall J., Street D., & Viney R. (2013). Efficiency and equity: a stated preference approach. *Health Economics,* **22**, 568–581.

Otsuka M. & Voorhoeve A. (2018). Equality versus priority. In **S. Olsaretti** (ed.), *The Oxford Handbook of Distributive Justice.* Oxford Univeristy Press, Oxford. pp. 65–85.

Ottersen T. (2013). Lifetime QALY prioritarianism in priority setting. *Journal of Medical Ethics,* **39**, 175–180.

Ottersen T., Mæstad O., & Norheim O. (2014). Lifetime QALY prioritarianism in priority setting: quantification of the inherent trade-off. *Cost Effective Resource Allocation,* **12**, 2.

Parfit D. (1997). Equality and priority. *Ratio,* **10**, 202–221.

Parfit D. (2002). Equality or priority? In **M. Clayton**, & **A. Williams** (eds), *The Ideal of Equality.* Palgrave, Macmillan, New York. pp. 81–125.

Petrou S., Kandala N., Robinso A., & Baker R. (2013). A person trade-off study to estimate age-related weights for health gains in economic evaluation. *Pharmacoeconomics,* **31**, 893–907.

Robson M., Asaria M., Cookson R., Tsuchiya A., & Ali A. (2017). Eliciting the level of health inequality aversion in England. *Health Economics,* 26(10), 1328–1334. DOI: 10.1002/hec.3430.

Rowen D., Brazier J., Keetharuth A. , Tsuchiya A., & Mukuria C. (2016a). Comparison of modes of administration and alternative formats for eliciting societal preferences for burden of illness. *Applied Health Economic Health Policy,* **14**, 89–104.

Rowen D., Brazier J., Mukuria C., Keetharuth A. , Risa Hole A., Tsuchiya A., et al. (2016b). Eliciting societal preferences for weighting QALYs for burden of illness and end of life. *Medical Decision Making,* **36**, 210–222.

Sen A. (1997). *On Economic Inequality.* Expanded edition with a substantial annexe by James E. Foster. Clarendon Press, Oxford.

Shah K., Tsuchiya A., & Wailoo A. (2014). Valuing health at the end of life: an empirical study of public preferences. *European Journal of Health Economics,* **15**, 389–399.

Shah K., Tsuchiya A., & Wailoo A. (2015). Valuing health at the end of life: a stated preference discrete choice experiment. *Social Science Medicine,* **124**, 48–56.

Tsuchiya A. & Dolan P. (2005). The QALY model and individual preferences for health states and health profiles over time: a systematic review of the literature. *Medical Decision Making*, 25, 460–467.

Tsuchiya A. & Dolan P. (2007). Do NHS clinicians and members of the public share the same views about reducing inequalities in health? *Socical Science Medicine*, 64, 2499–2503.

Wolfson M. & Rowe G. (2001). On measuring inequalities in health. *Bulletin of the World Health Organization*, 79.

Chapter 14

Direct equity weights

Mike Paulden, James O'Mahony, and Jeff Round

Direct equity weights are indicators of relative importance applied to effects and opportunity costs for specific subgroups of the population—such as people with or without a severe or rare or terminal illness—giving higher priority to some and lower priority to others. This chapter shows how two different forms of direct equity weighting can be used: 'health weighting', in which weights are applied directly to the health-adjusted life year (HALY) effects and opportunity costs on each side of the equity-weighted net health benefit equation; and 'threshold weighting', in which an adjustment is instead made to the cost-effectiveness threshold. The latter approach is a simple approximation to the former, though can be misleading because it fails to account for the distribution of health opportunity costs between people with different equity-relevant characteristics. In effect, threshold weighing is a one-sided form of equity weighting in which equity weights are only applied to benefits but not opportunity costs. The chapter then shows how net equity impact can be plotted on the equity-efficiency impact plane using direct equity weights. The chapter concludes by examining the circumstances under which threshold weighting can be misleading, with the aid of simple hypothetical examples that illustrate the importance of paying careful attention to the distribution of health opportunity costs.

14.1 **Introduction**

This chapter describes the use of direct equity weights to evaluate and rank decision options. Direct equity weights can be used to give priority to population subgroups based on disease categories, such as people suffering from rare or terminal or severe diseases. For example, national healthcare technology assessment processes in the Netherlands and Norway use direct equity weights that give priority to people suffering from severe diseases with a high burden or morbidity or mortality or both (Franken et al., 2015; Ottersen et al., 2016).

Direct equity weights can also be used to give priority to population subgroups based on social variables, as we show below by revisiting our example of nicotine replacement therapy (NRT) outcomes by deprivation and geographical groups.[1]

Direct equity weights can be set directly by the decision maker across the population subgroups in whatever *ad hoc* pattern is preferred. They are thus more flexible than the indirect equity weights described in Chapters 12 and 13, which are restricted to patterns that are logically consistent with the chosen social welfare function and the simulated distributions of baseline health by equity-relevant subgroups. This flexibility can be seen as an advantage, in allowing the analysis to provide a more precise reflection of the value judgments of the decision maker in the specific decision-making context. It can also be seen as a disadvantage, however, in allowing the analysis to be overly responsive to *ad hoc* special pleading and insufficiently constrained by the requirements to consider the logical implications of value judgments and to be consistent from one decision to another.

The application of direct equity weights has potentially important implications for the allocation of health sector resources. It may tilt the balance between a specific intervention appearing desirable or not, and hence meriting funding or not. It may also raise questions as to whether specific programmes should be re-designed to reduce barriers to access for certain subgroups with specific characteristics.

This chapter covers two different forms of direct equity weighting: health weighting and threshold weighting. Forms of both approaches are used in practice. For example, a recent economic evaluation of meningitis B vaccination conducted to inform policy in the UK applied a health weight to the subgroup of children receiving vaccination, such that their HALYs were valued three times higher than the rest of the population (Christensen et al., 2014). Meanwhile, the UK's National Institute for Health and Care Excellence (NICE) routinely applies threshold weighting in its appraisals of treatments for 'end of life' conditions and very rare diseases (NICE, 2009, 2017).

The application of direct equity weights raises a number of questions. Have the applications used to date adequately reflected equity concerns regarding the opportunity costs of health services forgone? Under what conditions are threshold weighting and health weighting equivalent? If these conditions are not met, what are the potential biases associated with using threshold weights as

---

[1] In principle, direct equity weights could also be defined as a function of a continuous variable such as income, rather than splitting into groups.

an approximation to health weights? In addition to addressing these questions, this chapter also considers how the results of a distributional cost-effectiveness analysis (DCEA) may be presented on the equity impact plane, creating a visual interpretation of which health programme is the most desirable.

The structure of the chapter is as follows: It begins with an overview of standard cost-effectiveness analysis, without the use of equity weights, to introduce some basic notation. Direct weighting of health effects and health opportunity costs is then introduced, first using health weighting and then threshold weighting. The equity impact plane is used as a means of visualizing the results of a DCEA. The penultimate section examines the conditions under which health weighting and threshold weighting are equivalent, and the potential biases and pitfalls associated with using threshold weights and health weights interchangeably when these conditions are not met. The chapter concludes with some guidance for decision makers regarding the recommended weighting approach to use. The accompanying exercise 14 shows students how to conduct health weighting and present the findings in the equity impact plane and can be downloaded at this website: https://www.york.ac.uk/che/research/equity/handbook

14.2 Standard cost-effectiveness analysis

In a standard cost-effectiveness analysis, a health programme is considered desirable if:

$$\frac{c}{h} < k \quad [1]$$

where c represents the estimated incremental cost of the programme versus the comparator (in monetary terms), h represents the estimated incremental health benefit of the programme versus the comparator (in HALYs) and k is a positive value that represents the cost per HALY of displaced activity, allowing the analysis to account for the opportunity cost of health forgone by funding the programme. As noted in Chapter 9, k is a supply-side concept of the cost-effectiveness 'threshold' value. This equation can also be written to illustrate the case of a demand-side cost-effectiveness threshold value, which may be set at a higher level than k to reflect individual willingness to pay for healthcare and additional social and political considerations such as the value of industrial innovation. As discussed in Chapter 2, however, we focus in this handbook on the opportunity cost of displaced activities for people's health.

Equation 1 may be rearranged to give:

$$h - \frac{c}{k} > 0 \quad [2]$$

As noted in Chapters 2 and 9, the c/k term in equation 2 represents the 'health opportunity cost' of the programme, that is, the estimated HALYs forgone if the programme is funded and resources are diverted from other activities that would otherwise have generated health benefits. For example, if c is $300,000 and k is $30,000 per HALY then ten HALYs are forgone if the programme is funded. In this example, a supply-side estimate of $30,000 per HALY implies that one HALY is forgone for every additional $30,000 spent on a health programme rather than other activities.

It follows that the left-hand side of equation 2 represents the 'incremental net health benefit' of the programme (hereafter denoted n, as in Chapter 9), reflecting the estimated incremental health benefit (h) minus the estimated health opportunity cost ($\frac{c}{k}$):

$$n = h - \frac{c}{k} \qquad [3]$$

The right-hand side of equation 2 and the inequality sign imply that the programme is only desirable if the incremental net health benefit is positive, that is, if the expected HALY gain exceeds the expected HALY loss.

Critically, a standard cost-effectiveness analysis does not consider *who* stands to gain or lose HALYs if the programme is funded. Each HALY gained or forgone is given the same value, regardless of the characteristics of those affected. The implicit equity position is that the potential health gains of all people are (or ought to be) valued equally by the decision maker.

14.3 Health weighting

If instead a decision maker wishes to prioritize people with specific equity-relevant characteristics, one approach is to apply an *equity weight* to the health gained and forgone by those people in terms of HALYs. In what follows we explore the implications of 'even-handed' health weighting, in which the same equity weights are applied to everyone with the same equity-relevant characteristics, irrespective of whether they are programme recipients who gain health benefits or non-recipients in the wider population who bear health opportunity costs. Later we discuss the implications of 'one-sided' equity weighting, in which equity weights are applied to health benefits only.

Suppose that each individual within the population belongs to one of two mutually exclusive groups, which we will generically label A and B. In principle, there is no limit to how many groups we may consider, but we will limit ourselves to two for simplicity. We will not restrict what these groups might be or whether they are disease groups or social groups or other kinds of group. For example, each person might be considered to be young (A) or old (B), or to be poor (A) or rich (B), or to have a rare disease (A) or a common disease (B), or a severe disease (A) or a non-severe disease (B). All people with characteristic A are considered together as a group, which we will call 'subgroup A', while all people with characteristic B comprise 'subgroup B'. As these subgroups are mutually exclusive, each patient is assigned to one subgroup only.

A key consideration is whether a subgroup specific resource allocation decision can be made. It may not be feasible or desirable to target a particular intervention exclusively at a specific equity-relevant subgroup. For instance, it is generally not possible to target supplemental fluoridation of mains water to specific families within a water supply area. Moreover, although some interventions such as cancer screening are commonly restricted to specific individuals likely to benefit the most, it might be discriminatory or stigmatizing to restrict on the basis of equity-relevant characteristics such as poverty, age, or disability alone. Accordingly, the decision maker needs to consider whether specific resource allocation decisions are going to be made separately for each equity-relevant subgroup or whether a common decision has to be made that will differentially impact all equity-relevant subgroups. For the remainder of this chapter we assume the latter.

If the decision maker wishes to apply equity weights to HALYs they need to determine which subgroups and the size of the weight to apply to each. For example, if the decision maker wishes to apply twice the 'value' to HALYs for patients with a severe disease (subgroup A) compared to those with a non-severe disease (subgroup B), then the decision maker may assign a weight of 2 to HALYs for patients in high priority subgroup A and a weight of 1 to HALYs for patients in low priority subgroup B.

The next step is to estimate how many HALYs are gained and forgone by patients in each subgroup if the programme is funded. This calculation requires consideration of the distribution across groups A and B of both the health gain and the health opportunity cost. This adds a layer of complexity to equation 2: rather than simply simulating the total HALYs gained (h) and the total HALYs forgone ($\frac{c}{k}$), the decision maker must simulate the HALYs gained and forgone by people in each subgroup.

In the example given in Table 14.1, funding a cost-ineffective programme results in 6000 HALYs gained by recipients in high priority subgroup A (hereafter denoted as h^A), and 2000 HALYs gained by recipients in low priority subgroup B (h^B). The total health gained by all programme recipients is therefore 8000 HALYs ($h = h^A + h^B$).

Table 14.1 Example programme with incremental costs and HALYs disaggregated by subgroup

Incremental health benefit (HALYs)		Incremental cost	Determinants of the health opportunity cost		
h^A	h^B	c	k	p^A	p^B
6000	2000	$300m	$30,000	0.2	0.8

Meanwhile, the incremental cost in this example is $300m ($c$). Since the cost-per-HALY of forgone activity (k) is $30,000 per HALY, a total of 10,000 HALYs are forgone if the programme is funded $\left(\frac{c}{k} = 10,000\right)$. The net health benefit is thus negative for this cost-ineffective programme: 8000 HALYs gained minus 10,000 HALYs lost equals negative 2000 HALYs.

Next we must consider the distribution of this opportunity cost across subgroups A and B. This distribution may depend on the relative size of the two subgroups, their relative usage of healthcare services, and the likelihood that the services they used are subject to displacement when funding new technologies. All else equal, the larger the relative size of the subgroup, the greater their healthcare usage, and the more likely their care is subject to displacement, the higher the proportion of the total opportunity cost falling on the subgroup in question. In our example, we will assume that 2000 HALYs are forgone by people in subgroup A and 8000 HALYs are forgone by people in subgroup B, such that subgroup A bears 20% of the total health opportunity cost ($p^A = 0.2$) and subgroup B bears the remaining 80% of the health opportunity cost ($p^B = 0.8$). Using this notation, the HALYs forgone by people in subgroup A are $p^A \cdot \frac{c}{k}$, while the HALYs forgone by people in subgroup B are $p^B \cdot \frac{c}{k}$.

This expanded notation allows us to rewrite equation 2 in disaggregated form, separating out the health gains minus the health opportunity costs for subgroups A and B:

$$n = \left(h^A - p^A \cdot \frac{c}{k}\right) + \left(h^B - p^B \cdot \frac{c}{k}\right) > 0 \qquad [4]$$

Equations 2 and 4 are identical. They are equivalent ways of expressing standard net health benefit (n), with all HALYs equally weighted as in a standard cost-effectiveness analysis, since differential equity weights have not yet been applied.

Now that the net health effects for each of the subgroups have been disaggregated, the third step is to apply equity weights to the health gained and forgone by each subgroup. In the following steps, we denote the equity weight applied to HALYs for people in subgroup A as α, and the equity weight applied to HALYs for people in subgroup B as β.

Table 14.2 expands on Table 14.1 by including potential equity weights for the example considered earlier. The weight applied to HALYs for high priority subgroup A is 2 ($\alpha = 2$), while the weight applied to HALYs for low priority subgroup B is 1 ($\beta = 1$).

We can now modify equation 4 to provide a decision rule based upon equity-weighted incremental net health benefit:

$$n^Q = \alpha\left(h^A - p^A \cdot \frac{c}{k}\right) + \beta\left(h^B - p^B \cdot \frac{c}{k}\right) > 0 \qquad [5]$$

where n^Q denotes the equity-weighted incremental net health benefit following the application of health weighting. Each equity weight is applied to the HALYs gained and forgone by patients in each respective subgroup; for subgroup A the HALYs gained (h^A) and forgone $\left(p^A \cdot \frac{c}{k}\right)$ are both weighted by α, while for subgroup B the HALYs gained (h^B) and forgone $\left(p^B \cdot \frac{c}{k}\right)$ are both weighted by β. The intuition for this is that any weight assigned to any subgroup must be applied not only to the HALYs gained by programme recipients in that subgroup, but also to any HALYs forgone by recipients or non-recipients in that subgroup due to opportunity costs.

In a standard cost-effectiveness analysis, the standard (i.e. equally-weighted) incremental net health benefit for the example in Table 14.2 is given by this expression derived from equation 4:

$$n = \left(h^A - p^A \cdot \frac{c}{k}\right) + \left(h^B - p^B \cdot \frac{c}{k}\right) = (6000 - 2000) + (2000 - 8000) = -2000 \qquad [6]$$

Table 14.2 Example treatment with equity weights applied to HALYs

Incremental health benefit (HALYs)		Incremental cost	Determinants of the health opportunity cost			Equity weight applied to HALYs	
h^A	h^B	c	k	p^A	p^B	α	β
6000	2000	$300m	$30,000	0.2	0.8	2	1

However, in a DCEA, the equity-weighted incremental net health benefit for the same example is given by this expression derived from equation 5:

$$n^Q = \alpha \cdot \left(h^A - p^A \cdot \frac{c}{k} \right) + \beta \cdot \left(h^B - p^B \cdot \frac{c}{k} \right)$$
$$= 2*(6000 - 2000) + (2000 - 8000) = 2000 \qquad [7]$$

A standard cost-effectiveness analysis would find that the programme is *not* desirable, since the standard incremental net health benefit in equation 6 is negative. Yet a DCEA would find that the treatment *is* desirable, given the specified equity weights, since the equity-weighted incremental net health benefit in equation 7 is positive.

In the analysis of meningitis B vaccination in the UK, the decision maker applied a health weight of 3 to the subgroup in question, which tripled the relative weight assigned to HALYs for children receiving vaccination compared to the rest of the population (Christensen et al., 2014). However, the decision maker did not apply an equivalent adjustment to the opportunity cost, thereby failing to account for how much of the health forgone was also incurred by children and hence potentially overestimating the net value of vaccination. Accordingly, the analysis may be considered to be incomplete, ethically inconsistent, or as embodying an implicit differentiation between children who gain and children who lose by bearing the health opportunity costs.

14.4 **Threshold weighting**

An alternative approach, often used in practice, is for decision makers who wish to prioritize patients with specific characteristics to apply a weight to the cost-effectiveness threshold value, rather than directly to HALYs. We assume a supply-side threshold concept as in the rest of the handbook, though the same approach can be used for a demand-side threshold value.

We will hereafter denote the 'threshold weight' as σ. This is multiplied by the cost-effectiveness threshold value (k) to derive an equity-weighted threshold, such that the programme is considered desirable in a DCEA if:

$$c/h < \sigma.k \qquad [8]$$

The threshold weight (σ) and the cost-effectiveness threshold (k) are both generally assumed to be positive ($\sigma > 0$ and $k > 0$), such that the equity-weighted threshold is also positive ($\sigma.k > 0$).

In the UK, for example, NICE uses a standard threshold of £20,000–£30,000 per HALY for appraising standard clinical treatments, an equity-weighted threshold of £50,000 per HALY when appraising 'end-of-life' treatments, and an equity-weighted threshold of between £100,000 and £300,000 per HALY when appraising treatments for 'very rare diseases' (NICE, 2009, 2017). In its 2014 'value-based-pricing' (VBP) proposals, NICE indicated that it regards its £50,000 per HALY 'end-of-life' threshold as reflecting a higher weight on the health benefits of patients at the 'end of life'. NICE noted that, 'No specific instruction was given to the Appraisal Committees with regard to the magnitude of this additional weight they should consider reasonable, but over time, practice has led to the application of a maximum weight of 2.5 from a starting point of £20,000 per QALY' (NICE, 2014). This conflation of health weights and threshold weights rests on the implicit assumption that all of the health benefits accrue to end-of-life patients and all of the health opportunity costs fall on non-end-of-life patients, as explained in more detail later in the chapter. Using the notation above, it follows that, for NICE's consideration of 'end-of-life' treatments, σ is assumed to be 2.5 and k is assumed to be £20,000 per HALY, such that the equity-weighted threshold is £50,000 per HALY.

Suppose NICE were to appraise an 'end of life' treatment with an incremental cost of £200,000 and an incremental benefit of five HALYs, such that the incremental cost-effectiveness ratio (ICER) is £40,000 per HALY. In the absence of a threshold weight ($\sigma = 1$), this ICER would be compared to NICE's standard threshold of £20,000–£30,000 per HALY, and the treatment would not be considered desirable (equation 8). However, if instead a threshold weight of 2.5 were applied to the lower bound of NICE's standard threshold (£20,000 per QALY), following the practice articulated in NICE's VBP proposals, then this ICER would be compared to an equity-weighted threshold of £50,000 per HALY, such that the treatment would be considered desirable.

We may rearrange equation 8 to obtain a decision rule expressed in terms of equity-weighted incremental net health benefit:

$$n^T = h - \frac{c}{\sigma.k} > 0 \qquad [9]$$

where n^T denotes the equity-weighted incremental net health benefit using threshold weighting.

Returning to the example of the 'end-of-life' treatment with an incremental cost of £200,000 and an incremental benefit of 5 HALYs, in the absence of a threshold weight the equity-weighted incremental net health benefit would be 5 − 10 = −5 HALYs, such that the treatment would not be considered desirable (equation 9). Alternatively, if a threshold weight of 2.5 were applied, then the equity-weighted incremental net health benefit would be 5 − 4 = 1 HALY, such that the treatment would be considered desirable.

The equity adjustment in equation 5 was made using health weighting (α and β), whereas the equity adjustment in equation 9 was made using threshold weighting (σ). Although either approach may be used to conduct a DCEA, there are reasons why health weighting may be preferred to threshold weighting, which will be explored later in the chapter. For clarity, throughout the remainder of this chapter, we will denote equity-weighted net health benefit as n^H if the equity adjustment is made using health weighting, or n^T if the equity adjustment is made using threshold weighting.

14.5 The equity impact plane

Following the application of health weighting or threshold weighting, the equity-weighted net health benefit of a programme (n^H or n^T) may differ from the standard (equally-weighted) net health benefit considered in standard cost-effectiveness analysis (n).

The difference between the equity-weighted and standard net health benefit will hereafter be referred to as the 'incremental equity benefit'. The magnitude of the incremental equity benefit will depend on the equity weights used as well as the distribution of health benefits and burdens; and if equal weights are used, then the equity benefit will be zero.

Following health weighting, the incremental equity benefit (denoted as eq^H) is defined as:

$$eq^H = n^H - n \qquad [10]$$

For example, when the programme summarized in Table 14.2 was considered earlier in the chapter, the standard net health benefit (n) was *negative* 2000 HALYs (equation 6), yet, following health weighting, the equity-weighted net health benefit (n^H) was *positive* 2000 HALYs (equation 7). From equation 10, the incremental equity benefit (eq^H) is therefore:

$$eq^H = n^H - n = 2000 - (-2000) = 4000 \qquad [11]$$

Also, from equation 10, it follows that the equity-weighted net health benefit is the sum of the standard net health benefit and the incremental equity benefit:

$$n^H = n + eq^H \qquad [12]$$

Alternatively, if threshold weighting is applied instead of health weighting, the incremental equity benefit (denoted as eq^T) is:

$$eq^T = n^T - n \qquad [13]$$

such that the equity-weighted incremental net health benefit (n^T) is:

$$n^T = n + eq^T \qquad [14]$$

The equity impact plane introduced in Chapter 3 allows for a graphical interpretation of the standard net health benefit (n), incremental equity benefit (eq^H or eq^T), and equity-weighted net health benefit (n^H or n^T). In economic evaluations of multiple decision options, all options may be represented and interpreted on a single equity impact plane, allowing for a ranking to be made in terms of their desirability.

For example, Fig 14.1 plots the right-hand quadrant of an equity impact plane for a DCEA of the three NRT options considered in the exercise accompanying this chapter: 'No NRT' (solid black line), 'Universal NRT' (dotted dark grey line), and 'Proportional Universal NRT' (dashed light grey line). In this example, a positive health weight of 3 has been assigned to patients in each of the two least advantaged social groups (N1 and S1), with all other HALYs unweighted (i.e. weighted at one).

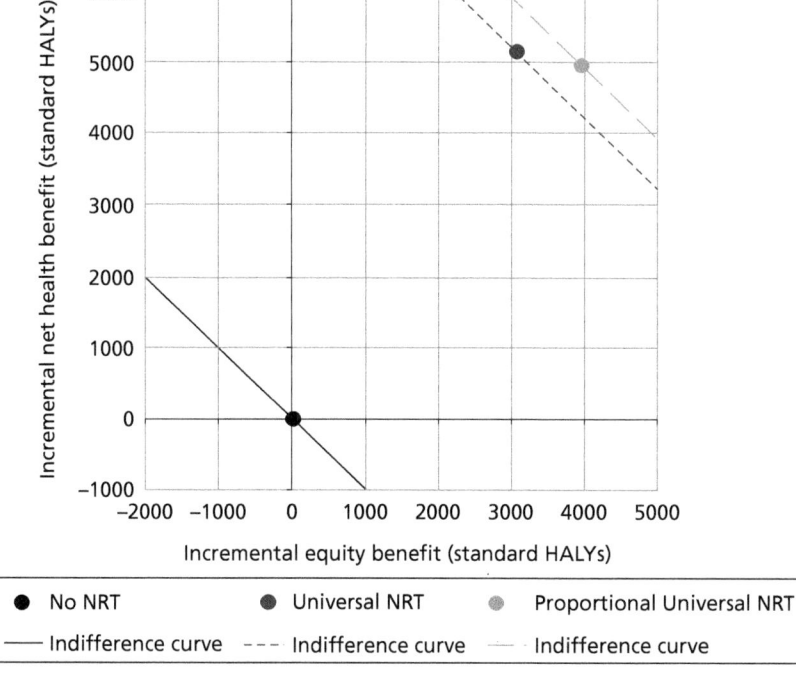

Figure 14.1 Equity-efficiency impact plane with health weights prioritizing N1 and S1.

The vertical axis of the equity impact plane reports the output of a standard cost-effectiveness analysis with no equity adjustment. The incremental net health benefit (n) of each option is compared to a common baseline comparator plotted at the origin. Options in the top half of the equity impact plane are cost-effective compared to this comparator, while those in the bottom half of the plane are not.

In the example in Fig 14.1, the baseline comparator is No NRT. Universal NRT and Proportional Universal NRT are both cost-effective compared to No NRT, since they both lie in the top half of the plane. In evaluations with multiple policy options, the relative location of each policy option on the vertical axis can be used to rank the options in terms of cost-effectiveness, with the most cost-effective policy option at the top of the plane and the least cost-effective at the bottom. In this example, the most cost-effective policy is Universal NRT (with a standard net health benefit of 5146 HALYs, reflected by the vertical distance of the dark grey point from the horizontal axis), followed by Proportional Universal NRT (4955 HALYs, such that the light grey point is slightly closer to the horizontal axis than the dark grey point), and finally No NRT (zero HALYs, since this is the baseline comparator, such that the black point is touching the horizontal axis).

The horizontal axis of the equity impact plane reports the incremental equity benefit of each option compared to the baseline comparator. A key question is what units to use when quantifying this incremental equity benefit. There is an advantage to using the same units as those used on the vertical axis, since this allows direct comparisons between cost-effectiveness (on the vertical axis) and equity impact (on the horizontal axis) and a straightforward 1:1 trade-off between the two using straight line diagonal indifference curves with a slope of minus 1. Because the purpose of the vertical axis is to report the results of a standard CEA, the most appropriate units to use for this axis are 'standard' HALYs. It follows that the most convenient units to use on the horizontal axis are also standard HALYs.[2]

---

[2] Although, in principle, analysts may choose to use other units on the horizontal axis; for example an analyst may wish to 'normalize' the incremental equity benefit (such that it is no longer measured in standard HALYs). These same units would also need to be used for the vertical axis in order to permit direct trade-offs between cost-effectiveness and equity considerations. This would then raise the issue that the vertical axis no longer reports the output of a conventional cost-effective analysis (CEA) in terms of standard HALYs, which is one of the primary purposes of the equity impact plane. In order that the vertical axis retains its intended meaning, while allowing for direct trade-offs between cost-effectiveness and equity consideration, we therefore recommend that analysts use standard HALYs as the unit of measurement for both axes.

There is a further question about how to choose the reference group with an equity weight of 1.

In mathematical terms the choice does not matter; the indifference curves will still give the correct answer. However, for communication purposes we generally recommend that analysts assign a health weight of 1 to the best-off subgroup, since this ensures that the incremental equity impact of a 'progressive' programme that disproportionately benefits worse-off groups is positive so long as the weights are 'progressive' (i.e. assign higher weights to worse-off groups).

In the example in Fig 14.1, the baseline comparator is No NRT. The incremental equity benefit of Universal NRT is 3065 HALYs, reflected by the horizontal distance of the dark grey point from the vertical axis. This means that Universal NRT is regarded as more equitable than No NRT (the baseline comparator), with this incremental equity benefit assigned the same value by the decision maker as 3065 standard HALYs worth of net health benefit. Meanwhile, the incremental equity benefit of Proportional Universal NRT is greater, at 3950 HALYs, implying that this policy is even more equitable than Universal NRT, such that the light grey point is plotted even further away from the vertical axis. It follows that, while Proportional Universal NRT is less cost-effective than Universal NRT (with lower incremental net health benefit, as illustrated on the vertical axis), it is considered more equitable (with a greater incremental equity benefit, as illustrated on the horizontal axis). Determining which policy is the more desirable therefore requires trading-off the cost-effectiveness and equity benefit of each.

From equation 12, the equity-weighted incremental net health benefit of each option is the sum of the standard incremental net health benefit (vertical axis of the equity impact plane) and the incremental equity benefit (horizontal axis). Since both axes are reported in the same units (standard HALYs), these can be summed to give the equity-weighted incremental net health benefit.

The indifference lines in Fig 14.1 allow for interpretation of the equity-weighted net health benefit of each option. Each line slopes down and to the right at a 45-degree angle and cuts through a different option. The line passing through each policy option represents all combinations of standard incremental net health benefit (vertical axis) and incremental equity benefit (horizontal axis) that sum together to give the same equity-weighted incremental net health benefit as the option in question.

For example, Universal NRT has a standard incremental net health benefit of 5146 HALYs and an incremental equity benefit of 3065 HALYs, which sum together to give an equity-weighted incremental net health benefit of 8211 HALYs. The dotted dark grey line cutting through Universal NRT therefore represents all possible points on the equity impact plane associated with an equity-weighted incremental net health benefit of 8211 HALYs. This includes the point on the vertical axis where the standard incremental net health benefit is 8211 HALYs and the incremental equity benefit is zero, the point 1 HALY to the right and 1 HALY below this, where the standard incremental net health benefit is 8210 HALYs and the incremental equity benefit is 1 HALY, and so on for all possible combinations of standard incremental net health benefit and incremental equity benefit that sum to 8211 HALYs. The dashed light grey line cutting through Proportional Universal NRT has a similar interpretation, except that it plots all combinations of points that sum to 8905 HALYs, representing the equity-weighted incremental net health benefit for Proportional Universal NRT. Finally, the solid black line cutting through No NRT plots all combinations of points with an equity-weighted incremental net health benefit of zero, the same as No NRT.

These lines can be interpreted as social indifference curves, since each represents a set of points on the equity impact plane between which the social decision maker is indifferent. Critically, although the decision maker is indifferent between all points on the same line, the decision maker prefers points located on lines further towards to the top right of the equity impact plane. In the example in Fig 14.1, this means the decision maker prefers any policy on the dashed light grey line to any policy on the dotted dark grey line, which in turn is preferred to any policy on the solid black line. It follows that the decision maker prefers Proportional Universal NRT to Universal NRT, which in turn is preferred to No NRT. This is the same conclusion that would be reached by comparing the numerical estimates of equity-weighted incremental net health benefit for each option. Using social indifference curves on the equity-efficiency impact plane allows this comparison to be made visually.

The same principles can be used to compare tens or hundreds of different options on the same equity-efficiency impact plane. A linear indifference curve is plotted through each, angled down and right at a 45-degree angle to the vertical axis, and then the options can be ranked with the most desirable option lying on the indifference curve closest to the top-right corner, and the least desirable option on the indifference curve closest to the bottom-left. Although all options in the top-right quadrant of the plane (positive standard incremental net health benefit and positive incremental equity benefit) are preferred to all options in the bottom-left quadrant of the plane (negative standard incremental net health benefit and negative incremental equity benefit), there may be cases where an option in the top-left or bottom-right quadrants is preferred to one in the top-right quadrant. The use of social indifference curves allows for simple visual determination of such cases, in a way that may not be visually obvious otherwise.

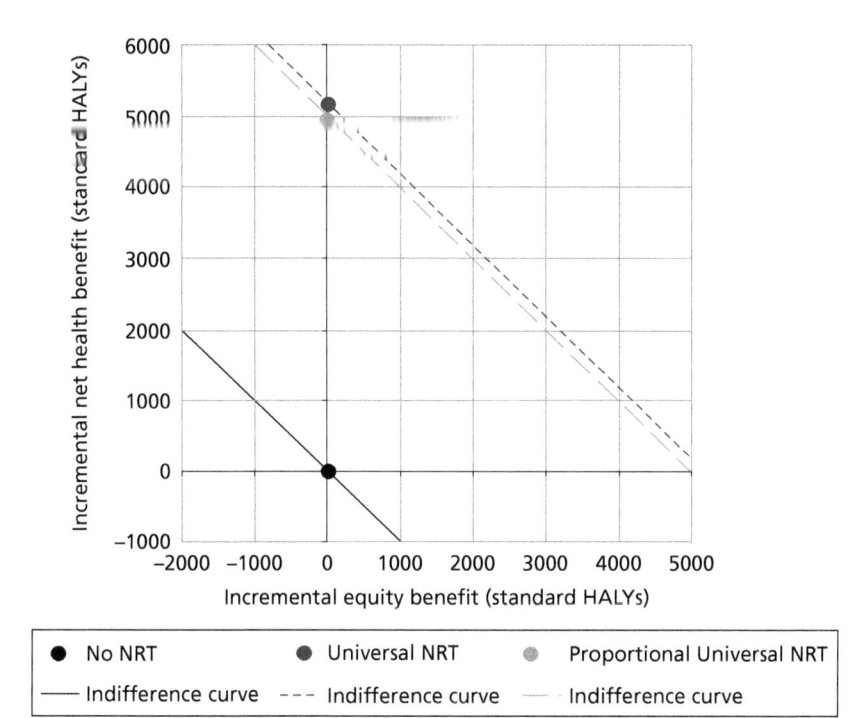

Figure 14.2 Equity-efficiency impact plane with no health weights (equal weighting).

We will now consider how the equity-efficiency impact plane in Fig 14.1 might change in response to the application of different health weights.

Fig 14.2 plots an equity-efficiency impact plane for the same comparison of three NRT policies except that no health weights are applied, such that the economic evaluation is equivalent to a standard cost-effectiveness analysis. Since there is no incremental equity benefit associated with any of the policy options, all policies are plotted on the vertical axis. Indifference curves are not needed because the ranking of policies can be read from the vertical axis: Universal NRT is the most cost-effective (and hence the most desirable, since there are no equity benefits to consider), while No NRT is the least cost-effective and hence least desirable.

Fig 14.3 plots an equity-efficiency impact plane for the same comparison of three NRT policies, except that the decision maker is assumed to adopt 're-gressive' equity weights, assigning a lower health weight of 0.5 to patients in the two most disadvantaged social groups (N1 and S1). This means that policies which favour these disadvantaged groups are valued relatively less than policies which provide equivalent benefits to more advantaged groups. Since Proportional Universal NRT provides the greatest standard incremental net

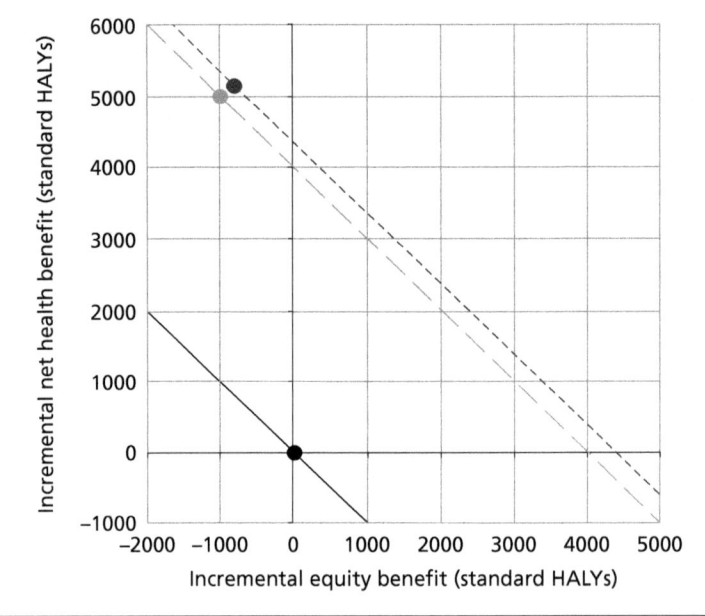

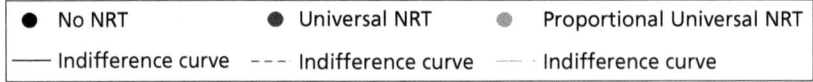

Figure 14.3 Equity-efficiency impact plane with 'regressive' health weights applied to N1 and S1.

health benefit for patients in disadvantaged social groups, it has the most negative incremental equity benefit (-987 HALYs), resulting in an equity-weighted incremental net health benefit of 3967 HALYs vs No NRT. Universal NRT also has a negative incremental equity benefit (-766 HALYs), resulting in an equity-weighted incremental net health benefit of 4380 HALYs vs No NRT. It follows that Universal NRT is the most desirable option and Proportional Universal NRT is the second most desirable, a reversal of the ordering from when 'progressive' equity weights were adopted earlier (Fig 14.1). Note that both options are plotted to the left of the vertical axis in Fig 14.3, since the incremental equity benefit of both is negative, that is, both appear relatively less desirable than they did before the application of equity weights.

14.6 Are health weights and threshold weights equivalent?

Earlier in the chapter we considered two approaches for conducting a DCEA: health weighting (using α and β) and threshold weighting (using σ).

This raises a question as to the conditions under which health weights and threshold weights are interchangeable. Can a health weight be used directly as a threshold weight, and, if so, does a threshold weight result in equivalent equity-weighted incremental net health benefit as an identical health weight?

In this final section we will answer this technical question. We will demonstrate that, while it is possible to construct hypothetical situations where health weights and threshold weights are interchangeable, in practice they are typically not interchangeable. Furthermore, there are some cases where it is impossible to specify a positive threshold weight which leads to equivalent equity-weighted incremental net health benefit as a desired health weight. As a result, where equity weighting is desired, we recommend that decision makers avoid using threshold weights and use health weights instead.

We recommend this even in the extremely simple special case where programme recipients are all high priority individuals and the health opportunity costs are all borne exclusively by low priority individuals. In this case there is no need to apply equity weights to health opportunity costs because they are all borne by low priority individuals with a weight of 1 – and so 'one-sided' equity weighting of health benefits yields the same result as 'even-handed' equity weighting of both benefits and opportunity costs. Although threshold weighting will then yield the same ranking of options as health weighting, it will nevertheless yield a lower equity-weighted net health benefit.

If health weights are applied to more than two equity-relevant subgroups (i.e. implying more than one 'exchange rate' between HALYs for different subgroups) then it is impossible to find a threshold weight that will exactly replicate health weighting. A single 'exchange rate' between programme recipients and non-recipients cannot capture the more intricate implications of many different HALY weights applied to multiple equity-relevant subgroups. We will therefore constrain ourselves to considering the simple case in which a single health weight (α) is applied to HALYs for people in subgroup A only, while the HALYs for people in subgroup B remain unweighted (i.e. the weight is set to one).

From the left hand side of equation 5, the equity-weighted incremental net health benefit (n^H) that arises through the application of a single health weight (α) for subgroup A, where subgroup B is unweighted (such that $\beta=1$), is given by:

$$n^H = \alpha.\left(h^A - p^A.\frac{c}{k}\right) + \left(h^B - p^B.\frac{c}{k}\right) \qquad [15]$$

Meanwhile, from the left hand side of equation 9, the equity-weighted incremental net health benefit (n^T) that arises through the use of a threshold weight (σ) is given by:

$$n^T = h - \frac{c}{\sigma.k} \qquad [16]$$

In order for the application of a single health weight to result in an equivalent equity-weighted net health benefit as the use of an identical threshold weight, equations 15 and 16 must be equal ($n^H = n^T$), and α and σ must also be equal ($\alpha = \sigma$), such that:

$$\alpha.\left(h^A - p^A.\frac{c}{k}\right) + \left(h^B - p^B.\frac{c}{k}\right) = h - \frac{c}{\alpha.k} \qquad [17]$$

Solving equation 17 in terms of α yields a single general solution, which holds provided that the incremental cost of the programme and the net health benefit for subgroup A are both non-zero ($c \neq 0$ and $h^A \neq p^A.\frac{c}{k}$):[3]

$$\alpha = \frac{c}{\left(h^A.k - p^A.c\right)} \qquad [18]$$

In general, equation 18 must hold in order that α may be used interchangeably as either a health weight for subgroup A or a threshold weight. That is, the incremental cost (c), incremental health benefit for subgroup A (h^A), cost-effectiveness threshold (k), and the proportion of the total health forgone incurred by subgroup A (p^A) must all take values that, when combined as in equation 18, coincide exactly with the desired equity weight (α).

It is unlikely in any specific economic evaluation that the values of these parameters will coincide in the way required for equation 18 to hold. For example, in the hypothetical scenario considered earlier, based upon the parameters in Table 14.2, the equity-weighted incremental net health benefit using a health weight of 2 for subgroup A is (from equation 15):

$$\begin{aligned} n^H &= \alpha.\left(h^A - p^A.\frac{c}{k}\right) + \left(h^B - p^B.\frac{c}{k}\right) \\ &= 2*(6000 - 2000) + (2000 - 8000) = 2000 \end{aligned} \qquad [19]$$

---

[3] There are also two 'special case' solutions: (1) If the equity weight applied to subgroup A is exactly 1, as in standard CEA, then it does not matter whether this is applied to HALYs or to the threshold, since it has no impact on the equity-weighted incremental net health benefit in either case; (2) If the programme provides zero incremental health benefit to subgroup A and also has no incremental cost, then: (a) the health weight applied to subgroup A is irrelevant, since no HALYs are gained or forgone by subgroup A; and (b) the threshold weight is irrelevant, since there is no incremental cost. In this special case, because the health weight and threshold weight are both irrelevant, *any* health weight can be used interchangeably as a threshold weight.

Whereas the equity-weighted incremental net health benefit using an identical threshold weight (such that $\alpha = \sigma$) is (from equation 16):

$$n^I = h - \frac{v}{\sigma . k} = 8000 - 5000 = 3000 \qquad [20]$$

In this example, the equity-weighted incremental net health benefit is lower using a health weight (equation 19) than using an identical threshold weight (equation 20). In other cases, the equity-weighted incremental net health benefit may be lower using a threshold weight. It is also possible that the treatment appears desirable when applying a health weight but not when applying a threshold weight (or vice versa).

To demonstrate this, we will now consider another hypothetical example adapted from the one shown in Table 14.2. The only change from the previous example is that the proportion of the total health loss incurred by subgroups A and B has been switched, such that subgroup A now forgoes 8000 HALYs and subgroup B forgoes 2000 HALYs (Table 14.3). The equity-weighted incremental net health benefit using a health weight for subgroup A is now:

$$n^H = \alpha . \left(h^A - p^A . \frac{c}{k} \right) + \left(h^B - p^B . \frac{c}{k} \right)$$
$$= 2 * (6000 - 8000) + (2000 - 2000) = -4000 \qquad [21]$$

Whereas the equity-weighted incremental net health benefit using an identical threshold weight remains unchanged from equation 20:

$$n^T = h - \frac{c}{\sigma . k} = 8000 - 5000 = 3000 \qquad [22]$$

Note that treatment now appears undesirable when a health weight is applied (equation 21), whereas an identical threshold weight makes the treatment appear desirable (equation 22). If a decision maker faced this scenario, the naive

Table 14.3 Example in which health weighting and threshold weighting yield different recommendations

Incremental health benefit (HALYs)		Incremental cost	Determinants of the health opportunity cost			Equity weight applied to HALYs	
h^A	h^B	c	k	p^A	p^B	α	β
6000	2000	$300m	$30,000	0.8	0.2	2	1

application of a threshold weight would result in an erroneous conclusion about which option is more desirable.

It is possible to conceive of hypothetical cases where health weighting and threshold weighting are identical. For example, if each parameter takes the values given in Table 14.4, which exactly satisfy equation 18, then the equity-weighted incremental net health benefit is the same regardless of whether α is applied as a health weight or a threshold weight.

In this special case, the equity-weighted incremental net health benefit using a health weight of 2 for subgroup A is:

$$n^H = \alpha.\left(h^A - p^A.\frac{c}{k}\right) + \left(h^B - p^B.\frac{c}{k}\right)$$
$$= 2*(2000 - 1000) + (5000 - 1000) = 6000 \qquad [23]$$

Meanwhile, the equity-weighted incremental net health benefit using an identical threshold weight is the same:

$$n^T = h - \frac{c}{\sigma.k} = 7000 - 1000 = 6000 \qquad [24]$$

However, any change in c, h^A, k, p^A, or α from the values in Table 14.4 will generally result in equation 18 no longer holding, such that α cannot be used interchangeably as a health weight or a threshold weight. Nevertheless, h^B can be changed freely without impacting on whether equation 18 holds; for example, if h^B changes from 5000 to 8000 HALYs then this increases the equity-weighted incremental net health benefit by 3000 HALYs under both approaches, such that α can still be used interchangeably as a health weight or a threshold weight (provided other parameters are not changed).

Since equation 18 is unlikely to hold in any real-world economic evaluation, decision makers wishing to use a threshold weight should proceed with caution, since the appropriate threshold weight to use in any specific evaluation will typically differ from the desired health weight.

Table 14.4 Example in which a health weight may be used interchangeably as an identical threshold weight

Incremental health benefit (HALYs)		Incremental cost	Determinants of the health opportunity cost			Equity weight applied to HALYs	
h^A	h^B	c	k	p^A	p^B	α	β
2000	5000	$60m	$30,000	0.5	0.5	2	1

To derive the threshold weight (σ) that corresponds to the desired health weight (α), we must respecify equation 17 after relaxing the assumption that $\alpha = \sigma$, such that:

$$\alpha.\left(h^A - p^A.\frac{c}{k}\right) + \left(h^B - p^B.\frac{c}{k}\right) = h - \frac{c}{\sigma.k} \quad [25]$$

Rearranging equation 25 in terms of σ gives:

$$\sigma = \frac{c}{\alpha.\left(p^A.c - h^A.k\right) + p^B.c + h^A.k} \quad [26]$$

This allows for determination of the required threshold weight (σ) corresponding to the desired health weight (α), given the other parameters specified.

For instance, in the earlier hypothetical example based upon the parameters in Table 14.3, the equity-weighted incremental net health benefit using a health weight of 2 for subgroup A was (from equation 21):

$$\begin{aligned} n^H &= \alpha.\left(h^A - p^A.\frac{c}{k}\right) + \left(h^B - p^B.\frac{c}{k}\right) \\ &= 2*(6000 - 8000) + (2000 - 2000) = -4000 \end{aligned} \quad [27]$$

From equation 26, the corresponding threshold weight (σ) is:

$$\sigma = \frac{300m}{2*(240m - \$180m) + 60m + 180m} = 0.833 \quad [28]$$

Applying the threshold weight from equation 28 results in an equity-weighted incremental net health benefit that is equivalent to that where a health weight was used (equation 27):

$$n^T = h - \frac{c}{\sigma.k} = 8000 - \frac{300m}{0.833 * 30,000} = 8000 - 12,000 = -4000 \quad [29]$$

Since equation 27 and equation 29 result in the same equity-weighted incremental net health benefit, both have identical implications for decision-making (in either case treatment appears undesirable). Recall, however, that when the health weight of 2 was naively used as a threshold weight (equation 22), treatment appeared instead to be desirable.

Finally, in some cases it is impossible to derive a positive threshold weight that corresponds to a desired health weight. In the hypothetical example given in Table 14.5, the treatment is 'dominated' by its comparator (it is more expensive but provides less total health benefit) and so would be considered undesirable in a standard cost-effectiveness analysis. (To avoid ambiguity with alternative uses of the term 'dominated', we were hereafter refer to this as 'CEA dominated'.)

Table 14.5 Example of a health weight with no corresponding threshold weight

Incremental health benefit (HALYs)		Incremental cost	Determinants of the health opportunity cost			Equity weight applied to HALYs	
h^A	h^B	c	k	p^A	p^B	α	β
3000	−4000	$60m	$30,000	0.5	0.5	3	1

Yet, if a health weight of 3 is applied to subgroup A, the equity-weighted incremental net health benefit is positive so the programme appears desirable:

$$n^H = \alpha\left(h^A - p^A.\frac{c}{k}\right) + \left(h^B - p^B.\frac{c}{k}\right)$$
$$= 3*(3000-1000) + ((-4000)-1000) = 1000 \qquad [30]$$

A decision maker wishing to apply an equivalent threshold weight would need to find a weight that results in the programme appearing desirable (with an equity-weighted incremental net health benefit of 1 HALY), despite having positive incremental costs and negative overall incremental health benefits. Since the threshold itself is positive, it is evident from equation 9 that a positive threshold weight does not exist that satisfies this requirement.

It follows that, if the decision maker uses a threshold weight instead of health weighting, then there will be some scenarios where erroneous conclusions are drawn about the desirability of different programmes. It is impossible for a 'CEA dominated' treatment to appear desirable following application of a positive threshold weight, yet it may appear desirable through the use of health weighting. Similarly, a treatment which 'CEA dominates' its comparator cannot appear undesirable using a positive threshold weight but may appear undesirable using health weighting. In all such cases, health weighting is required to make the correct determination about the ranking of different programmes.

14.7 Conclusion

In this chapter we considered the application of two forms of direct equity weighting in DCEA: health weighting and threshold weighting. With the aid of simple examples, we explored how the application of direct equity weights under either of these approaches can result in departures from the findings of standard economic evaluations, with potentially important implications for decision-making. Throughout, we emphasized the importance of 'even-handed' application of direct equity weights to health opportunity costs as well as to health effects. This requires explicit simulation of the distribution of opportunity costs by equity-relevant characteristics. It is easy to fall into the implicit presumption that all of the programme recipients are high priority individuals and all of the opportunity costs fall on low priority individuals. This assumption may be reasonable in some cases. However, whatever assumptions are made it is important to make them explicit and to think through their implications for decision-making.

Next, we considered the equity-efficiency impact plane which allows for a visual interpretation of the results of a DCEA, including trading-off the incremental net health benefits with the incremental equity benefits. We showed how simple straight-line social indifference curves can be used to enable decision makers to visualize which policy option is the most desirable, and that there is no limit to the number of policy options which may be compared on a single equity-efficiency impact plane using this approach. When using direct equity weighting, we recommend that analysts use standard HALYs on both the horizontal and vertical axes to allow direct comparisons to be made between cost-effectiveness and equity impact, and that the lowest priority group is used as the reference norm for defining a score of 1 HALY.

Finally, we considered some important differences between health weighting and threshold weighting. Although threshold weighting is more common in practice, we identified several limitations compared with health weighting. First, attempting to apply a desired health weight as a threshold weight will generally result in biased estimates of equity-weighted incremental net health benefit; this might, in turn, result in a programme appearing desirable when it is not, or *vice versa*. Second, although it is possible in some circumstances to adjust the threshold weight so that it has equivalent implications for decision-making as a desired health weight, such an adjustment is complex (see equation 26) and requires the same information as that required to implement health weights directly. Third, in some circumstances it is impossible to specify a threshold weight that has identical implications for decision-making as a desired health weight.

There are further limitations of threshold weighting beyond those described in this chapter. In comparisons of multiple programmes, there may be no possible threshold weight that preserves the correct ranking in terms of equity-weighted incremental net health benefit. Also, if the decision maker wishes to conduct probabilistic analysis, a different threshold weight may be required for every Monte Carlo simulation in order to maintain consistency with a desired health weight.

In summary, threshold weighting is a simple approximation to health weighting but is potentially biased. Except in the special cases set out in the previous section[4], threshold weighting results in biased estimates of the equity-weighted incremental net health benefit with potentially misleading implications for decision makers. For this reason, we recommend that analysts explicitly simulate the distribution of opportunity costs as well as the distribution of effects and use health weighting rather than threshold weighting.

14.8 Further reading

An introduction to direct equity weighting is provided by Williams and Cookson (2006) and an introduction to the equity-efficiency impact plane by Cookson et al. (2017). Readers who wish to consider practical examples of the use of direct equity weighting in health technology assessment should read Franken et al. (2015) and Otterson et al. (2016), in addition to the NICE 'end-of-life' guidelines referred to throughout the chapter, though bearing in mind that these examples all involve either threshold weighting or 'one-sided' health weighting of health benefits but not health opportunity costs. Examples of specific studies incorporating direct equity weighting include Christensen et al. (2014) and Baeten et al. (2010). Readers interested in the technical challenges associated with direct equity weighting may wish to read Wailoo et al. (2009), Paulden et al. (2014), and Round and Paulden (2017).

References

Baeten S., Baltussen R., Uyl-de Groot C., Bridges J., & Niessen L. (2010). Incorporating equity-efficiency interactions in cost-effectiveness analysis-three approaches applied to breast cancer control. *Value Health*, 13, 573–579. https://doi.org/10.1111/j.1524-4733.2010.00718.x

Christensen H., Trotter C., Hickman M., & Edmunds W. (2014). Re-evaluating cost effectiveness of universal meningitis vaccination (Bexsero) in England: modelling study. *British Medical Journal*, 349, g5725. https://doi.org/10.1136/bmj.g5725

Cookson R., Mirelman A., Griffin S., Asaria M., Dawkins B., Norheim O., et al. (2017). Using cost-effectiveness analysis to address health equity concerns. *Value Health*, 20, 206–212. https://doi.org/10.1016/j.jval.2016.11.027

Franken M., Stolk E., Scharringhausen T., de Boer A., & Koopmanschap M. (2015). A comparative study of the role of disease severity in drug reimbursement decision-making in four European countries. *Health Policy*, 119, 195–202. https://doi.org/10.1016/j.healthpol.2014.10.007

National Institute for Health and Clinical Excellence (2009). *Appraising Life-extending, End of Life Treatments*. NICE, London. https://www.nice.org.uk/guidance/gid-tag387/documents/appraising-life-extending-end-of-life-treatments-paper2

---

[4] When equation 18 holds or the threshold weight has been adjusted in accordance with equation 26.

National Institute for Health and Care Excellence (2014). *Consultation Paper: Value Based Assessment of Health Technologies.* https://www.nice.org.uk/Media/Default/About/what-we-do/NICE-guidance/NICE-technology-appraisals/VBA-TA-Methods-Guide-for-Consultation.pdf

National Institute for Health and Care Excellence (2017). *Changes to NICE Drug Appraisals: What You Need to Know.* https://www.nice.org.uk/news/feature/changes-to-nice-drug-appraisals-what-you-need-to-know

Ottersen T., Førde R., Kakad M., Kjellevold A., Melberg H., Moen A., et al. (2016). A new proposal for priority setting in Norway: open and fair. *Health Policy,* **120,** 246–251. https://doi.org/10.1016/j.healthpol.2016.01.012

Paulden M., O'Mahony J., Culyer, A., & McCabe C. (2014). Some inconsistencies in NICE's consideration of social values. *Pharmacoeconomics,* **32,** 1043–1053. https://doi.org/10.1007/s40273-014-0204-4

Round J. & Paulden M. (2017). Incorporating equity in economic evaluations: a multi-attribute equity state approach. *European Journal of Health Economics,* 19, 489–498. https://doi.org/10.1007/s10198-017-0897-3

Wailoo A., Tsuchiya A., & McCabe C. (2009). Weighting must wait: incorporating equity concerns into cost-effectiveness analysis may take longer than expected. *Pharmacoeconomics,* **27,** 983–989. https://doi.org/10.2165/11314100-000000000-00000

Williams A. & Cookson R. (2006). Equity-efficiency trade-offs in health technology assessment. *International Journal of Technology Assessment Health Care,* **22,** 1–9. https://doi.org/10.1017/s026646230605077x

Part IV

Next steps

Chapter 15

Uncertainty about facts and heterogeneity in values

Susan Griffin

This chapter covers methods for describing how lack of knowledge impacts on the conduct and findings of distributional cost-effectiveness analysis (DCEA). It also sets out methods for describing how different value judgments can alter the findings. DCEA supports decisions by providing information about the desirability of options with different distributional consequences. The ability to discriminate between options depends on our level of knowledge about how each would change any distributions of health-related outcomes—potentially including financial protection and opportunity costs, as well as health. Estimating distributions of health-related outcomes produced by different options can be thought of as a factual exercise subject to uncertainty. Determining which distributions and outcomes to estimate, and choosing between options, relies on value judgments about what is desirable. The existence of different views about what is desirable signifies heterogeneity in values. This chapter will explain why and how to distinguish uncertainty about facts from heterogeneity in values, and the role of each in informing decisions.

The standard set of tools used for uncertainty analysis in economic evaluation—including deterministic and probabilistic sensitivity analysis, and value of information analysis—can be applied to DCEA. In cost-effectiveness analysis (CEA) these provide information on uncertainty in aggregate costs and health-related outcomes. In DCEA they can also provide information about uncertainty in distributional outcomes and summary measures of equity impact. These methods can help answer the question: for any given outcome (e.g. slope-index of inequality in healthy life expectancy, net health benefit, equity-weighted net health benefit), how certain it is that one option will produce a better outcome than another. The chapter will also discuss the costs of basing decisions on uncertain evidence, and how value of information analysis can be used to inform decisions aimed at reducing the incurrence of irrecoverable costs and failure to select the option with the best outcomes.

Different value judgments produce different pictures of health inequality. With perfect knowledge of the true impacts different options have on the health outcomes and opportunity costs for different individuals, the ranking of options can still differ depending on the chosen inequality metric and equity concern. This chapter explains how to use sensitivity analyses to investigate the impact of alternative value judgments, and in so doing make a DCEA relevant in a variety of different contexts. Sensitivity analysis can also be used to generate information about how building different views on equity into analysis can yield both different ranking of options and different findings about trade-offs.

15.1 **Uncertainty about facts**

Uncertainty about facts relates to lack of knowledge or imperfect information, and it is typically marked by an inability to assign a unique value to a quantity of interest from a range of many possible values. Uncertainty in the final outcome of interest—for example, an equity impact or net health benefit statistic—may reflect both uncertainty in various input parameter values and broader structural uncertainty about how inputs combine to produce final outcomes. All policy evaluations, including those undertaken with DCEA, are built upon inputs whose true values are uncertain. For example, the distributions of health effects and costs estimated in Chapter 8 rely on input values relating to need for healthcare, receipt of healthcare, immediate and long-term health effects of different health programmes, and healthcare costs. Uncertainty in these values can stem from the quantity of evidence, the quality of evidence, and the degree to which the evidence is generalizable from one setting to another. The 'true' empirical quantities cannot be measured with zero error. They are always estimated from incomplete or imperfect observations. Nonetheless, in order to estimate them, the analyst must select data, choose the estimation technique, and specify the estimation model. These choices are determined on the basis of producing the most accurate and plausible estimate. These are not merely matters of subjective preference but require scientific expertise and judgment.

This chapter does not address the problems caused by the incorrect use of evidence and methods. This would lead to the results of an evaluation being wrong (inaccurate) as well as uncertain (imprecise). We primarily focus on estimates that are accurate but imprecise. This applies both to the inputs, and to the output of the evaluation. That is, we assume the use of appropriate methods, including the decision analytic model structure, which produce an unbiased estimate of the aggregate population health impact and costs. Resolving the uncertainty would reveal the correct population value.

Taxonomies for the range of types of uncertainty met in economic evaluation often split it in two: those associated with the inputs (in modelling studies also referred to as the parameters) and those associated with the evaluative process (Briggs et al., 1994; Manning, 1996). Table 15.1 describes some different sources of input uncertainty and offers examples of further considerations

Table 15.1 Sources of uncertainty in inputs

Source	Definition	Potential issues for distributional analysis
Sampling uncertainty	Incomplete information due to observing only a fraction of the relevant data points. For example, the Demographic and Health Survey in Malawi collects data from about 32,000 individuals out of a population of 17.6 million.	The number of observations in each equity relevant subgroups is smaller than the whole, providing less statistical power to determine if estimated values differ between equity relevant groups only by chance.
Sampling bias	The completeness of information differs across the population, because groups differ in their likelihood of being in the sample. For example, lower likelihood of recruiting housebound individuals to a study. Unbiased estimation of population parameters relies on sample weights that describe the degree of group representation.	There may be an association between equity relevant characteristics and likelihood of being sampled. If the degree of group representation cannot be quantified, sample weights cannot be defined to correct for the problem.
Measurement error	Differences between the measured quantity and the true value of the quantity being measured. For example, data on diagnoses of malaria based on clinical judgment that includes false positives and false negatives.	The extent of measurement error may differ between population groups. For the example presented, it may be that clinical judgment is affected by the socioeconomic status of the presenting individual.
Extrapolation	The true value can only be estimated using data points outside the range observed. For example, the data include events observed over a period of two years, but the policy under evaluation affects survival and its benefit on life years gained is revealed only after all affected individuals have died. We define this separately to forecasting because the analyst knows the value of the input (e.g. time elapsed in the model or income levels of individuals) and wants to provide the appropriate model output for each value.	The value in some equity relevant groups may be extrapolated from an observed relationship between an equity relevant characteristic and the input in a data set that omits relevant observations. For example, if the relationship between income level and treatment efficacy is estimated from a data set that omits observations at the extreme of the income distribution.

Table 15.1 Continued

Source	Definition	Potential issues for distributional analysis
Forecasting	Imperfect foresight about future events for which no current observations exist. For example, the emergence of new diseases or development of treatment resistant pathogens. We define this separately to extrapolation because the analyst does not know the values for the input and wants to describe the expected outcome averaged across possible future values.	The need to consider whether the event will occur. For example, the impact of a volcanic eruption. Forecasting must be combined with extrapolation to infer how the event may differentially effect equity relevant groups. For example, the eruption may lead to more crop failure among subsistence farmers than commercial farmers.
Generalizability	Difference between true value in the population from which the sample is taken and the true value in the population for whom the decision is to be made. For example, the available data are from Malawi, but the decision to be informed is in Zambia.	The population for whom the decision is to be made differs in the available health services and epidemiology, but also in socioeconomic structure.

when going beyond estimating the population mean value to estimate distributional impacts. Sources of uncertainty in the evaluative process include the selection of evidence, the relationships between inputs (including choice of model structure), and the estimation techniques used, as described later in Table 15.2.

In general, the quantity and quality of evidence to support distributional analysis is often lower than that for assessing the impact on aggregate population health. One problem is that research studies often focus on the population average value rather than on how the value may differ between people with different equity-relevant characteristics (Petticrew et al., 2004; Welch et al., 2012). Whether a health programme increases absolute levels of population health can be determined without reference to baseline levels of population health. However, determining whether a health programme reduces relative inequality in health outcomes requires information about baseline health—as explained in Chapter 7. Uncertainty about baseline life expectancy and its distribution may be particularly substantial in low- and middle-income countries that lack vital registration systems.

Another problem is uncertainty about the distribution of health opportunity cost. Some cost-effectiveness analyses refer to a cost-effectiveness or decision threshold that represents a preference for health instead of health opportunity cost, and willingness to pay for health is a preference rather than an uncertain empirical quantity. However, in order to estimate a distribution of net health benefit an empirical estimate of the marginal productivity of resources is required to convert costs into health opportunity costs. While opportunity costs are inherent to any economic evaluation, information on their distribution is scarcer than information on the average marginal productivity of healthcare resources (Woods et al., 2016; Love-Koh et al. 2020).

DCEA requires estimates for a greater number of inputs (parameters) than a cost-effectiveness analysis focusing on average health. For example, instead of treating the effect of treatment on the risk of a health event as a single input, a distributional analysis calls for several inputs that describe how this effect varies with the equity-relevant characteristics. These inputs will typically be estimated from the same data sources that would have been used to estimate the overall population parameter. Asking more of a fixed number of observations by increasing the number of parameters to be estimated increases the degree of uncertainty in each. Simply, there are fewer observations per parameter. While ignoring variation between equity relevant subgroups may or may not affect estimates of the population average, it will certainly affect the estimated distribution of an outcome. Failure to characterize between group differences in the value of a model input is equivalent to assuming no variation. It is therefore important to highlight any such assumptions to prompt assessment of their validity and effect on the interpretation of the DCEA results.

The evaluative process includes the identification and selection of data, the assumptions made in specifying relationships between inputs, and the choice of estimation technique. Where an economic evaluation employs a decision analytic model, this includes structural uncertainty about the type of model (Markov cohort model versus individual patient simulation), the health states and events to represent in the model, and the possible transitions. We describe three broad sources of evaluative uncertainty in Table 15.2.

In general, there is nothing distinctive about evaluative uncertainty in DCEA compared to its use in any other form of economic evaluation. The skills and scientific judgment required in selecting data and conceptualizing models are the same. The estimation technique best able to simulate a distribution can, however, differ from that which most accurately estimates the mean, and so to populate a DCEA model different techniques are needed compared to those commonly applied in standard CEA.

Table 15.2 Sources of uncertainty in the evaluative process

Selection of evidence	Imperfect categorization of data into 'relevant' data that provide information on the true values, and 'irrelevant' data that do not contribute to identification of the true values.
Relationships between inputs	Uncertainty about the process by which final outcomes are generated. For example, incomplete information about which factors determine healthcare access, or incomplete information about how an intermediate outcome such as progression-free survival impacts on overall survival. Includes structural uncertainty in specifying models.
Estimation technique	The availability of different mathematical approaches to estimate a quantity, the accuracy of which cannot be fully assessed given ignorance of the true data generating mechanism.

Broadly, if the input value in each equity relevant group is estimated separately using subgroup or stratified analyses, the same estimation techniques apply as for the overall population mean. A stratified approach neither directly models nor allows testing of the differences between groups, but by using separately estimated inputs in a DCEA, the analyst can assume that the differences are attributable to the equity relevant characteristic. The analyst should highlight and justify such assumptions. Alternatively, the equity relevant characteristics can be included as predictors in statistical models so as to assess how an input varies with different levels of the equity characteristic and make this relationship amenable to statistical testing and examination. In DCEA there is a focus on how equity-relevant characteristics might modify the effect of a health programme on outcomes. Therefore, a suite of methods used for exploring heterogeneity in treatment effects is relevant. There are various ways of doing this, including the use of interaction terms to estimate how an effect changes according to the equity characteristic and more flexible semi-parametric and non-parametric approaches to estimating complex patterns of conditional average treatment effects (Robson et al., 2019). Estimation techniques such as quantile regression can explore whether the relationship between an equity characteristic and the outcome is constant for different levels of the outcome. For example, it may reveal whether increased deprivation increases the risk of death from smoking to a similar degree in any smoker, or only among people with higher than average risk of death. Techniques such as machine learning can identify subgroups that exhibit different relationships between predictors and outcomes.

15.2 Heterogeneity in values

Evaluation of decision options inevitably relies on value judgments, including what are the outcomes of interest and the social significance attached to changes in the outcomes. An example of a value judgment in the calculation of outcomes from an economic evaluation is the discount rate, which reflects the social rate of time preference for future relative to current outcomes. Institutions that use economic evaluation as part of their decision making process often specify their chosen discount rate, and it varies between institutions. For example, in Estonia a discount rate of 5% for both costs and health outcomes is specified, whereas in the UK a lower rate of 3.5% would be recommended, and in the Netherlands a rate of 4% is recommended for costs and 1.5% for health outcomes (van de Wetering et al., 2013; Attema et al., 2018).

Intrinsic to DCEA is the need for a specific value judgment about what are the equity relevant groups in the population. Chapter 4 describes in detail the set of value-laden choices that determine which health distribution to produce as the output of a DCEA. Each alternative represents a different viewpoint on what constitutes unfair health inequality.

While there exists heterogeneity in views on equity between people, only one choice of health distribution captures the preferences of a particular person. The DCEA must reflect the choices that correspond with the underlying social principles of those with the legitimate authority to decide which option to pursue, such as decision makers who decide on behalf of the people they represent. In many circumstances, the notion of a single decision-making authority does not reflect the variety of actors involved in the authorization of a health programme. Nonetheless, there may be many factors leading to consensus about major value judgments, in which case it is possible to assert a common set of underlying principles. If the actors are, however, likely to have different perspectives, for example an international donor agency and the ministry of health in one of the donor's aid recipient countries, their underlying principles may differ and may, indeed, clash. It would be a mistake to represent a choice that neither actor would make in an attempt to describe a 'halfway' viewpoint. Instead, a separate analysis is required to embody each distinctive viewpoint.

Where equity informative economic evaluation becomes routine practice, institutions may formalize and specify their equity principles. This is exemplified by the Netherlands, where priority is given to health outcomes by disease area according to the degree to which sufferers exhibit proportional shortfalls from a standardized disease-free life expectancy (van de Wetering et al., 2013). Such routine conventions need to be observed unless there is good reason for not doing so, otherwise an analyst may be in the position of conducting a DCEA from a perspective that is not the decision maker's. Where decision makers have not fully articulated their concern, their principles are unknown to the analyst, but are not an uncertain quantity.

When health programmes change a chosen health distribution, the decision may depend on the degree of inequality reduction preferred relative to increases in overall health. In principle, one could study choices that people have made in order to estimate this value empirically. However, this is rarely done, and may be characterized in less than fully quantified form, thereby requiring a more general judgment about the extent to which the data may be relied upon or can be used to provide quantitatively scaled measures.

15.3 Distinguishing uncertainty about facts from heterogeneity in values

Scientific judgments about factual matters that can in principle be settled by scientific investigation fall within the remit of the analyst, and should be included in uncertainty analysis. In contrast, value judgments about normative matters fall within the remit of those with legitimate authority to make the decision; they are choices to be made and not quantities to be discovered through measurement of the physical world. That is not to say, however, that value judgments cannot sometimes be measured. In such cases, the role of sensitivity analysis is not so much as to reflect uncertainty about facts as to reflect heterogeneity and disagreement in ethical views. Because of the different remits, and the different role of sensitivity analysis in each case, analysts should be careful to distinguish between the two.

Some examples of facts about which we are uncertain, and which may require scientific judgment are:

- The sources of data that provide information on the inputs to a DCEA;
- The value (magnitude) of inputs that represent empirical quantities; and
- The relationships between the inputs.

Some examples of normative choices or value judgments include:

- Value judgments employed in economic evaluation, such as the discount rate;
- The factors that determine which health distribution to estimate, that is, in what, between whom, and how differences are to be measured;
- Willingness to accept lesser health outcomes to improve equity in a health distribution.

15.4 Why analyse uncertainty in DCEA?

Uncertainty in the components of DCEA can give rise to *decision uncertainty*, where the results of the evaluation can lend support to different conclusions about which is the preferred option. Presenting and communicating the overall level of uncertainty in potentially complex modelling studies is an important step in evaluation. Failure to do so risks treating strong and weak evidence as having equal importance. Decisions based on limited or poor quality evidence are more likely to be proven wrong compared to decisions based on large amounts of high quality evidence. This has consequences for outcomes, because if the wrong option is pursued the result will be inferior population health outcomes, that is, lower and/or more unequal. Evaluating these consequences can influence the timing of decisions and the collection of further research.

Analysis of decision uncertainty is not concerned with the width of confidence intervals or frequentist inference about whether the evidence base is consistent with a hypothesis that a particular option is optimal. It takes a Bayesian interpretation and concerns the probability that each option is preferred. Imprecision in the results of a DCEA will not always translate into decision uncertainty. One may be unable to pinpoint the magnitude of a change in inequality, but be reasonably confident about the direction of change. If there are wide uncertainty intervals around the point estimate of equity impact, including the possibility that the equity impact may be zero, the inclusion of equity impacts may still alter the conclusion about which option is preferred compared to consideration of aggregate population health impacts alone.

When faced with poor quantity or quality of evidence, one option is to invest in collecting further information. More evidence reduces the likelihood of a decision proving wrong and reduces the likelihood of incurring inferior health outcomes. If the decision about which health policy to implement can be altered instantly and without penalty whenever new information arrives, it can be made separately from decisions about evidence collection and based on expected values (Claxton, 1999). However, if the decision to implement a health policy affects the ability to collect further information (Griffin et al., 2011), or cannot be changed without penalty, it may be useful to subject the results of the DCEA to further analysis that takes account of this irreversibility in order to inform the optimal timing of decisions (Claxton et al., 2016).

15.5 Sensitivity analysis

Presenting and communicating the impact of uncertainty requires sensitivity analysis. Sensitivity analysis involves changing the components of the evaluation to alternative plausible values supported by the evidence, and studying the impact on the model output (Andronis et al., 2009). Changing the value of one component while keeping the remaining components constant is called one-way, or univariate, sensitivity analysis. Changing the value of more than one input at the same time is termed multivariate sensitivity analysis. These are forms of deterministic sensitivity analysis, in which the analyst determines which components to investigate and the set of alternative values to use. The choice of alternative values may, for example, be informed by available data, or by experts, or be based on analysts' own assumptions. Deterministic sensitivity analysis is relatively easy to perform but is not comprehensive. Because it fails to reflect all possible combinations of values for all components of the analysis, it provides an incomplete picture of decision uncertainty which may, in some circumstances, also be inadequate. Whether it is inadequate will usually depend on the context and whether decision makers value a more complete analysis which may in the event have no impact on their decision.

If the likelihood and range of alternative input values can be quantified from the data, uncertainty in these inputs can be represented using statistical distributions. Sets of correlated inputs will be a common feature in equity-informative economic evaluation as when regression methods are used to determine the relationship between the input of a model and an equity relevant characteristic. Correlated inputs require the use of multivariate probability distributions, which can be complex to implement. Knowledge about correlation is often lacking, especially where the evaluation combines evidence from different sources (as opposed to a single data set that provides simultaneous measures for all parameters). In the presence of correlation between two parameters, knowing the value of one provides information about the likely value of the other. In general, ignoring correlation leads to an overestimate of the level of uncertainty.

When inputs are given probability distributions, probabilistic sensitivity analysis can be undertaken by repeated sampling of values for every component simultaneously and recording the corresponding results each time. Statistical analysis of uncertainty in the distribution of results produced by probabilistic sensitivity analysis summarizes the impact of all alternative input values for all components of the analysis. However, some sources of uncertainty, particularly those relating to evaluative methods, may not be readily amenable to statistical analysis. For example, the range of plausible model structures and the likelihood that each is appropriate may be difficult to specify in a way that can be represented by a probability distribution.

15.5.1 Presenting the results of uncertainty analysis

Uncertainty analysis focuses on judging whether a decision based on a DCEA might prove to be wrong rather than on whether the analysis is incorrect. To communicate uncertainty, the analyst can describe the probability of error, for example the probability that a preferred option does not match specified decision criteria. If an option is selected because the results indicate it is expected to reduce health inequality compared to an alternative, one investigates the probabilities that it has nil impact or increases health inequality. To communicate the importance of uncertainty, the analyst can describe the consequences of error. For example, one can describe how much lower health inequality would have been if the best option had been correctly identified. The two combined, the probability of error and the consequences if a wrong option were pursued, give an expected cost of uncertainty. This cost may be expressed in terms of lower aggregate health outcomes, higher health inequality, and—in the case of trade-offs—trading less inequality reduction for a given overall health improvement (or more health improvement for a given inequality reduction).

15.5.2 Probability of error

The dominance analyses described in Chapter 11 can be applied to the distribution of results generated from probabilistic sensitivity analysis to calculate the proportion of the results in which a particular policy meets the dominance criteria. While this can describe the probability of error in terms of the likelihood of pursing an option that does not have stochastic dominance, it cannot indicate the importance of uncertainty with respect to the consequences of a wrong decision. This is because dominance analysis informs a binary judgment about whether one distribution is better than another, not a measure of how much better or worse.

15.5.3 Probabilistic sensitivity analysis in the equity-efficiency impact plane

If the DCEA employs a summary measure quantifying the extent of inequality in each distribution of health, a simple way of visualizing the uncertainty is to present the distribution of results from a probabilistic sensitivity analysis as a scatter plot on the health equity-efficiency impact plane. It is possible to provide information about the uncertainty in the estimated policy impacts on overall population health and on health inequality by reporting a credible interval for each. A 95% credible interval provides the range that has 95% probability of containing the true policy impact. However, the two summary measures of policy impact are not independent. Presenting separate credible intervals for each may not assist decision makers who want to know what the two combined imply for the overall level of decision uncertainty. A credible ellipse can be constructed using covariance information from the probabilistic sensitivity analysis to define a joint normal distribution for the change in overall health and change in health inequality (Fenwick et al., 2004; Collins et al., 2019). This visually depicts a region with a specified probability of containing the two summary measures of policy impact. In doing so, the analyst should consider whether the normal distribution is suitable given the logical constraints and underlying distribution of the chosen inequality metric.

314 | UNCERTAINTY ABOUT FACTS AND HETEROGENEITY IN VALUES

A simple summary report of the proportion of points that fall into each of the quadrants describes:

- The probability that the policy increases overall population health (proportion of points in the upper left plus upper right quadrant);
- The probability that it reduces health inequality (proportion of points in the upper right plus lower right quadrant);
- The probability that it is dominant (proportion of points in the upper right quadrant); and
- The probability that is dominated (proportion of points in the lower left quadrant).

Fig 15.1 shows four equity-efficiency impact planes for the comparison of two health policies. The incremental impact of a health policy compared to the alternative is uncertain, but in panel (a) the majority of points are in the 'win-win' quadrant, so there is little decision uncertainty and the consequence or cost of basing the decision on current evidence is small. In panel (b) the impact on overall population health is uncertain but highly likely to be positive; however, there is marked variation in terms of whether there would be an increase or reduction in health inequality. In panel (c) the magnitude of the reduction

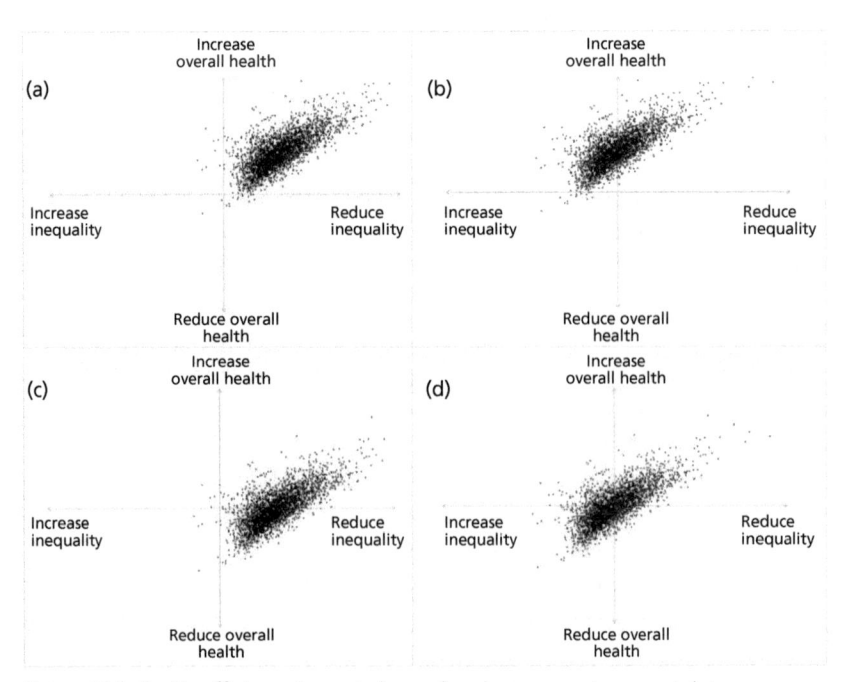

Figure 15.1 Equity-efficiency impact planes showing parameter uncertainty.

in health inequality is uncertain, but the consequences of uncertainty are primarily in terms of the direction of change in overall population health.

A proportion of points fall in the 'win win' quadrant (44% for (b) and 47% for (c)). The full extent of decision uncertainty, or the probability of error, in panels (b) and (c) depends on the relative value of changes in health inequality to changes in overall population health. That is, it depends on the proportion of points in the trade-off quadrant that would favour each alternative policy. Similarly, in panel (d) a proportion of points (42%) fall in the 'lose-lose' quadrant, but the probability of the decision being in error will be higher than this depending on the proportion of points in the trade-off quadrants that support different policy options.

15.5.4 Results for specified inequality aversion

If the decision maker's aversion to inequality can be quantified with an equity parameter (Chapters 12 and 13), or by direct equity weights (Chapter 14), this determines the rate at which they would trade overall health improvement for a particular reduction in health inequality (the rate of exchange between overall health and health inequality). In such case, the DCEA has a single objective, for example to maximize equity weighted or equally distributed equivalent health (EDEH). In this case, the uncertainty analysis can proceed with the same toolkit as used for cost-effectiveness analyses that focus on a single objective of health maximization (Briggs et al., 2006).

Uncertainty in EDEH naturally incorporates the correlation between impacts on overall population health and on health inequality, and so a 95% credible interval around equity weighted net benefit would reflect this correlation. Credible intervals and depictions of uncertainty on the equity-efficiency impact plane are useful when only two options are being compared. With more than two options, it is better to directly describe the probability that each provides the highest equity weighted net benefit. This can be in a table, or using graphs such as cost-effectiveness acceptability curves that are used in cost-effectiveness analysis to display the probability for a range of cost-effectiveness threshold values. The reduction to a single objective facilitates the use of value of information analysis to combine both the likelihood of a wrong decision and the consequences of a wrong decision to estimate the cost of uncertainty in terms of the equally distributed equivalent health that could be achieved if further evidence were collected to reduce the uncertainty.

15.6 Why analyse heterogeneity of values?

As a consequence of different value judgments, conclusions about which decision option is best can differ. This is distinct from the decision uncertainty.

For example, with complete certainty about the impact of alternative policies, heterogeneity of values may still lead to different conclusions. The appropriate process for addressing heterogeneity in preferences and values accordingly differs from that for dealing with poor or absent information.

Good communication about value judgments and their effect on conclusions about differences in population health outcomes assists decision makers in selecting a policy that is compatible with their principles. Presenting the consequences of alternative value judgments is relevant where the analyst does not know in advance the set of value judgments that describe the equity concern. It can make a single DCEA useful to different decision makers in different contexts. Similarly, it can reveal whether a common option could satisfy a disparate group of stakeholders who must agree.

Heterogeneity in preferences does not have implications for the timing of decisions or the collection of further evidence. Gathering further evidence might better describe the range of alternative viewpoints, but would not consolidate them. Plurality of values cannot be reduced with evidence collection and may not reduce over time. Equity informative economic evaluation can, however, provide information on the population health consequences of adopting one set of values over another.

15.6.1 Analysing heterogeneity

Accounting for uncertainty about facts and heterogeneity in values both require that the analyst assign alternative values to particular components of the DCEA in order to evaluate the impact on the results. However, the interpretation and actions that can arise from variation in results differ. It is usually inappropriate to assign a probability distribution to describe the range of different preferences or social values, for example to describe the range of alternative viewpoints about what is considered fair or unfair inequality. We may, however, assign a distribution to describe a lack of precision, for example to describe the uncertainty around the size of a general population average inequality aversion parameter estimated in a discrete choice experiment.

The impact of different choices and values can also be analysed and reported using scenario analysis. In essence, the results can be presented for different scales of measurement of health inequality and for different viewpoints. This is equivalent to deterministic sensitivity analysis. Table 15.3 shows scenario analyses from a DCEA of bowel cancer screening in the UK (Asaria et al., 2016). This compared the standard screening programme with the gFOBT test to a policy that aimed to increase uptake overall ('gFOBT + universal') and a policy that aimed to increase uptake in deprived areas with higher percentages of individuals of South Asian ethnicity ('gFOBT + targeted'). Table 15.3 includes

Table 15.3 Social value judgment scenario analysis in bowel cancer screening

	No screening	No intervention gFOBT	Targeted gFOBT	Universal gFOBT
Relative Inequality Indices				
Relative Gap Index (ratio)	0.17527	0.17592	0.17586*	0.17596
Relative Index of Inequality (RII)	0.18607	0.18674	0.18668*	0.18678
Gini Index	0.03101	0.03112	0.03111*	0.03113
Atkins on Index ($\varepsilon = 1$)	0.00171	0.00172	0.00172*	0.00172
Atkins on Index ($\varepsilon = 5$)	0.00918	0.00924	0.00923*	0.00924
Absolute Inequality Indices				
Absolute Gap Index (range)	10.98604	11.03064	11.02726*	11.03325
Slope index of inequality (SII)	12.88747	12.94123	12.93691*	12.94438
Kolm Index ($\alpha = 0.025$)	0.20281	0.20430	0.20416*	0.20439
Kolm Index ($\alpha = 0.125$)	1.12234	1.13028	1.12955*	1.13075

* denotes option with lowest inequality.

Social value judgment			Preferred strategy based on social welfare index			
Area level deprivation	Area level ethnic diversity	Sex	Atkinson EDE ($\varepsilon = 1$)	Atkinson EDE ($\varepsilon = 30$)	Kolm EDE ($\alpha = 0.025$)	Kolm EDE ($\alpha = 0.5$)
Fair	Fair	Fair	U	U	U	U
Fair	Unfair	Fair	U	U	U	U
Fair	Fair	Unfair	U	U	U	U
Fair	Unfair	Unfair	U	U	U	U
Unfair	Fair	Fair	U	T	U	T
Unfair	Unfair	Fair	U	T	U	T
Unfair	Fair	Unfair	U	T	U	T
Unfair	Unfair	Unfair	U	T	U	T

U = gFOBT + universal, T = gFOBT + targeted, EDE = equally distributed equivalent.

different summary measures of inequality, including measures of relative versus absolute inequality, and showing simpler measures such as the gap index alongside more complex and comprehensive summaries of the health distribution in terms of the Gini index and slope index. It summarizes which policy would be preferred given different viewpoints on what represents unfair inequality in terms of whether in the differences between people of different area level deprivation (Index of Multiple Deprivation, IMD), ethnicity and gender are

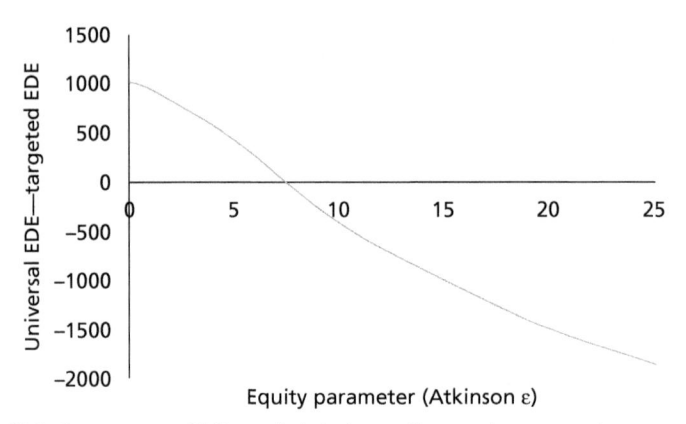

Figure 15.2 One-way sensitivity analysis to inequality aversion parameter.

regarded as unfair. It also shows how different strength of aversion to inequality would impact on choices, by varying the inequality aversion parameter used to calculate the Kolm and Atkinson indices.

Fig 15.2 shows a one-way sensitivity analysis from the same bowel cancer screening DCEA. This graph shows the difference in EDEH between a universal screening policy and a targeting screening policy for different strengths of inequality aversion. Several useful pieces of information can be gleaned from this graph. An inequality aversion parameter of zero represents no aversion to health inequality. The difference in EDEH health at this point is equivalent to the difference in aggregate population health. This shows that the universal screening policy provides the greatest amount of health. It demonstrates the relationship between the strength of inequality aversion and the desirability of the different options, showing that the distribution of health offered by the targeted screening programme is more desirable to the more inequality averse. The point at which the difference in EDEH crosses zero on the x-axis shows the threshold, which is the level of inequality aversion at which the desired option would switch from the universal screening programme to the targeted programme.

In some cases it may be that one option is preferred for all alternative viewpoints. In other cases a different ranking of options would result. Looking at the differences in overall population health and health inequality across the different scenario analyses can inform the health consequences that are implied by adopting one set of values over another. In the bowel cancer screening example, if the strength of inequality aversion is high enough to prefer targeted screening, Fig 15.2 indicates that the decision would result in over 1000 fewer quality-adjusted life years among the population compared to offering universal screening (i.e. compared to zero inequality aversion). If instead, the strength of inequality aversion is low enough for universal screening to be preferred, the slope index of inequality in Table 15.3 indicates that this would widen the gap in health between the least and most healthy compared to the current screening policy. If the evaluative process is reflexive and interactive, informing decision makers of these consequences may be useful in debate about the underlying social choices.

Sensitivity analysis can combine analysis of uncertainty with analysis of heterogeneity of values. For example, one might construct cost-effectiveness acceptability curves that display the probability that each option provides the highest equity weighted net benefit for a range of equity parameter values.

15.7 Conclusion

Uncertainty analysis for DCEA can proceed on a similar basis to that for any other cost-effectiveness analysis. Similarly, deterministic sensitivity analysis or scenario analysis can express the impact of alternative beliefs and values. Uncertainty analysis assesses whether the outcomes of a desired option might differ from what is expected. It concerns the probability or the likelihood of alternative outcomes, and addresses how far the evidence allows us to discriminate between the impacts of alternation options. Analysing heterogeneity of values looks at how the desired option might differ for different viewpoints. It concerns normative choices which are subject to ethical disagreement and addresses the implications of the differing ethical views that may be taken by different stakeholders.

15.8 Further reading

Those interested in an overview of uncertainty in economic evaluation can read Chapter 11, 'Characterizing, reporting, and interpreting uncertainty', in the authoritative guide to health economic evaluation by Drummond and colleagues (2015).

Those interested in the process of undertaking sensitivity analysis can read the report by Andronis and colleagues (2009).

Those interested in how uncertainty analyses informs the set of decisions about which option to pursue, whether to collect further evidence, and whether to alter the timing of decisions can read the paper by Claxton and colleagues (2016).

References

Andronis L., **Barton P.**, & **Bryan S.** (2009). *Sensitivity Analysis in Economic Evaluation: an Audit of NICE Current Practice and a Review of its Use and Value in Decision-making.* Prepress Projects Limited, Perth.

Asaria M., Griffin S., & Cookson R. (2016). Distributional cost-effectiveness analysis: a tutorial. *Medical Decision Making*, 36, 8–19.

Attema A., Brouwer W., & Claxton K. (2018). Discounting in economic evaluations. *Pharmacoeconomics*, 36, 745–758.

Briggs A., Sculpher M., & Buxton M. (1994). Uncertainty in the economic evaluation of health care technologies: the role of sensitivity analysis. *Health Economics*, 3, 95–104.

Briggs A., Sculpher M., & Claxton K. (2006). *Decision Modelling for Health Economic Evaluation*. Oxford University Press, Oxford.

Claxton K. (1999). The irrelevance of inference: a decision-making approach to the stochastic evaluation of health care technologies. *Journal of Health Economics*, 18, 341–364.

Claxton K., Palmer S., Longworth L., Bojke L., Griffin S., Soares M., et al. (2016). A comprehensive algorithm for approval of health technologies with, without, or only in research: the key principles for informing coverage decisions. *Value Health*, 19, 885–891.

Collins B., Kypridemos C., Cookson R., Parvulescu P., McHale P., Guzman-Castillo M., et al. (2019). Universal or targeted cardiovascular screening? Modelling study using a sector-specific distributional cost effectiveness analysis. *Preventative Medicine*, 105879.

Drummond M., Sculpher M., Claxton K., Stoddart G., & Torrance G. (2015). *Methods for the Economic Evaluation of Health Care Programmes*. Oxford University Press, Oxford.

Fenwick E., O'Brien B., & Briggs A. (2004). Cost-effectiveness acceptability curves–facts, fallacies and frequently asked questions. *Health Economics*, 13, 405–415.

Griffin S., Claxton K., Palmer S., & Sculpher M. (2011). Dangerous omissions: the consequences of ignoring decision uncertainty. *Health Economics*, 20, 212–224.

Love-Koh J., Cookson R., Claxton K., & Griffin S. (2020). Estimating social variation in the health effects of changes in health care. *Medical Decision Making*, 40(2), 170–182. https://doi.org/10.1177/0272989X20904360

Manning W. (1996). Reflecting uncertainty in cost-effectiveness analysis. In M. Gold, J. Seigal, L. Russell, & M. Weinstein (eds), *Cost-effectiveness in Health and Medicine*. Oxford University Press, New York.

Petticrew M., Whitehead M., Macintyre S., Graham H., & Egan M. (2004). Evidence for public health policy on inequalities: 1: the reality according to policymakers. *Journal of Epidemiology and Community Health*, 58, 11–16.

Robson M., Doran T., & Cookson R. (2019). Estimating and decomposing conditional average treatment effects: the smoking ban in England. HEDG Working Papers, 19/20. https://www.york.ac.uk/media/economics/documents/hedg/workingpapers/1920.pdf

van de Wetering E., Stolk E., van Exel N., & Brouwer W. (2013). Balancing equity and efficiency in the Dutch basic benefits package using the principle of proportional shortfall. *European Journal of Health Economics*, 14, 107–115.

Welch V., Petticrew M., Ueffing E., Benkhalti Jandu M., Brand K., Dhaliwal B., et al. (2012). Does consideration and assessment of effects on health equity affect the conclusions of systematic reviews? a methodology study. *PLoS One*, 7, e31360.

Woods B., Revill P., Sculpher M., & Claxton K. (2016). Country-level cost-effectiveness thresholds: initial estimates and the need for further research. *Value in Health*, 19, 929–935.

Chapter 16

Future challenges

Richard Cookson, Alec Morton,
Erik Schokkaert, Gabriela B. Gomez,
Maria W. Merritt, Ole F. Norheim,
Susan Griffin, and Anthony J. Culyer

16.1 Introduction

In this chapter we discuss some of the challenges facing the field of distributional cost-effectiveness analysis (DCEA). Some are scientific challenges to do with simulating distributions in more detailed and credible ways, some are ethics-related challenges to do with evaluating distributions in ways that address a broader range of equity concerns, and others are practical challenges to do with facilitating more widespread and systematic use of DCEA in decision-making and then learning from this experience where future methods and empirical work may best be done. We focus on describing the challenges rather than trying to address them—that task we leave to the reader.

DCEA is more data demanding than standard cost-effective analysis (CEA). In particular, there are usually too few data to populate the various steps on the 'staircase of inequality' (see Chapter 8) and to estimate the distribution of health opportunity costs (see Chapter 9). However, the routine data challenges facing DCEA analysts have already been extensively discussed in the relevant methods chapters, so this chapter focuses on special challenges relating to the development of new methods.

We cover four methodological challenges for ongoing research: (1) complex modelling; (2) *ex post* DCEA; (3) cross-sectoral DCEA; and (4) fair shares. The first of these challenges is primarily scientific, the fourth is primarily ethics-related, and the middle two involve a mix of scientific and ethics-related issues. We also discuss the practical challenge of making DCEA more useful to decision makers. We first summarize the challenges in broad terms below, before describing them in more detail in the rest of the chapter, together with references to further reading.

16.1.1 **Complex modelling**

Some health technologies and programmes are complex by virtue of their many components, which can interact differently in different contexts and so generate different distributional consequences. Inadequacies in the available data, together with shortages of research skills and time, mean that important complexities currently often have to be left out—for example economies of scale and scope, spillovers, behavioural responses, multiple morbidity and disadvantage, and general equilibrium effects.

We discuss the challenges of complex modelling under three broad health policy topic headings, each of which raises a distinctive set of complexities: system-level health policies (e.g. economies of scale), infectious disease control (e.g. infection spillover effects), and non-communicable disease prevention (e.g. behavioural responses). These are all important challenges for health economic evaluation in general, as well as DCEA in particular, and addressing them will facilitate the more detailed and accurate modelling of distributional consequences needed to tackle some of the more specific DCEA challenges listed below.

16.1.2 *Ex post* **DCEA**

The realized lifetime health of an individual or group, that is, the number of health-adjusted life years (HALYs) they will actually experience from birth until death, is uncertain. Various lifetime health outcomes are possible *ex ante* (i.e. before death), only one of which is ultimately realized *ex post* (i.e. after death). Currently, the usual approach to equity analysis in DCEA and the wider health services research literature is to focus on expected lifetime health, that is, the probability weighted mean of all the possible outcomes. This is also the approach adopted in this handbook and is known as the *ex ante* approach to evaluating distributions. Another approach, however, would be to look at the *ex post* lifetime health outcomes. Rather than focusing on a single distribution of expected health outcomes, one could instead simulate and evaluate various possible distributions of *ex post* lifetime health and their probabilities of occurring. The *ex ante* and *ex post* approaches to evaluating distributions can yield different conclusions about equity, as we illustrate later with a simple example.

Many distinguished experts in economics and ethics have examined this issue from a theoretical perspective and concluded that *ex post* evaluation of distributions is more coherent than *ex ante* evaluation. Addressing this disconnect between theory and practice by developing practical ways of conducting *ex post* DCEA is an important future methodological challenge, raising technical and data availability challenges as well as ethical challenges.

16.1.3 Cross-sectoral DCEA

As we have seen, DCEA currently focuses on (expected) distributions of health-related outcomes, including distributions of health itself, health service delivery, and financial protection from the cost of health services. It can evaluate distributions of these three outcomes separately but cannot integrate this into an overall assessment of distributional equity. Nor can it handle distributions of other non-health outcomes, for example consumption, education, employment, adverse experiences, stigma, life satisfaction. These limitations are usually unimportant when the aim is to inform health sector decision-making designed from a health sector perspective. They are more problematic, however, if the aim is to inform decision-making about cross-sectoral programmes which are designed to improve both health and non-health outcomes and have opportunity costs that fall on both health and non-health budgets, or if there are concerns about the consequences of health sector decisions for non-health outcomes.

Various approaches to evaluating multidimensional outcome distributions are being developed. These include disaggregate approaches that keep health and non-health outcomes separate, such as the presentation of separate quantitative and qualitative information about wider equity impacts on non-health dimensions of well-being, and the use of multidimensional inequality and welfare indices, as well as aggregate approaches which combine health and non-health outcomes into a general composite outcome.

16.1.4 Fair shares

DCEA currently evaluates distributions by seeking an optimal trade-off between efficiency and equity objectives—the 'value maximizing' way of thinking. However, another way of evaluating distributions is the 'fair shares' or 'proportionality' way of thinking. This seeks to distribute resources in proportion to strength of claim, rather than to maximize social welfare or equity-weighted net benefit. As explained in Chapter 2, the logic of proportionality differs from the logic of maximizing. Maximizing implies that the needs of individuals with relatively weak claims—for instance those who need cost-ineffective care—should be completely overridden in the pursuit of maximum value. By contrast, proportionality implies that the needs of individuals with relatively weak claims should still be met to some extent—if only partially—even if this means failing to maximize value. Fair share concerns which do not fit comfortably within the existing DCEA framework and which we discuss later include:

- The 'fair chances' argument for healthcare lotteries;
- The 'realization of potential' argument;
- The 'negligible claims' problem.

These concerns can be addressed through a deliberative process and considered alongside, without being integrated into, a DCEA. A future challenge, however, is finding analytical approaches to inform deliberations about these non-maximizing concerns.

16.1.5 Making DCEA more useful in practice

Key practical challenges for DCEA research commissioners and users include:
- Identifying and involving stakeholders;
- Institutionalizing the use of DCEA;
- Improving underpinning data sources (e.g. surveys, administrative data linkage);
- Improving evidence synthesis (e.g. for simulating distributions of opportunity costs and for parameterizing steps on the staircase of inequality);
- Improving simple low-cost approaches.

Our list of DCEA management challenges is by no means exhaustive. There are many other challenges facing the wider community of people interested in helping decision makers to make fairer decisions with better health outcomes—not least the challenge of developing deliberative decision-making processes that address equity concerns and that both use and supplement the fruits of DCEAs.

16.2 Complexity

16.2.1 System-level health policies

The focus of the current volume has mostly been on decisions about specific health services for specific population groups. There are also, however, important equity concerns about system-level health policies—the general infrastructure 'platforms' supporting the delivery of many different health services. For equity to be possible, health workers, clinical facilities, and medical equipment have to be distributed to match local population need; information systems have to be sufficiently widely available that there are no 'invisible' populations, whose ill health goes unrecognized by planners; and there has to be a robust system for ensuring that financial resources are distributed equitably among geographical areas.

The WHO has produced guidance on health system strengthening which describes six 'health systems building blocks': services, workforce, information, technologies, financing, and leadership and governance (WHO, 2007). This provides a useful map of the terrain but falls short of providing a clear analytical framework for decision makers wanting to turn general aspirations into specific expenditure priorities. In principle, health economic evaluation can help to set specific priorities for health system strengthening. However, health system dynamics are complex and raise substantial modelling challenges that are often assumed away in conventional modelling exercises. For example, analysing health systems strengthening almost always necessitates examining economies of scale and scope and geographical and social differences in delivery cost (Morton et al., 2016; Hauck et al., 2019). There are also likely to be important behavioural response feedbacks in terms of how providers, such as individuals like doctors or institutions like hospitals, respond to changes in prices and incentives.

System-level policies intended to benefit disadvantaged groups can have unintended consequences for other—perhaps hitherto unrecognized— disadvantaged groups. For example, e-health technologies designed to reach geographically remote communities will probably exclude the less computer-literate; when bednets are distributed in the most high-risk parts of a village, the mosquitos shift their attention to the moderate-risk areas; funding uplifts for the most deprived territorial health authorities can disproportionately benefit affluent enclaves within these generally deprived regions. The idiosyncrasies, the coarseness of institutional mechanisms for service delivery and the vagaries of human behaviour and biology, mean that well-intentioned policies can sometimes have unintended consequences that harm equity.

16.2.2 Infectious disease modelling

The modelling of indirect spillovers to the wider population from infectious disease prevention, as well as direct impacts on programme recipients, raises important challenges for DCEA. A changed risk of infection and disease for one person at one time will influence risk of transmission to others for many years to come, including transmission to future generations (Vynnycky & White, 2010). Allowing for these dynamic spillover effects and further opportunity costs in the wider population substantially complicates DCEA. Some equity-relevant groups are more likely to be infected, and hence to infect others, due to adverse environments (e.g. poverty-related undernourishment, crowded living spaces, poor sanitary conditions) and exposure to behavioural risks (e.g. unprotected sex). Progression from infection to various stages of disease may also vary by equity-relevant group due to co-morbidities (e.g. influenza may exacerbate chronic obstructive pulmonary disease) and physiological characteristics that influence disease incubation and progression. Counter-intuitive things can happen when programme recipients are not the only beneficiaries and health opportunity costs are not distributed uniformly across non-recipients, for example some groups can suffer an increased risk of disease even if the total community infection rate is reduced (Panagiotopoulos et al., 1999). Models of infectious disease transmission dynamics capable of handling these issues have been developed but have only recently started to be used to conduct distributional analysis by equity-relevant group (Verguet et al., 2017; Chang et al., 2018).

16.2.3 Non-communicable disease modelling

Modelling distributions in the context of non-communicable disease prevention raises further complexity challenges, including:

- Behavioural responses of individuals (e.g. in relation to diet, physical activity, and the consumption of tobacco, alcohol, and narcotics);
- Behavioural responses of producers (e.g. food and drinks industry, tobacco industry);
- Multimorbidity and multiple disadvantage (e.g. understanding the individual-level clustering, compounding, and interaction of multiple mental and physical illnesses, alongside multiple developmental, educational, financial, and social risk factors);
- Long-term change over the life course and between generations in equity-relevant variables (e.g. income, neighbourhood deprivation, education);
- Disentangling the influence of neighbourhood-level environmental factors (e.g. air and noise pollution, crime, obesogenic environment) from individual and household factors (e.g. education, household income).

Addressing these complexity challenges will require the development and validation of scientifically credible life course microsimulation models for economic evaluation, which synthesize a large body of interdisciplinary theory and evidence about the long-term social determinants of health and well-being over the life course. Such models will also be useful in providing the detailed information on distributional consequences needed to handle further challenges outlined below, including both *ex post* DCEA and cross-sectoral DCEA.

16.3 *Ex post* DCEA

In this book, we have adopted an *ex ante* perspective, focusing on expected outcomes. We have quantified efficiency impacts in terms of expected net benefit and equity impacts in terms of inequality in the distribution of expected lifetime health by equity-relevant variables. However, prominent economists and philosophers have argued that it may also be useful to evaluate equity from an *ex post* perspective that focuses on realized outcomes (Diamond, 1967; Fleurbaey, 2010; Adler, 2012; Fleurbaey & Voorhoeve, 2013). The analyst may have some information about the probable distributional pattern of *ex post* outcomes, even if it is not known who will benefit.

Table 16.1 Level and distribution with limited information

		Life expectancy
Programme U	Person 1	76
	Person 2	76
Programme E	Person 1	75
	Person 2	75

16.3.1 A simple example

Consider the following simple example, with just two individuals to make things easy. Person 1 has a life expectancy of 70 and person 2 of 65. A decision maker is comparing two health programmes, both remarkably effective (Table 16.1).

Programme U will equalize expected lifetime health at 76; programme E will equalize expected lifetime health at 75. A decision maker concerned with both the level and distribution of health may find this choice easy: programme U is as egalitarian as programme E but will improve health even more. Programme U is better, all things considered. That is, if we adopt the *ex ante* perspective.

However, the decision maker is curious, they have heard about the *ex post* perspective, and ask for more information. As it happens, both programmes have been rigorously evaluated and the possible *ex post* outcomes are shown in Table 16.2.

In programme U, there is a 50 per cent chance of person 1 benefiting a lot and a 50 per cent chance of person 2 benefiting a lot. In programme E, by contrast, both will experience 75 life years for certain. The possible *ex post* distributional patterns and their probabilities of occurring are known, even though it is unknown who will benefit under programme U.

A key principle for *ex post* egalitarians is that: 'when one lacks information, but can infer that there is a particular alternative one would invariably regard as best if one had full information, then one should choose this alternative'

Table 16.2 Level and distributions with more information

		Life expectancy	State of the world (equiprobable)	
			State α	State β
Programme U	Person 1	76	100	52
	Person 2	76	52	100
Programme E	Person 1	75	75	75
	Person 2	75	75	75

(Fleurbaey & Voorhoeve, 2013). In our example, we can infer that the distributional pattern under programme E is more equal than that under programme U, whatever the state of the world. From the *ex post* perspective, programme U would be more effective, but also more unequal in terms of realized outcomes. The decision makers may therefore want, with the help of the analyst, to explore a trade-off between improving health and reducing unequal *ex post* outcomes. If the decision maker has strong aversion to *ex post* inequality, they may even rank programme E over U.

16.3.2 Ethical and technical challenges

The *ex post* perspective raises interesting ethical challenges. For example, it violates the principle of *ex ante* Pareto (for good discussions, see Fleurbaey, 2010; Adler, 2012). *Ex ante* Pareto says that: 'if an alternative has higher expected utility for every person than every other alternative, then this alternative should be chosen' (Fleurbaey & Voorhoeve, 2013). Consider again Table 16.2. Expected lifetime health is 76 in programme U compared to 75 with programme E, for both individuals. Both have higher expected lifetime health under programme U. The *ex ante* Pareto principle therefore recommends choosing programme U, even though it will ultimately involve much worse outcomes for one of the individuals.

The *ex post* perspective also raises important technical and data availability challenges for DCEA. *Ex ante* DCEA requires information about the likely mean health outcome of a programme and how this depends upon equity-relevant characteristics. By contrast, *ex post* DCEA requires information about likely variability in the health outcomes of a programme and how this depends on equity-relevant characteristics. In some cases, standard probabilistic decision models may provide enough information for simple *ex post* analysis (Samson et al., 2018). More generally, however, the information demands are considerably stronger. For example, in the NRT example used in our spreadsheet training exercises, there is substantial and right-skewed individual-level variability in effectiveness, whereby some individuals gain many HALYs but most gain little or nothing (see Chapter 8). To simulate the *ex post* distributional pattern we would need to know how this variability in health effects depends upon baseline health, that is, are worse-off individuals with poor baseline health more or less likely than others to lie in the right tail of the distribution of programme effects with large HALY gains? To analyse 'unfair' *ex post* inequality relating to deprivation and region, as well as 'pure' *ex post* inequality, we would also need to know how the variability of health effects depends upon deprivation and region.

Addressing these issues requires further research into methods of causal inference for looking at programme effects on the variance and skewness of outcomes, as well as effects on the mean outcome (Chernozhukov et al., 2013). It also requires careful conceptual analysis of different kinds of uncertainty in outcomes and how far these sources of uncertainty may be 'fair' or 'unfair' (Asada et al., 2015; van der Bles et al., 2019). Evaluation of distributional consequences from an *ex post* perspective is thus a fascinating and important challenge for DCEA and for health services and public health research more generally.

16.4 Cross-sectoral DCEA

We saw in Chapter 10 how to simulate distributional impacts on financial protection from healthcare costs, alongside distributional impacts on health. Decision makers may also be interested in distributional impacts on other non-health outcomes. Difficult challenges arise, however, when seeking to evaluate multidimensional outcome distributions. Analytical methods are starting to be developed for evaluating programmes with distributional impacts on both health and non-health outcomes, but they are diverse and embryonic in form. We sketch out some of the promising lines of enquiry and the challenges faced in developing these into routinely applicable approaches in the coming years.

We label this section 'cross-sectoral DCEA', since the most obvious application of these methods is to programmes that cut across multiple policy sectors. Education and social protection policies, for example, will often influence distributions of income as well as distributions of health. Cross-sectoral issues also arise in relation to expenditure on health care and public health. One obvious question, for example, is how much health care should be financed through the government budget, that is, through taxes or social security contributions. An increase in the government budget might lead to a decrease in private consumption of healthcare and other goods. This trade-off raises important questions of distributive justice in terms of who gains and who loses. This issue cannot be addressed merely by looking at health impacts; it requires analysis of the distribution of both health and non-health outcomes. Furthermore, priority setting within the public healthcare budget can have distributional consequences for household finances, which in turn has consequences for well-being beyond health. Treatments that are not covered in the collective system have to be funded privately or forgone. Co-payments and deductibles for publicly funded care have been introduced in many countries, and so the health effects of reimbursement decisions have to be weighed against the consumption effects of co-payments.

16.4.1 Disaggregate approaches

One approach is to present decision makers with separate information about wider equity impacts concerning the distribution of non-health outcomes, without aggregating health and non-health outcomes into a general composite outcome measure. For example, this is the approach currently taken in extended cost-effectiveness studies, which look separately at distributions of health and financial protection (Verguet et al., 2016). Disaggregate approaches can go some way towards formal evaluation through use of multidimensional dominance criteria (Atkinson & Bourguignon, 1982) and systematic approaches to designing dashboards of distributional consequences (McKnight et al., 2019). However, they stop short of constructing general composite indices and analysing potential trade-offs and compensation between health and non-health outcomes, for example the possibility that increased inequality in non-health effects (e.g. tobacco tax contributions as a proportion of income) may be offset by reduced inequality in health effects (e.g. smoking-related deaths) to yield an overall improvement in equity.

Disaggregate information may take the form of a quantitative distributional breakdown, for example a distribution of financial protection outcomes alongside a distribution of health outcomes. It may also take the form of qualitative data about the lived experiences of programme recipients, which can be translated into an overall subjective rating of wider equity impact. For example, treatment regimens requiring frequent clinical visits may generate social stigma and disrupt family life in ways that are particularly burdensome for people already suffering multiple disadvantages. A new treatment that reduces the frequency of clinical visits may then have a beneficial wider equity impact (Zwerling et al., 2017). Qualitative data may help decision makers to consider the nature and importance of this wider equity impact and weigh it up informally against impacts on total health and equity in the distribution of health. Selecting the relevant non-health outcomes and placing qualitative information about those outcomes into 'level of importance' categories requires explicit value judgments by decision makers and stakeholders, and the resulting disaggregate information provides some, albeit limited, guidance for decision makers.

16.4.2 Aggregate approaches

There are three main approaches to constructing a general composite outcome measure for economic evaluation that combines and values both health and non-health outcomes:

- Full income (i.e. income plus the monetary value of health and non-health outcomes);

- Equivalent income (i.e. income adjusted for health and non-health outcomes);
- Well-being QALYs (i.e. life-years adjusted for health and non-health-related quality).

Each of these measures can then be used in distributional analysis, both to simulate distributions and to evaluate them using the methods described in Part III of this handbook (i.e. dominance analysis, rank and level-dependent equity weights based on social welfare functions and direct equity weights).

Full income is perhaps the simplest approach: one takes a standard measure of income and then adds to this the monetary value of health and other outcomes. A drawback of this approach is that it assumes a common constant exchange rate between income and health, that is, the monetary value of health. Equivalent income refines this approach by allowing more carefully for heterogeneity in individual preferences between income, health, and other outcomes within an explicit welfare theoretical framework. An individual's equivalent income is the hypothetical level of income that, if combined with reference levels of health and other outcomes, would place the individual in a situation that they consider as good as their current actual situation. The reference level is a normative choice for the decision maker, but a convenient choice is often a maximal value such as full health.

If reference levels are set at maximal values, then equivalent income is always lower than actual money income unless the individual reaches the maximal reference values for all other outcomes. In a two-dimensional case focusing on income and health only, the difference between equivalent and actual income reflects the decrease in well-being that results from not reaching full health. This decrease is measured as the willingness-to-pay of the individual for full health. Equivalent income can be measured using information on individual preferences from stated preferences techniques such as contingent valuation or discrete choice modelling, or using derivation of marginal rates of substitution from life satisfaction data (Decancq et al., 2015).

Both full income and equivalent income can then be equity weighted to allow for distributional concerns. Fleurbaey and colleagues provide an illustration of how to derive distributional weights in a framework with equivalent incomes (Fleurbaey et al., 2013), and Samson and colleagues illustrate the use of equity-weighted equivalent income as a metric for distributional cost-benefit analysis (Samson et al., 2018).

Another approach is the well-being QALY (Brazier & Tsuchiya, 2015; Cookson et al., forthcoming), which is also known as the equivalent health approach (Canning, 2013). The basic idea is to measure policy outcomes in terms of years of good life, rather than years of healthy life. Rather than adjusting only for health-related quality of life, a broader adjustment is made for all relevant dimensions of quality of life. Years of good life capture both health and non-health benefits, whereas years of healthy life only capture health benefits.

Like the equivalent income approach, the well-being QALY approach requires individual-level information on multiple health and non-health outcomes. Producing this detailed underpinning information itself raises substantial microsimulation modelling challenges, as explained above in the section on complex modelling. Once this detailed information is available, however, the challenge is then how to convert individual-level measures of income, health, and other specific outcomes into a general composite outcome. We can distinguish three broad ways of doing this:

- A well-being index that combines and weights multiple specific outcomes using various sources of evidence and value judgment—the 'mash-up' approach;
- Questionnaire data on life satisfaction (or some other one-dimensional quality of life questionnaire score)—the 'life satisfaction' approach;
- Questionnaire data on multidimensional quality of life—the 'multidimensional questionnaire' approach.

The latter two approaches do not necessarily require programme effects to be measured directly using questionnaire data on life satisfaction or multidimensional quality of life. Instead, the available programme-specific outcome measures can be valued indirectly by mapping them onto life-satisfaction or quality of life outcomes.[1] For example, one can define a 'WELLBY' as a one-point improvement in life satisfaction for one person for one year (Fijters and Krekel, forthcoming). Any policy outcome can then in principle be valued indirectly in terms of its expected effect on life satisfaction—for example the effect of changes in employment, income, and morbidity can all be estimated by applying robust causal inference methods to life satisfaction data from longitudinal surveys or (preferably) well designed quasi-experiments relevant to the decision-making context. When the questionnaire approaches are used indirectly in this way, they move a step closer to the mash-up approach insofar as they do not rely exclusively on questionnaire data but combine outcomes data of various different kinds. However, the remaining difference is that the 'conversion rate' between each outcome measure and well-being is based exclusively on questionnaire data, rather than a well-being function that combines different kinds of data and social value judgment. Combining different kinds of data has

---

[1] A limitation of indirect mapping is that it only captures programme effects on the general outcome (e.g. life-satisfaction) via effects on the set of specific outcomes (e.g. income and health) and so may not capture the full effect.

advantages, insofar as it makes use of a wider range of information. It also has disadvantages, of course, insofar as it runs the risk of incoherence if diverse forms of data are mashed together in an unstructured and inconsistent manner. To guard against this, care is needed to make all value judgments explicit and to provide a coherent structure for any mash-up approach.

The development of general composite measures of benefit for cross-sectoral evaluation is thus a lively ongoing research endeavour, where the key challenge, as ever, is to find methods that are credible and useful to decision makers rather than merely being intellectually appealing to researchers.

16.5 Analysing fair shares

Chapter 2 distinguished three different ways of thinking about equity with importantly different logical structures:

- Value maximization (e.g. maximize health, reduce health inequality);
- Moral rights (e.g. right to non-discrimination);
- Fair shares (e.g. distribution in proportion to need).

Part III of this handbook focused on evaluating distributions based on the 'value maximization' approach. Economic analysis can also play a role in examining moral rights, for example by examining the health opportunity cost of respecting a moral right for one group of people in terms of the forgone health benefits for other groups. However, an unresolved future challenge is how to analyse the third kind of principle: fair shares. In this section we discuss three different ethical arguments about health equity claims and how they might be analysed using DCEA methods—the fair chances argument, the realization of potential argument, and the aggregation of small benefits argument.

16.5.1 Lotteries and the 'fair chances' argument

According to the fair chances argument, everyone should have a fair chance of accessing needed healthcare—not a guarantee, just a fair chance—including people who need care that is cost-ineffective, and including people who are relatively well off in terms of baseline health or other equity-relevant characteristics (Broome, 1994; Brock, 2003). If this proposition is accepted, a practical implication is that scarce health care resources should sometimes be allocated using lottery mechanisms that provide fair chances. Explicit lottery mechanisms are indeed sometimes used to help allocate rare and indivisible healthcare resources, such as organs for transplantation. And some authors argue for more widespread use of healthcare lotteries, for example co-payment lotteries to ensure that low-income families have a fair chance of accessing high-cost specialized hospital services (Wagstaff, 2013).

If decision makers are convinced by the fair chances argument, the question then arises: how could DCEA methods be used to help design and evaluate healthcare lottery mechanisms? Existing DCEA methods could be used to examine the impact of different lottery designs on unfair inequalities in the distribution of health, healthcare delivery, and financial protection. Plausibly, analysis of this kind and formal evaluation based on maximizing equity-weighted net health benefit would find in favour of spending the lion's share of the public healthcare budget on care that is cost-effective and/or disproportionately benefits disadvantaged groups. It would not fundamentally get to grips with the logic of proportionality and the argument that people who need care that is cost-ineffective should still receive a fair chance of treatment. Nor would it help to clarify the potential conflicts and trade-offs between maximizing and proportionality ways of thinking. A future challenge, therefore, is to develop quantitative approaches to defining and measuring the strength of need claims and the appropriate lottery weights for different kinds of people with different strengths of claim. A judgment would then be required as to which objective is more important—increasing total health, reducing unfair inequality in health, or delivering fair chances—and a further challenge would arise about how to analyse trade-offs between these three different objectives.

16.5.2 Realization of potential

According to the 'realization of potential' argument, each individual has a claim to the healthcare resources that will allow them to achieve their full potential to benefit. This 'fair shares' way of thinking yields different recommendations to the 'value maximizing' way of thinking. For example, imagine patient A gains 50 expected discounted HALYs from a treatment that costs the same as treating ten patients B-K who each gain 2.5 expected discounted HALYs. Assume they are the same in all other potentially equity-relevant respects, including age, severity of illness, socioeconomic status, and so on. Maximizing net health benefit would recommend treating patient A, since this delivers twice as many HALYs—50 rather than just 25. However, the 'realization of potential' argument is that the claim of patient B should not be completely over-ridden by the claim of patient A, merely because their capacity to benefit is 20 times smaller. Collectively, the ten patients B-K may have a greater claim on public resources than patient A alone, and so it may be fairer to treat them, or divide the resources 11 ways in proportion to strength of claim, or hold a lottery as per the fair chances argument described above.

One way of addressing the realization of potential argument is a system of direct equity weights with diminishing marginal returns to capacity to benefit (Nord, 2019). In this system, social value is not a simple linear function of capacity to benefit but is instead a concave function. However, this approach is still based on a 'value maximizing' way of thinking according to which the aim is to maximize equity-weighted net health benefit, and it does not address the question of how to ensure that no legitimate claims are completely over-ridden. A future challenge is to develop approaches that explicitly adopt a 'fair shares' way of thinking by specifying how individual fair shares are to be defined and measured, rather than seeking to maximize equity-weighted net health benefit.

16.5.3 Negligible claims

It might be argued that people with small health benefits have a negligible claim on public resources if this means forgoing large health benefits for others (Kamm, 2005). In the Netherlands, for example, decision makers have proposed withdrawing public funding for treating minor ailments to ensure funding is available for treatments with larger benefits (Voorhoeve, 2018, 2020). This is a variant of 'fair shares' thinking—it implies that some people's strength of claim is so negligibly weak that their 'fair share' of healthcare for the ailment in question is zero.

This differs from the argument that priority should be given to worse-off patients with poor baseline health. The negligible claims argument focuses not on baseline health but on capacity to benefit. Someone in good health may have substantial capacity to benefit from preventive care, whereas someone in poor health may have low capacity to benefit. It also differs from the financial protection argument that priority should be given to covering high cost treatments, since those who need low cost treatment can pay privately out of pocket without suffering hardship (Smith, 2013). The negligible claims argument is about the size of the health benefit, not the size of the financial protection benefit.

A future challenge is developing analytical methods that operationalize the concept of a negligible claim and draw out the implications of adopting a 'fair shares' principle alongside health maximization and health inequality reduction objectives.[2]

16.6 Making DCEA more useful in practice

The fundamental aim of DCEA is to provide decision makers and stakeholders with useful information that helps them make better decisions with fairer

---

[2] This challenge interacts with the challenge of *ex post* DCEA, insofar as it is often uncertain whether an individual's realized health benefit will be large or negligibly small.

outcomes. The most important challenge facing this embryonic field is thus a practical one: how can DCEA become more useful to decision makers and stakeholders? It took standard CEA four decades to develop from the stage of invention in the 1960s and 1970s through to early application in the 1980s and methodological standardization in the 1990s, before moving on to widespread use in health decision-making around the world from the 2000s onwards (Williams & Cookson, 2006). How can DCEA emulate this success and become a routine part of decision-making in healthcare and public health?

We expand on this challenge below under five principal headings:

- Identifying and involving stakeholders;
- Institutionalizing the use of DCEA;
- Optimizing data sources and evidence synthesis;
- Removing barriers and facilitating implementation;
- Research into better DCEA theory, methods, and practice.

While these categories matter in all forms of CEA, we concentrate on those we conjecture to be most important in its distributional aspects.

16.6.1 Stakeholders

How can analysts work together effectively with decision makers and stakeholders to co-produce useful information? Who else, besides the analysts, ought to be involved in the analysis and its application in any specific case; who else might have a useful role in the implementation of the decision and the management of its roll out; and who else might have a useful role in learning from the process from start through to implementation in ways that enable suitable future revisions to be made in the light both of experience and any changes in the evidential or value foundations of the analysis?

Decision makers obviously need to be involved because they are the key customers for DCEA information. But without the appropriate involvement of a broader range of stakeholders, decisions, no matter how well-informed by evidence and how explicit about the value content, may lack public, professional, or political credibility and may be impossible to implement (Culyer, 2006; Li et al., 2017). CEA and DCEA can appear to be mechanistic and 'hard' technologies that are insensitive to individual and social nuances. This may be far from the truth in many applications. However, the perception of insensitivity, particularly with relatively nontransparent systems of decision-making, may be sufficient to bring the principles of DCEA into disrepute (Culyer, 2005). Involving 'real' people appropriately in the decision-making process is therefore a form of direct democracy that lends credence to the process. Stakeholder participation is also an important source of information about social values and about the lived experiences of those most affected by decisions. Identifying and involving stakeholders is thus fundamental to the successful application and use of DCEA in decision-making.

Box 16.1 contains a list of possible stakeholders (which are relevant in any application that is, of course, context dependent) and some roles they might

Box 16.1 Potential stakeholders and the roles they can play

Decision makers

Source of social value judgments, topic selection, process design, and development.

Technical advisors

Supporting decision makers in their roles.

Patients and the public

Validation of equity outcome measures, information about how decisions would affect their lives, knowledge brokers.

Informal carers

Same roles as patients and the public and can also represent patients.

Managers

Topic selection, implementation planning, local financing issues, local inequities.

Clinical professionals

Clinical experience, research expertise, expertise in minorities and multiple disadvantages.

Research and researchers

Research funding, research production, topic selection, data development, methods, systematic reviews and meta-analysis, generalization of evidence, quality assurance.

> **Potential stakeholders and the roles they can play** *(continued)*
>
> ### Manufacturers
>
> Information about products being evaluated and comparators, views on reasonableness of criteria, speed and rigour of process, design, and support for research.
>
> ### Insurers
>
> Information about the design of insured packages, issues of coverage, comprehensiveness and co-payments, liaison with researchers.
>
> ### NGOs, donors, development partners
>
> Multilateral and bilateral relationships, international standard setting, coverage issues, financing, consultancy, and advice.
>
> ### Politicians, including opposition politicians
>
> Democratic accountability, representation of opposition views and minority interests.
>
> ### Courts and the judiciary
>
> Consistency with rights to health, constitutional issues, legality of process, judicial review.
>
> ### Knowledge brokers and the media
>
> Communication skills, public and professional education.

play at various stages of a DCEA. The relevance of each will, of course, depend on social and political factors, local appraisal of what is possible, and the aims of the exercise. All of these groups might be invited to observe, comment on, or participate in particular stages of the process. As well as contributing useful information from various different perspectives, each group of course has its own set of vested interests and tendencies towards special pleading and bias.

16.6.2 Institutionalization

The next set of challenges are to do with the institutional and political contexts of decision-making and how these might be best designed to

> **Box 16.2 Institutional context for DCEA**
>
> *Social value judgments* (e.g. use of QALY/DALY, cost-effectiveness thresholds, focus on future or lifetime health for equity analysis, inequality aversion parameter values).
> *General cultural conditions* (e.g. religious taboos, prevalence and belief in the role of traditional medicine).
> *General political conditions* (e.g. stability of regime, acquiescence of formal opposition parties).
> *Professional politics of healthcare* (e.g. past and current medical attitudes, managerial attitudes, organized labour attitudes).
> *History of healthcare and public health* (e.g. memories of what seems to have previously worked and what not, continuity of movement towards universal healthcare coverage and healthy public policy).

support the fundamental purpose of DCEA, that is, better-informed decisions. Institutionalization has many advantages in CEA: achieving a critical mass of evaluative skills, economies of scale and scope, a single centre of excellence and communication (or a few), and close relationships and partnerships with other relevant institutions. These apply with equal force in DCEA. Institutionalization in DCEA also enables the creation of consensus and continuity in the value framework for DCEA, which comprises many interlinked elements including those listed in Box 16.2.

16.6.3 Strengthening the evidence base

There are several limitations in data sources and evidence available to support DCEA, as noted in each of the methods chapters. Institutionalization and networked research afford an opportunity for coherent programmes to prioritize and address research into DCEA methods and usage and, in connection with universities and independent research institutions, the development of both theoretical and empirical research to support future applications of DCEA. Having several linked centres of expertise in evaluating the quality of evidence submitted to the national or regional health technology assessment (HTA) agency (if one exists), and in conducting systematic reviews and in performing primary empirical research in DCEA, builds a powerful foundation for evidence-informed decision-making in distributional matters and also helps to build a wider culture of evidence-informed critical appraisal.

16.6.4 Political economy

A major absence in current DCEA research activity lies in what one might call 'political economy': research to investigate the cultural, historical, economic, and political environment in which policy is made and to understand why decisions are taken that seem irrational. In many cases, wise investment opportunities are missed not because they cannot be identified but because they are difficult to implement—for a range of reasons, from corruption and dishonesty in the political culture to rigidity in planning and managerial hierarchies. Locating and understanding barriers, removing them or mitigating their effects, and designing incentive-compatible systems of decision-making at all levels are three major possible research themes.

16.6.5 Methodological standardization

At present, the state of DCEA methods is rather like the state of computing in the 1960s: powerful tools exist but can only be deployed effectively by highly specialized research teams. Further research is needed to reduce the cost and increase the power and accessibility of DCEA in ways that make it suitable for widespread production and use.

At least five different kinds of research are needed to take the theory and methods of DCEA to the next level of mass production and routine use in decision-making:

- Fundamental research—policy-oriented rather than entirely curiosity-driven—to address methodological challenges, including the four outlined in this chapter.
- Comparative research into the values informing different systems and the various ways in which they have influenced decisions and decision-making processes.
- Primary research (short term) on topics of immediate policy relevance in the jurisdiction.
- Primary research (long term) on developing general data infrastructure (e.g. cohort studies and improved reporting of equity-relevant distributional breakdowns in intervention studies) and general evidential building blocks (e.g. estimates of the distribution of opportunity costs by equity-relevant group).
- Secondary research in the form of equity-related literature reviews and, where feasible, meta-analysis.

Training and capacity building are also key future challenges for the field of DCEA—both to develop the capacity of analysts to produce useful distributional analyses and to develop the capacity of decision makers and their technical advisers to understand, critically appraise, and use evidence and analysis to make fairer decisions with better health outcomes. Coordinated programmes of research and capacity building, for example by a consortium led by a ministry of health and local universities, together with funding sources, would help to glue together these different strands of work and ensure continuing relevance to decision-making.

References

Adler M. (2012). *Well-being and Fair Distribution: Beyond Cost-benefit Analysis*. Oxford University Press, New York.

Asada Y., Hurley J., Norheim O., & Johri M. (2015). Unexplained health inequality—is it unfair? *International Journal for Equity in Health,* **14**, 11.

Atkinson A. & Bourguignon F. (1982). The comparison of multi-dimensioned distributions of economic status. *Review of Economic Studies,* **49**, 183–201.

Brazier J. & Tsuchiya A. (2015). Improving cross-sector comparisons: going beyond the health-related QALY. *Applied Health Economics and Health Policy,* **13**, 557–565.

Brock D. (2003). Ethical issues in the use of cost effectiveness analysis for the prioritization of health care resources. *Making Choices in Health: WHO Guide to Cost-Effectiveness Analysis,* 289–312.

Broome J. (1994). Fairness versus doing the most good. *Hastings Center Report,* **24**, 36–39.

Canning D. (2013). Axiomatic foundations for cost-effectiveness analysis. *Health Economics,* **22**, 1405–16.

Chang A., Riumallo-Herl C., Perales N., Clark S., Clark A., Constenla D., et al. (2018). The equity impact vaccines may have on averting deaths and medical impoverishment in developing countries. *Health Affairs (Millwood),* **37**, 316–324.

Chernozhukov V., Fernández-Val I., & Melly B. (2013). Inference on counterfactual distributions. *Econometrica,* **81**, 2205–2268.

Cookson R., Skarda I., Cotton-Barrett O., Adler M., Asaria M., & Ord T. (forthcoming). Quality adjusted life years based on health and consumption: a summary wellbeing measure for cross-sectoral economic evaluation. *Health Economics,*

Culyer A. (2005). Involving stakeholders in health care decisions—the experience of the National Institute for Clinical Excellence (NICE) in England and Wales. *Healthcare Quarterly,* **8**, 54–58

Culyer A. (2006). NICE's use of cost effectiveness as an exemplar of a deliberative process. *Health Economics, Policy and Law,* **1**, 299–318. (Reprinted in R. Cookson and K. Claxton (eds) (2012), *Humble Economist,* 283–300. https://www.york.ac.uk/che/publications/books/the-humble-economist/

Decancq K., Fleurbaey M., & Schokkaert E. (2015). Happiness, equivalent incomes and respect for individual preferences. *Economica,* **82**, 1082–1106.

Diamond P. (1967). Cardinal welfare, individualistic ethics, and interpersonal comparison of utility: a comment. *Journal of Political Economy,* **75**, 765–766.

Fleurbaey M. (2010). Assessing risky social situations. *Journal of Political Economy*, **118**, 649–680.

Fleurbaey M., Luchini S. , Muller C., & Schokkaert E. (2013). Equivalent incomes and the economic evaluation of health care. *Health Economics*, **22**, 711–729.

Fleurbaey M., & Voorhoeve A. (2013). Decide as you would with full information! An argument against ex ante Pareto. In **N. Eyal, O. Norheim, & D. Wikler** (eds), *Inequalities in Health: Concepts, Measures, and Ethics*. Oxford Scholarship Online. pp. 113–128.

Frijter P. & Krekel C. (forthcoming). *Handbook for Well Being Policy*. Oxford University Press.

Hauck K., Morton A., Chalkidou K., Chi Y., Culyer A., Levin C., et al. (2019). How can we evaluate the cost-effectiveness of health system strengthening? A typology and illustrations. *Social Science & Medicine*, **220**, 141–149.

Kamm F. (2005). Aggregation and two moral methods. *Utilitas*, **17**, 1–23.

Li R., Ruiz F., Culyer A., Chalkidou K., & Hofman K. (2017). Evidence-informed capacity building for setting health priorities in low- and middle-income countries: a framework and recommendations for further research. *F1000Research*, **6**, 231.

McKnight A., Loureiro P., & Vizard P. (2019). Multidimensional Inequality Framework. http://sticerd.lse.ac.uk/inequality/the-framework/media/mif-framework.pdf

Morton A., Thomas R., & Smith P. (2016). Decision rules for allocation of finances to health systems strengthening. *Journal of Health Economics*, **49**, 97–108.

Nord E. (2018). Beyond QALYs: multi-criteria based estimation of maximum willingness to pay for health technologies. *European Journal of Health Economics*, **19**, 267–275.

Panagiotopoulos T., Antoniadou I., & Valassi-Adam E. (1999). Increase in congenital rubella occurrence after immunisation in Greece: retrospective survey and systematic review. *British Medical Journal*, **319**, 1462–1467.

Samson A., Schokkaert E., Thébaut C., Dormont B., Fleurbaey M., Luchini S., et al. (2018). Fairness in cost-benefit analysis: a methodology for health technology assessment. *Health Economics*, **27**, 102–114.

Smith P. (2013). Incorporating financial protection into decision rules for publicly financed healthcare treatments. *Health Economics*, **22**, 180–193.

van der Bles A., van der Linden S. , Freeman A., Mitchell J., Galvao A., Zaval L., et al. (2019). Communicating uncertainty about facts, numbers and science. *Royal Society Open Science*, **6**.

Verguet S., Kim J., & Jamison D. (2016). Extended cost-effectiveness analysis for health policy assessment: a tutorial. *Pharmacoeconomics*, **34**, 913–923.

Verguet S., Riumallo-Herl C., Gomez G., Menzies N., Houben R., Sumner T., et al. (2017). Catastrophic costs potentially averted by tuberculosis control in India and South Africa: a modelling study. *Lancet Global Health*, **5**, e1123–e1132.

Voorhoeve A. (2018). Balancing small against large burdens. *Behavioural Public Policy*, **2**, 125–142.

Voorhoeve A. (2020). Healthy nails versus long lives: an analysis of a Dutch priority-setting proposal. In **N. Schroeder, S. Hurst**, and **D. Wikler** (eds), *Global Health Priority-Setting: Beyond Cost-Effectiveness*. Oxford University Press, Oxford. pp. 145–161.

Vynnycky E., & White R. (2010). *An Introduction to Infectious Disease Modelling*. Oxford University Press, Oxford.

Wagstaff A. (2013). Cost-effectiveness vs. universal health coverage. Is the future random? https://blogs.worldbank.org/developmenttalk/cost-effectiveness-vs-universal-health-coverage-future-random

Williams A. & Cookson R. (2006). Equity-efficiency trade-offs in health technology assessment. *International Journal of Technology Assessment in Health Care,* **22,** 1–9.

World Health Organization (2007). *Everybody's Business—Strengthening Health Systems to Improve Health Outcomes: WHO's Framework for Action.* World Health Organization, Geneva.

Zwerling A., Dowdy D., von Delft A., Taylor H., & Merritt M. W. (2017). Incorporating social justice and stigma in cost-effectiveness analysis: drug-resistant tuberculosis treatment. *International Journal of Tuberculosis and Lung Disease,* **21,** S69–S74.

Glossary

This glossary provides brief definitions of the main terms needed to conduct and interpret distributional cost-effectiveness analysis (DCEA), excluding common cost-effectiveness terminology. We include familiar terms that are used in unfamiliar ways in DCEA (e.g. 'dominance') as well as terms that may be simply unfamiliar (e.g. 'level-dependent equity weights').

Italics indicate an entry in the glossary.

Adjusted univariate distribution: a distribution of an *outcome variable* that has been filtered to reflect *unfair inequalities* but not *fair inequalities*—for example a distribution of expected *lifetime health* based on socioeconomic status and geographical region only. Cf. *Bivariate distribution.*

Baseline distribution: a distribution of existing levels of an *outcome variable* prior to taking a decision. Cf. *Incremental distribution.*

Bivariate distribution: a joint distribution between two variables: for example an *outcome variable* and a single *equity-relevant characteristic* such as socioeconomic status.

Cost-effectiveness: in its most general sense, the outcome of a programme, intervention, or option compared with its cost. An option can be considered 'cost-effective' if it meets two conditions: first, it achieves a given outcome at the lowest possible cost or attains the maximum possible outcome for a given cost; and second, it is more cost-effective than a specific comparator, or more cost-effective than a general benchmark standard or threshold. In this handbook we often use the term cost-effectiveness in the more specific sense of *net health benefit*: total health benefits minus total health *opportunity costs*. An option can then be considered cost-effective if it has a positive *net health benefit*.

Dominance: in standard cost-effectiveness analysis (CEA), one option dominates another if it has lower cost and greater beneficial effect. In DCEA, by contrast, one option dominates another if it is more efficient (i.e. has greater net benefit) and more equitable (a 'win-win'). CEA dominance is neither necessary nor sufficient for DCEA dominance. For example, an option can improve total health and reduce unfair health inequality even if it does not reduce cost.

Furthermore, DCEA dominance is neither necessary nor sufficient for *Pareto dominance*. For example, investing in rural primary care rather than urban hospital care may improve total health and reduce unfair health inequality yet be worse for city dwellers.

Incremental distribution: a distribution of the costs and effects attributed to a decision compared with an alternative. An incremental distribution focuses on changes (gains and losses) whereas a *baseline distribution* focuses on levels.

Direct equity weights: direct *equity weights* are indicators of relative importance applied to effects and opportunity costs for specific subgroups of the population, giving more importance to some and less to others. Direct equity weights can be set directly by the decision maker in whatever ad hoc pattern is preferred. Cf. *Indirect equity weights*.

Discounting: a discount rate adjusts the value of costs and benefits for the time at which they occur. The value diminishes the more distant in the future they occur, to reflect, for example, pure time preference and consumption growth.

Distributional cost-effectiveness analysis (DCEA): a cost-effectiveness analysis that provides information about *equity* in the distribution of costs and effects as well as *efficiency* in terms of aggregate costs and effects. In its simplest form, DCEA just provides information about the incremental distribution of health effects and opportunity costs for two groups—programme recipients and everyone else served by the decision-making organization. However, DCEA can also provide information about incremental distributions broken down by one or more *equity-relevant characteristics*, about *baseline distributions,* about the distribution of non-health effects such as financial protection, and about *equity-efficiency trade-offs*. Cf. *Extended cost-effectiveness analysis*.

Efficiency: in this handbook we often use the term 'efficiency' informally in a specific sense as the maximization of *net health benefit*, regardless of *equity* in the distribution of health. In economics, efficiency is often defined as 'Pareto efficiency', which requires that no individual can be made better off without making another individual worse-off. More generally, efficiency is the avoidance of waste in pursuing an objective—potentially including an *equity* objective—and can be defined in different ways depending on the objective.

Efficiency impact: the total net benefit of a decision, allowing for *opportunity costs* as well as benefits. A convenient summary measure for health decision makers is *net health benefit*, where benefits and opportunity costs are both measured in *HALYs*. Cf. *Efficiency*.

Equally distributed equivalent health (EDEH): a way of measuring *social welfare* in units that are comparable with standard health metrics such as *HALYs*. EDEH is the (same or lower) average level of health in a perfectly equal health distribution that the decision maker considers to be as good as the current unequal health distribution.

Equity: although not the same as equality, equity frequently involves equality in the distribution of something (such as opportunity, health, access to healthcare). Horizontal equity requires reducing *unfair inequalities* in the treatment of people who are equal in relevant respects (such as being human or having the same need for healthcare). By contrast, vertical equity requires achieving *fair inequalities* in the treatment of people who differ in relevant respects (such as persons with different needs). Cf. *Efficiency*.

Equity impact: the effect of a decision on *unfair inequalities*. Equity impact can be evaluated formally using an *inequality index* or in terms of *equity-weighted HALYs*.

Equity-efficiency impact plane: a two-dimensional graph representing the *efficiency impact* and *equity impact* of one or more options compared with a baseline comparator at the origin.

Equity-efficiency trade-off analysis: analysis of the potential conflict that may occur in the context of a specific decision between an equity objective, such as reducing unfair inequality in health, and an efficiency objective, such as increasing *net health benefit*. Equity-efficiency trade-offs can be summarized in various ways, for example as the minimum value of an *inequality aversion parameter* or *equity weight* required to consider an equity-improving programme worthwhile, and as the corresponding sacrifice in *net health benefit*.

Equity-relevant characteristic: a characteristic of a population subgroup that is the focus of a concern about *equity*, such as socioeconomic status, geographical location, ethnicity, gender, age, disability, *severity of illness*, end-of-life, or orphan condition.

Equity weights: a numerical way of valuing benefits and *opportunity costs* more highly for some specific subgroups of the population than others. Typically, equity weights relate to some measure of disadvantage—for example greater weight to benefits and burdens for persons with poor health, low income, or other *equity-relevant characteristic*.

Equity-weighted HALY: a *HALY* that is weighted to allow for *equity* considerations. If all *equity weights* are set to one then an equity-weighted HALY is the same as an ordinary HALY.

Expected health: an anticipated health outcome based on information available at a time when future health is uncertain, for example health-adjusted life expectancy at birth. Expected health is calculated by multiplying each possible health outcome by the probability it will be realized and then summing. Cf. *Realized health.*

Extended cost-effectiveness analysis (ECEA): a cost-effectiveness analysis that provides information not only about costs and health effects but also about other relevant dimensions of a choice, such as financial protection effects and *equity* in the distribution of costs and effects. Cf. *Distributional cost-effectiveness analysis.*

Fair inequality: inequalities or differences are not always considered unfair. For example, differences in health arising from free informed choices are sometimes considered fair. See *Equity.*

Fair shares: a way of thinking about ethics as the distribution of scarce resources in proportion to strength of claim—for example the distribution of healthcare in proportion to need. Cf. *Fair processes, Moral Rights, Value maximizing.*

Fair processes: a way of thinking about ethics as a fair decision-making process, for example a process that is impartial, transparent, and accountable. Cf. *Fair shares, Moral rights, Value maximizing.*

Future health: the number of future *HALYs* remaining to an individual or group from the age of observation until death, setting aside past health. See *Lifetime health.*

Health-adjusted age at death (HAAD): the number of years lived from birth to death, adjusted for health-related quality of life. Cf. *Lifetime health, Realized health.*

Health-adjusted life expectancy (HALE): the expected number of years lived from birth to death, adjusted for health-related quality of life, based on information available at a time when *future health* is uncertain. Cf. *Lifetime health, Expected health.*

Health-adjusted life-year (HALY): a year of life, adjusted for health-related quality of life. We use this as a generic term for a quality adjusted life year

(QALY) or a disability adjusted life year (DALY). A DALY represents a health burden but DALYs averted can represent benefits, and lifetime DALY burden subtracted from a maximum lifespan norm can represent *lifetime health*. Some approaches to evaluation, such as the Atkinson index, can only be applied to distributions of 'goods' such as *lifetime health* rather than 'bads' such as lifetime health burden.

Health transfer principle: according to the health transfer principle, a hypothetical transfer of health from healthier to less healthy people that does not reverse their rank ought to lead to a more equal health outcome. This is a central axiom of all the inequality and *social welfare* indices that we describe in this book. In economics, the corresponding income transfer principle is known as the Pigou-Dalton principle.

Indirect equity weights: indirect *equity weights* are determined by an *inequality aversion parameter* in a *social welfare function*, in conjunction with information about the health and *equity-relevant characteristics* of the relevant population subgroups. Indirect equity weights, like *direct equity weights*, are set by social value judgments made by decision makers.

Inequality index: an inequality index summarizes the degree of variation in a distribution. Univariate indices like the Gini and Atkinson indices focus on the distribution of a single *outcome variable* (e.g. health). By contrast, bivariate indices like the slope and concentration indices examine the joint distribution of two variables (e.g. health and social status).

Inequality aversion parameter: a coefficient in a *social welfare function* representing the decision maker's degree of concern for reducing a specified inequality. In DCEA the focus is usually on aversion to *unfair inequality* rather than aversion to overall inequality including *fair inequality*.

Level-dependent equity weights: a class of *indirect equity weights* that gives priority to the worse-off according to their level of health and their *equity-relevant characteristics*. Level-dependent equity weights depend on health levels, rather than health ranks, and represent an ethical view known in philosophy as prioritarianism. See *Equity weights*. Cf. *Rank-dependent equity weights*.

Lifetime health: the total number of *HALYs* over a whole lifetime from birth to death. Realized lifetime health is uncertain until death. Expected lifetime health depends on the age at which the expectation is formed (e.g. at birth or at disease onset) and includes past health as well as *future health*.

Moral rights: a way of thinking about ethics as normative rules about what duties individuals owe one other. Typically, duty-bearing individuals (often termed 'agents') have obligations towards right-bearing individuals (often termed 'principals'). For example, a doctor may owe patients a duty of care, and a public policymaker may owe citizens a duty of non-discrimination. Cf. *Fair shares, Fair processes, Value maximizing.*

Net health benefit: a summary measure of the expected benefits of a decision minus the expected opportunity costs. Net health benefit measures both benefits and opportunity costs in terms of *HALYs* gained and forgone. Cf. *Efficiency impact, Cost-effectiveness.*

Opportunity cost: in general, the value of resources in their most valuable alternative use. When making health sector priority setting decisions, the opportunity cost is often health forgone—as, for example, when there is a fixed budget that can be used only for health services. In such circumstances, the opportunity cost of using resources one way rather than another is the health gain not secured through the other route. Health opportunity costs arise even when budgets are not fixed, and both forgone private consumption and public expenditure outside the health sector can have health effects.

Outcome variable: in DCEA, an outcome variable typically serves as both a maximand—an entity to be maximized—and a distribuendum—an entity to be distributed. The primary outcome variable is often *lifetime health* measured using a generic health outcome measure such as *HALYs*.

Pareto dominance: Pareto dominance exists when, as the expected consequence of a decision, at least one individual or group is better off and none worse-off.

Rank-dependent equity weights: a class of *indirect equity weights* that give priority to the worse-off according to their relative health rank compared with other people and their *equity-relevant characteristics*. Cf. *Level-dependent equity weights, Indirect equity weights, Separability.*

Realized health: a final health outcome after uncertainty about future health has been resolved, for example *health-adjusted age at death*. Cf. *Expected health.*

Separability: a *social welfare function* is additively separable or subgroup decomposable if it can be divided into separate components—one for each subgroup in the distribution—such that the whole is equal to the sum of the parts. *Level-dependent equity weights* are separable because the contribution of a subgroup to *social welfare* depends only on its own level of health. By contrast, *rank-dependent equity weights* are not separable because the contribution of a subgroup to *social welfare* depends on how its own level of health is ranked in relation to the health of other subgroups.

Severity of illness: the burden of ill health suffered by an individual or group. Different concepts of health can imply different severity rankings of the same disease or risk factor, depending, for example, on whether the focus is on *lifetime health* or *future health*, on short-term or long-term future health, and on mortality or morbidity or both.

Social indifference curve: points in the *equity-efficiency impact plane* that are considered equally good in terms of *social welfare*. Options to the right are better; options to the left are worse. The slope and curvature of a social indifference curve usually depend on the *equity weights* used. However, when *equity impact* and *efficiency impact* are both measured in comparable *HALY* units, social indifference curves are straight lines with a fixed slope of -1.

Social welfare: a criterion for ranking alternative courses of action in order of desirability according to the social value judgments of the decision maker, which can be a useful tool for analysing trade-offs between equity and efficiency. See *Equity impact, Equity-weighted HALY*.

Social welfare function: a mathematical formula that converts many numbers representing the distributions of one or more *outcome variables* between different individuals or groups into a single number representing *social welfare*.

Subgroup analysis: subgroup analysis examines differences in effectiveness and cost-effectiveness within different sections of a population. Subgroup analysis in the context of trials and quasi-experiments usually focuses on subgroups within the population of programme recipients, whereas in DCEA the focus is usually on subgroups within the broader population served by the decision-making organization. Cf. *Distributional cost-effectiveness analysis*.

Staircase of inequality: a framework for thinking about the main steps in the causal pathway leading to inequality between social groups in the costs and effects of a decision. The main steps include: need (e.g. who smokes), receipt (e.g. which smokers use smoking cessation services and how delivery costs vary), short-term effect (e.g. which service users succeed in quitting), and long-term effect (e.g. which short-term quitters become long-term quitters and how many healthy life-years different kinds of people gain from quitting).

Unfair inequality: while not all inequalities or differences are unfair (see *Equity*) people often agree that certain kinds of equality are fundamentally desirable, such as equality before the law, equality in life chances, or equality in ability to access healthcare when it is needed. Inequalities in respect of these would then be seen as unfair. Cf. *Fair inequality.*

Value maximizing: a way of thinking about ethics as the efficient pursuit of objectives—for example the maximization of health or the minimization of health inequality, or an optimal combination of both objectives. Value maximizing may conflict with other ways of thinking about ethics, such as *moral rights, fair shares,* and *fair processes,* requiring compromises to be made.

Index

Note: Tables, figures, and boxes are indicated by *t*, *f*, and *b* following the page number.

absolute health achievement
  concept 108, 108*t*, 110, 111*t*, 112
  by disease categories 113
    league tables 122*t*, 125*t*
absolute health shortfall
  concept 108, 108*t*, 110, 111*t*, 112
  by disease categories 113, 128
    league tables 122*t*, 125*t*
absolute inequality indices 83, 84–5
accountability for reasonableness
    (A4R) 24–5
adjusted univariate distribution 74*f*, 75*f*
  dominance analysis 227, 232–3
  inequality indices 84
  selecting distributional breakdowns 73–5
age factors
  fair inequality 76, 134, 232
  health by disease categories 120, 124
aggregate approach 55–6
alcohol harm paradox 156
anonymity principle, dominance analysis 217, 219, 221, 224, 232, 233
  unfair inequality 227, 229
Arrow, Kenneth 35
Atkinson, Anthony 81, 258, 261
Atkinson index 79, 81, 84, 254, 258–61, 259*f*, 262–3, 270
  equity-efficiency trade-off
    analysis 266, 267–8
  health by social variables 131
  heterogeneity in values 317*t*, 317
attainment inequality indices 83

baseline distribution 92, 105, 128
  by disease categories 120–7
    league tables 122*t*, 124, 125*t*, 127
    calculation methods and data inputs 112–20
    colorectal cancer screening 158*b*
    concepts of health and severity 106–12
    costs and health effects 164, 165
  designing a DCEA 54, 56, 60
    equity in health between social groups 61, 62
    partial vs full DCEA 65
  dominance analysis 215
  ex post DCEA 328
  financial protection 195, 196–7, 207

    applying weights to the distribution 200–1
    catastrophic healthcare expenditure 198–9
    impoverishing healthcare expenditure 199–200
    Lebanese tobacco tax example 205
  health by social variables 130, 147–8
    analysing and presenting distributions 143–6
    Ethiopia 136*b*
    measurement choice 132
    need for baseline distributions 130–1
  health frontier diagrams 85
  inequality indices 84
  level-dependent equity weights 266, 270
  metrics 108–9, 108*t*
  opportunity costs 177*b*
  uncertainty 306
  using this book 14
  value maximizing 21
bedside rationing 105
benefit incidence analysis (BIA)
  marginal 189
  opportunity costs 187–9
Beta distribution 143
bivariate distribution 74*f*
  health by social variables 143–4
  inequality indices 84
  selecting distributional breakdowns 73–5
bivariate downside positional transfer sensitivity (DPTS)
  dominance analysis 230n28, 232–3, 234n33
  rank-dependent equity weights 248, 249
'blue book' 6, 159
'bottomless pit' problem 35–6
bowel cancer *see* colorectal cancer screening
breast cancer, baseline health league tables 122*t*, 125*t*
bronchus cancer, baseline health league tables 122*t*, 125*t*

catastrophic healthcare expenditure 197, 198–9, 200–1, 207
  Lebanese tobacco tax example 205, 205*f*, 206, 207*f*
cervical cancer, baseline health league tables 122*t*, 125*t*

change egalitarianism
  distributional breakdowns, selecting 71
  inequality indices 84
Chiang II life tables 137t, 137, 142b
chronic kidney failure, baseline health league
  tables 122t, 125t
chronic obstructive pulmonary disease
  (COPD) 141t
Cochrane, Archibald 36
Cochrane Reviews 167
cohort measures 134–5
comorbidities 110
complexity 321, 322
  infectious disease modelling 325–6
  non-communicable disease modelling 326
  system-level health policies 324–5
concentration curve dominance 231n29,
    234n34, 249, 249n22
  generalized 229–31, 230f, 232, 248
concentration index 271
  financial protection 200–1
  rank-dependent equity weights 249
continuous welfare loss measures, financial
    protection 196–7
cost-benefit analysis 8
  total health benefit maximization 33
cost-consequence analysis 59
cost-effectiveness analysis (CEA) 3–4
  aims of book 6
  comparison with DCEA 5, 321
  cost-effectiveness plane 48f, 48
  cross-sectoral approach 330
  databases 56
  in DCEA process 19, 55, 56, 57, 59
    partial vs full DCEA 65
  development 336
  and direct equity weights 277–8, 284, 297
    comparison of health weights and
        threshold weights 292, 292n3, 295–6
    equity impact plane 286, 286n2, 287, 289
    health weighting 281, 282
    threshold weighting 282–4
  dominance analysis 214, 217
  economic evaluation 7–8
  efficiency 4, 8, 19, 26, 106
  equity 4, 8, 10–11, 50–1
    in health 36
  equity-efficiency impact plane 52
  fair shares 334
  financial protection 195, 203
  health by disease categories 112
  heterogeneity in values 318
  incremental changes, focus on 71
  informal equity concerns 25, 28–9
  institutionalization 339, 339b
  level-dependent equity weights 257,
      268, 271
  moral rights 21, 22
  net health benefit 47–51, 49f, 50f, 278
  nicotine replacement therapy 95, 96
  opportunity costs 175, 181
  social welfare function 80
  staircase of inequality 157, 159–64, 170
  total health benefit maximization 29, 32, 33
  uncertainty 303, 307, 318
    sensitivity analysis 315
  value maximizing vs fair shares 23b
  visualizing equity trade-offs 87, 89
  see also incremental cost-effectiveness ratio
cross-sectoral DCEA 323, 326, 329
  aggregate approaches 330–3
  disaggregate approaches 330
Culyer, Anthony 38
current health
  concept 106, 107f, 107, 108, 108t, 109, 110
  costs and health effects 153, 170
  designing a DCEA 61
  by disease categories 113, 128
    league table 122t
  level-dependent equity weights 257

Dalton, Hugh 82
Daniels, Norman 24
dashboards 56, 64, 70, 83, 90, 330
databases 56
decision-making context 44, 45–7
decision trees 96, 161
decision uncertainty 310–11, 312, 315–16
dementia, baseline health league
    tables 122t, 125t
demographic surveys 185t
diarrhoeal diseases 141t
direct equity weights 93–4, 275–7, 297–8
  comparison of health weights and threshold
      weights 290–6
  cross-sectoral DCEA 331
  designing a DCEA 57
    equity in health between disease
        categories 61
    equity in health between social groups 63
    partial vs full DCEA 64, 65
  dominance analysis 233
  equally distributed equivalent health 89
  equity impact plane 284–90
  fair shares 335
  health weighting 278–82
  informal equity concerns 29
  social welfare indices 81–2
  and standard CEA 277–8
  threshold weighting 282–4
  uncertainty 315
  using this book 15
direct unfairness 147, 149
disability-adjusted life years (DALYs)
  CEA 48
  economic evaluation 7

INDEX

future health 109
Global Burden of Disease 117
health by social variables 132, 140, 141*t*
health metrics 108
institutional context for DCEA 330*b*
opportunity costs 175
and QALY, relationship between 132, 133*f*
total health benefit maximization 29, 32
discounting 30, 262, 309, 310, 334
Discrete Event Simulation 161
Disease Control Priorities 56
disposable income 198
distributional breakdowns, selecting 69–71
   adjustments 76–8
   equity-relevant populations 73–6
   incremental changes or levels or both? 71
   observation timing 78
   outcome variable(s) 71
   population 71–3
distributional cost-effectiveness analysis (DCEA) 4, 8–12
   aims of book 5–6
   applications 5
   comparison with CEA 5, 321
   costs and health effects 156, 161, 171
   designing 44, 60–1, 83
      components 53–60, 54*f*
      decision-making context 45–7
      equity-efficiency impact plane 47–53
      equity in financial protection 63–4
      equity in health between disease categories 61
      equity in health between social groups 61–3
      equity in health service delivery 63
      flowchart 58*f*
      partial vs full DCEA 60, 64–6
   direct equity weights 277, 296–7
      equity impact plane 285
      health weighting 282, 284, 290
      threshold weighting 282, 284, 290
   distributional breakdowns, selecting 69, 71, 72, 76, 78
   dominance analysis 214, 228
   and ECEA, relationship between 59–60, 59*f*
   equity 4, 9–11
      principles 18–20, 22, 25, 28–31, 36–40
   financial protection 195
   future challenges 321
      complexity 322, 324–6
      cross-sectoral DCEA 321, 323, 326, 329–33
      ex post DCEA 321, 322, 326–8
      fair shares 321, 323–4, 333–5
      increasing usefulness in practice 321, 324, 335–41
   heterogeneity in values 303, 304, 309, 316, 317
   limitations 10
   misconceptions 10
   nicotine replacement therapy exercises 94–9
   rank dependent equity weights 250
   uncertainty 303, 304, 307, 308, 318
      reasons for analysing 310–11
      sensitivity analysis 312, 313, 315
   unfair inequality focus 253n1
   using this book 14, 15
   visualizing equity trade-offs 87
dominance 93, 213–14, 232–5
   CEA 48
   cross-sectoral DCEA 330, 331
   designing a DCEA 57, 60, 62
   equity trade-offs 85
   evaluating equity impacts 84
   health monotonicity (Pareto) and health transfer (Pigou-Dalton) principles 214–22
   higher order generalized Lorenz dominance 222–6
   level-dependent equity weights 270
   limitations of analysis 237
   rank-dependent equity weights 237–41, 243–4, 248, 250, 270
   uncertainty 313, 314
   unfair inequality 226–32
   using this book 15
   see also concentration curve dominance; generalized concentration curve (GCC) dominance; generalized Lorenz (GL) dominance; Lorenz dominance; Pareto dominance; second order generalized Lorenz dominance
donor-financed healthcare 190
downside positional transfer sensitivity (DPTS)
   bivariate *see* bivariate downside positional transfer sensitivity
   dominance analysis 223*f*, 223–4, 225–6, 226*f*, 234
      unfair inequality 229–31
   rank-dependent equity weights 239–40, 241–2, 243–4, 248
   second order 240n9, 241–2, 244, 249
downward social selection 171

economic evaluation 6–8
efficiency 90
   CEA 4, 8, 19, 26, 106
   DCEA 10
      designing 54, 57, 60
      dominance analysis 214, 221
   vs equity 3, 3n1
   evaluating equity impacts and trade-offs 77–8, 82
   financial protection 196

efficiency (*cont.*)
  informal equity concerns 25, 28
  meanings 3n1, 51–2
  nicotine replacement therapy exercises 94
  opportunity costs 181
  rank-dependent equity weights 251
  total health benefit maximization 29
  value maximizing 20
  see also equity-efficiency trade-off analysis; net health benefit
efficiency impact 51, 79
  defined 52
  designing a DCEA 57, 60
  economic evaluation 8
  nicotine replacement therapy exercises 98
  scale, choice of 85
  visualizing equity trade-offs 87
  see also equity-efficiency impact plane; equity-efficiency trade-off analysis
end-of-life criterion 35
epilepsy, baseline health 114*f*
  across countries 120, 121*f*
  league tables 122*t*, 125*t*, 127
equally distributed by income equivalent health (EDIEH) 248–9
equally distributed equivalent (EDE) 258–9
equally distributed equivalent HALY 87
equally distributed equivalent health (EDEH)
  heterogeneity in values 317
  level-dependent equity weights 259–62, 260*f*
  equity-efficiency trade-off analysis 264–5, 267–8, 268*t*, 269*f*, 270
  rank-dependent equity weights 240, 242*t*, 242–3, 247
  uncertainty 315
  visualizing equity trade-offs 88–9
equity 3n1
  CEA 4, 8, 10–11, 50–1
    in health 36
  costs and health effects 159, 161, 170
  DCEA 4, 9–11
    components 53–4, 56–60
    cross-sectoral DCEA 323, 330
    decision-making context 45–7
    design 44, 51–3, 60–5
    ex ante DCEA 322
    ex post DCEA 322, 326
    principles 18–20, 22, 25, 28–31, 36–40
  differing opinions on 213
  direct equity weights 276
  distributional breakdowns, selecting 71–2, 73–6
  dominance analysis 219, 227, 231–3
  vs efficiency 3, 3n1
  ethical controversies 6
  financial protection 195, 196, 204
  future challenges 321, 324
  complexity 324, 325
  ex post DCEA 322, 326
  health by social variables 130, 148–9
    estimation 143, 145–6
    Ethiopia 136*b*
  heterogeneity in values 309, 316, 318, 321
  importance 3
  institutional context for DCEA 339*b*
  level-dependent equity weights 246
  metrics 70
  nicotine replacement therapy exercises 94–9
  opportunity costs 174, 175–83, 177*b*, 192
  principles 18–19, 40
    ethics 19–25
    financial risk protection 38–9
    health 33–7
    health service delivery 37–8
    informal equity concerns 25–29
    total health benefit maximization 29–3
  rank-dependent equity weights 246, 251
  severity of illness 99, 105–6
  uncertainty 310
    sensitivity analysis 304, 312, 315
  using this book 14
  ways of thinking about 19–20, 22, 25, 333
equity-efficiency impact plane 82
  designing a DCEA 44, 47, 51*f*, 51–3
  direct equity weights 275, 277, 284–90, 297
  dominance analysis 215–16, 215n2, 216*f*, 217n6, 219, 221
  level-dependent equity weights 268, 269*f*
  nicotine replacement therapy exercises 98, 98*f*
  probabilistic sensitivity analysis 313–15, 314*f*
  social indifference curve 87, 89–90, 89*f*, 288, 297
equity-efficiency trade-off analysis 85–6, 213
  dominance analysis 221
  level-dependent equity weights 245, 253, 254, 257, 264–70, 271
  nicotine replacement therapy exercises 98–9
equity impact 4, 8, 51, 69
  costs and health effects 153, 159
  cross-sectoral DCEA 323, 330
  DCEA 10
  designing a DCEA 57, 60
    equity in health between social groups 62
    equity in health service delivery 63
    partial vs full DCEA 64, 65
  distributional breakdowns, selecting 71, 75
  evaluating 78–9, 90
    ethical axioms 82–3
    inequality indices 79–82, 83–5
    social welfare indices 79–82
  financial protection 195

health by social variables 130–1, 148
level-dependent equity weights 265, 267–8
nicotine replacement therapy exercises 98
opportunity costs 190
uncertainty 303, 304, 311
using this book 14
visualizing equity trade-offs 87, 88, 89
see also equity-efficiency impact plane
equity-relevant characteristics 4
  costs and health effects 152, 159, 161–2
  DCEA 9, 11
  designing a DCEA
    components 53–8
    partial vs full DCEA 64–5, 66
  direct equity weights 275, 276, 278–9, 291
  distributional breakdowns, selecting 70, 72, 73–8
  dominance analysis 214, 227–8, 231–3
  equally distributed equivalent health 88–9
  equity
    in financial risk protection 39
    in health 35
    in health service delivery 37
  ex post DCEA 328
  fair shares 333, 334
  financial protection 197, 203
  health by social variables 147, 148
    determinants of health inequality 132–4
    estimation 135, 138, 139, 139f, 140
  heterogeneity in values 309
  infectious disease modelling 325–6
  level-dependent equity weights 253n1
  methodological standardization 340
  nicotine replacement therapy exercises 98
  non-communicable disease
    modelling 326
  opportunity costs 174, 175
    distributions 181, 185, 185t, 188–9
  PROGRESS-Plus acronym 73
  rank-dependent equity weights 247, 250
  uncertainty 306, 307–8
    sensitivity analysis 312
equity trade-offs 69
  evaluating 79, 85–7, 90
  visualizing 87–90
  see also equity-efficiency trade-off analysis
equity-weighted HALYs 275, 276, 278–82, 280t, 281t
  comparison with threshold weights 290–6
  distributional breakdowns, selecting 71
  equity impact plane 284
  inequality indices 85
equity-weighted net health benefit
  plot 87–8, 88f
equity weights 4
  CEA 10
  DCEA 11
    cross-sectoral 331

designing 57, 59
misconceptions 10
fair shares 334, 335
health by disease categories 113
heterogeneity of values 318, 321
informal equity concerns 29
nicotine replacement therapy exercises 99
social indifference curve 87, 89–90
social welfare indices 81
value maximizing 21
see also direct equity weights; indirect equity weights; level-dependent equity weights; rank-dependent equity weights
equivalent income, cross-sectoral
  DCEA 331, 332
estimation technique, and uncertainty 308t
ethics, ways of thinking about 19–25, 20f, 333
evidence base, strengthening the 339
evidence selection, and uncertainty 308t
exercises 92
  NRT example 94–7
  policy questions addressed by 98–100
  summary 92–4, 93f
expected health 34
  absolute health achievement 110
  concept 109
  DCEA 10
  distributional breakdowns, selecting 76
  equally distributed equivalent health 88
  equity
    in health 35
    in health service delivery 38
  ex ante DCEA 322
  level-dependent equity weights 266
  opportunity costs 177b, 181
ex post DCEA 321, 322, 326
  ethical and technical challenges 328–9
  example 327–8
  and fair shares 335n2
extended cost-effectiveness analysis
  (ECEA) 4, 165b, 196
  and DCEA, relationship
    between 59–60, 59f
extended Gini index 79
  rank-dependent equity weights 241, 242, 244f, 244, 249
extrapolation, and uncertainty 305t

fair chances argument 333–4
fair inequality 76–7, 227n22, 316
  by social variables 134, 146–7, 148t
'fair innings' argument 35
fair processes 20f, 20, 24–5, 28
fair shares 20f, 20, 22, 24, 25
  equity in health service delivery 38
  evaluating equity impacts and trade-offs 78
  future challenges 321, 323, 333

fair shares (cont.)
    lotteries and the 'fair chances'
        argument 333–4
    negligible claims 335
    realizing of potential 334–5
informal equity concerns 29
and value maximizing, comparison
    between 22, 23b
financial protection 99–100, 195, 207–8
    baseline 196–7
        applying weights to the
            distribution 200–1
        catastrophic health expenditure 198–9
        impoverishing health
            expenditure 199–200
    distribution of effects 201–2
    distribution of opportunity costs 202–3
    equity in 38–9, 59
        designing a DCEA 63–4
    fair shares 335
    heterogeneity in values 303
    Lebanese tobacco tax example 203–7
    staircase framework 196
first order stochastic dominance
    (FOSD) 216–17, 216n3, 217n4,
    233, 243
forecasting, and uncertainty 305t
fractional rank 145, 145n1, 149t
full income, cross-sectoral DCEA 330, 331
future challenges 321
    complexity 322, 324–6
    cross-sectoral DCEA 323, 329–33
    ex post DCEA 322, 326–9
    fair shares 323–4, 333–5
    increasing usefulness of DCEA in
        practice 324, 335–41
future health 33
    absolute health shortfall 112
    concept 106, 107f, 107, 108, 108t, 109,
        110, 111t
    costs and health effects 158, 170
    designing a DCEA 59, 61, 65
    by disease categories 113, 115–16, 128
        league table 122t
    distributional breakdowns, selecting 71
    equally distributed equivalent health 88
    equity-efficiency impact plane 52n1
    equity in health 35
    Global Burden of Disease 117
    level-dependent equity weights 257
    relative health shortfall 112
    by social variables 135
    total health benefit maximization 29

gap statistics 144–5
gender factors, life expectancy 77
generalizability, and uncertainty 305t
generalized concentration curve (GCC)
    dominance 229–31, 230f, 232, 248

generalized concentration index 79, 249
generalized Lorenz (GL) curve
    dominance analysis 219, 220f, 222f
    orders of GL curves 225t
    rank-dependent equity weights 239
generalized Lorenz (GL) dominance 219–26,
    234, 235f
    level-dependent equity weights 270
    rank-dependent equity weights 240, 241,
        243, 270
    second order 224, 225t, 226, 234,
        239–40, 243
Gini, Corrado 80
Gini coefficient 80, 84, 271
    equally distributed equivalent health 240
    extended 79
        rank-dependent equity weights 241, 242,
            244f, 244, 249
    health by social variables 131
    heterogeneity in values 317
Global Burden of Disease (GBD)
    health by disease categories 113, 115,
        116–19, 120
        absolute health shortfall 112
        league tables 124
    health by social variables 135, 136b
    LMICs 185t
    opportunity costs 186b
global health partnerships 190
'green book' 7, 161, 171

health
    concepts 24
    and costs 92, 152, 170–1
        applying staircase to a cost-effectiveness
            model 159–64
        extending the staircase 156–8
        NRT example 164–9
        staircase of inequality 152–5
    by disease categories 92, 105, 128
        calculation methods and data
            inputs 112–20
        comparisons 120–7
        concepts of health and severity 105–12
        league tables 122t, 124, 125t, 127
    equity in 33–7
        designing a DCEA 61–3
        between disease categories 61
        between social groups 61–3
    metrics 108–9, 108t, 111t
    right to 35–7
    by social variables 92, 130, 147–9
        baseline distributions 130–1
        deriving additional distributions 147
        determinants of health inequality 131–4
        estimation 134–46
        fair inequality adjustments 146–7
    total health benefit maximization 29–3
health-adjusted age (HAA) 109

INDEX 359

health-adjusted age at death (HAAD)
　designing a DCEA 61
　by disease categories 113, 114f, 115f, 116,
　　117f, 119
　　epilepsy 120, 121f, 124
　　league table 125t, 127
　individual 113, 115f, 115, 117f, 121f
　by social variables 134-5, 137-44, 148-9
　　fair inequality 147
health-adjusted life expectancy (HALE)
　absolute health shortfall 112
　designing a DCEA 61
　by disease categories 115-16
　　league tables 122t, 125t, 127
　future health 109-10
　health metrics 108t, 109, 111t
　level-dependent equity weights 253, 257,
　　267t, 268t
　　equity-efficiency trade-off
　　　analysis 267t, 268t
　lifetime health 109
　opportunity costs 177b
　relative health shortfall 112
　by social variables 134-46, 144f, 146,
　　148, 149t
　　Ethiopia 136b
　　fair inequality 147
health-adjusted life years
　(HALYs) 237, 256n2
　absolute health shortfall 112
　CEA 10, 48-50, 277-8
　costs and health effects, NRT
　　example 167-8, 169f
　designing a DCEA 55, 63
　direct equity weights 297
　　comparison of health weights and
　　　threshold weights 291, 293, 293t, 294,
　　　294t, 296t, 296
　　equity impact plane 285, 286, 287-8, 290
　　threshold weighting 282-4
　　see also equity-weighted HALYs
　by disease categories 116
　distributional breakdowns, selecting 71
　dominance analysis 224, 229
　　Pareto and Pigou-Dalton principles 214,
　　　215t, 215, 216, 216n3, 217n4,
　　　218-19, 219n11
　economic evaluation 7, 8
　equally distributed equivalent 87
　equity-efficiency trade-off analysis 86
　equity in health 33
　ex ante DCEA 322
　ex post DCEA 328
　fair shares 334
　health by social variables 132
　health metrics 108, 108t
　health monotonicity, principle of 82
　health transfer, principle of 82
　inequality indices 83, 85

　level-dependent equity weights 254-6, 258,
　　259f, 259-61, 262f
　Lorenz curve 79
　opportunity costs 177b, 180t, 181t, 182, 187
　rank-dependent equity weights 230, 246n16
　social welfare function 80
　total health benefit maximization 29-2
　value maximizing vs fair shares 23b
　visualizing equity trade-offs 87, 88, 89
　see also disability-adjusted life years; equity-
　　weighted HALYs; quality-adjusted
　　life years
health frontier 85-7, 86f
health monotonicity, principle of (Pareto
　principle) 82
　dominance analysis 215-17, 219-22,
　　224, 232-3
　unfair inequality 228-9
　ex post DCEA 328
　level-dependent equity weights 246, 270
　rank-dependent equity weights 238-9, 241,
　　246, 247, 248, 249, 270
health poverty 146, 148
health-related quality of life 35
　current health 109
　HAAD 113
　HALYs 31
　by social variables 61, 131-2, 138-400, 139f
　estimation 135
health service delivery
　costs 157-8
　equity in 37-8, 59
　designing a DCEA 63
　health surveys 185t
health systems strengthening 96, 325
health transfer, principle of (PHT, Pigou-
　Dalton principle) 82
　dominance analysis 217-22, 223, 224n18,
　　225, 234
　unfair inequality 227, 228-9, 231
　inequality indices 84
　level-dependent equity weights 258, 270
　rank-dependent equity weights 239-40,
　　241, 243, 248, 270
health weighting 275, 276-7, 278-82, 297-8
　equity impact plane 284
　and threshold weighting compared 290-6
heterogeneity of values 303, 304, 308-10, 319
　analysing 316-18
　reasons for 315-16
　uncertainty distinguished from 310
high-income countries (HICs)
　financial protection 198
　health by social variables 132, 138-9
　opportunity costs 178
horizontal equity
　financial risk protection 39
　health service delivery 37-8
household budget 198, 207

household surveys
  financial protection 198
  LMICs 185*t*
  opportunity costs 185

impoverishing healthcare expenditure 197, 199–200, 201
incidence
  limitations as data source 185
  opportunity costs 185–6, 186*b*
income-related health transfers, principle of (PIRHT)
  dominance analysis 228–9
  rank-dependent equity weights 247–8, 249
incremental cost-effectiveness ratio (ICER) 283
incremental distribution 14, 60, 84
incremental equity benefit 284–90, 297
independence axiom 238n1, 245n15
indirect equity weights 57, 61, 62
  comparison with direct equity weights 276
  see also level-dependent equity weights; rank-dependent equity weights
individual health-adjusted age at death (iHAAD) 113, 115*f*, 115, 117*f*, 121*f*
inequality aversion parameter
  Atkinson index 81
  designing a DCEA 59
  equity-efficiency trade-off analysis 86–7, 88
  heterogeneity in values 316, 317, 318*f*, 318
  institutional context for DCEA 339*b*
  level-dependent equity weights 253, 254, 258, 260, 263, 271
    equity-efficiency trade-off analysis 264, 264*f*, 267, 268, 269*f*, 270
  rank-dependent equity weights 240–4, 250
  value maximizing 21
inequality gradients 161, 162, 162*f*, 164, 170–1
inequality indices 8, 79–82, 83–5
  designing a DCEA 57, 60, 62
  distributional breakdowns, selecting 71
  equally distributed equivalent health 89
  level-dependent equity weights 261–2
  levelling down objection 146
  rank-dependent equity weights 241
infectious disease modelling 325–6
informal equity concerns 25–29, 27*b*
innovation 26
institutionalization of decision-making 338–9, 339*b*
instrumental variables 182
insurance
  financial protection 196, 202–3
  opportunity costs 175–6, 178, 189–90
interaction terms 308
International Classification of Diseases (ICD) 132

International Covenant on Economic, Social and Cultural Rights 36
intervention-generated inequality 53, 153
  colorectal cancer screening 158*b*
inverse care law 152
inverse prevention law 153
ischaemic heart disease, baseline health league tables 122*t*, 125*t*
ischaemic stroke, baseline health league tables 122*t*, 125*t*

Kolm-Pollak social welfare function 79, 260–1, 262*f*, 262, 270
  equity-efficiency trade-off analysis 266
  heterogeneity in values 317*t*, 317

level dependence 234
level-dependent equity weights 93, 253–61, 271
  aversion to unfair health inequality 263–4
  comparison with rank-dependent equity weights 244–7, 253, 266
  cross-sectoral DCEA 331
  equity-efficiency trade-off analysis 264–70
  health inequality measures derived from SWFs 261–2
  social welfare indices 81
  using this book 15
  utility function 32n1
level egalitarianism
  distributional breakdowns, selecting 71
  inequality indices 84
life expectancy (LE) 35
  costs and health effects 155, 158
  disability-free 140
  by disease categories 120
  ex post DCEA 327
  fair inequality 76
  future health 109
  gender factors 77
  heterogeneity in values 309
  lifetime health 78, 131
  NHS objectives 47
  quality-adjusted 142*f*, 158*b*
  by social variables 131, 133
    distributions 135–8
    estimation 140
  uncertainty 303, 306
  see also health-adjusted life expectancy
life tables
  absolute health shortfall 112
  Global Burden of Disease 117, 124
  health by social variables 136–7, 137*t*
  morbidity adjustment procedure 140–3
lifetime health 33
  absolute health achievement 110
  concept 106, 107*f*, 107, 108, 108*t*, 109–10, 111*t*

INDEX | 361

costs and health effects 152, 155, 164, 169f
designing a DCEA 47, 59, 63
  equity in health between disease categories 61
  equity in health between social groups 61–2
  partial vs full DCEA 65
by disease categories 113, 116, 128
  epilepsy 120, 121f
  league table 125t, 127
distributional breakdowns, selecting 69, 71, 76, 78
dominance analysis 214, 227–8, 232
equally distributed equivalent health 88
equity-efficiency impact plane 52
equity in health 35
ex post DCEA 322, 327, 328
health frontier diagram 85
inequality indices 83, 84
informal equity concerns 29
institutional context for DCEA 339b
level-dependent equity weights 254, 255f, 256f, 257, 258n4, 259f, 259–60
  equity-efficiency trade-off analysis 266
NHS objectives 46
NRT exercises 98
by social variables 130, 131–2, 134, 147–8
  estimation 134–5
Lorenz, Max 79
Lorenz curve 79–80, 80f
  defined 218n8
  dominance analysis 218f, 218, 220f, 221n13
Lorenz dominance 84, 218–19, 222–6
  see also generalized Lorenz (GL) dominance; second order generalized Lorenz dominance
lotteries 333–4
low- and middle-income countries (LMICs)
  financial protection 99–100, 196, 198
  health by disease categories 120
  health by social variables 132
  household surveys 185t
  NRT exercises 94, 97
  opportunity costs 178, 180t
    benefit incidence analysis 188
    donor-financed healthcare 190
    tobacco taxes 165b
  uncertainty 306
lower respiratory infections 141t
lung cancer, baseline health league tables 122t, 125t

machine learning 308
marginal benefit incidence analysis (MBIA) 188
marginal productivity of health systems

opportunity costs 179, 180t, 180, 192
  between-country estimates 187–9
  equity variables, incorporation of 182–3
  NGO expenditure 190
  within-country estimates 183–9
  uncertainty 307
Markov models 96, 97, 161, 307
mathematical programming 8
measurement error 305t
meningitis B vaccination 276, 282
methodological standardization 340–1
microsimulation models 6, 96, 134, 326
  cross-sectoral DCEA 332
  health by social variables 137–8
  staircase of inequality 161, 170
moral rights 20f, 21, 24, 25, 333
  evaluating equity impacts and trade-offs 78
  informal equity concerns 29
morbidity adjustment procedure 140–3
mortality data 135–6
multi-criteria decision analysis 8
multiple indicator cluster surveys 185t

national health surveys 139
negligible claims 335
net health benefit
  CEA 47–51, 49f, 50f, 278
  designing a DCEA 53, 55
  direct equity weights 275, 297–8
    comparison of health weights and threshold weights 291–6
    equity impact plane 284–90
    health weighting (n^H) 280–2, 284, 292–5
    threshold weighting (n^T) 283, 284, 285, 292–5
  distributional breakdowns, selecting 71, 72
  economic evaluation 8
  efficiency 3n
  equity-efficiency impact plane 52
  equity-weighted net health benefit plot 87–8, 88f
  fair shares 334, 335
  inequality indices 84
  informal equity concerns 28
  level-dependent equity weights 267–8
  meaning 3n1
  opportunity costs 175, 177b, 181, 190
  uncertainty 303, 304, 307
  visualizing equity trade-offs 87, 88
  see also efficiency
nicotine replacement therapy (NRT)
  assumptions
    about delivery 95–7
    about key model inputs 97
  costs and health effects 160f, 160, 164–9, 166f, 167f, 168f
  designing a DCEA 46–7, 53

nicotine replacement therapy (NRT) (*cont.*)
 direct equity weights 276, 285–90
 ex post DCEA 328
 level-dependent weights 265–70
 modelling approach 96
 policy options 94–5
  No Public NRT 95, 97, 98–9, 98*f*
  Proportional Universal NRT 95, 96, 98–9, 98*f*
  Universal NRT 95, 97, 98–9, 98*f*
 policy questions addressed 98–9
 reasons for choice as exercise 94
 summary of exercises 92–4, 93*f*
no levelling down principle 82
non-communicable disease modelling 326
non-food expenditure 198, 199
non-governmental organizations (NGOs), opportunity costs 190
normal distribution 143

opportunity costs 92, 174, 192, 250
 beyond 191–2
 CEA 49–50, 277–8
 DCEA 10
 designing a DCEA
  components 54, 55, 56, 57, 60
  equity in financial protection 63
  equity in health between social groups 62
  equity in health service delivery 63
  partial vs full DCEA 64, 65, 66
 direct equity weights 276, 296–7, 298
  comparison of health weights and threshold weights 291, 293*t*, 294*t*, 296*t*
  health weighting 275, 278–82, 280*t*, 281*t*
  threshold weighting 275, 283
 distributional breakdowns, selecting 69, 72
 dominance analysis 215
 efficiency impact 52
 in equity-informative evaluation 175–8
 estimating
  distributions 181–9
  total opportunity costs 178–81
 financial protection 195, 202–4, 207
 future challenges 321
  cross-sectoral DCEA 323
  increasing DCEA usefulness in practice 324, 340
  infectious disease modelling 325
 health by social variables 130
 heterogeneity in values 303
 insurance and donor-financed healthcare 189–90
 level-dependent equity weights 247, 257
 moral rights 22
 NRT exercises 95, 97
 quasi-experiments, limitations of 7
 scenario analysis 190–1
 staircase of inequality 156
 total health benefit maximization 29, 32, 33
 uncertainty 304, 307
 using this book 14
 value maximizing 333
 what they are 174–5
Ordinary Least Squares regression 145
outcome variables 25, 79, 85, 187
 cross-sectoral DCEA 323
 distributional breakdowns, selecting 69–70, 71, 73
out-of-pocket (OOP) expenses 3
 CEA 8
 designing a DCEA 59, 63
 health equity objectives 46
 opportunity costs 176
 see also financial protection
overseas development aid 190

Pareto, Vilfredo 82
Pareto dominance 84, 86, 87, 93
Pareto principle *see* health monotonicity, principle of
period measures 134–5
period of increased disability (PID) 113, 125*t*
period of increased mortality (PIM) 113, 125*t*
philanthropic financing of healthcare 190
Pigou, Arthur 82
Pigou-Dalton principle *see* health transfer, principle of
pluralist egalitarianism 81, 258
political economy 340
potential, realization of 334–5
poverty gap 200
poverty line 197, 199–200
prevalence
 limitations as data source 185–6
 opportunity costs 185–6
prevention paradox 161
prioritarian equity weights *see* level-dependent equity weights
prioritarianism 81, 257, 271
production function, health system 178–9, 179*f*

quality-adjusted life expectancy (QALE) 142*f*, 158*b*
quality-adjusted life years (QALYs)
 CEA 48
 colorectal cancer screening 158*b*
 cross-sectoral DCEA 331–2
 and DALYs, relationship between 132, 133*f*
 direct equity weights 283
 economic evaluation 7
 equity in health 35
 health by social variables 132, 138–40
  England 142*b*
 health metrics 108, 108*t*
 heterogeneity in values 318

institutional context for DCEA 339b
opportunity costs 175
rank-dependent 238n3
total health benefit maximization 29, 32
well-being 331–2
quality-adjusted years of life lost
   (QAYLL) 142b, 142f
quantile regression 308
quasi-experiments 7

randomized controlled trials 7
rank dependence 234
rank-dependent equity weights 93,
   237–8, 250–1
   aversion to socioeconomic-related health
      inequality 247–50
   comparison with level-dependent equity
      weights 244–7, 253, 266
   cross-sectoral DCEA 331
   quantification of welfare and inequality 240–4
   social welfare indices 81
   transfer principles and dominance 238–40
   using this book 15
rank-dependent HALY model 238
Rawls, John 81
Rawlsian social welfare function 81, 226, 237,
   239n5, 259, 263
realization of potential 334–5
realized health 34
   DCEA 10
   by disease categories 113, 116
   distributional breakdowns, selecting 76
   equally distributed equivalent health 88
   equity in health 35
   fair shares 335n2
relationships between inputs, and
   uncertainty 308t
relative health shortfall
   concept 108, 108t, 110, 111t, 112
   by disease categories 113, 128
   league tables 122t, 125t
relative index of inequality (RII) 79, 83,
   145–6, 249n23
relative risk 162, 163
rescue, rule of 61
respiratory illness 186b
rotavirus vaccination 136b, 191, 191f
rule of rescue 61

Sabin, James 24
sampling bias 305t
sampling uncertainty 305t
scale invariance 261
scenario analysis
   heterogeneity in values 316–18, 319
   opportunity costs 180, 181, 190–1, 191f
schizophrenia, baseline health 106, 114f, 120
   league tables 122t, 125t, 127

second order downside positional transfer
   sensitivity 225–6, 226f
rank-dependent equity weights 240n9,
   241–2, 244, 249
second order generalized Lorenz dominance
   (SOGLD) 224, 225t, 226, 234,
   239–40, 243
second order stochastic dominance 219n10
selection of evidence, and uncertainty 308t
Sen, Amartya 9
sensitivity analysis 6, 72, 303, 310, 311–12
   deterministic 311–12, 316, 319
   dominance analysis 222
   equity impact 51, 90
   equity weights 11, 29, 90
   financial protection 199, 200, 203
   heterogeneity of values 318
   level-dependent equity weights 57,
      264–70, 271
   multivariate 311
   opportunity costs 50, 181, 203
   presenting the results of 312–13
   probabilistic 312, 313–15
   probability of error 313
   rank-dependent equity weights 57, 250–1
   specified inequality aversion results 315
   staircase of inequality 167, 170
   univariate 311
separability 81, 247, 270
severity of illness 99
   concepts 105–6, 109
   costs and health effects 153–4, 155
   designing a DCEA 57, 58, 61, 65
   direct equity weights 275, 279
   by disease categories 116, 117
   league tables 122t, 125t, 127
   distributional breakdowns, selecting 72
   dominance analysis 214, 231
   equity in health service delivery 38
   informal equity concerns 29
   level-dependent equity weights 245, 246, 251
   opportunity costs 184
   rank-dependent equity weights 245–6
   value maximizing vs fair shares 23b
shortfall inequality indices 83
slope index of inequality (SII) 79, 84, 145–6,
   249n23, 303, 317–18
   heterogeneity in values 317, 318
   regional inequalities calculated from
      national distribution 149t
smoking cessation see nicotine replacement
   therapy
Smoking Toolkit Study 166
social determinants of health 3
social distribution of health see health: by
   social variables
social indifference curve 87, 89–90, 89f,
   288–9, 297

social welfare 80
  designing a DCEA 54, 60
  dominance analysis 215, 217, 223, 228, 229
  evaluating equity impacts and trade-offs 78
  health by social variables 146
  level-dependent equity weights 245, 245n14, 254, 255–9, 262, 264
  rank-dependent equity weights 240, 241, 250
  value maximizing 21
  visualizing equity trade-offs 87, 88
social welfare function (SWF) 80–1
  cross-sectoral DCEA 331
  designing a DCEA 57, 62
  dominance analysis 221–3, 231n30, 234
  equity-efficiency trade-off analysis 86
  indirect equity weights 276
  informal equity concerns 29
  level-dependent equity weights 245, 253–61, 271
    aversion to unfair health inequality 263–4
    comparison with rank-dependent equity weights 253, 266
    equity-efficiency trade-off analysis 264–70
    health inequality measures derived from SWFs 261–2
  rank-dependent equity weights 237–8, 250–1
    aversion to socioeconomic-related health inequality 247–50
    comparison with level-dependent equity weights 244–7
    quantification of welfare and inequality 240–4
    transfer principles and dominance 238–40
    violating Pareto and Pigou-Dalton principles 82
social welfare indices 79–82, 89, 146, 317t
staircase of inequality 152–3, 154f, 155, 170–1
  application to cost-effectiveness model
    building staircase into the model 161
    designing the staircase 159
    distributions selection 159–61
    populating the staircase 161–4
  designing a DCEA 55, 63
  distributional breakdowns, selecting 69
  extension
    adding more steps 156
    delivery costs 157–8
    downstream healthcare savings 158
    healthcare costs 156–7
  financial protection 196, 201–2, 202f, 208
    Lebanese tobacco tax example 204, 204f
  future challenges 321, 324
  key steps

  lifetime health benefits 155
  need 153–4
  receipt 154
  short-term effects 154–5
  NRT example 164–5
    effects 166–7
    healthcare costs 168–9
    lifetime health benefits 167–8
    need 165–6
    receipt 166
stakeholders
  decision-making context 45, 46
  participation 336–8, 337b
Stepwise Approach to Surveillance Surveys 185t
subgroup analysis
  costs and health effects 161, 167
  designing a DCEA 47
  direct equity weights 275, 276
    comparison of health weights and threshold weights 291–6
    equity impact plane 287
    health weighting 278–82, 280t
  distributional breakdowns, selecting 74–5
  financial protection 200, 203
  health by social variables 130, 147–9
    baseline distributions 130–1
    deriving additional distributions 147
    determinants of health inequality 131–4
    estimation 134–46
    fair inequality adjustments 146–7
  level-dependent equity weights 247, 253
  opportunity costs 177b, 180, 183, 184, 186b
  rank-dependent equity weights 253
  social welfare indices 81
  uncertainty 307–8
survivor costs 158
Sustainable Development Goals (SDGs) 196, 199
system-level health policies 324–5

third order inverse stochastic dominance 224n17
third-party payments 175–6
threshold hardship measures, financial protection 196–9
threshold weighting 275, 276–7, 282–4, 297–8
  equity impact plane 284–5
  and health weighting compared 290–6
tobacco tax 99, 165b, 195, 202, 203–7
Tobin, James 9
total health benefit maximization 29–3
tracheal cancer, baseline health league tables 122t, 125t
training exercises *see* exercises
Tudor-Hart, Julian 152

Tufts Global Health Cost-Effectiveness Analysis Registry 56
Tugwell, P. 153

uncertainty 303–8, 318–19
 ex post DCEA 329
 financial protection 206
 heterogeneity in values distinguished from 310
 reasons for analysing 310–11
 sensitivity analysis 311–12
  presenting the results of 312–13
  probabilistic 313–15
  probability of error 313
  specified inequality aversion results 315
 sources
  in evaluative process 306, 307, 308t
  in inputs 304–6, 305t
 staircase of inequality 171
unfair inequality
 costs and health effects 152
 designing a DCEA 46, 60
 distributional breakdowns, selecting 73, 76–7, 78
 dominance analysis 226–32
 equally distributed equivalent health 88
 heterogeneity in values 316, 317
 level-dependent equity weights 253n1, 254, 263–4
 lotteries 334
 NRT exercises 98
 by social variables 130, 133–4, 146–7, 149
Universal Health Coverage (UHC)
 equity concerns 3
 financial protection 196
urgency of treatment vs severity of illness 106

value maximizing 20f, 20–1, 24, 25–6, 333
 evaluating equity impacts and trade-offs 78
 and fair shares, comparison between 22, 23b
 informal equity concerns 29
 and realization of potential 334, 335
values, heterogeneity of see heterogeneity of values
vertical equity
 financial risk protection 39
 health service delivery 38

Wagstaff, Adam 38
Walzer, Michael 9
well-being QALY, cross-sectoral DCEA 331–2
Williams, Alan 22
Wilson, James 36
World Bank
 poverty line 200
 tobacco taxes 165b
World Health Organization (WHO)
 CHOICE 56
 Consultative Group on Equity and Universal Health Coverage 33
 financial protection 196, 199
 global ageing and adult health study 185t
 health systems building blocks 324
 Health Systems Building Blocks framework 196
 Life Expectancy database 136b
 tobacco taxes 165b

years lived with disability (YLDs) 117, 119
years of life lost (YLLs) 112, 117